Writing the Female Voice

WRITING THE FEMALE VOICE

Essays on Epistolary Literature

Edited by ELIZABETH C. GOLDSMITH

Northeastern University Press
BOSTON

Northeastern University Press

Copyright © 1989 by Elizabeth C. Goldsmith

Library of Congress Cataloging-in-Publication Data
Writing the female voice.
  Bibliography: p.
  Includes index.
    1. Letters—Women authors—History and criticism.
2. Letters—History and criticism. 3. Women in
literature. I. Goldsmith, Elizabeth C.
PN6131.W75 1989   809.6'088042   88-12528
ISBN 1-55553-038-9 (alk. paper)

Designed by Ann Twombly.

Composed in Garamond #3 by The Composing Room of Michigan, Grand Rapids, Michigan. Printed and bound by the Maple Press, York, Pa. The paper is Sebago Antique, an acid-free sheet.

MANUFACTURED IN THE UNITED STATES OF AMERICA
94 93 92 91 90 89   5 4 3 2 1

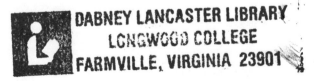

Contents

Introduction

THE LITERARY history of women's epistolary writing is a
fascinating survey of cultural views of both the female gender and the letter genre. Since the sixteenth century, when
the familiar letter was first thought of as a literary form, male
commentators have noted that the epistolary genre seemed particularly
suited to the female voice. Newly educated women could easily learn to
write letters, and, as epistolary theory became more adapted to worldly
culture, women's letters began to be considered the best models of the
genre. But the new admiration for a "natural" feminine style clashed with
old arguments about female virtue: to be virtuous was to be modest, self-
effacing, above all not talked about, and most certainly not published.[1]
To publish a woman's letters, even if the purpose of publication was to
praise female epistolary style, was in some way to violate her personal
integrity. Published epistolary writing by women was therefore rarely
signed, and was often in fact produced by male writers "imitating" the
way women wrote. Publishers, though, were quick to recognize the easy
marketability of a woman's private correspondence, and ultimately of a
literary genre based on women's letters. By the eighteenth century the
practice of male authors appropriating the female voice in their fictions
had become a popular and innovative narrative ploy. The most famous
epistolary novelists of France and England—Laclos, Rousseau, Richardson—perfected this technique.

Any study of the female voice in epistolary literature, then, must
examine male ideas of what it means to write as a woman, along with the
writings of real women. All the contributors to this collection have approached the topic with a similar series of questions in mind: How has
the female epistolary voice been defined by those who write it and those
who read it? Has it been an ideological as much as an aesthetic construct?
What have been the prescribed parameters for feminine self-expression
in letters? Can the figure of the woman letter writer be seen as an
emblem of changing cultural notions of both sexuality and textuality?

The essays are presented in chronological order, beginning with
three pieces on the early emergence of women as skilled letter writers in

the sixteenth and seventeenth centuries. The longest section is devoted to studies of epistolary writing of the eighteenth century, when the popularity of the letter novel form was at its height; the essays in the closing section examine the use of the epistolary form in more recent contexts. Several contemporary novelists and critics have used the letter genre to express the impossibility of describing a unitary, integrated self. Women's voices have again been chosen in these new epistolary experiments, sometimes to portray female stories as fragmented residues that others must reconstruct (as in Atwood's *The Handmaid's Tale*), other times to show women excluded from the dominant culture writing letters to reinscribe or relocate themselves in the world (as in Puig's *Heartbreak Tango* or Walker's *The Color Purple*).

One of the most unexpected results of compiling this collection has been the dialogues evoked among essays that are not linked by a common historical context. It is striking, for example, to observe how both Madame de Graffigny and Alice Walker, writing more than two hundred years apart, use the epistolary form to suggest an analogy between female confinement and the predicament of minority cultures, or to see how Jane Austen's subversion of conventional epistolary tropes in *Lady Susan* seems to echo Veronica Franco's efforts to forge new epistolary models for female intellectual exchange.

Several of the essays in each section focus on what has been a standard *topos* of epistolary literature since Ovid—the female letter of suffering and victimization. The association of women's writing with the love-letter genre has been perhaps the most tenacious of gender-genre connections in the history of literature.[2] Katharine Jensen's close analysis of rules for feminine writing in seventeenth-century France reveals how male editors of letter collections, by extolling the female love letter of abandonment and despair, contributed to a narrowing of the concept of women's writing and to a limitation of its practice to the social (as opposed to the literary) arena. Alicia Borinsky's essay on *Heartbreak Tango* argues that Puig reverses a familiar epistolary scenario—the series of letters telling the story of a woman who has been seduced and betrayed—by constructing a letter novel based on two women who begin to write to each other when a man whom they both have loved dies. In Puig's ironized version of what has been termed the "exquisite cadaver" motif,[3] the female voice of passion turns out to be highly self-conscious and ultimately false, and the body of the beautiful but inarticulate Juan Carlos becomes the pretext for a female bonding based on mutual distrust and manipulation. Carolyn Williams shows how Alice Walker in *The Color Purple* ironizes traditional epistolary situations by introducing a protagonist who writes letters to God until she decides that she has been rejected by both God and men. Walker ties the conventional scenario of female abandonment to her heroine's experience of isolation from interaction with other women.

The use of a love-letter exchange to represent, paradoxically, the failures of both epistolary and erotic interaction is not restricted to contemporary texts, as Suzanne Pucci shows in her essay on Montesquieu's *Persian Letters*. While the letters exchanged between the traveling Usbek and his harem women seem simply to represent female sentiment and passion in terms of a male voyeuristic fantasy, the progression of this correspondence and its apocalyptic conclusion may be read as a metaphor for the violent experience of exile and self-estrangement that is central to Montesquieu's philosophical point. Epistolary duplicity comes to signify the failure of language to sustain a reliable or authoritative system of communication.

In examining both the constructions and the subversions of conventional epistolary form, several contributors have addressed the question of how women writers responded to reader expectations about female letter writing. Patricia Spacks argues that the plots of letter novels by eighteenth-century English women writers tended to reinforce social restrictions on female enterprise. A stunning exception is Jane Austen's *Lady Susan,* which Spacks shows is a unique and bold experiment in the real, subversive possibilities of the letter novel form. Sally Winkle's study of two letter novels by the German writer Sophie La Roche traces some of the troubling contradictions in La Roche's experiments with the newly popular genre, contradictions that seem to reflect her reluctance to sustain a challenge to prevailing gender ideology. For La Roche, the woman-centered novel must ultimately adopt the myths of a feminine destiny as created by men. Yet her second, more conventional novel seems nonetheless to express the author's anxiety about the tension between the public and private selves inherent in the contemporary ideal of womanhood, as she splits the conflicting voices of her first heroine into two separate characters. The essays by Margaret Rosenthal and myself both examine how women writers responded to early definitions of the ideal female epistolary voice. Rosenthal studies the Renaissance poet Veronica Franco's fascinating and subtle variations on models provided by Ovid's *Heroides*. The autobiographical thrust of Franco's poetry, Rosenthal argues, has been overemphasized by readers who have neglected the complex intertextual system of references that she uses to suggest a specifically feminine literary tradition. The double standard faced by early women writers, aptly described by Ann Jones as "the tension between public accessibility and private chastity,"[4] was particularly strong for writers of the sixteenth and seventeenth centuries. But interpretive models provided by the earliest editors of letter collections continue to influence the way women's letters are read. My own essay on seventeenth-century attitudes toward the publication of women's letters takes a closer look at some of the historical consequences, for women writers, of reading female letters as "natural," "authentic," and essentially nonliterary. The legacy of seventeenth-century theorizing about female epistolary writing is particularly strong in the editions of numerous correspondences that have not been reedited in the last century.

Domna Stanton has recently pointed out that the term "autobiographical" is often applied pejoratively to women's writing and positively to men's. Women are not represented in the major theoretical studies of autobiography, yet women's writing is often read as being exclusively concerned with the personal and private.[5] Historically, women's letters have been subjected to a similar process of misreading. The two essays in our collection dealing with real correspondences expose the fallacy of labeling even the most intimate of letter exchanges as transparent expressions of the private self. Kathryn Crecelius finds in George Sand's letters to her mother, written over a twenty-five-year period, an astonishing gap between Sand's epistolary enactment of their relationship and the story she presents in her autobiography. For Sand there is, moreover, an essential quid pro quo between her private epistolary contacts with her mother and her public development as a writer—she discovers that to strengthen her public voice she must repress her expression of filial need in the letters. Julie Hayes's reading of Sade's correspondence from prison with his wife and his intellectual "sister," Milli Rousset, reveals a systematic disruption of standard literary concepts of epistolary relationships. In this letter triangle it is the man who writes from confinement and the women who are at liberty to provide him with news of the world outside and information about what might eventually become of him. Yet the "free" Marquise de Sade can write only with the voice of a cloistered nun, in a naïve and untutored style; she refuses to attempt the more sophisticated speculations her husband demands of her and grants only the most obvious level of meaning to her text. The consequences of this ironic situation for her correspondent's strategy of reading and writing are dramatic, as he transforms the circuit of epistolary communication into a fantastic mechanism for verbal aggression and intimidation.

Male authors of epistolary novels have often used female voices as forms of disguise, and literary critics have recently focused much attention on the notion of "transvestitism" in letter fiction.[6] The essays in this volume by James Carson, Julia Epstein, and Susan Jackson examine cross-gender narration in the eighteenth-century letter novel. Looking at the epistolarity-sexuality equation in *Memoirs of a Woman of Pleasure,* Epstein argues that Cleland creates a female voice that is not simply a projection of masculine heterosexual desire, but instead is a thin disguise for a homosexual male voice. Fanny's narrative uses the female voice as a veil, supposedly celebrating female sexuality but actually subordinating it to male narcissism. At the same time, Cleland's combined parroting and distortion of established novelistic devices—in the epistolary form of his story, its plot structure, and its unconventional ending—constitute a complex critique of both conventional novel plots and the sociosexual ideologies they sustain.

Carson's study views the use of the female voice in Richardson's epistolary novels as a method of authorial self-criticism wherein Richardson expresses his desire to transcend the boundaries of the self and, at the same time, his recognition of the impossibility of such a gesture. This reading challenges the adequacy of the traffic-in-women paradigm, which views cross-gender narration as subjecting women to a male homosocial structure. In so doing he reassesses both the dramatic force of female resistance in Richardson's novels and the reasons for authorial identification with the male villain. Jackson's analysis of the "virtuoso ventriloquism" in *Les Liaisons dangereuses* reveals how Laclos causes the female voices in his text to proliferate, only to bring them all back under the authority of the editor's third-person commentary. Laclos's own epistolary conversations with Madame Riccoboni about the novel further expose the contradictions inherent in his views of what it means to "write as a woman."

One of the oldest letter narrative situations—the cloistered woman resorting to letters as a way of reorienting her life—forms the basis of two novels studied by Linda Kauffman and Janet Altman. The narrator of Margaret Atwood's nightmare of the future, *The Handmaid's Tale,* addresses herself to an unknown listener. But, as Kauffman clearly shows, the recorded trace of the narrator's voice is appropriated by her scholarly editors just as surely as her body had been enlisted in the service of a gynophobic political regime. The vision of feminine destiny that the novel offers is in the end no more hopeful than the cries of Ovid's abandoned heroines. Interestingly, an epistolary novel written by Madame de Graffigny some two hundred years earlier manages a far more optimistic transformation of the same conventions of the genre. Like *The Handmaid's Tale, Letters of a Peruvian Woman* presents a female narrator who uses the epistolary mode to reconnect with a world from which she has been violently exiled. In her thoroughly original reading of this text, Janet Altman demonstrates how the novel challenges the dominant view of history as a record of male conquests, and posits an equivalence between the place of the female and the place of "new world" peoples in European culture. Graffigny's Peruvian lady ultimately uses her various environments of captivity to develop a critical understanding and personal autonomy that had no model in earlier epistolary tales of female confinement.

One of the most interesting, and perhaps surprising, results of bringing these essays together has been the evidence they have accumulated to show to what extent the female voice in the epistolary tradition has been a history of restrictions or failed interactions. The one genre with which women have been persistently connected has specialized in narrowing the range of possible inflections for feminine expression. Our collection may seem to suggest that female epistolary voices tend to describe confinement more than liberation, isolation more than interaction. For an author like Margaret Atwood, this is because feminine experience has not fundamentally changed in the modern age. Not the least of the depressing moments in *The Handmaid's Tale* is the postscript, when an officious historian seems to echo, three centuries later, Laclos's arguments in his letter to Riccoboni that a woman's voice can at best be only an increment, an embellishing ornament to the more solid, male powers of observation. To study the history of the female epistolary voice, it would seem, is to record the ways it has been silenced.

Yet to write about the female voice is also to propose new ways of reading that force a reconsideration of the critical assumptions behind our understanding of the epistolary genre and its traditions. Several of the essays in this book argue for radical rereadings of texts by women writers that have long been pigeonholed as inferior imitations of epistolary works by men. Others propose new critical approaches to the traditionally acknowledged masterpieces of epistolary literature. It is hoped that this collection will provoke readers to return to familiar texts, to reexamine the mechanisms of epistolary representation, and to construct new frameworks for the study of women's letters.

NOTES

I wish to thank the Boston University Humanities Foundation for a semester's leave from teaching, which gave me the time to develop this collection. I am most grateful, too, for many fruitful discussions with Deborah Kops of Northeastern University Press.

1. As Hortense Mancini ruefully writes: "I know that a woman's honor (*gloire*) depends on her not being talked about." *Mémoires d'Hortense et de Marie Mancini* (Paris: Mercure de France, 1965), p. 31.

2. See Linda Kauffman, *Discourses of Desire: Gender, Genre, and Epistolary Fictions* (Ithaca: Cornell University Press, 1986).

3. See Nancy Miller, "The Exquisite Cadavers: Women in Eighteenth-Century Fiction," *Diacritics* 5 (1975):37–43.

4. In "Surprising Fame: Renaissance Gender Ideologies and Women's Lyric," in *The Poetics of Gender,* ed. Nancy K. Miller (New York: Columbia University Press, 1986), 74–93.

5. See her "Autogynography: Is the Subject Different?" in *The Female Autograph* (Chicago: University of Chicago Press, 1987), 4–5.

6. See, for example, Nancy K. Miller, "I's in Drag: The Sex of Recollection," *Eighteenth Century* 22 (1981): 45–57; Robert Markley, "Language, Power, and Sexuality in Cleland's *Fanny Hill*," *Philological Quarterly* 63 (1984): 343–56; Terry Castle, *Clarissa's Ciphers: Meaning and Disruption in Richardson's 'Clarissa'* (Ithaca: Cornell University Press, 1982), 148–80; Terry Eagleton, *The Rape of Clarissa: Writing, Sexuality and Class Struggle in Samuel Richardson* (Oxford: Basil Blackwell, 1982), 36–39.

I

Women and the art of letter writing:
Origins of a gender–genre connection
in France and Italy

1

A Courtesan's Voice: Epistolary Self-Portraiture in Veronica Franco's Terze Rime

MARGARET F. ROSENTHAL

You may ask why my verses alternate, when I am better suited to the lyric mode. I must weep, for my love—and elegy is the weeping strain; no lyre is suited to my tears.

Sappho to Phaon, 15:5–8, Ovid, *Heroides*

 IN A SENSE, all of the works of Veronica Franco, the famous sixteenth-century Venetian courtesan, evoke an epistolary genre.[1] Many of her poems composed as *capitoli* in terza rima (*Terze Rime* 1575), and her personal letters designed for publication (*Lettere familiari a diversi* 1580), directly address members of a tight-knit Venetian "academy of virtuous men" in letter form; she requests that her addressees enter a poetic collaboration, dialogue, or friendly conversation with her.[2] While in the *Terze Rime* an anonymous male lover politely responds to her rigorous poetic and ideological challenges by vehemently defending his love for her, in her prose letters we hear her voice alone.[3] Orchestrated as an elegant duet between male and female lovers, the dialogue in the *Terze Rime* is rudely interrupted, however, by a third dissonant extratextual voice, which seeks to undermine both the male lover's adulatory verses in praise of his beloved, and the courtesan's repeated claims to fidelity, virtue, and intellectual abilities. This third voice denounces her as a vulgar and common whore. A confusion of identities generates eloquent retorts and propels Franco, the female persona of the *Terze Rime*, to publicly challenge her

3

4 MARGARET F. ROSENTHAL

interlocutor to a poetic duel. In this duel she defends her personal honor and reputation and speaks in support of all courtesans and other women victimized by men. After a superb poetic skirmish in *capitoli* 13 and 14, she emerges victorious in *capitolo* 16.[4]

Her verse epistles and personal letters, both published from 1575 to 1580, when read together as an epistolary narrative, combine to form a portrait of the courtesan's livelihood in sixteenth-century Venice and of Franco's personal concerns. She constructs this portrait by exposing and then overturning misogynists' and moral satirists' claims, exemplified by the defamatory voice in the *Terze Rime*, that courtesans are duplicitous, venal, greedy, and sexually rapacious. Franco redefines the courtesan's profession as contrary to mercenary and duplicitous love; she portrays herself as a devoted friend and mother uninterested in financial gain, a faithful companion and partner in love, and a professional writer and editor ambitiously engrossed in literary projects.[5]

The epistolary genre was ideally suited for this kind of self-portraiture. The familiar letter permitted Franco to correct satirists' charges against courtesans, and it offered her a public forum for articulating her personal complaints openly, informally, and directly to a male interlocutor or to an "absent friend."[6] The familiar epistolary genre, inherited from the Ciceronian, Stoic, and Christian moral traditions, was widely imitated and discussed in Venetian literary academies and private intellectual circles during the sixteenth century.[7] Translated into the vernacular and commented on by Renaissance theorists, the classical epistles designed for publication displayed an individual's knowledge of correct civic, moral, and social conventions.[8] Franco capitalizes on the familiar aspect of classical epistolography in order to characterize the nature of the courtesan's voice as unmediated and truthful.

The conversational and personal tone in her poems and letters also adheres closely to the tenets of the Renaissance letter genre, which advocated the use of "plain," unadorned speech, uncorrupted by rhetorical flourishes.[9] Critics have consistently misread this personal and often intimate voice in Franco's works as implying nothing more than a confessional autobiography. They have collapsed the life into the works and thus failed to see how Franco manipulates classical and Renaissance literary genres in order to give prominence to the woman's voice.[10] Indeed, much of the strength of Franco's poems arises from their high degree of intertextual reference to contemporary literary traditions.

Franco's amorous verse epistles and familiar letters do not simply record the successes and failures of a courtesan's life within a five-year period.[11] Rather, they constitute fictional models (dialogue, poetic exchange, debate, verse epistle, elegiac lament) that point to, act out, and contain the tensions present in Franco's ongoing polemical dialogue with a misogynist society. Bolstered by the authority of classical literary traditions, she contests satirists' claims that women embody dissimulation. She dramatizes and reinterprets scenes drawn from classical elegy of a woman's betrayal in love by switching traditional gender roles: in her version the male lover is duplicitous and unfaithful.[12]

Whereas her amorous verse epistles theatrically stage scenes of betrayal and duplicity in love and highlight the destructive effects of obsessive passions on male and female lovers, her familiar letters comment and reflect upon these scenes from a retrospective point of view. Further, in the *Lettere familiari* the woman speaker takes on the role of moral advisor. She espouses, by mimicking her male addressees' past advice to her, a correct and virtuous behavior between friends and lovers that is based on mutual respect and reciprocity of feeling:

> My speaking to you on this subject is perhaps redundant and, as the saying goes, like carrying water to the sea, for I refer to matters that you profoundly understand and have explained to me; nevertheless a duty born of love and gratitude compels me to say to you that virtue lies in its own practice rather than in being aspired to: so when it comes to things that you so often taught me, you will prove how you neither understand nor own them unless you practice them when the need occurs.[13]

Throughout her letters, she reminds an allegedly superior aristocracy to live up to its avowed claims to fairness, justice, moderation, and honesty. She invests a humanist social vocabulary, however, with new meaning by calling attention to her self-assumed role as courtesan/advisor. In letters 3, 28, and 30, for example, she warns her male addressees of the havoc that unbridled passions such as anger, jealousy, and obsessive love can play on a human's power of reason.[14] This she does as a loyal friend, grateful colleague, and affectionate companion who conscientiously returns the advice offered to her in times of adversity in the manner and spirit in which she had originally received it. She reflects and theorizes in letters 36, 47, and 48 on the causes of the deceit, cruelty, slander, and abuse perpetrated against her and other women lovers. And she warns her addressees in letters 8, 14, 17, and 18 of the moral dangers and destructive effects that repeated calumny, victimization of innocent women, and feigned and calculated emotions can have on one's acquired skills and talents:

> I do not know who deserves greater blame for the malicious rumors spread abroad; I, whom you tax so unduly or you, who—despite the nobility you profess and into which you were indeed born—go about

slandering me. There is no doubt that when unjustice is done, the one
on whom it is inflicted suffers the damage while the one who inflicts it
must bear the burden of a wicked deed. The sin of calumny taints me
not.[15]

By teaching Venetian nobility to meet its own high standards, she
threatens an established social balance that had carefully positioned
women, and especially courtesans, on the margins of cultivated society as
merely decorative borders. Sanctioned and protected, however, by the
familiar letter form, Franco ascribes to herself the role of educator and
counselor for both men and women.

As discursive literary reflections, Franco's familiar letters are closer
to the Senecan epistle or the essay by Montaigne than to the humanist's
occasional missive, which was calculated to document personal connections and to exhibit the rewards of achieved social status.[16] Her letters
do not specifically name her addressees, except for letter 21 in which she
thanks "signor Tentoretto" for the portrait he has done of her. Her
letters also do not include date or place of composition. Many of her
letters call into question the very tenets of a humanist circuit of epistolary exchange, one that assigns intellectual accomplishments and social
and literary refinements exclusively to men. Thus, in the familiar letter
Franco found a literary arena suitable for envisioning a more satisfactory
existence for courtesans, one defined not by sexual performance and
economic reward, but rather by intellectual collaboration and virtuous
exchange.[17]

To which models could she turn to legitimize this appropriation of a
female epistolary authority in her poems and letters? Which texts were
available to a sixteenth-century woman and which would have been considered acceptable models for a courtesan writer?[18] Franco appropriates
for her own, and thereby intensifies, the ventriloquized female voice in
the elegies of Ovid and Propertius. By adopting as a courtesan the kind
of epistolary denunciatory voice found in Ovid's *Heroides,* she transfers
any moral superiority from the distant male lover to the lamenting
female and she questions the textual stereotype of the deceitful whore.[19]
In the *Terze Rime* distinctions between author and narrator are collapsed;
the "Franca" persona emerges as the enactor of her own fate.[20]

She further evokes the epistolary exchange of the second book of the
Heroides by including in her *Terze Rime* a few of the male responses to the
woman's accusations. While in Book One of the *Heroides* the woman's
narrative airs only her side of the story of betrayal, with the double
letters in Book Two both sides of the love dialectic are presented. The
male hero finally has the chance to tell his story. His account often vies
for authority with his beloved's narrative. The reader is left to judge

which version is not only the more pitiful but also the more truthful. Similarly, with the inclusion of the male-authored poems in her volume, he presents, as does Franco in *capitolo* 4, his account and insists that his love for her is not duplicitous.[21]

It is beyond the scope of this essay to discuss both the verse epistles and the familiar letters, although they can in fact be read as forming one epistolary narrative. I will focus here on an analysis of only one element of this epistolary "love story": the elegiac verse epistles in the *Terze Rime*. I maintain that Franco elects to present the women lovers' complaints in classical elegy as a means to empower her literary voice on the one hand, and to undermine satirists' claims against courtesans on the other.

Ovid's works were carefully studied, annotated, and projected for translation during the years 1555 to 1561 when the Accademia della Fama assembled in Venice.[22] However, the *Heroides* were translated and published not by a Venetian member of the academy but by a Florentine writer, Remigio Fiorentino, in 1555.[23] The entry in the academy's *Somma delle opere* attests not only to a study of the *Heroides* but also to an investigation of all Ovid's elegiac texts, as well as the elegies of Tibullus and Propertius.[24]

A translation of Ovid's *Heroides* into *capitoli* in terza rima during the years that Franco was composing her poems must have suggested to her a powerful rhetorical and vernacular model.[25] The textual and exegetical studies of the classical elegists within the Venetian academy, and in Domenico Venier's literary salon, also contributed the philological basis for accurate metrical translations of the elegiac distich into the vernacular tercet.

In the elegiac verse epistles in the *Terze Rime*, the reader is drawn into a sophisticated contest of verbal performance that is interlaced with comic and tragic devices inherited from classical elegy, ancient Senecan tragedy, the lyrics of the women troubadours, and Renaissance comedy.[26] The shifts between verbal virtuosity, and the range and articulation of profound and disturbing emotions, interlaced with a highly charged Venetian sensuality, transport the reader into an Ovidian arena of passionate and erotic love.

Whereas Franco's familiar letters include a variety of topics such as deceit in friendship, the effects of adverse fortune, invitations to her home for musical entertainment and friendly conversation, and the courtesan's role as literary collaborator and moral counselor, her verse epistles, especially *capitoli* 3, 17, and 20, center on the effects of duplicitous and obsessive love. What further distinguishes these *capitoli* from the other poems in the *Terze Rime* that include elegiac laments on the pain of unrequited love is their precise function as verse love letters; it is in these poems that we see most clearly the influence of Ovid's *Heroides*. Each *capitolo* opens with an address to an unnamed "sir" and identifies the speaker as either "Veronica" or "Franca." Within this three-line exordium, the woman speaker's psychological state and the attributes of the male recipient are introduced. At times, the exordium defines and prefigures the letter's dramatic turn of events; often the relationship between the two people establishes the thematic content of the entire poem.[27]

In the *Heroides* the women speakers recount their betrayal drama retrospectively, assigning blame to specific figures drawn from myth or ancient history. The addressee in Franco's verse epistles remains anonymous.[28] The classical epistles produce an ironic effect because the reader already knows that the woman's lament is in vain; the outcome of her story predates her narrative. Thus, the reader's attention is drawn not to the narrative's resolution but rather to the pathos of the woman's lament as it unfolds and to the expressive tension created between an urge to fulfill passionate desire and a need to resolve the conflicts of unrequited love. The words of the elegiac lament, including most particularly their sounds and textures, lure the reader into a realm of verbalized sorrow.[29] This language of lament is closely connected to Franco's passionate repudiation of male duplicity in *capitoli* 3, 17, and 20; in addition, many of the conventional themes of Ovid's *Heroides* are present in these verses.

There are no preexisting narratives, however, that inform or determine the fiction of *capitoli* 3, 17, and 20, nor do they recount episodes drawn from the stories of heroes or heroines of antiquity. In Franco's amorous verse epistles there is no authorial ventriloquist who speaks through the woman; here, the letter writer and the author are the same subject. She is the suppliant and her lover the recipient. Moreover, it is she, as both writer and narrator, who acts (rather than is acted upon) and therefore has a role in determining her own fate; she leaves her beloved in *cap.* 3 and intercepts him upon her return to Venice in *cap.* 17 in the moment of publicly disclosing his unfaithfulness to her.

Many of the rhetorical devices of Ovid's *Heroides* are employed in her text. Abrupt changes in emotion disrupt the speaker's narrative. At times a poem that begins as an accusation condemning her beloved on the grounds of infidelity, ends conversely, for example in *cap.* 20, in a plea for his mercy, pity, and compassion.[30]

If we view *capitoli* 3, 17, and 20 as an epistolary narrative, we may read the first *capitolo* as an introduction to a love "story" that culminates in *cap.* 20. What begins in *cap.* 3 as an intimate, personal confession of love and desire ends in *cap.* 20 with a proclamation against male cruelty, deceit, and infidelity. *Cap.* 17 stands as the mediator between the two. In a melodramatic scene reminiscent of Renaissance comedy, the woman apprehends her beloved as he is textually, and not physically, unfaithful to her. In classical elegy, what often followed a lovers' quarrel and accusations of infidelity was the male lover's forced exile from the woman's home. This, in turn, prompted him to compose a song or a poetic address to his beloved's door. In Franco's version it is the woman lover who denounces her beloved and charges him with cruelty, deceit, and betrayal in love. She reworks the *exclusus amator* and *paraclausithyron* traditions of classical elegy in *cap.* 20 by having the woman lover wander the Venetian streets at night, unable to sleep because of the relentless pain of unreciprocated love. Drawn to her lover's home, accompanied by a faithful male companion, she is barred entrance by the doorkeeper; her lover is not at home, he tells her, but sleeps in the bed of a woman more fortunate than she. This drives the woman speaker to address the door, mediated by the doorkeeper; Propertius's *paraclausithyron* of Book 1.16, in which the door is the sole speaker throughout, and Ovid's *Amores* 1.6 function as intertexts.[31] In these poets' texts it was the woman who prevented the man from entering because, it was implied, she entertained another lover. Her sexual rejection unleashed the male lover's invectives against his courtesan lover's dissolute ways. Made popular by Roman comedy, above all in the plays of Plautus and Terence, this theme was widely employed as well in Renaissance comedies by such playwrights as Bernardo Pino da Cagli, Ludovico Dolce, and Girolamo Parabosco.[32]

Franco reconstructs these roles by rearranging the referents in Ovid to point to the man's infidelity and corrupt sexual mores. But her agonistic stance reverts at the close of *cap.* 20 to an appeal for his pity and for a recognition of her intrinsic virtue and merit. Praise and blame, the rhetorical paradoxes of Ovidian elegy and the Petrarchan love lyric, inform her speech.[33]

The male lover adopts the same rhymes proposed by the woman in his response in *cap.* 4. This exchange in *capitoli* 3 and 4, the only exchange between male and female speakers in the three elegiac epistles, evokes the alternating discourses in Book Two of the *Heroides*.[34] She claims that she has been forced to leave her city, and he retorts in an ironic rejoinder, in which he plays with verbal ambiguity, that her departure was unnecessary and was probably motivated not by his cruelty but by another man. A tension stretching from her accusations of infidelity to his denial of her suspicions is eroticized in a play of absence and presence; physical pleasure is celebrated in both poems as a natural resolution to love's passions. She exclaims, "I live only for the hope of seeing you again soon in the sweet site." The woman speaker reminds

her interlocutor of the sensual pleasures that they once shared by drama-
tizing in her verses an imagined physical reunion. She takes on the
traditional rhetorical stance of the wounded lover and then appeals to
her lover's virtue by comparing him to Apollo.

> The moment I will enter that coveted-for room
> my knees will touch the ground and I will bow
> to my Apollo in knowledge and mien.
> Then vanquished by him in amorous war,
> my soul shattered by fear, I will follow him
> on the path of valor whence he does not stray. (3.58–66)

He adopts in his response the role of the courtly love poet who pleads
with his cruel lover to diminish his anguish by recognizing the extent of
his suffering.

Driven from her adored virginal city, "the maiden of Adria," because
of the pain of unrequited love and once exiled in a pastoral setting, she
laments the effects of this separation. Separation serves only to intensify
the anguish that she now experiences. Proceeding from a praise of her
beloved to extolling her virginal city, uncorrupted and protected from
outside enemy forces, she identifies herself as a courtesan with its pure
and unviolated origins.[35]

In the opening verses of *cap.* 3, the woman speaker acknowledges her
error: "Alas how I do curse my parting from you dear soul though in my
thoughts you are still joined to me." She has left her lover and by
extension her beloved city, and has mistakenly believed that she could
find refuge from love's travails in nature's landscape. Her words are
mirrored and transformed into "sorrowful cries."

> so that from uttering grieved, sorrowful cries
> and weeping alone I draw supreme delight
> Alas, I say and I shall say everywhere
> That life without you is cruel death
> and my pleasures are torments and ills. (3.10–15)

Nature responds to the woman's lament by echoing and duplicating
her internal passions. Nature is not an alien force; rather, it evokes
human sentiment that has the power to distort reason into a destructive
emotion—jealousy.

> but possessed by jealousy which,
> when I am far from you, slowly
> consumes me with its ice-cold
> gloomy and vicious flame. (3.55–57)

It is this irrational emotion that ultimately transfigures the mental landscape (already a projection of her mental state) into an unyielding nar-

cissistic mirror in which all of nature reproduces and intensifies her lament as it sings in unison with her. Her sorrow is metonymically answered by two female mythological victims of deceit, Echo and Philomel. Echo, whose voice had been taken away from her because of Juno's vindictive anger and jealousy, responds to her lament with "truncated calls" and Philomel and Procne's sorrowful "song" accompanies her as she wanders in search of pastoral comfort.

> Often when I cried aloud the dear name
> Echo was stirred to pity by my lament
> and answered it with brief truncated calls.
> At times the sun and sky did halt
> intent on listening in midcourse
> and even earth bowed to my plangent tones.
> Emerging from their lairs the tigers yet
> would weep to see the torments and the tears
> that pierce my heart and take my life away.
> Procne and Philomel accompany my words'
> sad melody and support my song through day and
> night. (3.16–27)[36]

Her tears, the simulated words of love that stain the page on which she records the anguish of her soul (a topos ubiquitous in classical elegy),[37] cathartically expiate her pain:

> The tears I shed quench the fire in part
> but hope of seeing you soon in that
> sweet site again, keeps me alive. (3.58–60)

If she loses her beloved to another woman, as her suspicions of his infidelity keep reminding her, she may also forfeit, paradoxically, the pretext for composing her verses. If the strength of her plea does not effectively convince her beloved of her pathetic condition, she asks that the "small god, the blindfolded archer" who initially wounded her, intercede on her behalf.

In the closing verses of *cap.* 3, she evokes the original scene of their love and their intimate encounters in the "coveted-for room" enclosed within the boundaries of the protected and virginal city: "my nest" and "sweet site." This eulogy of her city as the locus of natural "pleasures" is the witness, in her revery, of the union of a terrestrial and profane Venus with her divine Apollo, who in "knowledge and in mien" excels all other lovers. Or is this the reunion of lovers in the "stanza" of love poetry—a love that exists solely in the lover's imagination and on the blank page?

The setting switches from the country back to the city in *cap.* 17. A reunion of lovers constitutes the dramatic focus of this poem. The woman speaker's jealousy switches to passionate anger, which precipitates a quarrel that has as its backdrop the literary salon, presumably in her lover's own home. It is here that she catches him unawares, as he holds (or possibly discusses with friends) his new edition of poems in praise of another woman.

> But also your endeavors were unkind
> for of another woman you dared think
> and you limned verses offering her praise;
> you hoped to do this on the sly but
> suddenly I came upon you when
> you least suspected that I might. (17.31–36)

Her courtly evocation of the "coveted-for room" (*bramata stanza*) that closed *cap.* 3 transforms in this verse epistle into *stanze* that turn against her. In their praise of another woman, her beloved has externalized and made public his exaltation and celebration of another muse.

> The book praising another against
> his breast the scoundrel hid from me.
> Alas, divided and at odds
> are the desires of Love! (17.64–66)

A rejection conceived in textual terms, much more severe than a sexual betrayal, radically reworks by intertextual allusion a scene of male betrayal in Propertius's *Elegies*.[38] In elegy eight in Book Four, Cynthia, overwhelmed by suspicions of her beloved's infidelity and by anger, catches her lover unaware and physically assaults him as he entertains and makes love to two courtesans.

> It was the creaking of the door hinges I heard first,
> and the hum of voices in the entrance hall,
> but it wasn't long before Cynthia burst
> in, flattening the doors against the wall,
> with her hair unkempt, but beautiful
> in the wildness of her fury; and the cup slipped
> from my paralysed fingers, my jaw dropped
> and my wine-stained lips grew pale.[39]

In Propertius's view, male infidelity provokes female passion, the ultimate sign and manifestation of female love and desire. Thus, Cynthia's fury belies sublimated sexual desire and physical longing.[40]

Franco alters this scene in order to emphasize not the woman's physical passion but her lack of faith in and impatience with her lover's repeated proclamations of fidelity. She denounces the deceptive power of his language, which has falsely convinced her of the validity of his professed love. She decries: "Your eloquent discourse is full of endearments and affectations." Here, the elegiac laments of Ovid's heroines inform the pathos of the woman speaker's lament. The amorous love epistle composed by Phyllis and addressed to her beloved Demophoon, who is away at sea, might have suggested to Franco the means by which radical switches in emotion and tone may be expressed by a deceived woman.[41]

Hence, in the exordium to *cap.* 17 the male attributes have changed radically from the "valorous lover" of *cap.* 3 to the now "disloyal lover."

> Veronica writes this letter to you,
> thankless master and disloyal lover,
> whom while she lives, she will suspect.
> Perfidious as you are you know quite well
> the many things I did to assure you of
> my love and never had expressed before to
> another. (17.1–6)

What began as an accusation of male infidelity is substituted by a courteous reminder of the appropriate form that his love for her should assume in an epistolary relationship with a woman: "You would not have written to me, when it happened that for so many days you weren't able to speak to me, proving yourself to be sad and afflicted, as I am now courteously writing to you" (17.22–25). One must, she dogmatically asserts, follow the correct mode of prescribed behavior dictated by society's code for a public amorous discourse. At the very least, she implies, this behavior can substitute for true feeling an appropriate courtly demeanor. In a reversal of received notions about the unfaithful, uneducated, and vulgar courtesan, she checks her lover's chivalric posture by assuming the kind of moral and even superior tone that she later employs in her *Lettere familiari*.

An ambiguously seductive allusion to and deliberate polysemy of the many "ways" in which her love had expressed itself to him quickly switches to a *captatio benevolentiae* in which she champions and praises her beloved's virtues.

> I certainly would not deny
> that you possess great merits
> of wisdom, valor, gentleness
> and innocent devices
> in which you are most practiced. (17.7–9)

She coyly reminds him that there are many others who appreciate and take delight in her grace and beauty.

> But my charm too, my beauty
> —whatever it might be in itself—
> is prized by many noble souls. (17.10–12)

To continue to show him her love, she knows, is to prolong her error. Nonetheless, she proceeds "against reason" to persuade him of why other "noblemen" deem her worthy of their admiration.

Her scolding alternates between erotic double entendres ("I live tied to you in a tender bond"), tongue-in-cheek coyness, and respectful submissions to her beloved's mastery of a chivalric poetic code. Altering the erotic nature of the classical elegists' scene of betrayal, this scene of infidelity in *cap.* 17 assumes comic proportions. We watch the struggle between male and female lovers as it unfolds in the woman speaker's narrative in the same manner that we might participate as spectators in the unraveling of a love-intrigue plot. The courtesan lover snatches from her disloyal lover a volume of poems that praise another woman.

> The book clasped in my hand
> I turned from you in flight
> but you were not out-distanced
> and at my side again
> presenting your excuses
> you were and begged in vain
> that I should yield the book. (17.71–75)

She publicly exposes, as a means of retaliation, the nature of their amorous relationship. She responds to her beloved's public betrayal by uncovering their private commitment in love. Whereas Ovid's heroines' laments are confined to a two-way trajectory and never exceed the letter's insular boundaries, Franco's woman speaker's accusations refer and appeal (in the tradition of satire) to a recognizable and tight-knit Venetian society. Both the opinions of his "good neighbors" and the prompting of Ovid's *Amores* have convinced her to assume the benevolent rhetorical stance of the courteous lover who permits her beloved another chance to redeem himself.

> through my offices and on his behalf
> the good and courteous Lomellini
> bids you a good night and
> greets you and commends himself to you.
> You have, I cannot see why, good neighbors
> who praise you and plead all the best for you
> even though you walk a crooked path. (17.94–102)

But by the third and final verse epistle in this group, *cap.* 20, "Veronica" no longer feels any intimacy with her beloved, nor is she convinced that the rhetorical power of her verses will succeed in changing his cruelty into love.

In the exordium to *cap.* 20 she calls herself "that one," and she further estranges herself from her lover by employing the formal and courteous *voi* in her address. Here the opening extends beyond the third line to the end of the next tercet.

> This letter is written to you by that Veronica
> who lives now neither free nor frank
> but as a slave of unrequited love;
> turned for your sake from the righteous
> onto the wrongful path, o thankless
> cruel man, in misery she hastens
> where sorrow thrives and hope does not abide. (20.1–6)

She posits one definition of the act of loving, "free and frank," against its converse, "enslaved," by referring to the multivalent interpretations of her name. By playing with verbal resonances, she creates a tension between society's traditional notion of the free and unfaithful courtesan who loves more than one man, and her own self-identification as a faithful and devoted lover.[42]

To call further attention to this role reversal, Veronica Franco adopts a stock scene of the classical elegiac tradition in which the male lover, the *exclusus amator,* is refused access to the woman's home; standing at the threshold of her home, he sings a song to the unyielding door that divides her from him.[43] The *paraclausithyron,* the lover's lament to and before the door, was widely employed in Roman comedies, and constituted an important parodic and comic component of Renaissance versions and translations into terza rima of the plays of Aristophanes, Plautus, and Terence.[44]

Franco's rendition collapses three scenes into one. The Propertian rejected and drunken lover's lament is mirrored in an ironic reversal in the swooning woman's reaction to the doorkeeper's report that her beloved sleeps with another woman. Instead of swooning under the effects of inebriation, as was common practice among scorned male lovers of classical elegy, she falls into the arms of her faithful companion overcome by emotion, in much the same manner as Dante the pilgrim swoons when he hears Francesca's pathetic and tragic tale. Compare the description in *cap.* 20 with Dante's in the closing verses of *Inferno,* Canto 5.

> And thus carried by no frail a foot
> I fall almost bereft of life
> into the arms of he who
> walks at my side. (Franco 20.52–54)

> While the one spirit said this,
> the other wept, so that for pity
> I swooned, as if in death,
> and fell as a dead body falls. (Dante 5.139–42)[45]

But this faithful companion accompanies her, she suggests, not only out of devotion but because he loves her. She exclaims, why can she not love him who loves her?

> Fierce, inequities of cruel love;
> for I chase after one who detests me
> and shun the one who pines
> and dies of love for me. (20.58–60)

The Ovidian confrontation with and dialogue between the excluded lover and the doorkeeper occupy a central position in her address. In Ovid's text the male lover's address is no longer directed solely to an inanimate object (the door), but to a real person, a situation that increases the potential for dramatic action. In a series of *captatio benevolentiae*, the lover tries various tactics in order to convince the doorkeeper of the urgency of his request. Ovid's parody of both Propertius's self-absorbed lover's lament and the role of the door (he introduces a servile doorkeeper) stand at the farthest extreme of the *paraclausithyron* tradition in classical elegiac poetry.[46]

As in *cap.* 17, the characters presented in Franco's verse epistle are placed within an intimate and identifiable Venetian stage set. The woman's wandering the street at night in a quest to consummate her desire alludes not only to the classical elegists' *exclusus amator,* but perhaps also to the restless wanderings of the foreigner Julio in the popular and sensually charged Venetian dialect play *La Venexiana.* He comes to Venice in search of female companions and ends up moving through the streets at night between one woman and another.[47]

In a comic switch of roles in *cap.* 20, albeit intersected by a language of pathos and desperate lament, the courtesan is barred from her lover's home by the doorkeeper. She becomes the *exclusus amator* and thus condemns her lover's cruelty and infidelity. Rather than the courtesan's entertaining many lovers, it is the male who betrays her trust by making love to another woman. His refusal to reciprocate her love only reinforces and intensifies the bond, now conceived as an imprisoning force, that pulls her to him. He is the one who tyrannizes and she, by contrast, the one who pleads for his love. Not only is she chained by *Amor's* playful and irresponsible will, she is also "a slave" to a merciless lover.

In Propertius's 1.16, the door is the speaker throughout. As Catullus had done before him in *carme* 67, the door attests to the woman's lack of fidelity:[48]

> My mistress doesn't seem to care
> though she's the loosest girl in Rome,
> and you know what modern Romans are.

And I can't stop her doing wrong.
Alas that I should come to this:
the subject of a dirty song.
And then, what makes it even worse,
there's always someone left outside
who tries to woo me with his verse.

The lover is chained to his beloved as the door who, contrary to his
wishes, is forced to listen to the frustrated lovers' "dirty songs."[49]
   The stern, moralistic door exploits the situation to unburden itself
and comments upon the hundreds of drunken male lovers' erotic laments
that it has endured and recorded over the years. In a reciprocal and
empathetic dialogue with the rejected male lover, who remains silent
throughout the monologue, the door confirms the corrupt ways of the
woman of the house.
   While the male lover's lament in Propertius 1.16 does not succeed in
softening the stern door's rigidity,

O cruel, cruel door, more heartless than my mistress,
   will you never open up and let me in?
Will nothing ever move you to break your stubborn silence
   and snuggle in a message to my love?

her lament in *cap.* 20 is more successful. The unhinging and groaning of
the door bolts as the woman lover's lament forces it to yield calls to mind
Dante's description of the majestic opening of the gates of Purgatory,
sealed from human access for hundreds of years.[50]
   Unlike Propertius 1.16, in Ovid's *Amores* 1.6 and Franco's *cap.* 20—
each of the roles—the *exclusus amator,* the door, and the doorkeeper—
has a distinct and separate voice. No longer is the door the sole focus.
Thus, in Franco's version the exchange among the lover, the door, and
the beloved's doorkeeper oscillates from one voice to the other in an
operatic trio.

—Would that in love you were my benign guides
who accustomed to my nightly errand
might cut for me a path to locked-in-joy,
and you, custodian, steeped in mortal sleep
aroused by the bark of your watchful dogs
do not reject and disappoint my plea
but lift your hand and merciful unlock
your servile shackles then will fall away
forever gone and loosened from your feet.
   But what do you demand of this poor soul?
—Be gone in peace—the watchman says—

my master does not reside here at night:
with another woman he lies and sleeps
to make her gay and happy with his love
While you poor wretch stand here consumed in vain.
    So leave, there is no hope; and though you can't
find peace, you must endure with steadfast heart
what irrevocable destiny has willed. (20.31–48)

Franco's doorkeeper does not refuse her access to his master's home; he simply warns her that his master sleeps with another woman. Even though there is no extended development of the concept of the doorkeeper's servility, as in Ovid's transformation of the Propertian servile lover, there is a reference to servility when she exhorts the custodian to "unlock your servile shackles . . . from your feet."

The *paraclausithyron* in *cap.* 20 introduces, as a kind of theatrical prologue, the rest of the *capitolo,* which consists of a lengthy lament on the woman's misfortunes in love. Her insistence on mutual respect and courteous behavior throughout this verse epistle echoes the ancient elegists' insistence on correcting the corruption of sexual mores rampant in Roman society.

This corrective and advisory voice signals the language of Franco's *Lettere familiari a diversi,* published five years after her volume of poems. In these elegiac verse epistles, her voice, empowered by the authority of classical elegy, is passionate, plaintive, accusatory, and erotic. She restores a language of desire for Renaissance women poets by providing a voice for the "truncated calls" of Ovidian heroines. She also aligns herself with the women's denunciatory complaints in the *Heroides.* This she does by reappropriating a female ventriloquized voice as her own. Thus, Veronica Franco retrieves an authentic woman-authored voice—a courtesan's voice—in an elegiac epistolary discourse on love.

NOTES

Research for this essay was aided by support from a summer fellowship from the Gladys Krieble Delmas Foundation, to which the author expresses her gratitude.

    1. I refer here to two modern editions of Franco's works which discuss their textual history and her activities as editor. For the poems, see Abdelkedar Salza, *Rime: Gaspara Stampa e Veronica Franco* (Bari: Laterza, 1913); and for the letters, see Benedetto Croce, *Lettere dall'unica edizione del MDLXXX con Proemio e nota iconografica* (Naples: Ricciardi, 1949). All translations of Franco's poems and letters are my own.

    2. This reference to the *accademia degli uomini virtuosi* is taken from letter 17. See Croce, *Lettere,* 28.

    3. Salza argues that this anonymous poet is Marco Venier, a cousin of

Domenico Venier, Franco's friend, supporter, and literary counselor. Why his name was removed from the Marciana *esemplare* is uncertain, although a few hypotheses have been advanced. See Alvise Zorzi, *Cortigiana veneziana. Veronica Franco e i suoi poeti* (Milan: Camunia, 1986), 115–26.

4. This third extratextual voice has been identified as Maffio Venier, another member of the powerful Venier clan. Franco discusses her mistaken identification of the enemy-poet in letter 48. See Croce, *Lettere*, 29–31. I argue in a forthcoming essay in *Renaissance Quarterly* that this confusion of identities generates a poetic debate and provokes Franco's defense of her position as courtesan in Venetian society.

5. The satirical literature in Venice that uses the courtesan as the target for a moralistic and often misogynist arsenal is best exemplified in the following works: Pietro Aretino, *Aretino's Dialogues,* trans. Raymond Rosenthal (New York: Stein and Day, 1971); Sperone Speroni, "Contro le cortigiane," in *Orationi del Sig. Speron Speroni* (Venice: Ruberto Meretti, 1596), 168–213; Isabella Andreini, "Della mala pratica delle Meretrici," in *Lettere,* (Venice: Zaltiere, 1607), 85–86.

6. On the vernacular epistolary tradition in Italy and France in the Renaissance, see Judith Rice Henderson, "Erasmus and the Art of Letter-Writing," in *Renaissance Eloquence: Studies in the Theory and Practice of Renaissance Rhetoric,* ed. James J. Murphy (Berkeley: University of California Press, 1983), 331–55; Ann Jacobson Schutte, "The *Letter Volgari* and the Crisis of Evangelism in Italy," *Renaissance Quarterly* 28 (1975): 639–85; Amedeo Quondam, *Le 'carte messaggiere': Retorica e modelli di communicazione epistolare: per un indice dei libri di lettere del Cinquecento* (Rome: Bulzoni, 1981); Janet Gurkin Altman, "The Letter Book as a Literary Institution 1539–1789: Toward a Cultural History of Published Correspondences in France," *Yale French Studies* 71 (1986): 17–62.

This reference to an "absent friend" is taken from François Rigolot's essay on Montaigne, whom he refers to as a frustrated epistolographer. See "Montaigne's Purloined Letters," *Yale French Studies* 64 (1983): 145–66.

7. On the many editions of familiar letters published in Venice during the sixteenth century, and on the translations of ancient epistolographers into the Italian vernacular, see Quondam, *Le 'carte messaggiere,'* 13–150, 177–98. Luigi Groto's definition of the familiar letter in his *Lettere famigliari* (Venice: Valentini, 1606), 13–14, supports the concept of evoking an absent friend when he says that "he who writes a letter imagines that he is listening to him who writes it."

8. For a discussion of these translations of Cicero, Seneca, and other classical authors, see Marc Fumaroli, *Age de l'éloquence: Rhétorique et "Res literaria" de la Renaissance* (Geneva: Droz, 1980); R. R. Bolgar, *The Classical Heritage and Its Beneficiaries* (London: Cambridge University Press, 1954), 508–41; Carlo Dionisotti, *Geografia e storia della letteratura italiana* (Turin: Einaudi, 1967), 125–78, and Quondam, *Le 'carte messaggiere,'* 59–80. For the acquisition of correct modes of behavior from the study of classical epistles, see Quondam, *Le 'carte messaggiere,'* 120–49, 177–97.

9. Franco refers to rhetorical theories on familiar letter writing (which echo Erasmian principles) in letters 38 and 39. See Croce, *Lettere,* 55–56.

10. This critical stance characterizes many evaluations of women's subjective poetry. On this problem, see Peter Dronke, *Women Writers of the Middle Ages* (Cambridge: Cambridge University Press, 1984), 84–143; *Oeuvres complètes de Louise Labé*, ed. François Rigolot (Paris: Garnier Flammarion, 1986), 22; *A Renaissance Woman. Helisenne's Personal and Invective Letters*, trans. Marianna M. Mustacchi and Paul J. Archambault (Syracuse: Syracuse University Press, 1986), 8–33; Peggy Kamuf, "Writing Like a Woman," in *Women and Language in Literature and Society*, ed. Sally McConnell-Ginet, Ruth Borker, and Nelly Furman (New York: Praeger, 1980), 284–89, and *Fictions of Feminine Desire: Disclosures of Heloise* (Lincoln: University of Nebraska Press, 1982). For Veronica Franco, see among others Arturo Graf, "Una cortigiana fra mille: Veronica Franco," in *Attraverso il Cinquecento* (Turin: Loescher, 1888), 232; Riccardo Scrivano, "Veronica Franco," in *Cultura e letteratura nel Cinquecento* (Rome: Ateneo, 1966), 204–6; Giuseppe Tassini, *Veronica Franco. Celebre poetessa e cortigiana del XVI secolo* (Venice: Alfieri, reprint ed., 1969), 99–105; A. Giovanni Frugoni, "I capitoli della cortigiana Veronica Franco," *Belfagor* 3 (1948): 44–59.

11. Veronica Franco's career as "honest courtesan" was well established by 1575, although she was still subject to vindictive treatment from neighbors, jealous lovers, or revenge-seeking servants. She participated in Domenico Venier's literary salon and through his support was active as poet and editor. At one extreme, when the triumphal entry of King Henry III of France and Poland was celebrated in Venice in 1574 he visited Franco in her home—a fact she documents in her letters and poems. At the other extreme, she was denounced before the Venetian Inquisition courts as a "public whore" by her son's tutor, Ridolfo Vannitelli, in 1580, and accused of performing heretical magical incantations in her home. The outcome of the trial is uncertain, but it is most likely that she was excused or perhaps asked to abjure publicly.

On Domenico Venier and his role as poet and counselor, see the informative yet outdated biography by Pierantonio Serassi, *La vita di Domenico Venier* (Bergamo: Lancelotto, 1751), and for his literary activities, see Edoardo Taddeo, *Il Manierismo letterario e i lirici veneziani del Cinquecento* (Rome: Bulzoni, 1974); Zorzi, *Cortigiana Veneziana*, 57–60, 69–90, and 163–64, for further bibliography; Martha Feldman, "Venice and the Madrigal in the Mid-Sixteenth Century," 2 vols. (Ph.D. diss., University of Pennsylvania, 1987), esp. chap. 6, 428–88. On the Inquisition trials against Franco, see Marisa Milani, "L'incanto di Veronica Franco," *Giornale storico della letteratura italiana* 262:518 (1985): 250–63; Alessandra Schiavon, "Per la biografia di Veronica Franco. Nuovi documenti," *Atti dell'Istituto Veneto di Scienze, Lettere, ed Arti* 137 (1978–79): 243–56.

12. On the charge of women as embodying dissimulation, and in relation to Ovid's Sappho in the *Heroides*, see Linda S. Kauffman, *Discourses of Desire: Gender, Genre, and Epistolary Fictions* (Ithaca: Cornell University Press, 1986), 50–61.

13. Croce, *Lettere*, 14.

14. On restraining an individual's passions in order to preserve social harmony according to the tenets of Venetian humanism, see Margaret L. King, *Venetian Humanism in an Age of Patrician Dominance* (Princeton: Princeton University Press, 1986), 175–78.

15. Croce, *Lettere,* 18.

16. On the distinction between letters designed for publication, letters dispatched, and letters that adhere to formulated "conceits," see Altman, "The Letter Book as a Literary Institution," 17–31.

17. On Franco's editorial activities and her compilation of encomiastic anthologies in the years 1570 to 1580, see Salza, *Rime,* 383–84.

18. For a comprehensive list of Italian sixteenth-century women epistolographers extending from Vittoria Colonna (1544) to Isabella Andreini (1607), see Quondam, *Le 'carte messaggiere,'* 255–76, 279–316; and for a recent analysis of the fifteenth-century personal letters of Alessandra Macinghi Strozzi, see Maria Luisa Doglio, "Scrivere come donna: fenomenologia delle 'Lettere familiari' di Alessandra Macinghi Strozzi," *Lettere Italiane* 36:4 (Oct.–Dec. 1984), 484–97.

19. On Ovid's ventriloquized female voice in his elegies, and above all in the *Heroides,* see Howard Jacobson, *Ovid's Heroides* (Princeton: Princeton University Press, 1974); Kauffman, *Discourses of Desire,* 17–61; Susan Lee Carrell, *Le Soliloque de la passion féminine ou le dialogue illusoire: étude d'une formule monophonique de la littérature épistolaire* (Paris: Laplace, 1981); Janet Gurkin Altman, "Portuguese Writing and Women's Consciousness: the Loneliness of the Long-Distance Lover," *Degré Second* 7 (July 1983): 163–75.

20. Of the twenty-five *capitoli,* seven are by the *incerto autore* (anonymous author). For a discussion of these poems, see my doctoral dissertation, "Veronica Franco: The Courtesan as Poet in Sixteenth-Century Venice" (Ph.D. diss., Yale University, 1985), 92–235; and Ann R. Jones, "City Women and Their Audiences: Louise Labé and Veronica Franco," in *Rewriting the Renaissance: The Discourses of Sexual Difference in Early Modern Europe,* ed. Margaret W. Ferguson, Maureen Quilligan, and Nancy J. Vickers (Chicago: University of Chicago Press, 1986), 299–316.

21. On the double letters, see Jacobson, *Ovid's Heroides,* ix, 317.

22. For an overview of this academy, see Michele Maylender, *Storia delle accademie d'Italia,* 5 vols. (Bologna: L. Capelli, 1926–30), 5:36–43; Pier Pagan, "Sulla Accademia 'Venetiana' o della 'Fama,'" *Atti dell'Istituto Veneto di Scienze, Lettere, ed Arti* 132 (1973–74): 359–92; Paul L. Rose, "The Accademia Venetiana: Science and Culture in Renaissance Venice," *Studi veneziani* 2 (1968): 191–242; Lina Bolzoni, "L'Accademia Veneziana: Splendore e decadenza di una utopia enciclopedica," in *Università, accademie e società scientifiche in Italia e in Germania dal Cinquecento al Settecento,* ed. Laetitia Boehm and Ezio Raimondi (Bologna: Il Mulino, 1982), 117–69.

23. Remigio Fiorentino's translation, *Epistole d'Ovidio di Remigio Fiorentino. Divise in due libri. Con le dichiarationi in Margine delle Favole e dell'Historie* (Venice: Oratio de' Gobbi, 1581), was also published earlier in 1555. For an analysis of the popularity of Ovid's *Heroides* during the Renaissance in France, see Anne Moss, *Ovid in Renaissance France: A Survey of the Latin Editions of Ovid and Commentaries Printed in France Before 1600* (London: Warburg, 1982).

24. This *Summa* of all the projected publications and studies undertaken by this academy is discussed in Bolzoni, "L'Accademia Veneziana," 135*n.*61.

25. In my definition, a verse love letter (or *epistola amorosa*) differs from a

capitolo that is merely elegiac (plaintive or deplorative of love's misfortunes) in nature or theme. In the first type, the fiction claims that the poem is sent to a specific lover who then responds in turn with another letter, whereas in the second no answer is requested. These verse epistles represent both the speaker's inner psychological state and the interpersonal dynamic between lovers.

26. Marianne Shapiro, "The Provençal *Trobairitz* and the Limits of Courtly Love," *Signs* 3:31 (Spring 1978): 560–71, suggests the intersection of Ovid's *Heroides* and the women troubadours' lyric poems.

27. The exordia in Ovid's *Heroides* are discussed in Jacobson, *Ovid's Heroides,* 349–56, 365–66, 401–6. The exordia in Book One of Ovid's *Heroides* perform this same function.

28. Jacobson, *Ovid's Heroides,* 349–70.

29. It is important to note that not all elegies are conceived as laments or poems of mourning. Perhaps only Ovid's elegy on the death of Tibullus could be specifically viewed as a funeral lament, for even Catullus's *carme* 68 blended mourning with other themes. Many amorous elegiac poems, however, often deplored the misfortunes of love. Franco's *capitoli* may be seen as both plaintive and declarative love poems.

On the notion of the self-reflexive lament that precludes any possibility of an outside referentiality, most evident in pastoral elegy, see Ellen Z. Lambert, *Placing Sorrow: A Study of the Pastoral Elegy Convention from Theocritus to Milton* (Chapel Hill: University of North Carolina Press, 1976). For a discussion of this theoretical confusion of the nature and uses of classical elegy during the French Renaissance, see Gertrude Hanisch, *Love Elegies of the Renaissance: Marot, Louise Labé, Ronsard* (Saratoga, Cal.: Stanford French and Italian Studies, 1979), 10–29.

30. On rhetorical devices in Ovid's *Heroides,* see Jacobson, *Ovid's Heroides,* 79–82, 87–89, 151–52, and passim.

31. On Ovid's *Amores,* see John Barsby, ed. and trans., *Ovid: Amores Book One* (Oxford: Clarendon Press, 1973), 71–81.

32. Some of the sources for Propertius's lament in 1.16 are the plays of Plautus (*Curculio*), Terence (*Eunuctius*), and Aristophanes (*Lysistrata*). For examples in antiquity in which a woman sings the lament before the door, see Barsby, *Ovid: Amores Book One,* 18–21. For Ovid's appropriation of parodic elements from Plautus and others, see 71–81. On this Cinquecento tradition, see Giulio Ferroni, *Il testo e la scena. Saggi sul teatro del Cinquecento* (Rome: Bulzoni, 1980), 76–84.

33. On the Renaissance rhetorical tradition of praise and blame as also connected to oratory, see James J. Murphy, ed., *Renaissance Eloquence,* 199, 204, 239, 241, 377.

34. An example of some of the rhyme schemes proposed by Franco in *cap.* 3 and then followed by the *incerto autore* in *cap.* 4 are: *scrive/amante/vive; piante/core/sembiante; vigore/aspetto/dolore* (*cap.* 3), and *s'ascrive/tante/descrive; sante/ardore/diamante; fore/petto/amore* (*cap.* 4).

35. For the myth of Venice's origins as a personification of the Virgin and as a vehicle in a distinctly Venetian humanist rhetoric, see respectively Ellen Ro-

sand, "Music in the Myth of Venice," *Renaissance Quarterly* 30 (1977): 511–37, and King, *Venetian Humanism*, 174–76.

36. For this myth, see Ovid's *Metamorphoses* 3.359–98; as adopted by women writers, see Patricia Klindienst Joplin, "The Voice of the Shuttle Is Ours," *Stanford Literature Review* 1 (1983): 25–53; Ann Rosalind Jones, "Surprising Fame; Renaissance Gender Ideologies and Women's Lyric," in *The Poetics of Gender*, ed. Nancy K. Miller (New York: Columbia University Press, 1986), 80–81. On the use of myth as a poetic device in Renaissance lyric poetry, with particular reference to the Petrarchan tradition's use of the Ovidian texts, see, among others, Nancy J. Vickers, "Diana Described: Scattered Woman and Scattered Rhyme," in *Writing and Sexual Difference*, ed. Elizabeth Abel (Chicago: University of Chicago Press, 1982), 95–111; Giuseppe Mazzotta, "The *Canzoniere* and the Language of the Self," *Studies in Philology* 75 (1978): 271–96.

37. For the *topos* of the tear-stained letter, see Jacobson, *Ovid's Heroides*, 388–90, and Kauffman, *Discourses of Desire*, 36–37. For other conventional themes of elegiac poetry, including the *exclusus amator topos*, see Frank O. Copley, *Exclusus Amator: A Study in Latin Love Poetry* (Madison, Wis.: American Philological Association, 1956), 20–85 and passim, and Robert E. Hallowell, *Ronsard and the Conventional Roman Elegy* (Urbana: University of Illinois Press, 1957).

38. *The Poems of Propertius*, trans. John Warden (Indianapolis and New York: Bobbs-Merrill Co., 1972). All quotations taken from Propertius are from this edition.

39. Ibid., 219.

40. For another scene of male sexual betrayal in Propertius, see ibid., 1.3, 8–9.

41. On switches in rhetorical tone, see Jacobson, *Ovid's Heroides*, 356. In the second letter in Book Two of the *Heroides* (lines 49–52 and 61–66), Phyllis remembers the force of Demophoon's words and the conviction with which he expressed them in his declarations of love for her. By reconstructing his discourse, first in her mind and then on the page, she uncovers the original language of deceit.

42. On the semiotic value of a proper name in Renaissance poetry, see François Rigolot, *Poétique et Onomastique. L'exemple de la Renaissance* (Geneva: Droz, 1977). For the many definitions of *franco*, see *Vocabolario degli Accademici della Crusca*, 11 vols. (Florence, 1889), 4:441–45. For the possible derivation from, or connection to, the Provençal attributes for the epithet *franc*, see Glynnis M. Cropp, *Le vocabulaire courtois des troubadours de l'époque classique* (Geneva: Droz, 1975), 83–88.

43. The source for this theme comes from Ovid's *Ars Amatoria* 2:523–28 and 3:579–88.

44. On this tradition, see Giulio Ferroni, *Il testo e la scena. Saggi sul teatro del Cinquecento* (Rome: Bulzoni, 1980), 76–84; Giorgio Padoan, "Città e campagna. Appunti sulla produzione rinascimentale a Padova e a Venezia," in *Il teatro del Rinascimento*, ed. Maristella de Panizza Lorch (Milan: Edizioni di Comunità, 1980), 36–49.

45. Dante Alighieri, *The Divine Comedy, Inferno,* trans. Charles S. Singleton (Princeton: Princeton University Press, 1970), 1:57.

46. For Ovid's treatment of this theme, see Kathleen Morgan, *Ovid's Art of Imitation: Propertius in the Amores* (Brill: Lugduni Bavatorum, 1977).

47. See Ludovico Zorzi, trans. and ed., *La Venexiana* (Turin: Einaudi, 1979). On the double roles of the women characters and on sexual doubling, see Franca Angelini, "La Venexiana: spazi e tempi dello 'sperimentare,'" *Letteratura e società,* ed. G. Petronio (Palermo: Palumbo, 1980), 129–39.

48. Catullus, *Carme* 67, 134–39.

49. Propertius, *The Poems of Propertius,* 1.16, 34–35.

50. Dante, *The Divine Comedy. Purgatory,* 3:95.

2

Male Models of Feminine Epistolarity; or, How to Write Like a Woman in Seventeenth-Century France

KATHARINE A. JENSEN

Tell me, when you looked upon the characters from my eager right hand, did your eye know forthwith whose they were—or, unless you had read their author's name, Sappho, would you fail to know whence these brief words come?

Sappho to Phaon, Ovid, *Heroides*

CAN PHAON recognize the woman author on the basis of her (hand)writing, apart from her signature? In asking Phaon this question, Sappho prefigures some of the most insistent questions in feminist criticism to date: what links a woman's identity, her writing, and her signature? How may a woman's identity be read through her signature, and how does a woman construct herself in writing for her readers?

A poet of the sixth century B.C., Sappho has been renowned for her erotic preference for women. Ovid, the male author behind the woman's signature in our epigraph—writing five centuries after Sappho—vitalizes a legend well known by the fourth century B.C. According to this legend, Sappho fell in love with Phaon for whom she left all women lovers; when Phaon abandoned her, she committed suicide. In Ovid's version, Sappho places her male lover at the center of her life and testifies to his power to determine her fate as a woman and as a writer. Her identity under the influence of his betrayal contrasts with who she was and how she wrote before she knew him. Previously renowned for her lyric verse and love of women, Sappho writes in elegiac couplets to Phaon, the man who has

25

reoriented her desire and broken her heart. Identity thus intersects with genre.

> Perhaps, too, you may ask why my verses alternate, when I am better suited to the lyric mode. I must weep, for my love—and elegy is the weeping strain; no lyre is suited to my tears. . . . [U]nworthy one, the love that belonged to many maids you alone possess.[1]

Sappho also expresses her pain at Phaon's betrayal in the epistolary genre. Indeed, all the heroines of the *Heroides,* most of whom have been seduced and abandoned, write their laments to the men they love in letters, which leave the indelible trace of their desire and the disorder it has wrought. The women often write as the penultimate gesture before willing death upon themselves, death being the inevitable consequence of a woman's broken heart and disillusioned spirit. Ovid's representations of these writing, suffering heroines thematize feminine sexual fatality as the natural outcome of woman's passion for man. Yet if Ovid's letter-writing women inscribe a sexual power structure that makes it man's right to seduce and abandon and woman's place to weep and die, this structure is not naturalized by the women's signatures, for it is Ovid who openly authors the *Heroides* as literature in his name.

We find in Ovid's *Heroides* a gap, then, between textual production and representation of women; while woman's amorous suffering is presented as plausible and, moreover, as necessary to writing—for it is out of pain and anger that the heroines write—this writing and suffering are not presented as real, biographical extensions of actual women. In France many hundreds of years later, on the other hand, the gap between textual production and feminine representation narrowed. Seventeenth-century men of letters promoted what they claimed to be "authentic" female writing to heighten the public's interest in love letters as literature.

The Ovidian heroine's passion and pain cast a long shadow, and in 1669 the French reading public was presented with the *Lettres portugaises*. In these five letters Mariane, the Portuguese nun, writes to the Frenchman who has seduced and betrayed her. In her violent and excessive emotion, she oscillates between accusations against her faithless lover and submission to the force of an overwhelming passion. Ultimately, convinced of her lover's treachery and desiring to cure herself of her amorous and epistolary obsessions, Mariane says she will stop writing, and the letters end.

As many critics have noted, the *Lettres portugaises* acted as a litmus test for the public's reading of female identity in love. Mariane's letters of torment and desire met with enormous enthusiasm upon their publication, and their popularity has extended through the following centuries to our own. The *Lettres portugaises* were reissued twenty-one times in the five years after their first publication and elicited a number of imitations and *réponses*.[2] From the seventeenth to the nineteenth centuries, with the exception of Rousseau,[3] readers heralded Mariane's letters as the true and plausible expressions of a woman who had loved and lost. Yet research in the twentieth century has revealed the author to be a man, Guilleragues, who subsequently became one of Louis XIV's secretaries.[4] F. C. Green traced Guilleragues's authorship to a 1668 *privilège* accorded to the publisher Claude Barbin for *Les Valentins, Lettres portugaises, Epigrammes et Madrigaux de Guilleragues.* This collection did appear, but the *Lettres portugaises* were replaced by *Questions d'amour.* The letters were published separately without any author's name and only a publisher's preface. The preface, directed to readers "who are specialists in the matter of emotion,"[5] refers to the letters' addressee, an unknown Frenchman, and to their translator, a similarly unknown (French) man. No mention is made of the letter writer. If a woman, Mariane, *had* written these letters,[6] their preface would have effaced her as their author. As Joan DeJean observes, the preface designates the *Lettres portugaises* as an arrangement "among publisher, translator, and recipient, an arrangement that denies the writer all rights to her story, eliding her scriptive authority even as it makes her betrayal public."[7]

Mariane's authorial erasure—first in the notice and then as a function of Guilleragues's authorship—in view of three centuries' readings of her emotional veracity, revives the question Ovid's Sappho asks of Phaon: Can one recognize a woman through her writing, and in what ways does her signature matter? Guilleragues's *Lettres portugaises* has prompted many feminist and deconstructionist readings and rephrasings of this question.[8] In this essay, I shall focus on several male representations of feminine letters—prescriptive pronouncements and published models—in order to consider what it meant in seventeenth-century France to write as a woman.

Caught Between Coeur *and* Esprit: *Feminine Writing and Male Literariness*

The trafficking in "women's" letters by men—publisher, "translator," and author—in the *Lettres portugaises* is part of a larger, more subtle story of men's appropriation and publication of the feminine epistolary text. The art of letter writing, along with the art of conversation, was strongly influenced by the seventeenth-century salons. As a social art, the letter genre is ascribed to woman. La Bruyère claims, for example, in his *Carac-*

tères, published in 1684: "The fair sex surpasses ours in this genre of writing."[9] Despite such assertions of feminine superiority, the numerous and widely read epistolary manuals ("secretaries") and collections that codify and exemplify the art of letter writing included model letters by women but offered far more examples by and for men. All the collection manuals were, of course, edited by men. Women's purported epistolary excellence principally concerned the practice of the genre as a social art while men, however less predisposed toward the genre, exercised it socially *and* literarily.

In an illuminating article, Janet Altman attributes male domination of the literary letter in seventeenth-century France to a consolidation of absolutism: "Letters published as 'art' under Classicism are always transformed into the 'art' of writing letters, typically construed to position the writing subject as a loyal (male) servant of an aristocratic order revolving around an absolute monarch."[10] I would suggest that the inclusion of women's letters in men's collections reflects a concern about woman's power and an interest in controlling it. To include women's texts as tokens is a more effective strategy for the consolidation of male supremacy than to exclude them. While Altman studied the exceptional, male-edited letter collections devoted entirely to women and found that they position woman either in the nonliterary social domain or in private, erotic space, I will examine this positioning of woman in the same period from *within* collections featuring both men's and women's letters. The social and sexual marginalization of the woman writer by the men who included her letters in their privileged space of publication uncovers a tension in the male, monarchical, supremacist position.

The view of women as superior letter writers related to the power they exercised in the salon as arbiters of language and social interaction. If men's publications of women's letters circumscribed the woman writer within the social or sexual domain at the very period when salon women were consolidating power of their own over language and behavior, what might such circumscription indicate about men's reaction to female power? I would argue that male theories and models of feminine epistolarity reveal an anxiety about woman's power. By presenting women's letter models and offering through them a social or sexual thematics for imitation, male publishers may have been addressing this anxiety by attempting to limit women's access to the literary. Rather than omit women's texts altogether, men contended with the phenomenon of female power by seeking to contain it through "representative" texts.

Before turning to these representative texts, let us return to La Bruyère's theory of gendered letter writing to delineate how men's advocacy of feminine epistolarity subordinated it to masculine literary pursuits. La Bruyère provides, it seems, an explanation for the underrepresentation of women's letters in published collections. Some women's letter writing could, according to him, exemplify not only better letter writing than men's but the best in the French language. In reality, however, women did not attain such exemplary national status because they made mistakes in writing: "If women were always correct, I would dare say that some of their letters would be some of the best writing we have in our language" (32–33). La Bruyère's previous assertion that the female sex surpassed the male in epistolary expression suggests that the opposition here between *they* ("their letters") and *we* ("our language") maintains sexual distinctions—to women's literary detriment. The French language belongs to men, and if women write well enough to be admitted to this masculine domain, even theoretically, women's access to the linguistic and literary "nation" is highly qualified. Only *some* women's letters would *perhaps* achieve an illustrative place in men's language.

As La Bruyère has indicated, women's "incorrectness" prohibited them from entering into competition for a place among men. La Bruyère does not define women's mistakes[11] but lets it be understood that they are gender-specific and intricately bound to the very basis of women's epistolary success: femininity. For it is woman's nature—characterized by emotion—that produces her art. Women's emotional makeup, La Bruyère maintains, permits them to express "naturally" what men must work to convey. Whether or not they write *about* emotion (*coeur*), women write through it, while thought and wit (*esprit*)[12] and rhetorical consciousness (*style*) mediate men's writing. From his late-century perspective, La Bruyère contrasts two male exemplars of the literary, that is, published, letter tradition, Guez de Balzac (published in 1624) and Voiture (published in 1650), to women's superior emotional expressiveness.

> I do not know if one could ever put into letters more *esprit*, more turns of phrases, more charm, and more style than what we see in those of Balzac and Voiture; the letters are empty of the emotion which has reigned since their time and which owes its birth to women. *Women* find under their pen turns of phrases and expressions which *in us* are the result only of long labor and painful searching. . . . It is women who can make an entire emotion be read in a single word. (32; emphasis added)

While women alone can eloquently communicate feeling effortlessly and unself-consciously, men, La Bruyère implies, are not prohibited from such eloquent communication but only from its effortlessness. If Balzac and Voiture wrote letters devoid of emotion, this lack is due not to their gender but to their historical period—before the reign of feelings. Again, maintaining the separation between "women" and "us" to contrast women (writers who remain outside the national, literary club) to men (writers on the inside), La Bruyère infers that while women introduced emotion into letter writing and surpassed men in facility of emotional expression, men with "long labor" and "painful searching" could approximate this feminine expressiveness. More than that, if women, writing spontaneously through emotion, also wrote incorrectly, then however much "we" may praise women's epistolary gift, this gift did not win women any literary prize. Conversely, if men, after much thought and work, were able to imitate women's letters, these imitations from the standpoint of literary correctness could only be an improvement on women's texts. The implications, then, in La Bruyère's theories are that femininity produces imperfect epistolary models of a superior emotional quality, models upon which masculine stylistic travail can improve. Men, then, can turn women's social art into literature, if they choose.

The question might be: Did they choose? Are women's letters published in the collections largely works by men writing "as" women but "correctly," or are they most often real women's letters that men edited to a greater or lesser extent? The anonymity of the letters and the absence of originals against which to compare them make it impossible to know what editing may have been done. At the same time, the anonymity of the women's letters does bear upon their male editor-publishers' choice to limit the literary possibilities of feminine epistolary writing. For the letters' anonymity signals their "authenticity," which in turn serves as a marker of an emotional femininity. On the one hand, this emotional femininity functions, as for La Bruyère, to preclude a woman's stylistic self-consciousness and thus to differentiate and exclude her "natural" writing from male literariness. On the other hand, femininity is seen to predispose women to write of their love and suffering for men. While women's love letters in the collection manuals are not presented as stylistically inferior to men's love letters, femininity determines the generic boundaries of women's epistolary representation: women's letter writing is limited to writing of love. Whether men actually wrote the feminine letters they published, as Guilleragues did Mariane's, or simply corrected real women's texts, in promoting female authenticity they reinforced an ideology of femininity that kept woman in her social and sexual writing place.

The abbé Cotin, in his 1665 *Galant Works in prose and in verse,* situates women's letter writing in the social domain while his own is carefully shown to extend to the literary realm. The first part of Cotin's collection presents letters the author claims to have received from women during his youth. Although he includes his own responses, he does so, he maintains, only to "add luster" to the women's texts. For women, in his opinion, write better and more naturally in these encounters of gallantry than all our modern orators. I hereby declare that I yield to the likable persons of the fair sex all the advantages of genius and those even of the art they have learned without thinking of it in frequenting High society.[13]

Underscoring women's epistolary art as unself-conscious and socially acquired, Cotin goes on in a second preface, "To one of my illustrious Friends," to specify the emotional nature of this art.

> The glory of representing well the thoughts of the *coeur* is in the beautiful and blessed hands of women. Nature has given to them to express without affectation and without art nature's emotion. You know, Monsieur, that beautiful women have only to let themselves be seen to be loved. I even believe that they have only to want to write to write well. Without effort and without violence, all they desire is presented to them, and they never desire anything but what is most beautiful. *Be it inspiration of chance, call what you please the cause of these "Lettres galantes," all is natural and chosen, all is clear and intelligible.* (n.p.; emphasis and quotation marks added)

How women's emotional spontaneity can yield writing that is, among its other characteristics, "chosen" and therefore in some degree self-conscious causes Cotin some concern, however. He foresees in his preface that the ungenerous reader will doubt the authenticity of these published women's letters, attributing them to him, the man who would gain literary glory by showing off his gift for self-conscious stylistic aplomb.

> Since one does not always love one's neighbor as oneself, many people will proclaim that these alleged Ladies' letters are intended for my own honor. I know that you will answer for me obligingly that if I had written them and not Axiamire, Armelinde, Iris, and Lucelle, I would have to have had a *marvelous esprit* to be capable of such different characters. (n.p.; emphasis added)

Thus we are to understand that because women write differently from one another, whether only from the *coeur* or also through the *esprit,* Cotin's *esprit* is insufficiently "marvelous" for the task of female epistolary impersonation. Moreover, it would appear that his confidence in his women's epistolary diversity as proof of female authenticity is such that, with the single exception of Iris, the women's "signatures" do not accompany their letters. The discerning reader, we infer, can perceive the legible traces of the variety of women's emotions among the letters. Yet one woman, to whose letter Cotin responds but which he does not reproduce, reproaches Cotin (on what grounds is not clear) for not naming his women letter writers in his own letters that extol and describe these women's art. Cotin responds that "the modesty of a hermit" prevents him from revealing the names of women whose illustrious identities would confer too much glory upon *him* (11). In effacing female signatures in the name of feminine epistolary diversity and masculine modesty, Cotin maintains authority over the texts he publishes. Whatever glory is to be conferred upon the writers of these feminine examples of unself-conscious, social, emotional art necessarily goes to him.

While these feminine letters of emotional art, as Cotin has categorized them, all fall within the genre *lettre galante*—broadly defined as "the art of expressing trivialities well"—Cotin makes it clear that his letter writing labors under no such generic limitation. In a letter entitled "The True Style of Letters," he also implies that his *esprit* is indeed "marvelous." Addressing this letter to "His Dangerous [Woman] Friend," he responds to the woman's praise of his epistolary mastery, "the beautiful productions of [his] *esprit*." Modestly denying that he attaches any value to these productions, Cotin admits that he does, in fact, try to write as "admirably" as his friend would have him believe he does. Now, if the adjective "admirable" resonates with "marvelous" on the one hand,[14] on the other, Cotin, in depicting his ("the true") epistolary style, indicates that he can certainly write as women do. His writing, like theirs, is "natural, clear, and intelligible." Not only can he write as a woman, but this stylistic consciousness enables him to write in a myriad of manners and genres. He can write seriously and academically, and delicately, wittily, respectfully, playfully, and modestly.

> It is not that I do not try to do what you would have me believe I do *admirably*. . . . I wish indeed for my Letters to be lofty (*relevées*) where they should be and that gibberish (*le galimatias*) never enter in; that the texture (*tissure*) be equally strong and delicate, the connection facile and ingenious, that my style be natural, free, and respectful at the same time, playful and modest, without vulgarity (*bassesse*), without buffoonery, neither too bold, nor too timid; that my style be scholarly if the encounter calls for it, but that it be clear and intelligible, far from pedantry and affected obscurity. (154–55; emphasis added)

Cotin's descriptions of his own style and that of his women writers place value on what is "natural, clear, and intelligible"; the similarity testifies to what a number of critics of seventeenth-century language and literature note as qualities used in defining the French language in general in the mid-to-late seventeenth century.[15] This "feminization" of the French language deserves a study of its own in relation to the female art of conversation in the salon and the elitist nationalism fostered under absolutism. In the scope of this study, I am concerned with the discrepancy between the positive emphasis men place upon feminine naïveté, spontaneity, and emotion, and the relationship women have to these qualities. As we can see in Cotin's epistolary breakdown of natural, emotional expression, women remain limited to such expression; men do not. The productions of the *coeur* do not attain the status conferred upon those of marvelous *esprit,* for however authentic and different from one another and however similar in natural, naïve, and intelligible style they may be to Cotin's, his women's *lettres galantes* do not demonstrate "true" epistolary style. Woman's exceptional art, even when published, is relegated to the social space where it was acquired. By extolling woman's natural epistolarity, Cotin retains the literary letter for men.

The Insistent Trope of Female Suffering

If Cotin makes it clear that men have a stake in defining feminine epistolarity as a social, nonliterary art, La Bruyère makes it equally clear that men have a stake in defining that social art as amorous. In a key La Bruyère provides for his passage on letter writing and women's superior emotional expressiveness, he refers the reader to the letters of the Portuguese nun, Mme Delamet, and Mme Ferrand (cited in Deloffre, vi, n. 1). Mme Delamet is unknown to modern scholarship, but the Portuguese nun of course is known. As for Mme Ferrand, Gabrielle Verdier has recently rediscovered her letters and compares her passionate expressions of love for the man who abandons her to Mariane's emotional excess. What La Bruyère had in mind, then, when praising woman's emotional expression, according to at least two of the "women's" letters cited in the key, was her inherently amorous and passionate nature. Indeed, the majority of feminine models in the collections fall under the love-letter genre. The underlying key in La Bruyère's theory seems to provide a telling link between a femininity conceived as emotion and amorous epistolarity. If a woman writes through emotion, then the logical consequence is that she will also write about it, that is, about love.

A woman's writing about love, moreover, carries with it a thematics of pain caused by seduction and betrayal. The Portuguese nun had, in the seventeenth century, precursors and followers. The theme of feminine betrayal and suffering characterizes Ovid's *Heroides,* and several seventeenth-century collections feature translations of these agonized epistolary heroines.[16] Whereas Ovid supplies a trope of feminine abandonment, Petrarch provides one of feminine amorous control and self-restraint. The Petrarchan tradition, in which man suffers from unrequited love and woman remains unassailable, remote, virtuous, and usually silent, plays a large part in seventeenth-century amorous codes. *Galanterie,* which, as we shall see later in greater detail, regulated relationships between the sexes in the salons, is based on Petrarch. Accordingly, Puget de la Serre in his 1623 *Court Secretary* offers letter models for both the Petrarchan lover and his mistress. The majority of feminine love letters published in the collections, however, leave the Petrarchan woman out. In her place, we find not only the Ovidian heroine, but a *revitalized* version of "female" seduction and betrayal. For it is "real" women who have authored these letters of nonreciprocated love and painful longing. This epistolary suffering relies upon a structure of sexual victimization, and when women are victims, indeed willing and writing victims, of unreciprocated desire, men are masters of amorous relations. This theme of victimization, etched in letters that men provide for imitative use by real women, would seem to represent a male assertion of sexual privilege.

In 1605, François Des Rues published *The Flowers of beautiful speaking . . . to express the amorous passions of the one as of the other sex.* In this collection, in addition to translating eight of Ovid's *Heroides,* Des Rues presents one group of letters written by a man to a woman and another group called "Passionate Letters of a Lady extremely in love." While the man's letters express Petrarchan commonplaces, the feminine models stand at a distinct remove from that tradition. If the *Heroides* clearly place feminine passion and emotional extremity within a literary tradition, the "Passionate Letters" place such passion and emotion within everyday reach. The female reader of Des Rues's manual finds, in counterpoint to the male reader's only literary epistolary choices, models of "authentic" emotional abandon and sexual abandonment.

In the first genre study of the *type portugais,* feminine letters of failed love, Susan Lee Carrell signals how closely the "Passionate Letters" prefigure the nun's story.[17] The letters paint a portrait of a woman who gives all to a love that is of course nonreciprocal: "At times she even shows herself subjugated enough to permit her lover to love another provided that she 'always remain his good cousin and greatly affectionate friend and servant'" (25–26). On the other hand, Carrell points out, the letters also give glimpses of reciprocated love, and the overall impression is one of a stormy relationship fraught with mutual jealousy and disagreement (28). I would nevertheless underscore what Carrell also notes to be the fundamentally *unresolved* status of the lovers' relationship at the end of the letters (28). The letters trace no dramatic progression; the lady at the end is as attached to passion's painful pleasure as she was at the beginning. In view of the stormy amorous imbalance, which produces the suffering and which in turn generates the lady's letters, we find in the unresolved ending what Nancy K. Miller has called in the context of the *Lettres portugaises,* "the trope of a *penultimate* masochism, the always renewable figure of feminine suffering" ("I's in Drag," 56). When a woman has once subjugated herself to passion, when she willingly endures its pain, nothing precludes her return to the scene of her seduction and its aftermath of victimization. She has internalized her unreciprocated desire and made herself responsible for the amorous imbalance, legitimizing her betrayal again and again.

In publishing, for his female readers, the "authentic" "Passionate Letters" in juxtaposition to the literary, fictional letters of the Petrarchan lover, Des Rues renews the figure of penultimate masochism as emphatically feminine *and* female. Male suffering, on the other hand, clearly aligned with the Petrarchan tradition, remains at a reassuring distance from real life.

François de Grenaille, in his 1642 *New Collection of Ladies' Letters both ancient and modern,* leaves the Petrarchan tradition altogether to concentrate on the domain of feminine epistolary "reality."[18] His collection offers letters in various genres from women of history such as Mary Stuart, Joan of Arc, and Héloïse, and letters from contemporary women, such as the famous Italian actress, Isabelle Andréini. Critics have seen in both Héloïse's and Andréini's epistolary passion important sources for the *Lettres portugaises.*[19] Carrell remarks that although Andréini writes to different lovers, the theme of amorous imbalance and feminine suffering distinguishes the letters (26). Bernard Bray highlights the theme of infidelity as the cause of Andréini's pain and the source of certain letters. Letter writing, for example, provides Andréini the masochistic means to relive her seduction and betrayal. Swayed by her urge to reread one of her perfidious lover's letters, she admits: "It is that my soul, ever anticipating a deceptive remembrance and a vain hope, commands me to represent to myself the ardent promises you made me, but does not permit me to see that you gave me your word only to break it" (quoted in Bray 19–20). Like Mariane, Andréini internalizes her passion and her pain; her letters can be self-generating. Similarly, as in the relationship traced in Des Rues's "Passionate Letters of a Lady extremely in love," Andréini's relationships remain unresolved. With this absence of resolution and Andréini's willing internalization of passion's pain, her exemplary letters of "female" amorous life figure an always renewable suffering and victimization.

In his preface to Andréini's letters, Grenaille brings their authentic and reflective nature to his female readers' attention as reason for pleasure: "I offer to Ladies a collection [of letters] which must be *all the more agreeable since I take from their cabinet ("study") itself the material from which they can write letters ("une pièce de Cabinet")* (2:20; emphasis added). Emanating from the same everyday space (the study) as the female reader's own writing, Andréini's letters are all the more seductive as models for a polished epistolary product, *une pièce de Cabinet*. But what comes out of Andréini's *cabinet* is not only writing, but passionate writing, and, through that, an image of a woman committed to love and repeatedly lost in its pain. If the reader is to find narcissistic pleasure in Andréini's letters, then Grenaille implies that the reader will recognize the epistolary image of the woman in love and in pain as herself. At the very least, in inviting the reader to imitate Andréini's letters, Grenaille asks that this image of female suffering continue.

Des Rues's and Grenaille's early-century models of "female" suffering and victimization reinforce an ideology of an emotional femininity that correlates to masculine sexual supremacy. As Ortigue de Vaumorière's late-seventeenth-century publication of "authentic" women's writing further indicated, the sexual themes and ideology of the *Lettres portugaises* and its predecessors continued to gain recognition and reinforcement.

In what we shall see to be his contradictory presentation of feminine suffering in love, Vaumorière points us toward what may be the logic behind men's concern to reinstate sexual control through so-called real women's letters: fear of phallic woman. In his 1690 *Letters on all sorts of subjects with advice on the manner to write them,*[20] under the section entitled "Passionate and Tender Letters," Vaumorière makes a critical allusion to the *Lettres portugaises*. According to Vaumorière, the love letter genre is to be divided by gender. Men may write ardently and openly of their passion, provided, of course, that their ardor is accompanied by respect. Women, on the other hand, must display restraint and virtue appropriate to their sex.

> I would not like for a sex, which must be endowed with modesty, to evidence passion. I would like, on the contrary, for a woman to enclose the signs of her love, to be content with letting them be glimpsed, to blend her tenderness with a character of restraint and decency. Not that we have not seen Letters appear successfully in which love has exceeded the boundaries of propriety. (13)

In condemning the *Lettres portugaises,* the century's most vivid example of woman's amorous violence, on the grounds of its emotional excess and inappropriate femininity, and in prescribing a restrained feminine style that expresses tenderness rather than passion, Vaumorière distinctly echoes the most prominent spokeswoman of salon ideology, Madeleine de Scudéry.

In addition to presiding over a salon of her own, Scudéry wrote and published, under transparent anonymity, multi-volumed novels transmitting the ideals and conventions of salon life. In her novel *Clélie* she stages

a conversation that presents women's love letters as the height of epistolary art. The reason for women's superiority is their emotional discretion; feminine modesty and virtue define women's writing and produce
more a pleasurable, because subtler, text.

> For once a Lover [*Amant*] has resolved to write entirely openly of his
> passion, there is no longer any art in saying continually I am dying of
> love. *But, for a woman, since she never admits so precisely to being in love,
> and since she makes of love a greater mystery, this love which is only glimpsed
> is more pleasing than that which shows itself simply. . . .* Love and respect
> must carry away a Lover's letters, while modesty and fear must blend
> with tenderness in those of a Mistress. [*Amante*]²¹

This conversation in *Clélie* dates from 1657 and thus corresponds to what
scholars generally see as the golden age of the salon, spanning the first
half of the seventeenth century to 1660. Vaumorière, then, in invoking
Scudéry to the detriment of Guilleragues, reilluminates a social and
sexual phenomenon that by 1690 had been some thirty years on the
wane.

The salon and woman's privileged position in it as arbiter of language
and social conduct arose, according to scholarly consensus, in reaction to
the crude character of court life under Henri IV.²² Considered to be
more socially refined and morally restrained than man, whose traditional
occupation has been war, woman instills and fosters in those who seek
her company an invaluable sense of propriety. In the interest of propriety and worldly sophistication, social commerce in the salon must
distinguish itself from all that would resonate of the ordinary, vulgar, or
physical. A high price is placed on linguistic subtlety and indirection.
Galanterie regulates relationships, epistolary and otherwise, between the
sexes. Based on the medieval, neo-Platonic, and Petrarchan traditions of
courtly love, *galanterie* defines the lover as passionately yet respectfully
in thrall to the virtuous and inaccessible mistress, who, continually on
guard for her virtue, discreetly expresses tenderness for the lover by
accepting his submission.

Unlike Petrarchanism, *galanterie* accords woman a position as a
speaking, writing subject. The appropriate tone of voice is, for example,
of major import in the feminine love letter. To express herself in a
perfectly modest fashion requires a woman's skillful manipulation of
both *coeur* and *esprit*, for a woman cannot abandon herself to emotion,
nor can she abandon emotion on behalf of an overly self-conscious style.
She must maintain her distance and dominance while communicating
some favorable response to her lover. In the letter Clélie writes to her
lover, Aronce, which elicits the conversation about gendered letter writ-

ing, she reproaches herself "for having wanted to have *esprit* in writing to you" and not permitting enough tenderness to appear (1124). *Galanterie* not only places the woman in control of love, herself, and her lover, but it assumes that *esprit* and rhetorical skill are part of her identity. Scudéry and salon ideology endow femininity with reason, language, and emotion. The tenuous balance required between withholding emotion and modestly implying it earns the feminine love letter its reputation as ultimate art.

As an advocate of a neo-Petrarchan discreet femininity, Vaumorière would presumably offer models of the feminine love letter that reflect this artful modesty and control. Yet the Vaumorière woman, far from illustrating the ideal emotional repression prescribed à la Scudéry in the letter collection's preface, reveals an indomitably passionate nature, (un)cannily close to that of the decried Mariane. Vaumorière's examples clearly contradict his rules for feminine writing.

The Vaumorière woman is single-mindedly attached to the passion her lover arouses, however painfully disruptive it may be. The obstacles that keep her from him and from his desire are not internal, as a femininity consonant with virtue and morality would demand, but external. Parental restrictions and watchfulness confine this woman in love to her home, casting her desire within an aura of the illicit, much as the Portuguese nun's seduction within the walls of the convent endowed her passion with the same titillating quality.

> Neither absence, nor threats, nor captivity can make me change my emotion. . . . *But remember, I beg you, that I am wretched only because I love you.* Reflect sometimes upon this, and be persuaded that my love and the persecution I am forced to endure will make me expire soon if I do not find a way to steal away to our Friend's house to see you, or unless you let me know that you are truly sensitive to my woes. *Alas! who could have said that the first pleasures I tasted in loving you would be followed by such frightful pain?* (184; emphasis added)

This last reflection as well as the earlier appeal to the lover to recognize himself as cause of his mistress's suffering bear a striking resemblance to Mariane's entreaties and reflections. In her first letter, for example, she wonders, "How can it be that the memories of such pleasurable moments have become so cruel?"[23] At the end of her second letter, she indirectly beseeches, "I dare to hope that you will have some indulgence for a poor senseless woman, who was not senseless, as you know, before she loved you" (81).

Not only does the Vaumorière woman parallel Mariane in her testimony to the overwhelming force of passion with its consequent persecution and pain but, like Mariane, she turns this pain into an enormous value. Suffering becomes the means by which her lover shall be persuaded of her ardor and intensify his own. Mariane, before deciding that she writes her letters "more for herself" than for her faithless lover (88), hopes her agony, so assiduously transcribed in her letters, will convince him to care for her. She asks, then, for more and more pain.

> Goodbye, love me always, and make me suffer even more pain. (73)

> Treat me severely! Do not find that my emotions are violent enough. Be more difficult to satisfy! Write me that you want me to die of love for you! . . . a tragic end would probably make you think of me often, you would cherish the memory of me, and you would, perhaps, be deeply touched by an extraordinary death. (80)

Similarly, in her second letter, Vaumorière's woman reflects that the persecutions she suffers have increased her lover's passion. Masochistically, she desires her torture to continue.

> I even believe that I am indebted to the persecutions they have made me suffer. You had pity on me and your tenderness was more intense and more ardent. I noticed that you loved me less when you were permitted to speak to me of love. . . . [Love] made you more sensitive the unhappier I became, and knowing that my pain had this effect makes it so dear to me that I wish it would not end. I am afraid that you will cease loving me if I cease to suffer. (193–94)

This letter, which begins. "I surrender myself, I want to believe that you love me," follows one written by the Vaumorière man, which concludes: "In brief, you did not even deign to *fear* that I could be *unfaithful* to you. I tell you that your heart which lacks *ardor* and *delicacy* is not worthy of mine" (191; emphasis added). Whether or not the intermittent masculine and feminine love letters in the collection are meant to construct a narrative, the woman, by her own consistent accounts, would certainly seem to give her lover the ardor he wants. Moreover, the fear he accuses her of lacking—fear of his power to betray—communicates itself, if obliquely, in the last line of her last letter: "I am afraid that you will stop loving me if I cease to suffer." In view of the fear and ardor the lover demands, the mistress has responded appropriately. But what of the desired delicacy?

Recalling Vaumorière's amorous epistolary prescriptions, the lover's call for feminine ardor and delicacy constitutes a paradox. After all, while the code of *galanterie* allows the lover to speak openly and ardently of his passion and suffering, the mistress, who by definition does not suffer, filters the expression of her tenderness through her inveterate modesty and virtue. To ask a woman to write passionately violates the very nature of a femininity predicated on the delicacy of emotional sublimation. Such violation is, of course, precisely what Vaumorière's woman enacts in each of her passionate letters. While paying tribute to the salon ethos of *galanterie* in his epistolary prescriptions, Vaumorière in his models of feminine writing relegates feminine modesty, virtue, control, and power to the status of myth. From this standpoint, the delicacy the lover demands is second to his mistress's ardor and is merely a remnant of a fictitious femininity.

In her analysis of *galanterie* and the role it plays in the formation of the *honnête homme*—the seventeenth-century ideal of masculinity—Domna C. Stanton underscores the literary, fictional character of courtly love. A virtual "grammar of amatory behavior," *galanterie* in no sense implicated its male participant in a reality of suffering and submission to female dominance: "The mythic nature of the code of *galanterie* explains why the required submissive posture carried no real threat of subjugation and castration. Participation in the art of courtly love was viewed, rather, as an integral aspect of the self-reflexive strategy of seductiveness."[24]

If Vaumorière invokes the myth of courtly love only to have his models of both masculine and feminine love letters violate it, what does this transgression imply about the force of the myth as *mere* myth, that is, as a fiction that has no bearing on reality? I would suggest that in the epistolary expressions against it, *galanterie* is shown emphatically to carry a real threat of male subjugation and castration. If men can play out the myth of courtly love so securely in or as literature, then why does Vaumorière not strictly adhere to the literary rules of feminine power and privilege, and masculine suffering and submission, which he has taken such care to set out? Instead he sets up Scudéry to supplant her with Guilleragues and by thematic extension with Grenaille's and Des Rues's models of feminine suffering. While Grenaille and Des Rues did not allude to Scudéry or to the code of *galanterie*, they nonetheless provided their models for female pain in passion during a time when women were legislating love according to an entirely different thematics, one in which woman rules and man submissively suffers.

By 1690, furthermore, in fact as early as 1660, the salon rhetoric of *galanterie* and the general salon predilection for linguistic indirection and sophistication had fallen into disrepute. More than that, as Stanton argues in "The Fiction of *Préciosité* and the Fear of Women," by 1660 salon rhetoric along with the salon women, disparagingly termed *précieuses,* had been satirized by the male writers Scarron, Saint Evremond, and Molière.[25] According to Stanton, the satiric representations of salon women are evidence of men's fearful phantasm of woman, "which spells the loss of phallic primacy" (108). I would suggest that a similar dynamic of male anxiety may be at work in the publication of feminine love letters. Vaumorière's blatant violation of Scudéry's rhetoric of *galanterie* in favor of Guilleragues's ironically demeaned intertext might be considered, if not satire, then perhaps a form of ridicule, "proving" woman's emasculation. In choosing "authentic" love letters that assert man's right to infidelity and exemplify woman's ardent and willing suffering, Des Rues, Grenaille, Vaumorière, and Guilleragues may be attempting to subvert, through supposedly real women, the power that real women in the salon represent.

To Be or Not To Be a Letter Writer: Woman's Social-Sexual Dilemma

An analysis of male prescriptions for feminine letter writing and models of feminine love letters uncovers a vested male interest in asserting control over woman. The salon and women played, for a while in the early part of the seventeenth century, a major role in regulating the ideological and literary climate. Along with Stanton and Carolyn Lougee, who has studied the salon and antifeminist responses to it from a sociological standpoint,[26] I contend that women's power to prescribe social and linguistic behavior caused certain male temperatures to rise. To alleviate a concern over literary control, Cotin and La Bruyère defined women's demonstrated stylistic and epistolary skill as emotional and unself-conscious. To extol women's natural gift for epistolarity amounts to confining women's writing to letter writing and, moreover, limits their letter writing to its social practice. The male theoreticians thus asserted man's exclusive right to literary letters.

As the key to La Bruyère's epistolary theory indicated, moreover, by designating Mariane and Mme Ferrand as exemplary practitioners of feminine epistolarity, to define woman's writing as emotional seemed to overdetermine that this writing be about love. As La Bruyère further implied, women's love letters, even when published (as were Mariane's and Ferrand's), are inherently incorrect by literary standards. This inevitable incorrectness denies woman access to literary status and positions her as the victim of man's seduction and betrayal.

Des Rues, Grenaille, Vaumorière, and Richelet, who republished Guilleragues's letters in his end-of-the-century manual,[27] provided "authentic" letters of emotional and amorous femininity. These letters naturalized the trope of feminine suffering and victimization, which had as its corollary masculine sexual supremacy. While salon women legislated sexual relations according to a Petrarchan theory, removing woman from man's physical domination and positioning him as sufferer, male epistolary models of women's amorous pain reinstated the "natural" sexual hierarchy and provided reflections of a social reality that undermined the salon women's vision of a sexual world they could control.

If male literary models of feminine love letters waged an ideological battle with the salon, where did this leave the women who may actually have produced the models and those who put them to imitative use? Where, between the literary and the literal, do we place these women writing of love?

In an article on the language of passion in the *Lettres portugaises*, Jean-Michel Pelous observes, "Female victims of love are given an enviable place in literature."[28] In this context he names Héloïse, Madame de Sévigné's niece Madame de Coligny, and the Présidente Ferrand. While Héloïse's letters, especially in recent years, have received the critical attention usually accorded "literature," Coligny's letters of passion and pain are virtually unheard of. Gabrielle Verdier, on the other hand, in her fascinating study comparing women's love letters to Guilleragues's, has brought Ferrand's texts out of critical oblivion, as well as Desjardins's passionate *billets*—a collection of letters that her lover, Antoine de Villedieu, sold and had published against her will at a time of financial strain. The point, nonetheless, must be taken that these real letters of real women—Coligny, Ferrand, and Desjardins—have as yet no place in literature, much less an enviable one.

In our study, with the exception of Andréini, the women who may have produced the letters that men published entered the literary scene anonymously. Like Desjardins, they had no authority over their texts. If they wrote (out) of their amorous suffering with literary intent, that intention circles back to their publishers' purpose: to give privilege to the "authentic" sexual dispossession behind the letters. Meanwhile, Guilleragues, capitalizing on this theme of female suffering, constructed the mythical Mariane whose letters have long been given a place in the canon. We know that Mariane had no literal experience of passion's pain and of sexual dispossession. What of the other women who were literarily marginalized? How authentically did they earn the attribute: victims of love . . . and of (literary) men?

They, of course, are the only ones who know. But I ask the question because female pain and suffering from men's sexual privilege has never existed *only* in literature. While *as* literature, feminine suffering is valorized, glamorized, and naturalized—and offered for an ever-renewable, real-life imitation.

NOTES

My greatest thanks to Peggy Waller for her insights on an earlier draft of this essay.

1. Ovid, *Heroides and Amores*, trans. Grant Showerman, Loeb Classical Library (Cambridge: Harvard University Press, 1977), 181–82.

2. Frédéric Deloffre and J. Rougeot, "L'Enigme des *Lettres portugaises*," in *Lettres portugaises, Valentins, et autres oeuvres de Guilleragues*, ed. Deloffre and Rougeot (Paris: Garnier, 1962), xv*n*.1. All further references to this work will be included parenthetically in the text; Henri Coulet, *Le Roman jusqu'à la Révolution*, 1 (Paris: Colin, 1967): 223.

3. Rousseau, in a footnote to his 1758 *Lettre à D'Alembert sur les spectacles*, denies woman the emotional nature necessary to a true expression of passion. Natural passion and its artistic representation are man's province: "Women know neither how to describe nor how to feel love itself. Only Sappho, as far as I can tell, and another, deserve to be excepted. I would bet anything in the world that the *Lettres portugaises* were written by a man" (quoted in Nancy K. Miller, "I's in Drag: The Sex of Recollection," *The Eighteenth Century: Theory and Interpretation* 22 [1981]: 48).

4. I follow Deloffre and Rougeot ("L'Enigme," v-xxiii) in reconstructing the research into the *Letters portugaises'* authorship.

5. All translations are mine unless otherwise indicated.

6. The debate over Mariane's authentic authorship continues. In a recent edition of the *Lettres portugaises* (Paris: Librairie Générale Française, 1979), Yves Florenne argues for Mariane as author.

7. Joan DeJean, "Lafayette's Ellipses: The Privileges of Anonymity," *PMLA* 99 (1984): 887.

8. Elizabeth Berg, "Iconoclastic Moments: Reading the *Sonnets for Helene*, Writing *The Portuguese Letters*," in *The Poetics of Gender*, ed. Nancy K. Miller (New York: Columbia University Press, 1986): 208–21; Peggy Kamuf, "Writing Like a Woman," in *Woman and Language in Literature and Society*, ed. Sally McConnell-Ginet, Ruth Borker, and Nelly Furman (New York: Praeger, 1980): 284–329; Peggy Kamuf, "Writing on the Balcony," in *Fictions of Feminine Desire: Disclosures of Heloise* (Lincoln: University of Nebraska Press, 1982): 44–66; Linda S. Kauffman, "Disorder and Early Sorrow: *The Letters of a Portuguese Nun*," in *Discourses of Desire: Gender, Genre, nd Epistolary Fictions* (Ithaca: Cornell University Press, 1986): 91–118; Nancy K. Miller, "I's in Drag," 47–57. All further references to this article are included parenthetically in the text; Nancy K. Miller, "The Text's Heroine: A Feminist Critic and Her Fictions," *Diacritics* (Summer 1982): 48–53; Gabrielle Verdier, "Gender and Rhetoric in Some Seventeenth-Century Love Letters," *Esprit Créateur* 23 (Summer 1983): 45–57.

9. La Bruyère, "Des Ouvrages de l'Espirt," in *Les Caractères* (Paris: Gallimard, 1965): 32. All further references are included parenthetically in the text.

10. Janet Altman, "The Letter Book as a Literary Institution 1539–1789: Toward a Cultural History of Published Correspondence in France," *Yale French Studies* 71 (1986): 62.

11. Grammatical errors, in any event, are hardly grounds on which to distinguish literary letters from the nonliterary. The manuals and collections are full of such mistakes as a result of printing conditions or editorial oversights. Puget de la Serre, for example, in his preface to the 1646 edition of *The Court Secretary* (*Le Secrétaire de la cour*), simply excuses himself to the reader for such oversights: "This book was printed last year in my absence, which prevented me from correcting it and from bringing it to light in better state" (n.p.).

12. The word *esprit* carries multiple meanings in French. It connotes mind, intellect, thought, wit, spirit. Because this loaded word is used by male epistolary theoreticians and publishers to distinguish masculinity from femininity, which is defined by the simple term *coeur* (heart), I leave both *esprit* and *coeur* untranslated throughout this essay.

13. *Oeuvres galantes en prose et en vers de M. Cotin* (Paris, 1665). All further quotations from this work are included parenthetically in the text.

14. According to Webster's (2d ed., Springfield, Mass.: G. & C. Merriam, 1939): *admirable:* "exciting wonder: surprising: deserving the highest esteem"; *marvelous:* "causing wonder: astonishing: of the highest kind or quality."

15. See for example, Fritz Nies, "Un Genre féminin?" *Revue d'Histoire Littéraire de la France* 78 (1978): 994–1003; Marc Fumaroli, "L'Apologétique de la langue française classique," *Rhetorica* 2 (Summer 1984): 139–61.

16. François Des Rues, *Les Fleurs du bien dire, première partie, recueillies aux cabinets des plus rares esprits de ce temps, pour exprimer les passions amoureuses, tant de l'un comme de l'autre sexe, avec un nouveau recueil des traits plus signalés, rédigés en forme de lieux communs, dont on peut se servir en toutes sortes de discours amoureux* (Lyon, 1605); Pierre Deimier, *Lettres amoureuses non moins pleines de belles conceptions que de beaux désirs. Ensemble la traduction de toutes les Epitres d'Ovide* (Paris: Gille Sevestre, 1612); Jean-Baptiste de Crosilles, *Héroides, ou Epitres amoureuses à l'imitation des épitres héroiques d'Ovide* (1619).

17. Susan Lee Carrell, *Le Soliloque de la passion féminine ou le dialogue illusoire* (Paris: Jean-Michel Place, 1982). All further references to this work are included parenthetically in the text.

18. François de Grenaille, *Nouveau Recueil de lettres des dames tant anciennes que modernes* (Paris: Toussaint Quinet, 1642). All further references to this work are included parenthetically in the text.

19. Bernard Bray, *L'Art de la Lettre amoureuse: Des Manuels aux Romans* (Paris: Mouton, 1967). All further references are included parenthetically in the text; J. Chupeau, "Remarques sur la genèse des *Lettres portugaises*," *Revue d'Histoire Littéraire de la France* 69 (1969): 506–24; Frédéric Deloffre and J. Rougeot, "Les *Lettres portugaises:* miracle d'amour ou miracle de culture?" *Cahiers d'Association internationale d'études françaises* 20 (1968): 19–36.

20. Ortigue de Vaumorière, *Lettres sur toutes sortes de sujets avec des avis sur la manière de les écrire* (Paris: Jean Guignard, 1691). All further references are included parenthetically in the text.

21. Madeleine de Scudéry, *Clélie, histoire romaine* III (Geneva: Slatkine Rpts., 1973), 2:1145–46, emphasis added. All further references are included parenthetically in the text.

22. For an analysis of woman's role in the salon as arbiter of language and behavior, see Maurice Magendie, *La Politesse mondaine et les théories de l'honnêteté en France au XVIIe siècle, de 1600 à 1660*, 2 vols. (Paris: Alcan, 1925).

23. Gabriel de Guilleragues, *Lettres portugaises*, in *Lettres portugaises, Lettres d'une péruvienne, et autres Romans d'amour par lettres*, ed. Bernard Bray and Isabelle Landy-Houillon (Paris: Flammarion, 1981): 72. All further references are included parenthetically in the text.

24. Domna C. Stanton, *The Aristocrat as Art: A Study of the Honnête Homme and the Dandy in Seventeenth- and Nineteenth-Century Literature* (New York: Columbia University Press, 1980), 137–38.

25. Domna C. Stanton, "The Fiction of *Préciosité* and the Fear of Women," *Yale French Studies* 62 (1981). All further references are included parenthetically in the text.

26. Carolyn Lougee, *Le paradis des femmes: Women, Salons, and Social Stratification in Seventeenth-Century France* (Princeton: Princeton University Press, 1976).

27. Pierre Richelet, *Les plus belles lettres françaises sur toutes sortes de sujets, tirées des meilleurs auteurs, avec des notes* (Amsterdam: Wetstein, 1691).

28. Jean-Michel Pelous, "Une héroïne romanesque entre le naturel et la rhétorique," *Revue d'Histoire Littéraire de la France* 77 (1977): 557.

3

Authority, Authenticity, and the Publication of Letters by Women

ELIZABETH C. GOLDSMITH

"IF WOMEN were always correct," wrote La Bruyère in 1684, "I would say that the letters written by some of them would perhaps be the best writing in our language." Women, he reflects, have a special facility for epistolary expression, giving their letters a natural quality that men have to struggle to achieve: "They find at the tip of their pens expressions and turns of phrase that often, in men, are the result of long searching. . . . they have an inimitable way of putting words together that seems to come naturally and that is only held together by the meaning."[1] By the end of the seventeenth century in France, this notion of a feminine affinity for a certain kind of epistolary writing was becoming a critical stereotype. Compilers of model letters were including an increasing number of letters by women in their collections. Pierre Richelet, editor of a popular epistolary manual of the period, opened his 1689 collection of model letters with a series of "amorous and gallant notes" mostly by women.[2] He also provided instructions to his male readers on how to praise their female correspondents who wrote well, and to the third edition he added a lengthy section of "passionate letters," all but one of which were by female writers.

46

Over and over again we read that the female writing style is somehow particularly adapted to the epistolary form. The editor of a 1666 collection of letters by the Comtesse de Brégy writes that, along with occasional poetry, epistolary prose is a form at which ladies have proven their skill: "If you are often presented with works by men, it is not because ladies don't know how to produce them. . . . This collection shows that [the fair sex] knows, on occasion, how to spend a few hours writing letters."[3] Letters, like conversation, were increasingly valued for their "natural," "authentic," and purportedly inimitable qualities, and good letter writers were said to be those who could make their letters "seem to speak," in a plain and unpedantic style.

This belief put female writers of letters in a privileged relation to the letter genre. Women did not have to worry about shedding a scholastic rhetoric that they had never learned, and the only form they had to attend to was the loose structure of polite conversation, at which they were thought to excel. The attributes of feminine writing that were praised by male commentators—a charming carelessness, a facility of expression—reflected a growing antischolastic, aristocratic prejudice that suddenly gave new esthetic credentials to the discourse of women. But while Richelet, Grenaille, Puget de la Serre, and other editors of letter collections provided the public with new examples of feminine epistolary style, they almost never attached their female authors' names to their texts.[4] Du Plaisir's 1683 manual includes numerous examples from male authors, whom he names, but he writes that discretion and a sense of justice prevents him from naming any women either as authors or recipients of letters of gallantry.[5] Moreover, while in the last decades of the seventeenth century women's letters were touted as the best models of the genre, very few collections of letters by women were published during this period.[6] This is particularly striking in view of the fact that women had published their letters under their own names in the sixteenth and early seventeenth centuries.

Various explanations have recently been proposed for this apparent unwillingness to publish of late seventeenth-century women epistolary writers. Janet Altman writes of the repression of the private sphere that coincided with the reign of Louis XIV, and the consequent disappearance of women's signatures from published letter collections.[7] Fritz Nies has argued that the disdain professed by noble writers for the professional author compounded traditional skepticism about female writers who published, and would explain the small number of letters published by women during the seventeenth century. He points out that the notion that letters were particularly suited to women was "discovered" at a crucial moment in the history of sociable education, by male writers who found themselves rejecting scholastic training in favor of the aristocratic and feminine culture of the salon.[8] Joan DeJean has argued more generally that seventeenth-century female writers frequently viewed anonymity as a strategic self-defense against the typical betrayal of their authority once their texts were published.[9] These perspectives all present plausible explanations of one aspect of the decision not to publish, namely the fear of exposure that was motivated by new class attitudes, political realities, or restrictions on feminine conduct. But to arrive at a more detailed answer to the question of why women did not publish their own letters we need to look closely at both the first prescriptive texts telling women how to write and at what women who *did* write and publish during this period had to say about them. The question that will then remain is, what has the impact of these prescriptions for female epistolarity been on the history of published letters by women?

Katharine Jensen's article in this volume traces two crucial elements of the gender-genre connection proposed by seventeenth-century male writers. First, analyzing Cotin's argument that women are more suited than men to a natural and spontaneous epistolary style, she uncovers the implicit exclusion of women from "the orbit of the literary" that results from this praise of feminine style. Men, according to this new standard, could learn to write like women, but the opposite was not true. Second, Jensen notes that admiration for feminine epistolary style in the letter manuals quickly narrowed its focus to one kind of letter, the love letter. By choosing the discourse of the suffering, passionate woman as the model of female epistolarity, theorists of the letter were in effect excluding other forms of feminine self-inscription from the space of published writing.

When we consider these two important features of the new attention to feminine epistolary writing, it is not difficult to see how it could, paradoxically, act to *reduce* female scriptive authority rather than enhance it. A woman's special epistolary talent was seen to reside in her ability to produce convincing and authentic letters of passion, while such a letter was precisely the sort of text that a woman was not supposed to write in the first place, much less publish. Moreover, male writers were told that they could learn to produce plausible imitations of female love letters and thus improve the quality of their own texts, both real and fictional. La Fevrerie, for example, writes in 1683 that writers should model themselves after Ovid, who "never shines in his letters from heroes as he does in those from his heroines."[10]

Even before the publication of *Lettres portugaises* and the ensuing fascination with female love letters, Madeleine de Scudéry had expressed the fear that new reader expectations could inhibit rather than inspire women's writing. In one of her published "conversations," entitled "On how to write letters," she describes one woman's reaction to the notion that all cultivated women should be good letter writers. Aminte simply refuses to write letters, stating that "a lady can write mediocre verse without shame, but not a bad prose letter."[11] Furthermore, if women are so good at epistolary writing, why do so few letter collections include their letters? She is told that "the respect due to ladies does not allow their letters to be printed without their consent, which they rarely give out of pure modesty." Thus, Aminte concludes, women are confronted with a double standard: praised for their epistolary skill, they are also expected to hide it. This is especially true in the writing of love letters: "But after all, if one can praise a beautiful love letter in and of itself, one should never praise ladies who expose themselves either to receiving or answering them" (46).

Other women writers were to provide, in their published fictions, more elaborate warnings of the consequences of male prescriptive notions of female epistolary style. An anecdote by Madame d'Aulnoy in her *Mémoires de la cour d'Angleterre* (1695) melodramatically brings out the dangers (to both men and women) that such expectations can generate. A certain Duc de Bouquinkam hears about the recent success at court of a Portuguese lady, and he is shown a list of maxims on letter writing that she composed. After reading it, he is disappointed, for, he says, while the lady is obviously clever, her idea of good letter writing is too controlled, lacking in emotion, and in short, incapable of matching the image he has of her as a person: "I found a loose style, but it seemed quite useless to me for my heart's satisfaction, that a girl whom I wanted to love would know how to write letters of compliment . . . it all seemed too self-conscious."[12] He writes his friend at court to ask that the lady write to him again, but this time he offers a more specific idea of his expectations. Ask her to write, he says, like the Mariane of *Lettres portugaises*.

> Wouldn't it be better if she concerned herself with writing like that girl from her country, who is called Mariane, I think, whose *letters* we have read; you will agree that nothing is more touching, and if I had seen a letter from this lady like hers I would adore her, yes, I would go mad over her. . . . I had fabricated an image of Mandoza's character that I do not find realized. I beg you to write to our friend asking him to send us something else by her that would satisfy me better." (45)

In reply, his friend sends a tragic story written by Dona Maria, which includes the sort of love letters that the duke had hoped to read. He enthusiastically deduces that this sad story is her own autobiography and rushes to London to meet her, where she admits that she is indeed the heroine of the text. But here d'Aulnoy gives an abrupt and violent end to her fable, revealing Dona Maria to be in fact a ruthless and fickle woman capable of arranging the death of her former lover in order to make way for her new admirer. Ultimately the duke's idol is dishonored and returned to Portugal, the land of her cloistered predecessor Mariane.

Aulnoy's melodramatic story of the vast discrepancy between male expectations and female performance gives an exaggerated reality to Aminte's vague warnings against epistolary publicity. And it is the woman writer who is the biggest loser at this game, for while the duke is left with some good letters and a story to tell, the woman who has learned how to write like the Portuguese nun is carried away by her own success and finally exiled, returned to her original status in the story as an absent and anonymous figure.

A more moderate view of a situation involving a male fascination with female epistolary writing can be found in the third story of Marie-Catherine Desjardins's *Les Desordres de l'amour* (1675). A young officer (Givry) loses a packet of love letters sent to him by Madame de Maugiron, only to have them returned to him by a mysterious woman who has read them and added her own critical commentary on their prose style. Gradually he becomes obsessed with this unknown author and finds the letters, and the person, of his mistress increasingly unsatisfying. The unknown woman turns out to be a princess, Mademoiselle de Guise, who tolerates Givry's adoration but seems singularly incapable of expressing genuine affection herself. The story ends wtih Givry's death in battle, Maugiron's death of a broken heart, and Guise's unrepentant survival. Thus Desjardins, like Aulnoy, separates the woman who loves from the woman who writes; Mlle de Guise, like Maria Mandoza, knows how to write of love but not how to love, while Maugiron loves best but her sincerity is not enough to produce an esthetically correct love letter.

That female epistolary writing cannot claim any special power to express the unique and singular experience of the woman writing is perhaps most forcefully illustrated in the episode of the found letter in Madame de Lafayette's 1675 novel *La Princesse de Clèves*. A letter that the princess believes was written by a woman to the Duc de Nemours comes into her possession; reading it she is overwhelmed by both jealousy and a frightening sense that she is reading her own future, that by loving Nemours she is simply preparing to duplicate the experience of the unhappy author of the letter. The letter *seems* personal—even the excess of first-person pronouns in the text seem to insist on its intimate and singular nature—but what strikes Madame de Clèves is that its writer is like her, and its addressee like other men. And though Nemours, as it turns out, is not in fact the man to whom the letter was written, the idea that this kind of epistolary discourse is neither personal nor private in Madame de Clèves's world is repeated in the scene immediately follow-ing, where Nemours presses his friend to read aloud to a group of gentlemen the latest of his mistress's letters. As Suzanne Relyea has shown, the episode of the letter is a crucial moment in the heroine's progression toward her renunciation of society and discourse in favor of solitude and repose.[13] Madame de Clèves learns that the discourse of passion is neither unique nor inimitable, but generic and eminently transferable.

Letters by women, in these texts by four of the most prominent women writers of the seventeenth century, are shown to be either gener-ated or appropriated by masculine expectations that ultimately rob the female writer of any authority over the specificity of her own text. It is a female contemporary of these writers, though, who has historically been the most famous of all French letter writers. By surveying the publication history of Madame de Sévigné's correspondence, we can trace an impor-tant legacy, for both readers and writers of epistolary texts, of these seventeenth-century notions of women's writing.[14]

Female Epistolarity: Text or Context?

Sévigné's letters first appeared in print one year after her death, as part of the correspondence of her cousin Bussy-Rabutin. Their readers were, from the beginning, increasingly interested in discovering the person behind the letter texts.[15] Successive editions of her letters in the early eighteenth century proclaim, as does one editor, that "the essential foun-dation of her letters . . . [is] . . . the feeling that so deeply penetrates her."[16] The great merit of these letters, everyone agrees, is that they bring to life the woman who wrote them. But unlike Bussy, Sévigné never planned to publish her letters, and from the beginning this fact was regarded as a special guarantee of their authenticity. Pauline de Simiane, Sévigné's granddaughter, wrote that this authenticity was the basis for her grandmother's much vaunted "natural style": "Here is a mother writing her daughter everything that she thinks, just as she thought it, without ever having believed that these letters would fall into another's hands."[17]

While Pauline insisted on the authenticity of her grandmother's text, in the sense that the letters were real, private messages never intended for public consumption, she felt it necessary to edit the correspondence heavily. Her great fear, like that of Scudéry's fictional Aminte, was that the letters would be misinterpreted. In 1734, frustrated by the failure of her attempts to maintain control over publication of her grandmother's correspondence, she destroyed the letters written to Sévigné from her daughter, and left instructions that the originals of Sévigné's letters also be destroyed after her death. Fifty years later these wishes were carried out by Pauline's son-in-law, nearly one hundred years after Sévigné's death when, of course, none of the people mentioned in her letters were still alive to be offended by them.[18]

While the text of Sévigné's letters survived this destruction of the original autographs, eighteenth-century readers of the correspondence continued to display ambivalent attitudes toward her as an author. Voltaire criticized some of her moral and esthetic judgments, but also praised her natural style, which in fact he seemed to think was enhanced by her careless attitude toward "serious" subjects. "She wrote so well and judged so badly. . . . Men have too much art in their writing/ I prefer Sévigné to thirty lively wits."[19] For Voltaire, whose attitude had a strong influence on future generations of Sévigné readers, she was a model epistolary writer who easily displaced writers such as Voiture and Balzac, but her influence was that of a nurturing mother, not an authoritative master. In a letter to Frederick of Prussia he observes that his correspondent has made great progress in learning French epistolary style: "Your French style has reached such a point of precision and elegance that I imagine you were born in the Versailles of Louis XIV, that Bossuet and Fenelon were your teachers, and Madame de Sévigné your nurse."[20]

Prefaces to the earliest editions of Sévigné's letters declare her to be the new model letter writer, eclipsing her cousin Bussy-Rabutin. The editor of a 1726 edition remarks that Sévigné's letters also demonstrate the superiority of the female epistolary voice: "though they have had little reading or education, (women) leave the men way behind. . . . One finds in Madame de Sévigné's collection a charming naïveté. . . . The best letters that we have read until now are without a doubt those of Bussy-Rabutin. But in the collection of his letters, Madame de Sévigné's, which were included, surpass his."[21]

Another collection of her letters to Bussy-Rabutin, published in 1775, was presented to the public as liberated from the now obscure context of her cousin's correspondence: "These letters were buried here and there in ten huge volumes of Bussy-Rabutin's letters, which have been condemned to oblivion for so long."[22] Her style, we are told, is both exemplary and inimitable. The editor offers his readers "the surest and most practical model of epistolary style, if the style of Madame de Sévigné left some hope of being imitated" (2).

By the nineteenth century the view of Madame de Sévigné as a model of feminine sensibility was widespread among her editors, who were steadily increasing in number. "Madame de Sévigné," wrote one, "is happily not a literary lady. She is an excellent mother separated from her daughter, incessantly plagued by the desire to communicate with her . . . and whose sensibility has risen without effort to the utmost perfection of style."[23] One American scholar, in an essay on Madame de Sévigné as the model correspondent, argued that her letters were "a genuine literary development" of "the essential traits of womanly character." He contrasted this naturalness with other forms of writing by women.

> It is . . . the consciousness of a reputation for authorship or wit, on the part of literary ladies, that causes men of earnest feeling to turn from female celebrities. . . . The advantage of a letter as an exponent of a woman's nature is, that it is, after all, only written conversation, the artless play of her mind, the candid utterance of her sentiment, designed only to be interpreted by one she loves.[24]

That Sévigné was best known for the adoring letters she wrote to her daughter facilitated an extension of this metaphor of her writing as a pure expression of femininity. Her editors begin to describe her ability as something resembling instinct: "Madame de Sévigné did not leave one page that she wrote with design, for the public, out of a desire to write well. If she talks of books that she wants to write on ingratitude, or on friendship, she is being playful. She affected nothing, she loved nothing by imitation."[25] Sévigné's readers are now exhorted to view the letters as pure expressions of affection, unmediated because utterly without artistic purpose. "Madame de Sévigné was not a philosopher, and what cannot be said too often, she was not an author."[26]

Not surprisingly, nineteenth-century discussions of epistolary style also subscribed to the idea that women were superior letter writers. Their affinity to the genre was seen in quasi-biological terms, as in an essay by a member of the French Academy in 1849.

> Nature gave them a more mobile imagination, a more delicate organization. . . . Their sensibility is quicker, more lively, and touches a wider variety of objects . . . from this that suppleness and continual variety in everything, that we so often see in their letters; that facility for jumping from one subject to other completely diverse ones, without effort and with unexpected but natural transitions.[27]

By the beginning of the twentieth century commentators on Sévigné's letters were more interested in situating her in a literary tradition, while still subscribing to the standard view of her natural, feminine affinity to the letter genre. They no longer used the argument that women have a natural epistolary talent to explain their own aversion for "literary ladies" who write in other genres. Instead, they gave much attention to the literary *influence* of women like Sévigné, who never thought of themselves as authors. In a speech delivered on the occasion of the unveiling of a statue of Sévigné in 1911, Paul Deschanel, a member of the French Academy, reflected on the irony of honoring a great writer who would have been excluded from the academy because of her sex. He cited the many academicians who had "fallen in love" with Sévigné and who, over the centuries, had been inspired by her letters to write important works. Sévigné and other female writers "have avenged themselves by becoming much more surely immortal and by causing most of us to become passionately attached to them."[28] Finally, after reminding his audience that Sévigné's celebrated maternal love was, oddly, stronger for her daughter than for her son, Deschanel read a long letter from Charles de Sévigné written to his sister after their mother's death, in which he showed no resentment over his smaller share of the inheritance. Deschanel ended his speech with a gesture evoking the gratitude of Sévigné's real and her literary "sons": "In the presence of the noble family that faithfully maintains the cult of their illustrious ancestor, I place at the feet of the mother the noble and touching letter of the son" (15).

Virginia Woolf may have been the first reader of Sévigné to depart from the popular image of her as a letter writer by instinct. "In our age," Woolf wrote, (she) "would probably be one of the great novelists."[29] Since then, modern redefinitions of the text and the status of the author have generated new analyses of genres such as the familiar letter, which was traditionally excluded from the domain of "literature." Recent studies of the eighteenth-century novel have noted the close relationship between the feminine cultivation of letter writing as a vehicle for both practical and artistic expression, and the development of narrative techniques in the epistolary novel.[30] Janet Altman's formalist approach to letter fiction explores characteristics of epistolary discourse manifested in any letter exchange, real or imagined.[31] Essays on seventeenth-century epistolary practice have argued that any writer of Sévigné's milieu had to be aware that the potential readership of a message was likely to extend far beyond the primary addressee. More importantly, it is argued that in any act of writing a public is implied.[32]

But research such as Bernard Bray's on Sévigné's "epistolary system" has provoked considerable criticism from other Sévigné scholars. Roger Duchêne, in particular, has mounted a crusade against critics who approach her letters as a literary text. In the preface to his richly annotated correspondence he insists that any care she may have taken in writing her letters had no other purpose than to please or make herself understood by her correspondent. Her letters, he says, are being ravaged by the misinterpretations of strangers, and she has no one to defend her. "Alive, she could at least appeal to her friends to reestablish the truth against her enemies, but today? No one is there to answer in her name" (I, ix). Casting himself in the role of defender of the embattled "truth" about the lady, Duchêne closes his preface with an attack on textual approaches to the correspondence. He quotes Bray, who has argued that "in Madame de Sévigné's life, the most interesting thing is her correspondence." Then he retorts, "The truth is, one cannot consider separately Madame de Sévigné's 'epistolary system' . . . when Madame de Sévigné wants to say something better, she doesn't try to phrase it better, but rather to make herself better understood by her correspondent" (xviii).

While Duchêne does not explicitly endorse the views of his predecessors on the special authenticity of letters by women, it is difficult to imagine a debate such as this one taking place over a correspondence written by a man. His description of Sévigné's vulnerable text, "offered defenseless to the gaze of a stranger" (ix), echoes the fears of Aminte in Scudéry's conversation on letter writing and suggests that the publication of letters, especially love letters, still poses special risks to the female writer.[33]

Eighteenth-century epistolary novelists, of course, knew that their readers' interest would be piqued by the belief that they were reading letters written by women for the eyes of another reader. The belief that letters were ideally suited to a feminine style of discourse made epistolary writing by women particularly susceptible to clandestine publication. The enormous popularity of *Lettres portugaises* and *Lettres de Babet* made French publishers eager to print letters by women, and the fact that such exposure was usually against the writer's wishes only increased their marketability. Loss of authorial control, faced by every author who releases a text into the public domain, was particularly threatening to female writers, who knew, as Hortense Mancini wrote in her memoirs, that "a woman's glory consists in not being talked about."[34]

The seventeenth-century fascination with female epistolary voices, combined with the belief that the integrity of these voices depended on the writer's nonauthorial stance, made it inevitable that male authors would begin to use letters by women more often in their own writings. In giving a large place to female characters, epistolary novelists knew that their claim to an authentic text would be strengthened. For love letters in particular, the female voice was perceived as the superior vehicle of expression, even when it was not from a female author.

In the 1698 edition of an epistolary narrative called *Lettres de Babet,* first published in 1669, a series of letters exchanged between a young woman and her lover is presented anonymously by an editor who identifies himself as the male correspondent.[35] He assures his readers of the letters' authenticity, which, he remarks, should be evident from the different styles of his letters and those of Babet. Anticipating the disapproval of some readers who will criticize him for publishing messages "that were made only for me," he replies that Babet's death has permitted him to publish her letters along with his own: "If I thought that there were souls so base as to dare attack the conduct of a girl who no longer exists, I would sing the praises of the one I am talking about, and I would defy Truth to contradict me if I were to say anything that she were not in agreement with."[36]

Like *Lettres portugaises,* which also appeared in 1669, this early experiment in epistolary narration presents love letters by women as a badge of authenticity. The sincerity of a female writer is not difficult to accept, so long as she is not herself responsible for the letters' publication. The role of author is reserved for the editor, who in the case of *Lettres de Babet* is also Babet's lover. He interposes himself between Babet and her readers and personally vouches for the truth of his presentation.

In the case of *Lettres portugaises,* the three figures of the recipient, publisher, and translator collectively authorized the text. In the foreword to the first edition, the publisher offers no acknowledgment of the writer of the letters, and instead invokes the authority of the recipient and translator: "I have no idea of the name of the person to whom they were written, nor of he who translated them, but it seemed to me that I would not displease them by making them public."[37]

Mariane herself, if she existed, would no doubt have wanted her identity to remain unknown and her letters unpublished. Even a writer like Sévigné, with an established reputation as a letter writer among her friends, objected vigorously to the idea that her correspondence might be circulated more widely.[38] For her, as for many of her female contemporaries, the safest space from which to write letters was private, protected from the intrusions of all but a carefully chosen number of readers. And much of the commentary on her letters over the last three hundred years has continued to mediate the relationship between her text and its public by attempting to preserve her from the status of an author.

The legacy of the seventeenth-century connection between the female gender and the epistolary genre is perhaps today most strongly present in the letter collections of lesser known women writers of the period, who have not been reedited since the nineteenth century. A recent six-volume anthology of French correspondences cites, as its source for nearly all of the letters by seventeenth-century women, a number of nineteenth-century biographies by Victor Cousin.[39] Cousin's massive project, begun in the 1840s, to publish in modern editions the letters of those seventeenth-century ladies that were so admired by their contemporaries, was inspired by his belief in the notion of a particular kind of "feminine genius" that could serve as a model for modern women writers. He resurrected the letters of Madame de Longueville, Madame de Sablé, Madame de Chevreuse, Jacqueline Pascal, Madame Cornuel, Madame de Hautefort, and others by publishing excerpts from their correspondences along with lengthy biographical essays on their lives and writing. From the outset his intention, echoing his seventeenth-century predecessors, was to argue in favor of the *femme d'esprit* over the *femme auteur:* "We have," he wrote, "infinite respect for the former and little taste for the latter."[40] With few exceptions, none of these women's letters had been published before.

Nor have they been published since, which means that a reader interested in studying the texts that were so praised by seventeenth-century epistolary theorists must either go to the manuscript sources or wade through the heavy context of Cousin's editions, for nowhere does he simply present his model letters without interspersed commentary on the superiority of women "who never wrote for the public," or "whose happiness came only from pleasing."[41] In large part, then, the task of freeing the work of these seventeenth-century letter writers from prescriptive notions of "how women write" remains to be done.

NOTES

1. La Bruyère, *Les Caractères,* "Des Ouvrages de l'Esprit," (Paris: Garnier, 1962), 79–80. All English translations in this essay are my own.

2. Pierre Richelet, *Les Plus belles lettres des meilleurs auteurs français,* (Lyon: Benoit-Bailly, 1689).

3. *Les Lettres et poésies de Madame la Comtesse de B.* (Leyde: A. Du Val, 1666), preface.

4. See Jean Puget de la Serre, *Le Secrétaire à la mode* (Amsterdam: L. Elzevier, 1663), and François de Grenaille, *Nouveau Recueil de lettres tant anciennes que modernes* (Paris: T. Quinet, 1642).

5. Du Plaisir, *Sentiments sur les lettres et sur l'histoire avec des scrupules sur le style* (Geneva: Droz, 1975), 29.

6. The letters of the Comtesse de Brégy, cited above, were one of the few exceptions. Even so, the author remained anonymous, being named only as the "Comtesse de B." See Janet Altman's comments on the relative anonymity of

women's epistolary writing in the seventeenth century in "The Letter Book as a Literary Institution, 1539–1789: Toward a Cultural History of Published Correspondences in France," *Yale French Studies* 71 (1986): 42–49.

7. See Altman, "The Letter Book as a Literary Institution."

8. Fritz Nies, "Un Genre féminin?" *Revue d'histoire littéraire de la France* 78 (1978): 994–1003.

9. Joan DeJean, "Lafayette's Elipses: The Privileges of Anonymity," *PMLA* 99 (1984): 884–902.

10. La Fevrerie, "Du Style Epistolaire," Extraordinaire du *Mercure Galant*, July 1683, 43.

11. Madeleine de Scudéry, *Conversations nouvelles* . . . (La Haye: Abraham Arendeus, 1685), 28. The conversation on letters was first published as part of Scudéry's novel *Clélie*.

12. Aulnoy, *Mémoires de la cour d'Angleterre* (Paris: Barbin, 1695), 42–43.

13. See Suzanne Relyea, "Elle se nomme: la représentation et la lettre dans *La Princesse de Clèves*," in *Onze nouvelles études sur l'image de la femme dans la littérature française du dix-septième siècle*, ed. Wolfgang Leiner (Tübingen/Paris: Narr/Place, 1984), 109–19.

14. The publication history of Sévigné's letters has been massively documented by Fritz Nies to illustrate how successive editions of her letters have reflected changing standards of taste. While Nies argued that her editors have frequently misrepresented Sévigné's original intentions, he was not concerned specifically with the impact of prescriptions for feminine epistolary style on the way Sévigné has been presented. See Nies, *Gattungspoetik und Publikumsstrucktur: Sur Geschichte des Sévignébriefe* (Munich: Wilhelm Fink Verlag, 1972).

15. For discussions of the changing relationship between letter writer and letter reader during this period, see Roger Duchêne, "Le Lecteur de lettres," *RHLF* 78 (1978): 977–90; Bernard Beugnot, "Style ou Styles épistolaires?" *RHLF* 78 (1978): 939–52; and Altman, "The Letter Book as a Literary Institution."

16. Madame de Sévigné, *Lettres* (Paris: Hachette, 1862), XI: 488.

17. Ibid., XI: 16.

18. This history is surveyed in detail by Roger Duchêne in his edition of Sévigné's correspondence. See Madame de Sévigné, *Correspondance* (Paris: Gallimard, 1972–78), I: 755–92.

19. Cited in Catherine Montfort Howard, *Les Fortunes de Madame de Sévigné au dix-huitième siècle* (Paris: Place, 1982), 59–60.

20. Ibid., 60.

21. *Lettres de Madame Rabutin-Chantal, Marquise de Sévigné, à Madame la Comtesse sa fille* (La Haye: P. Gosse, 1726), 2–4.

22. *Lettres de Madame de Sévigné au Comte de Bussy-Rabutin, tirées du recueil des lettres de ce dernier* (Amsterdam/Paris: Delalain, 1775), 1.

23. *Lettres de Madame de Sévigné* (Paris: Furne et Cie., 1860), iii–iv.

24. Henry Tuckerman, "The Correspondent: Madame de Sévigné," in *Characteristics of Literature* (Philadelphia: Lindsay and Blakiston, 1851), 104–6.

25. *Lettres de Madame de Sévigné* (Paris: Lefèvre, 1843), 1: xxi.

26. *Lettres de Madame de Sévigné* (Paris: Furne et Cie., 1860), vi.

27. M. Suard, "Du style épistolaire," in *Lettres de Madame de Sévigné* (Paris: Firmin Didot Frères, 1849), iii.

28. *Discours de Monsieur Paul Deschanel prononcé à l'occasion de l'inauguration de la statue de Madame de Sévigné* (Paris: Firmin-Didot, 1911), 3.

29. Virginia Woolf, "Madame de Sévigné," in *Death of the Moth and other essays* (New York: Harcourt Brace Jovanovich, 1942), 51.

30. See Ruth Perry, *Women, Letters, and the Novel* (New York: AMS Press, 1980), and Laurent Versini, *Le Roman épistolaire* (Paris: Presses Universitaires de France, 1979), 182–209.

31. See Janet Altman, *Epistolarity: Approaches to a Form* (Columbus: Ohio State University Press, 1982), 117–42.

32. See Bernard Bray, "L'Epistolier et son public au 17e siècle," *Travaux de linguistique et de Littérature* 2 (1973): 7–17; and "Le Système épistolaire de Madame de Sévigné," *RHLF* 69(1969); 490–505.

33. The Bray-Duchêne debate is summarized by Louise K. Horowitz in "The Correspondence of Madame de Sévigné: Letters or Belles-lettres?" *French Forum* 6(1981): 13–27. Bernard Beugnot also discusses this exchange and its echoes in Duchêne's edition of the Sévigné correspondence in "Madame de Sévigné telle qu'en elle-même enfin?" *French Forum* 5(1980): 208–17. I would agree with the point made by both Beugnot and Horowitz that the antitheses of nature and artifice, sincerity and disguise, force an oversimplification of the interaction of text and life in Sévigné's writing. Moreover, in discussions of epistolary style, as we have seen, the polarization of nature and artifice has been traditionally linked to the idea that the letter is a particularly appropriate form for feminine discourse.

34. Cited in René Démoris, *Le Roman à la première personne* (Paris: Armand Colin, 1975), 111.

35. Edme Boursault, *Lettres de Babet,* first published in *Lettres de respect, d'obligation et d'amour* (Paris: J. Guignard, 1669).

36. Bernard Bray and Isabelle Landy-Houillon, eds., *Lettres Portugaises, Lettres d'une péruvienne, et autres romans d'amour par lettres* (Paris: Garnier Flammarion, 1983), 108–9.

37. Ibid., "Au Lecteur," 69.

38. This has been amply documented by Duchêne, most recently in "Texte public, texte privé, le cas des lettres de Madame de Sévigné," in *Ecrire au temps de Madame de Sévigné* (Paris: J. Vrin, 1982), 223–40.

39. The exceptions to this are published letters by women known for their public roles in political or religious history, such as Marie de Medecis, Marguerite de Valois, Louise de Coligny, Madame de Maintenon, Sainte Jeanne de Chantal, and Angélique Arnauld. See André Maison, ed., *Anthologie de la correspondance française* (Paris: Rencontre, 1969).

40. Victor Cousin, *Jacqueline Pascal* (Paris: Didier, 1845), 3.

41. Ibid., 13; Cousin, *Madame de Longueville* (Paris: Didier, 1853), 28.

II

*The female epistolary voice
in the eighteenth century*

4

Female Resources:
Epistles, Plot, and Power

PATRICIA MEYER SPACKS

EARLY IN *Northanger Abbey,* Jane Austen's Henry Tilney
explains to wide-eyed Catherine Morland the inadequacies
of female letter writers: "It appears to me that the usual style
of letter-writing among women is faultless, except in three
particulars. . . . A general deficiency of subject, a total inattention to
stops, and a very frequent ignorance of grammar." Although she responds with some pique, Catherine has given Henry his opening by
observing "doubtfully" herself, "I have sometimes thought . . . whether
ladies do write so much better letters than gentlemen! That is—I should
not think the superiority was always on our side."[1] At roughly the same
time that she wrote *Northanger Abbey,* however, Austen was probably
also working on the novel later to be published as *Lady Susan*—a fiction
composed of letters, mainly by women, which demonstrated no deficien-
cies of subject, grammar, or energy.

The conventional view of *Lady Susan* has it that Austen wrote awk-
wardly in the epistolary style. "It did not suit her talents," Margaret
Drabble writes. "The letter form is an artificial convention, and she felt
its limitations. . . . The epistolary form is in many ways open to ridicule,

especially from an essentially naturalistic writer like [Austen]."[2] Although Austen may have drafted early versions of *Sense and Sensibility* and *Pride and Prejudice* in letters, her published work composed after *Lady Susan* never again employed the mode. Yet by playing with epistolary convention in *Lady Susan,* I shall argue, Austen placed herself in a female tradition, then demonstrated subversive possibilities of a form that in previous uses by Englishwomen had reinforced literary and social restrictions on female enterprise. Earlier epistolary novels hint resentment and depression about the female situation, but they implicitly accept that situation as necessary. *Lady Susan* realizes the possibility of a woman's exercising agency, partly by the act of writing letters. The novel's innovative force becomes apparent by comparison with preceding epistolary fictions.

As Humpty Dumpty explains in *Through the Looking-Glass,* all use of language raises questions of mastery. Lady Susan quite understands. "Consideration & Esteem as surely follow command of Language," she writes, "as Admiration waits on Beauty."[3] Lady Susan means that she's a good talker, but the epistolary form emphasizes the "command" of her letter writing: she controls reality by her verbal representations of it. Conversely, Lady Susan's vigorous antagonist, her brother-in-law's wife Mrs. Vernon, suspects her opponent's integrity precisely because of her linguistic deftness: "She talks vastly well, I am afraid of being ungenerous or I should say she talks *too* well to feel so very deeply" (letter 15, *Minor Works* 267). The relative value of mastery and of feeling becomes deeply problematic in the representation of a woman who gains her power only by avoiding the trap of conventional "feminine" emotion.

Lady Susan speaks and writes always of feeling but seldom claims the emotion she really experiences. The short letter that opens the novel epitomizes her mastery and her implicit mockery of orthodox feeling and expression, as she invites herself to her brother-in-law's house and announces her hope there "to be introduced to a Sister whom I have so long desired to be acquainted with" and her impatience to be "admitted into your delightful retirement. . . . I long to be made known to your dear little Children," Lady Susan continues, "in whose hearts I shall be very eager to secure an interest" (*Minor Works* 243–44).

The letter supplies factual information: Lady Susan is determined to visit the Vernons; she will leave her daughter in London. It also contains misstatements, although the reader cannot yet know this. Lady Susan's real reasons for departing from her previous retreat involve not her proclaimed reluctance to engage in active social life but her excessive social activity: she has created a scandal, severely testing the "hospitable

& chearful dispositions" she attributes to her friends, that makes her departure imperative. Despite her claims, she feels neither "Duty" nor "affection" toward her daughter, who impedes her social freedom. She wants to visit Churchill not from eagerness to meet Mrs. Vernon but because she has nowhere else to go.

Before learning these facts, the reader may intuit the letter's falseness from its insistent emotional clichés. The repertoire of attitudes here invoked—wishes for attachment, need for solitude, longing for "delightful retirement," love for a daughter, interest in the "dear little Children" of others—belongs to the stereotypical lady of sensibility. Lady Susan recklessly, mockingly multiplies acceptable emotional postures. Mrs. Vernon suspects her falseness: "I am not quite weak enough to suppose a woman who has behaved with inattention if not unkindness to her own child, should be attached to any of mine" (letter 3, *Minor Works* 247). But she does not know how to resist.

I dwell on this first letter because it epitomizes Austen's daring in imagining her central character. In the 1790s, when Austen presumably wrote the book, the woman of sensibility was a virtually sacred stock figure. As a female letter writer in a novel published in 1789 puts it, "Poor Clara! she had always a tender and susceptible heart, which seldom fails of subjecting its possessor to many a severe pang: yet, who would wish to be destitute of sensibility?"[4] Austen answers that question. Lady Susan sees sensibility as weakness, manipulates its vocabulary, and avoids its substance. She feels contemptuous toward her daughter, who indulges in feeling rather than exercising control: "She is so charmingly artless in [her] display [of feeling], as to afford the most reasonable hope of her being ridiculed & despised by every Man who sees her" (letter 19, *Minor Works* 274). For Lady Susan herself, artifices of emotion supply instruments for domination. *Real* feeling must be denied, suppressed, disguised.

Yet real feeling—though hardly the kind associated with "sensibility"—rings through Lady Susan's letters, especially those written to her confidante, Mrs. Johnson, which vividly convey aggressiveness and will to power. Lady Susan's second letter, to Mrs. Johnson, reveals what remained latent in the first. Now, when she uses a phrase like "the sacred impulse of maternal affection," she dramatizes her rage: "If [my] Daughter were not the greatest simpleton on Earth, I might have been rewarded for my Exertions as I ought" (*Minor Works* 245). She urges Mrs. Johnson to keep up her husband's resentment against Mrs. Manwaring, declares that her brother-in-law "Charles Vernon is my aversion" (246), and acknowledges that she will never pay the bill at her daughter's new school. "There is exquisite pleasure in subduing an insolent spirit," she writes in a later letter (letter 7, *Minor Works* 254). Her accounts of her relations with Reginald, Mrs. Vernon's brother, formulate their exchanges as a struggle for mastery. Toward the novel's end, she suggests that she understands all relationships as contests of power. "Frederica shall be Sir James's wife before she quits my house. *She* may whimper, & the Vernons may storm; I regard them not. I am tired of submitting my will to the Caprices of others. . . . I have given up too much—have been too easily worked on" (letter 39, *Minor Works* 308).

Her pose of bravado, preserved with her closest friend, denies some emotional realities to reveal others. At this point in the narrative, most of Susan's plans have failed; instead of acknowledging defeat, she rapidly shifts ground. Her correspondent's persona resembles hers: when Mrs. Johnson explains that they can no longer write each other, her letter announcing the loss of Susan's one important alliance concludes offhandedly, "I dare say you did all for the best, & there is no defying Destiny" (letter 38, *Minor Works* 307). These women have established new conventions for themselves, rules that govern their correspondence as other rules control Lady Susan's decorous overtures in her initial letter to the Vernons. Mary Poovey claims that "Susan is able to manipulate others chiefly because she knows that the use of language is an art capable of generating plausible, internally consistent, but wholly malleable fictions—just as the manners of propriety can."[5] In fact, Lady Susan's use of language is itself controlled by various versions of "the manners of propriety." She and Mrs. Johnson have adopted consistent poses of flippant cynicism. Their self-protective personae allow no expression of tenderness, grief, regret, or melancholy—sensibility.

Austen modifies epistolary tradition by calling attention to the necessary artifice of letters, their inevitable participation in established decorums. "Perhaps the most distinctive aspect of epistolary language," Janet Altman writes, "is the extent to which it is colored by not one but two persons and by the specific relationship existing between them."[6] The difference between the correspondence of Lady Susan and Mrs. Johnson and that of Mrs. Vernon and her mother, Lady De Courcey, depends more vividly on opposed sets of convention than on dissimilar personal relationships. In a provocative essay on Austen's use of letters as a specifically female genre, Deborah Kaplan argues that the two sets of letters in *Lady Susan* represent oppositional female networks in and through which women struggle over possession of men. The rules of the game differ depending on which network one belongs to.[7]

Convention's decorums create conduits for impermissible feelings. Mrs. Vernon's aggressive impulses find respectable expression in her desire for the good of her family and ultimately in her wish to help

Frederica (thus foiling Lady Susan); Lady Susan's aggression constantly seeks acceptable forms. By writing, these women mobilize their forces, internal and external: they provide rhetorics of self-justification, make plans of action, record and interpret events in ways that help them decide what to do next. Writing becomes a form of agency for their wishes. Even as facts close in on Lady Susan ("Facts are such horrid things!" Mrs. Johnson rightly observes [letter 32, *Minor Works* 303]), she insists that her control of language will make all right: "Do not torment yourself with fears on my account. Depend upon it, I can make my own story good with Reginald" (letter 33, *Minor Works* 303).

She is wrong. No longer can she deceive Reginald; no longer can she even manipulate her daughter. With few financial resources, few friends, no family of her own, an alienated set of in-laws, she has no obvious recourse. From the beginning of the narrative her social situation has been precarious—and not altogether as a result of her wickedness. Her verbal aplomb disguises the bleakness of social and personal actuality for a woman destitute of profitable alliance. By sheer style she plays with reality. This aspect of her letter writing differentiates her not only from self-righteous Mrs. Vernon but also from other epistolary "heroines" before and after her. Indeed, her tenuous claim to the title of heroine rests almost entirely on her style of self-presentation, by which she demands the attention of others within and outside the text. No nonverbal action of Lady Susan's elicits the reader's unequivocal admiration as much as does the strength she shows in the letter's domain of more or less licensed fantasy.

> At present my Thoughts are fluctuating between various schemes. I have many things to compass. I must punish Frederica, & pretty severely too, for her application to Reginald; I must punish him for receiving it so favourably, & for the rest of his conduct. I must torment my Sister-in-law for the insolent triumph of her Look & Manner since Sir James has been dismissed . . . & I must make myself amends for the humiliations to which I have stooped within these few days. To effect all this I have various plans. (letter 25, *Minor Works* 293–94)

One can only admire her resilience.

To read earlier epistolary novels by women makes one realize how brilliantly Austen manipulated preoccupations of her predecessors. Every major formal and thematic issue raised by *Lady Susan* occurs frequently in earlier female fictions, but in a different key. Particularly interesting are the concerns central to Austen's novel: the problem of female power, the problem of feeling, the possibilities for women of writing as action. Although these forgotten works contain no such aggressive female character as Lady Susan, their plots suggest the resentment with which women internalized social norms.

Eighteenth-century epistolary novels by women often reflect explicitly on their own literary operations by emphasizing self-proclaimed inadequacies. "I am provoked at this natural incapacity of conveying my sentiments to you; words are but a cloak, or rather a clog, to our ideas," one fictional letter writer complains.[8] Characters within novels apologize for the insufficiencies of their epistolary style in comparison with the grace of others' writing.[9] Writers faced with the task of narrating intense experience resort to the trope of inexpressibility. My favorite example comes from a work called *Female Stability*. "The particulars of the former [scene] I cannot describe," a woman character writes, "but the latter, not being so very interesting, I will endeavour at."[10] If these novelists do not altogether confine themselves to the uninteresting, they certainly eschew conspicuous forms of emotional drama: proposal scenes, for instance, which Austen, too, notoriously avoided. This version of a proposal is allegedly written by the young woman who has just received it:

> I am not going to tire your patience with a repetition of what passed on the occasion: this would be absolutely unnecessary, as our modern novelists in general have favoured us with such florid discourses upon the subject. Too many of them, indeed, have given their dialogues in so romantic a style, as to render not only the parties concerned, but even the passion itself highly ridiculous. I have always had a great distaste to this sort of writing, and shall therefore only observe, that Mr. Dormer made the offer of his person and fortune in a manly, sensible, and delicate manner; and concluded with requesting my permission to make application to my father. (Timbury 1: 156–57)

Unlike Lady Susan, earlier characters in female epistolary fictions claim no verbal mastery.

If fictional correspondents draw back from scenes of intense emotion, they also worry about confining themselves to trivia. "I am seriously considering," one young woman writes another, "whether or not I can find any thing to amuse you, which I have not repeated to you five hundred times."[11] She then summarizes the daily events of her life, concluding that none of them justifies a written record. What can one write letters *about?* This woman's dilemma hints at a problem of the female novelist: daily life, the life she knows, lacks substance and interest as matter for public communication.

Two solutions for the problem emerge. One can lend interest to private letters by using them to report sensational episodes, sometimes from the writer's life, more often from other people's experience. "I . . . hope this letter, if it does not find you perfectly recovered, will, as you say you are so much interested in the story, be a means of dispelling for awhile, the ennui of your very solitary life."[12] For writers and for readers, stories dispel ennui. Within the nominally "realistic" context of an assemblage of letters, these novels construct lurid romance sequences, justifying their existence by emphasizing their story.

A second solution to the problem of subject entails assigning high value to feeling, like Mrs. Vernon and unlike Lady Susan. If writers fear their inability to convey intense emotion, they paradoxically appear to believe that writing can issue directly from the heart. "Let your pen, as your tongue has ever done, speak the language of your heart," one young woman writes another (Timbury 1: 13). Letters, in all these works, provide outlets for emotion. In *Felicia to Charlotte,* an early novel almost devoid of developed happenings through much of its length, Felicia announces at the outset her intent "to discover all the secret folds of my heart, and to unbosom myself to you without the least reserve."[13] "Unbosoming" provides the woman novelist's narrative staple.

Both uses of letters—as repositories for story, as registers of feeling—bear directly on issues of plot, the artifice that creates narrative out of events; in Paul Ricoeur's words, "the temporal synthesis of the heterogeneous."[14] Epistolary novels substantiate the female vocation of feeling by substituting notations of emotion for other kinds of happening and by making feeling the cause for all effects in the outer as well as the inner world. Feeling constitutes power rather than weakness, these works maintain. A good woman can be defined by her emotional capacity; female authors, evoking characters of sensibility, thus insist on their own female virtue. Here is a male character's description of his beloved: "As her mind has been adorned, not warped, by education, it is just what her appearance promises: artless, gentle, timid, soft, sincere, compassionate; awake to all the finer impressions of tenderness, and melting with pity for every human woe."[15] Artless, gentle, timid, soft, sincere, compassionate, *melting:* the perfect woman. The same adjectives apply to male letter writers imagined by woman authors in their own idealized image: men who not only elaborately extol female sensibility but who can also melt at others' woes.

Effusions of sensibility often strike the modern reader as meretricious. Lady Susan's letter about how much she looks forward to knowing her hostess's little children rings false because it *is* false, as is she; not so the corresponding protestations of earlier epistolary heroines, which their fictional recipients accept as authentic. At our emotional distance from the eighteenth century, though, we may prefer Lady Susan's lack of sentimentality in our need to resist the apparent intent of manipulation in earlier texts.

But the rhetoric of sensibility means more than manipulation. Feeling substitutes for agency in these books. Lady Susan's fictional predecessors write letters to communicate facts or feelings but not, characteristically, to make anything happen. That is not to say, however, that they do not exercise force. As fictional correspondences clarify women's claim to dominion over the realm of emotion they suggest how feeling can substitute for action to generate its own kind of plot. One woman character writes another, "To any one but my Lucy, the enclosed narrative would afford little entertainment; it is not a series of events, but a continued conflict of the mind, and is a history of passions, not of persons" (Griffith 2: 160). Most eighteenth-century epistolary novels by women indeed record passion rather than character. Women novelists claim competence as their women characters do: in summoning, accepting, creating emotion. Feeling *is* doing.

Consider this paradigmatic little story, contained in the opening letter of a novel called *The Male Coquet.*

> Poor Lucy Seymour was an unhappy instance of the fatal effects of platonic love. From supposing that she felt nothing more than friendship for the agreeable Mr. Selby, her heart was irretrievably lost before she was sensible of her danger: and, to complete this misfortune, the destroyer of her peace was on the point of marriage with her most intimate friend. The last time I heard any thing of her, she was supposed to be in a deep decline. (Timbury 1: 12)

The novel's reader, too, hears nothing of Lucy Seymour beyond her decline, but her story, which foreshadows subsequent events of the novel, typifies common technique. Lucy is endowed with no individual character; the figures who write the novel's letters reveal little more specificity; the asserted passion, recorded in a kind of shorthand, seems as unpersuasive as the character. *Telling* rather than *showing,* this tiny story (like the novel it inhabits and many other novels) violates a fundamental principle of writing we teach to freshmen. For two centuries critics have accordingly explained the curious emptiness of such narrative as the product of authorial ineptitude. Yet episodes of this sort, in all their bareness, supply fables of the female condition.

Although these novels contain elements of "the traditional narrative of resolution," in which events gradually work themselves out, they also exemplify what Seymour Chatman calls "the modern plot of revelation," in which "a state of affairs is revealed."[16] Diverse happenings reveal remarkably similar "states of affairs": men betray women, women go into declines, varied events reiterate the same assumed yet unacceptable realities. The female condition involves deprivation and offers cause for despair. The emotional notation of countless flatly rendered episodes underlines that despair.

The novelistic "history of passions" covers a limited emotional range. Love accounts for many consequences good and bad. "That powerful passion is never to be conquered," observes Adeline Belville, irresistible heroine of *Female Stability* (Palmer 5: 204). Its force reduces strong men to emotional dependence and elevates women to heroic status. It justifies anger (always rendered as the product of sexual jealousy) and grief. It elucidates women's fates.

Yet women's novels qualify their apparent sentimentality about love. What are we to make, for example, of this male rhapsody (the male in question imagined by a woman) on love's power? "When inspired by a worthy object, [love] leads to every thing that is great and noble: warmed by the desire of being approved by her, there is nothing I would not attempt. I will to-day write to my father for his consent, and embark immediately for the army" (Brooke 69). The lover, however, neither writes to his father nor embarks for the army: he only produces rhetoric about his exalted feelings. What should we make of a plot in which, after page upon page of vapid outpourings about love, a bride discovers that her doting husband has fathered an illegitimate child by a woman who crept into his bed one night? He never bothered to mention this episode, nor does he appear to feel guilty about it, since he thought the woman only a chambermaid. When he rather perfunctorily asks his wife's forgiveness, she points out that a woman in a comparable situation would never be pardoned; then she forgives him (Collyer). What else can she do? What can we make, finally, of the fact that these plots generated by love record mainly disaster, often caused by male lust and self-indulgence?

"All the privilege I claim for my own sex (it is not a very enviable one, you need not covet it) is that of loving longest, when existence or when hope is gone" (Austen, *Northanger Abbey and Persuasion* 235). Anne Elliott, in Austen's *Persuasion,* speaks these bleak words. In her complexity of tone—ruefulness, self-congratulation, hints of resentment—she epitomizes implications of many women's novels. Imagined letters in these texts stress misery and the need to endure it, and suggest pride as well as anger. One can only guess how much social criticism these structures of feeling imply, how self-consciously they *mean*.

Happening and feeling of course are closely related, in fiction as in life. The stories for which fictional letters claim attention differentiate these books from the eighteenth-century novels we have agreed to call *major* precisely by their emotional weight. With the exception of *Clarissa* and *Roxana,* all important novels of eighteenth-century England manifest a comic structure. They end in marriage, in financial security, or at least (I'm thinking of *Tristram Shandy*) in verbal triumph. Along the road to final success, nothing terrible happens. Tom Jones appears to have gone to bed with his mother, but he hasn't really; Matthew Bramble almost drowns, but not quite; Tristram converts a squashed nose into comedy.

One would not describe the epistolary novels in comparable terms. Although some—two of my sample of nine—end in marriage, dreadful happenings precede the happy endings. In Susannah Gunning's *Barford Abbey,* for instance, the heroine's guardian dies at the novel's start. The protagonist endures smallpox and near rape; her lover nearly dies from grief. More dramatically, Jane Marshall's *History of Alicia Montague* subjects its heroine to desperate poverty as well as severe sexual threats and almost universal rejection by family and friends. And most of these novels do *not* provide happy endings. *Agnes De-Courci, A Domestic Tale* presents a plot too intricate for summary, including complicated tales of sexual deceit and manipulation, and ends in narrowly averted incest, which causes the madness and death of the heroine and the suicide of her lover. *The Male Coquet* allows one of its two female protagonists to marry but dwells on the demise of the other, who is betrayed by a man. *The History of Lady Julia Mandeville,* a popular work, not only concludes with the deaths of Julia and her lover Harry, but implicitly attributes responsibility for those deaths to the system of patriarchy. Harry's father praises the British constitution, the British royal family, and the happiness of "virtuous industry" (Brooke 27); he imitates the national order he admires by arranging his son's life in every detail. His arrangements precipitate the final catastrophe.

As one would expect in works written by people who are officially relegated to domesticity, the family provides the main source of drama in these angry plots, which insist on the sins of fathers (particularly) and to a lesser extent of mothers (who, however, typically atone for their usually inadvertent evildoing). Patriarchal power both makes and conceals human misery; everything is not for the best in a world which, from a woman's point of view, seems far from the best possible.

The structures of these fictions differ markedly from those of such better known contemporary novels of sensibility by men as *The Fool of Quality* (1764–70), *A Sentimental Journey* (1768), and *The Man of Feeling* (1771), in which disjunctive episodic orderings of events deny causality and evade responsibility.[17] Both as "narratives of resolution" and as "plots of revelation," epistolary novels by women insist on cause and effect, sometimes on remarkably simple conceptions of final cause—male lust, love, parental dominance. But intricate epistolary structures deliberately obscure the novels' systems of causality. Plots center on the

dilemmas of young men and women forced into present misery by unknown happenings in the past. What they don't know hurts them. The
work of fictional correspondences is to unravel not such benign secrets
as the truth of Tom Jones's or Joseph Andrews's parentage, but bitter
secrets of illegitimacy, jealousy, lust, and power. To discover the past
emphasizes powerlessness in the present. As letters accumulate to make
a story, they tell, typically, of despair: of the painful weight of personal
history, the inescapability of the past.

Seldom do these novels corroborate common assumptions about the
epistolary. The correspondents only nominally respond to one another,
with little real interchange. No love letters appear. Letters between
women, between men, or between relatives evoke scant sense of intimacy. Rarely does one hear an individual voice, and the few instances of
distinctive tone seem imitations of Lovelace or Anna Howe borrowed
from Richardson. Storytelling and assertion of feeling replace the evocation of character and relationship that one normally anticipates in private
letters, fictional or literal.

Inasmuch as the device of letters itself participates in plot, then, it
helps to reiterate the sense of things gone awry that the reported events
confirm. The forms of intimacy contain little content; the narrators of the
past do not fully possess their own stories. Letters, those images of
connection, dramatize connection's impossibilities.

Should one connect the special aspects of these novels—their dark
tone; intricate, malevolent plots; emphasis on the power of families and
of the past; substitution of *feeling* for *doing;* employment of letters more
for narrative than for evocation of relationship—with the gender of their
authors? Perhaps we find occluded in these texts a peculiarly female
version of the social criticism abundant in the works of sentimental
writers like Sterne, Henry Brooke, and Mackenzie, as well as in Fielding
and Smollett: veiled reaction to the impoverished lives and the limited
power to which most women were doomed. Male as well as female
characters suffer in these novels; but the generating vision belongs to
women. The darkness of that vision, the incursion of darkness even into
so bland a plot as that of *Felicia to Charlotte,* may derive from female
consciousness of female actualities. One can only speculate.

In the context of these novels, *Lady Susan* becomes the more remarkable for its openness. The plot of Austen's novel derives not from revelations of the past but from a powerful woman's operations within the time
scheme defined by the letters that narrate events. Lady Susan, like Richardson's Lovelace, occupies herself mainly in plotting. Although her
plots, like Lovelace's, do not work out as she intends, the crucial fact
remains: she generates her own narrative. Never does her determination

to control events weaken. Her verbal activity, oral and written, constantly remakes her history; letters provide for her a form of force rather than of passivity. She refuses to accept the power of the past or to acknowledge, except as verbal form, the sacred ties of motherhood. Aware of the conventionality of convention, as none of its previous fictional victims is, she can turn it to her own ends. For her, a story is something you make rather than something that happens to you.

What an act of liberation, to imagine the bad mother not as inescapable nightmare but as center of consciousness, responsible for herself and capable of being defeated! Bad mothers in earlier fiction are represented from the child's point of view. Indeed, even almost two centuries after *Lady Susan,* few novelists have fully evoked a parent's perspective. (In our imaginations, we all remain children.) Lady Susan exists as a sketched rather than a fully developed character. Fully developed, she might become intolerable, might arouse too much fear and guilt in novelist and reader alike. In Austen's representation, her self-interested acts have no long-range devastating consequences. If she almost lures Reginald into marriage and almost destroys her daughter's happiness and almost takes a man from his wife, she yet misses all these achievements, not by the arrangement of Providence but largely because of the verbal effectiveness of women she has scorned. Reginald, the man Susan wants, believes the story of the wronged wife and abandons his temptress. Susan's daughter, whom the reader probably thinks as negligible a creature as her mother believes her (partly because of the childishness of her prose: "I would rather work for my bread than marry him. I do not know how to apologise enough for this Letter." [letter 21, *Minor Works* 279]), wins Reginald's heart through the intervention of his mother and his sister (see Kaplan). Lady Susan must marry the rich fool she chose for her daughter.

A *very* rich fool, though. Like the conclusions of Austen's later novels, this ending carries a sting in its tail. Its subtle poetic justice simultaneously rewards Lady Susan with the wealth and status her society values and punishes her by depriving her of the male wit and style she herself values. The huddled-up form of the conclusion, with its retreat from the epistolary, parodies the ineptitudes of such earlier works as *The History of Alicia Montague,* which recurrently abandons the artifice of letters for the sake of narrative economy. The narrator's playfulness not only asserts a new kind of verbal mastery but extends to conventional assumptions about the relative power of parents and children: the cruel mother meets the fate she has ordained for her daughter. Lady Susan, of course, will know how to control Sir James as her daughter could not. This is not a "sad" ending even for the mother, though it carries overtones of bitterness about the social necessities that require Susan's marriage.

Eighteenth-century epistolary novels by women are hard to come by now, rare even in great libraries. The only example of the genre most people know is Fanny Burney's *Evelina*—a work different from the others in virtually all respects, and far less disturbing than fictions that openly question the benignity of families and the possibility of carefree marriage. Their troubling message of despair and their demonstration of female ineffectuality may have ensured the disappearance of other epistolary works; perhaps *Evelina* survives because it appears more innocent. However disturbing the female epistolary tradition, though, however angry and despairing its fictional arrangements, its novels reinforced the status quo by assuming it. Declaring in their reliance on epistolary form their concern only with "private" matters, women novelists apparently accepted the necessity of the system from which they suffered.

Jane Austen, in contrast, understood letters as voice and as action and understood conventions as capable of manipulation. She imagined possibilities of female power within the sphere of the "private," and played with reversals of fictional patterns that portrayed conceivable social reversals. She questioned even the value of sincerity and its power and envisioned a female character capable of play and of mastery through play. Jane Austen, even in her adolescent novel, experimented with quiet modes of undermining.

NOTES

1. Jane Austen, *Northanger Abbey and Persuasion*, vol. 5 of *The Novels of Jane Austen*, 3rd ed., ed. R. W. Chapman (Oxford: Oxford University Press, 1969), 27.

2. Margaret Drabble, ed., *Lady Susan, The Watsons, Sanditon* (Harmondsworth: Penguin, 1974), 9.

3. Jane Austen, *Minor Works*, vol. 6 of *The Works of Jane Austen*, ed. R. W. Chapman (Oxford: Oxford University Press, 1982), Letter 16, 268.

4. Jane Timbury, *The Male Coquet* (London, 1789), 1:152.

5. See Mary Poovey, *The Proper Lady and the Woman Writer: Ideology and Style in the Works of Mary Wollestonecraft, Mary Shelley, and Jane Austen* (Chicago, University of Chicago Press, 1984), 175.

6. Janet Altman, *Epistolarity: Approaches to a Form* (Columbus: Ohio State University Press, 1982), 118.

7. Deborah Kaplan, "Female Friendship and Epistolary Form: *Lady Susan* and the Development of Jane Austen's Fiction," forthcoming in *Criticism*.

8. In Elizabeth Griffith, *The Story of Lady Juliana Harley* (London, 1776), 1:2.

9. See, for example, Susannah Gunning, *Barford Abbey, a Novel in a Series of Letters* (London, 1768), 1:61.

10. Charlotte Palmer, *Female Stability: Or, the History of Miss Belville. In a Series of Letters* (London, 1780), 4:28.

11. Jane Marshall, *The History of Alicia Montague* (London, 1767), 1:115–16.

12. Agnes Maria Bennett, *Agnes De-Courci, A Domestic Tale* (Bath, 1789), 2:49.

13. Mary Collyer, *Felicia to Charlotte* (New York: Garland, 1974), 1:2. Originally published in 1744.

14. Paul Ricoeur, *Time and Narrative* (Chicago: University of Chicago Press, 1985), 2:158.

15. Frances Brooke, *The History of Lady Julia Mandeville,* vol. 27 of *The British Novelists* (London, 1810), 3. Originally published in 1763.

16. Seymour Chatman, *Story and Discourse: Narrative Structure in Fiction and Film* (Ithaca: Cornell University Press, 1978), 48.

17. Henry Brooke, *The Fool of Quality* (London: Routledge, n.d.); Laurence Sterne, *A Sentimental Journey Through France and Italy,* ed. Graham Petrie (Harmondsworth: Penguin, 1967); Henry Mackenzie, *The Man of Feeling* (New York: Norton, 1958).

5

Innovation and Convention in Sophie La Roche's The Story of Miss von Sternheim and Rosalia's Letters

SALLY WINKLE

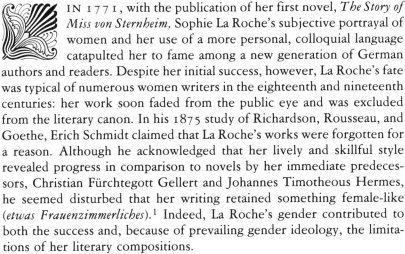

IN 1771, with the publication of her first novel, *The Story of Miss von Sternheim,* Sophie La Roche's subjective portrayal of women and her use of a more personal, colloquial language catapulted her to fame among a new generation of German authors and readers. Despite her initial success, however, La Roche's fate was typical of numerous women writers in the eighteenth and nineteenth centuries: her work soon faded from the public eye and was excluded from the literary canon. In his 1875 study of Richardson, Rousseau, and Goethe, Erich Schmidt claimed that La Roche's works were forgotten for a reason. Although he acknowledged that her lively and skillful style revealed progress in comparison to novels by her immediate predecessors, Christian Fürchtegott Gellert and Johannes Timotheous Hermes, he seemed disturbed that her writing retained something female-like (*etwas Frauenzimmerliches*).[1] Indeed, La Roche's gender contributed to both the success and, because of prevailing gender ideology, the limitations of her literary compositions.

As a product of the Enlightenment and of sentimentality, as an admirer of Richardson and Rousseau, and as a female author, Sophie La

Roche represents a woman in conflict with herself; she provided a new insight and a female perspective on women's lives, but she was also influenced by an emerging ideology that designated women as more passive than active, as more receptive than creative. The designation of supposedly natural masculine and feminine attributes denoted a shift in the philosophical arguments concerning gender difference in the latter third of the century from an emphasis on nurture to a focus on nature as the essential determinant of male and female character and function.[2] This shift is evident in La Roche's novels and marks her as a transitional author struggling to harmonize conventional ideas of gender distinction with her own desire to apply rational ideals of self-improvement and human dignity to the female as well as the male sex.

The idea of two distinct, complementary personalities based on gender emerged after 1760 in conjunction with the gradual change in middle-class family structure from the self-sufficient household, consisting of extended family as well as servants, apprentices, and the like, to the nuclear family, in which woman was increasingly defined in terms of her new role as household manager, consumer, reproducer, and nurturer within the domestic sphere.[3] Whereas previous theories utilized the Bible and social necessity to defend the separate roles of the sexes and the subordinate position of women, theories influenced by Rousseau described woman as destined by nature for her position as a self-effacing, gentle, devoted wife and mother.[4] A woman's desire to transgress her predetermined function in life was therefore no longer simply socially unacceptable, but could be denounced as unnatural and degenerate.

The idealization of traits ascribed as natural to the female sex was accompanied by a subtle devaluation of her work in the household and a repression of qualities that would enable her to openly fight mistreatment. As exemplified in the 1795 novel by Karoline von Wobeser, *Elisa or Woman as She is Supposed to Be*, the ideal woman was expected to apply her inborn kindness, generosity, and unselfishness to transform an abusive husband into a good, loving man. This ideology rapidly became established as social convention. German literature in the last decades of the century became the forum for the construction of a bourgeois feminine ideal suitable for middle-class woman's self-sacrificing, pleasing role within the nuclear family idyll.[5] This crippling idealization of women was accentuated by the simultaneous trend toward a literary depiction of more individualized male heroes as singular, struggling, developing characters.

Although Sophie La Roche's epistolary novels *The Story of Miss von Sternheim* (1771) and *Rosalia's Letters* (1779–81) reveal a tendency toward the construction of feminine ideals and the exaltation of sentimental love and marriage as indispensable to a woman's fulfillment and happiness, the author simultaneously undermines these ideas by creating proud female characters, narrative twists, and subplots that seem to subvert the more overtly didactic messages of the dominant story line. La Roche seems to celebrate a sentimental view of femininity, expressed in the self-denying love, modesty, and physical weakness of many of her fictional females, while also advocating a rational education for women and acknowledging their diverse talents. The contradictory aspects of La Roche's two best-known epistolary novels exhibit a conflicting mixture of literary innovation and convention, though the author's challenge to the bourgeois ideal of passive femininity in *Sternheim* is muted in *Rosalia's Letters*. La Roche's increasing conventionality in her second novel seems to reflect and reinforce the power in the late eighteenth century of a newly established ideology based on the distinction between inborn masculine and feminine characters.

It is not surprising that La Roche's first published literary accomplishment was an epistolary novel, nor is it surprising that she began writing in the period of sentimentality. The sentimental movement in the latter half of the eighteenth century simultaneously promoted and limited women's cultural development. Qualities highly valued in the age of sensibility were those increasingly being regarded as "feminine": sensitivity, modesty, compassion, moral goodness, self-denial, and the ability to express feelings. Sentimental friendships, letters, melancholy walks, and novels provided emotional outlets for middle-class women tired of the boredom and routine of their daily lives.[6] Recognition of women's particular aptitude for epistolary writing and the new value placed on "female" traits gave women of the educated bourgeoisie an awareness of their personal assets, which created the appearance of a "separate but equal" world for the "other sex." As the private virtues and the themes of love, family, and the heart edged into the public arena of literature, some women felt encouraged to take up the pen themselves as creators of poems, essays, travel journals, and even novels.[7]

The Enlightenment's emphasis on reading and education for both sexes led to substantial gains in the numbers of female readers by the end of the century. The result was twofold: greater influence of the female reading public in the book market on the one hand, and dire warnings against *Lesewuth*, or reading mania, as deleterious to the development of women as suitable wives and mothers on the other.[8] This ambivalent response to a more visible female role in German culture after 1750 corresponded to the paradoxical effects of sentimentality for women.

Many of the supposedly typical feminine traits celebrated in this era were private virtues more appropriate to devoted wives and self-sacrificing mothers in the developing nuclear family than to active creators of culture. In other words, characteristics valued in the age of sensibility may have given women a new sense of gender autonomy, but they also prescribed for the female gender the practice of receptivity rather than creativity, feelings rather than deep reflection or analysis, and unselfishness rather than self-love. Female authors thus found themselves in a perilous position. In order to avoid being labeled unnatural or unwomanly, many defended their writing as useful for the edification of young women, or as merely a peripheral part of their more important roles as wives and mothers. Women writers were thus limited to a mainly private, modest role in a society and culture still defined and dominated by men.

La Roche's strengths as a female author accounted for both her enthusiastic reception by the educated, middle-class reading public in the 1770s and her subsequent marginalization as a writer devoted to raising "paper girls," making fictional harmonious matches, and extolling feminine virtues. Recent reprintings of *Sternheim*, a 1983 publication of her collected letters, and a surge of articles and dissertations attest to the renewed interest in her work in the past fifteen years, especially among young scholars and feminist critics.[9] Current studies recognize La Roche's significance as the first prominent female novelist in Germany and as contributor to the development of the epistolary novel, the subjective novel, and the so-called "women's novel" that proliferated in the realm of popular literature at the end of the eighteenth century.[10]

La Roche's *The Story of Miss von Sternheim* is a transitional novel whose heroine presents a combination of conflicting rational and sentimental tendencies. Sophie Sternheim is simultaneously an outspoken, well-read, proud female role model and a modest, unselfish example of sentimental femininity. The result is the depiction of a conflicted female protagonist who has certain features of the bourgeois feminine ideal but, as a speaking subject, changes and develops within the narrative.

La Roche's contemporaries hailed *Sternheim* for its unique heroine, whose freer use of language (variously described as natural and heartfelt) contributed to an innovative use of the epistolary form.[11] The author's omission of addressees' letters in her first novel provided a compact narrative structure and a more subjective text, increasing the tension and excitement of the plot.[12] The reader of the novel is forced to take a more active role, as the reader adopts the position of the absent addressee. Letters by various characters provide the reader with different versions of events relevant to the motivation of the main characters and to the plot in which Sophie is entangled.

In contrast to Samuel Richardson's *Clarissa,* Hermes's *Sophie's Travels,* and Rousseau's *Julie ou la nouvelle Héloïse,* La Roche's *Sternheim* is neither cumbersome nor overloaded with subplots. La Roche did of course make use of many traditional epistolary techniques perfected by her predecessors: presenting the book as a collection of letters by the heroine's friend and former servant, as well as insisting on the authenticity of the letters and on their usefulness as moral edification for the eighteenth-century reading public.[13] Similarities to Richardson's *Clarissa* and *Pamela,* which are obvious in the plot and in the characterization of Lord Derby, reveal the influence of her forerunners.[14]

The novel begins with a biographical introduction of the heroine's parents and childhood by her friend and later servant/companion, Rosine. Sophie von Sternheim was raised with bourgeois values on a country estate, the only daughter of a noble family committed to the Enlightenment principles of the landholder as benevolent patriarch. La Roche carefully outlines her heroine's education and stresses the importance of learning and environment for the development of the individual character. The loss of her mother at the age of nine and her father at nineteen reinforced Sternheim's sentimental inclination toward melancholy and set the stage for the subsequent tests of her virtue, moral principles, and strength of character.

Sophie von Sternheim's letters begin a year after her father's death when she arrives at court D* with her mother's half sister, the haughty Countess of Löbau. Sophie becomes ensnared in her aunt's plan to further her husband's prospects at court by offering her unsuspecting niece to the prince as his new mistress. Sophie addresses her letters to her friend Emilie, Rosine's sister. Letters by two Englishmen at D*, the sentimental Lord Seymour and the diabolical rake Lord Derby, supply alternate perspectives of events and provide information unknown to the heroine. Although Sophie and Lord Seymour are depicted as related souls, their budding love is impeded by court intrigue. Despite her expressed virtue and austere ideal of sentimental love, Sternheim's role at court is mainly a sexual one: she is pursued by the prince, Count F*, Lord Seymour, and Lord Derby.

Alone at court, bereft of friends, and scorned by her aunt and uncle for thwarting their plan, she is easy prey for Lord Derby, who convinces her to marry him and secretly leave D*. After several unhappy weeks at an inn some distance from the court, Derby angrily leaves her. His farewell letter informs her that their marriage was false; Sophie falls ill and returns with Rosine to Emilie. Unlike some sentimental heroines with a similar fate, however, she does not languish and die; instead she assumes the sentimental name Madame Leidens,[15] and with the help of a rich widow founds a school to train poor girls as domestic servants.

An elderly Englishwoman, Lady Summers, convinces Madame Leidens to live with her and continue her good work in England. Their neighbor, the rational Lord Rich, falls in love with Sophie but, devastated by her first "marriage," she is determined to remain single. The plot thickens when Derby marries Lady Summers's niece. Afraid Sophie will betray him, he has her abducted and carried off to a destitute family in a desolate area of Scotland. Derby's evil servant nearly kills Sternheim when she refuses to become the lord's mistress.

Convinced that Sophie is dead, the dying Lord Derby remorsefully summons Seymour and Rich to erect a monument in her name. The two good lords, who are now revealed to the reader as half brothers, rush to Scotland to find Sophie alive and rescued by a kind Scottish lady. Lord Rich generously renounces his love for Sophie in deference to his sensitive, sentimental younger brother Lord Seymour. After some hesitation, Sophie agrees to the marriage, and the three live happily on Seymour's estate in England.

Throughout the novel, La Roche stresses the importance of women in Sternheim's life: her friends Emilie and Rosine; the widows she lives with in Germany and England, Madame Hills and Lady Summers; the woman who rescues her in Scotland, Lady Douglas; and numerous others of various ages and classes, who give her support and friendship. Sophie's success as teacher and social worker demonstrates La Roche's belief in the significance of women's accomplishments within and outside the private sphere and thus contradicts messages elsewhere in the narrative that project marriage as the only respectable goal for the female sex. Recent readings of the novel have emphasized the author's representation of a strong, active female protagonist, who serves as a "hero to her sex," and a plot that at least temporarily grants Sophie a free space outside the patriarchal society, before her virtue is rewarded with marriage to the man of her choice.[16]

The multifaceted perspective of the narrative provided by the epistolary form applies to gender as well. On the one hand, La Roche's novel offers a personal, subjective account of women as survivors. Her emphasis on the diversity of female skills and characters, and on personal development for women as well as men, imparts a female perspective to the action. Sophie Sternheim's letters and journal in Scotland form the core of the narrative, supplemented by Rosine's introduction and description of the heroine. Sternheim's "I" reveals to Emilie her inner doubts, moralistic observations, and struggles to accept both self-love and self-sacrifice. Her letters demonstrate her internal conflicts and growth as the offspring of a father of bourgeois background and a mother of noble birth, and as a woman defined according to an ideology in flux.

The female voice is counteracted, however, by the letters of the male protagonists, in particular Lord Seymour and Lord Derby, who judge Sternheim's actions from an androcentric perspective and superimpose their ideals of virtue and love upon her with disastrous results.[17] Seymour's letters present a view of Sophie's behavior based on court gossip and social definitions of feminine morality. Although he loves Sternheim "at first sight," he obeys his uncle's wish not to intervene in the intrigue surrounding the girl until she proves beyond all doubt her innocence, so as not to endanger his career by marrying a woman of questionable reputation.

Lord Seymour's exalted idea of Sternheim as an ominiscient goddess of virtue blinds him to her naïveté and prevents him from seeking to discover the truth behind activities which the court misinterprets as proof of Sophie's relationship with the prince. As he later regretfully admits: "First I did not want to speak of my love, until she had revealed herself completely in accord with my concepts in the full splendor of triumphant virtue. She went her own pretty way, and because she did not follow my ideal plan, I appropriated for myself the power to punish her in the most painful way."[18] Seymour's all-encompassing love for Sophie is possessive and selfish, since it is founded on his idealized image rather than on attempts to understand her thoughts, character, and behavior. Once his ideal of her is shattered, his love is overshadowed by rage at having loved an unworthy object, and he names himself judge and jury, nearly destroying her in the process.

Similarly, Derby's observations of Sophie are colored by his own view of women as objects of conquest and sexual pleasure. His reports of Sophie's experiences at court are interspersed with mocking comments on her generosity and modesty, whereas his account of their brief "marriage" is distorted by his unrealistic demands on Sophie's capacity to express ardent desire for a man she doesn't love. Ironically, Derby is the only one in D* who really attempts to know her character, even though his motives are selfish. He hopes that by feigning virtue and magnanimity he can win Sophie's affection. He mistakenly believes that he can convert her passion for good deeds and helping others to passion for enjoyment and pleasing him.

Deluded by his improbable ideal of Sophie as a sensuous lover, Derby can read his young bride's cool kisses and unhappiness only as signs of repressed love for another man, Lord Seymour. Derby's jealous assertion that he is not the man she loves is true, since the character he had originally revealed to her was nothing but pretense. When Sophie no longer fits his exaggerated conception of female sensuality, he considers himself free of all responsibility to her. "She is no longer the creature that I loved, therefore I am no longer committed to remain what I seemed to her to be at the time" (*Sternheim* 191).

Both these male protagonists set up ideals of the female character based on their own imagination and desires, rather than permitting her to define and reveal herself to them. When Sophie proves incapable of meeting their fantastic demands, both men react with rage and reject her. Although the shattering of each hero's ideal and her subsequent abandonment leave Sternheim broken and ill, it is significant that the heroine herself survives and that the author grants her at least some determination of her own existence. La Roche thus depicts and subsequently undermines the idealizations of her heroine by exposing them as destructive fantasies of Sophie's suitors, thereby providing a subtle critique of the projection of unattainable feminine ideals. The clear juxtaposition of male and female perspectives in the narrative provides added tension to the text.

Interestingly, although Sophie's and Rosine's voices predominate throughout the novel, Seymour's rational brother, Lord Rich, describes the final scene of the Seymour's marital bliss and family idyll. Nevertheless, Sophie's public role is not totally stifled by the confinement of marriage. Rich portrays Sophie's active involvement in the community on their estate, that is, in a sphere bridging the public and private.[19] In addition, Sophie enjoys the love of not one, but two men, forming an unconventional, though socially acceptable, ménage à trois, as Ruth-Ellen Joeres points out. Even though Rich's affection for his sister-in-law is strictly platonic, he refuses to marry, chooses to reside with his in-laws, and raises their second son as his own.[20] In this sense, La Roche's family idyll in *Sternheim* contrasts with the increasingly privatized function of women in the bourgeois nuclear family as experienced by many of her readers.

The fictional female narrator of the text, Rosine, is countered by a male editor, the well-known novelist and La Roche's friend, Christoph Martin Wieland. Despite his good intentions and his helpful role in advising Sophie La Roche on her first published work, Wieland's patronizing preface and critical footnotes run counter to the meaning of the text and evoke a male presence throughout the novel.[21]

Of greater significance, however, is the androcentric perspective that occasionally disrupts the female point of view. This is most obvious in Sophie's conversation with the rational scholar and author Mr. ***, whom she meets on a visit with her aunt. Conceived as a tribute to her friend Wieland, Mr. *** also reveals the strong influence of Rousseau's

Emile on Sophie La Roche. He warns Miss von Sternheim to avoid a "masculine tone" in her writing and speech, and prescribes for men and women different spheres and talents based on the distinct qualities endowed them by nature.

> Nature itself designated this by making man fervent and woman tender in the passion of love; by equipping the former with rage and the latter with sentimental tears in the face of insult, and by imparting for business matters and learning the masculine mind with strength and deep thought, and the feminine spirit with flexibility and grace; in misfortune the man with resoluteness and courage, the woman with patience and resignation. In domestic life nature has charged the former with the responsibility to obtain the resources for the family and the latter with the adept distribution of these funds, etc. (*Sternheim* 108)

The concept of neatly complementary, inborn masculine and feminine character traits in this passage contradicts La Roche's emphasis elsewhere on education and socialization as essential to the development of the heroine's character. Moreover, the homogeneous ideal of bourgeois femininity articulated in this conversation contrasts with La Roche's heterogeneous representation of women throughout the novel. The female characters in *Sternheim* represent all social classes. Whether married, widowed, or single, they lead useful lives, and their productivity and value are acknowledged. However, in an era in which the lower classes far outnumbered the bourgeoisie, and middle-class women were often unable to marry owing to lack of dowry, the ideas proposed by Mr. *** define the entire female sex as if all members were middle-class and married. These theories exemplify an androcentric perspective, which undercuts the author's recognition of women's varied contributions both within and outside the private sphere.

Like *The Story of Miss von Sternheim,* La Roche's *Rosalia's Letters* could be classified as a transitional novel, marked by an uneasy combination of rational and sentimental characteristics and contradictory definitions of women's character, abilities, and functions. On the one hand, La Roche's experiments with changes in narrative voice, open structure, and a more realistic depiction of country life,[22] as well as her intriguing portrait of Madame Gudens, are innovative aspects of her second novel. On the other hand, these elements are offset by an increasing conventionality in tone, didactic message, and idealization of marriage and motherhood.

Written in the years between 1773 and 1780, *Rosalia's Letters* differs sharply from *The Story of Miss von Sternheim.* Although Rosalia appears as the major protagonist and main correspondent, her travels and acquaintances primarily provide a framework for a series of interwoven and independent stories, which she relates in her letters in the third person, in dialogue form, or in the first person. Rosalia's tale is quite simple; she leaves her friend Marianne in order to accompany her uncle, a lawyer and privy councillor, on his official travels in Germany and Switzerland. She and her uncle settle in a city where she makes friends among the upper bourgeoisie and lower nobility and takes small trips into the countryside. In the second volume she marries her fiancé, Cleberg, a higher magistrate in a village nearby; volumes two and three trace her inner development as a wife and mother.

The purpose of *Rosalia's Letters* is more overtly didactic than that of the first novel and is almost overwhelmed by the subplots and stories of numerous characters, some of whom are more interesting than the protagonists, Rosalia, her uncle, and Cleberg.[23] La Roche frees her epistolary novel from the constriction of one major plot and thus approximates an actual correspondence or journal, with multiple topics and reports on events, conversations, and people surrounding the letter writer. These new uses of the epistolary form and shifts in the narrative voice lend the work an original quality, but also contribute to a loose, unwieldy structure. Even though Rosalia's letters far outnumber those by Madame Guden or Cleberg, her character lacks the depth and complexity of a heroine like Sternheim, and her correspondence often revolves around the lives and experiences of friends and acquaintances.

As in *Sternheim,* the female perspective in *Rosalia's Letters* stresses the value of women's work and directs the reader's attention to women's everyday lives. La Roche portrays a variety of women from different social classes, both single and married, but her idealized world centers on the educated upper bourgeoisie. Rosalia's letters offer insight into the feelings and experiences of a young woman of the upper middle class, and disclose aspects of women's existence usually overlooked in fiction of this era: adjustment to the commitment of marriage, fear of childbirth, problems with in-laws, and the like. The supporting characters, Mrs. Grafe and Madame Guden, nevertheless impart a female perspective much more rigorously than La Roche's designated bourgeois feminine ideal and major protagonist, Rosalia.

Mrs. G** (Grafe), is a sarcastic, witty woman who prefers a lightly mocking discourse and consistently subverts and interrupts serious discussion. Mrs. Grafe often directs her humor and criticism toward the male sex and the unjust rules of a male-dominated society.[24] She reacts with skepticism to Rosalia's enthusiastic accounts of female domestic bliss and feminine docility. In response to Rosalia's glowing praise of a woman who, after years of isolation from society because of the bitterness of her mother-in-law, chose to continue her reclusive life in devotion to her husband and children, Mrs. Grafe warns Rosalia of the risk of telling the story to men.

> There could be rich greedy devils, or other house tyrants among men who would go home and banish their wives and daughters to the miserable nests where the poor creatures already have to spend most of their lives; the men, however, would go prancing off every day, like that Councillor . . . , to their coffee house, and would have their freedom and their fun, while the poor woman would have to wait patiently by her whirring spinning wheel for her sullen and bull-headed master.[25]

Even though Rosalia often protests against Mrs. Grafe's comments, the latter is portrayed as a kind-hearted, sympathetic character, and the former usually recognizes the justification of the older woman's complaints. Mrs. Grafe thus functions as a dissenting voice to Rosalia's complete acceptance of self-sacrifice and willing submission to male authority.

Whereas in *Sternheim* La Roche created a complicated heroine who embodied both a sentimental feminine ideal and an active female protagonist, in *Rosalia's Letters* she split the conflicting halves of Sophie's personality into two separate characters. Determined by her desire to please the men in her life, Rosalia internalizes their ideals of woman as cheerful, devoted niece, wife, and mother. Madame Guden, however, La Roche's most original character, represents a stubborn, passionate counterpart to Rosalia.

Madame Guden is a wealthy, well-educated young widow with artistic and musical talents, irrepressible energy, and creativity. Still suffering from an unhappy love for a weak, extravagant man when she meets Rosalia, Madame Guden nonetheless enjoys a degree of autonomy that Rosalia has never known. Her independence has a high price in La Roche's world, that of renounced love and a tinge of melancholy, but Madame Guden achieves a full life because of her generosity and concern for the welfare of those around her. By the end of the novel she has gained in self-respect and accepted the differences that kept her and her beloved Mr. Pindorf apart, rather than blaming their unfulfilled love on fate, as he has done. Through Guden the author depicts the importance of self-love in the development of the female as well as the male character. It is not so much her magnanimous desire to help the poor Wolling family and to educate Pindorf's children that mark her as a unique woman, as it is her ability to create her own happiness, to construct her own world, and to define her own family.

A shift in narration emphasizes Guden's increasing significance in her heroine's fictional community. First described by Rosalia, then appearing in conversation, Guden's story is told in the third person before she begins writing to Rosalia and gains her own voice. In her letters, Guden subsequently becomes a narrator herself, relating her own experiences and repeating conversations in which others tell their stories, mirroring Rosalia's narrative role. Guden's growing recognition of Mr. Pindorf's weak, helpless character demonstrates her development as a woman aware of her own strengths.

La Roche's choice of Rosalia rather than Madame Guden as her main protagonist is crucial to the author's shift in favor of male-defined feminine ideals and conventional messages of female passivity and conformity. On the one hand, Guden is a more well-rounded, intricate character, her past and present experiences are more varied and interesting than Rosalia's, and her philanthropic activities and generosity serve as models for her class and sex. On the other hand, she is too unconventional, unique, and independent, her temperament is too strong, and her love too passionate to function as the major role model in La Roche's didactic novel. Even though Rosalia's ideas and experiences as a new wife and mother are presented as exemplary for her bourgeois readers, Madame Guden's significant role transmits a strong signal of women's multiple talents, intelligence, and active ways to achieve a meaningful life.

As in *Sternheim,* the female perspective in *Rosalia's Letters* is countered by an androcentric point of view, which is evident in Rosalia's thoughts on women's subordinate role in marriage, in her enthusiastic stories of blissful courtships, and in Cleberg's letters. Indeed, Rosalia's personality and behavior betray the author's growing adherence to the prevailing ideology that defined women merely in relation to men, children, and the intimate bourgeois family idyll, thus revealing the increasing conventionality in the content and tone of her work.

Throughout the novel, Rosalia's life is controlled and determined by dominant, strong-willed men. Modeled on La Roche's husband, Rosalia's uncle is depicted as a rational, generous, kind man, yet his patriarchal rule over his niece's life is absolute.[26] His decision that Rosalia be given only a moment's notice before her wedding is but one example of his well-intentioned but manipulative gestures.

Although Cleberg is depicted as a dedicated, hard-working husband, his schemes to observe his new wife under the adverse conditions of illness and jealousy indicate a concern governed by curiosity and the will to dominate. Even Cleberg's defense of women demonstrates a paternalistic attitude toward the "beautiful" sex, as he criticizes the injustice of men's expectations of women: "We inform ourselves so much with the superior power and talents of our minds; and yet our equanimity succumbs to the most minute offence in the course of business, fate, or due to a small accumulation of work. And from you frail children we demand a constant equal cheerfulness and serenity" (*Rosalia's Letters* 2:386). La Roche's fictional females applaud Cleberg's reproach of his own sex, yet the passage illustrates how important were vulnerability and weakness to the bourgeois ideal of femininity in the last decades of the eighteenth and throughout the nineteenth century.

Like Seymour's, Cleberg's love is genuine, but it is neither unselfish nor unconditional; it is a possessive, demanding love, based on an idealistic view of woman and marriage. Unlike in *Sternheim*, however, in which Seymour has to reassess his image of his beloved once his ideal is shattered, Cleberg's expectations are fulfilled, because Rosalia fits his concept of a feminine ideal. Rosalia passes his tests with flying colors, and even though she subtly indicates her displeasure with his obtrusive behavior, she nonetheless swallows her resentment and represses her anger. The heroine in La Roche's second novel clearly exemplifies resignation, patience, and unquestioning support of husband and children as essential qualities of a bourgeois feminine ideal. Whereas Sophie Sternheim expresses an inner conflict between opposing elements of self-determination and passive acceptance, Rosalia's sensitivity, willingness to please, and submissiveness easily prevail over any budding notions of obstinance or pride. Her sentimental soul is more harmoniously balanced, and her character approaches the innocent, self-sacrificing feminine ideals of the Storm-and-Stress dramas, the static idealized femininity of Goethe and Schiller's classical works, and the exalted image of woman as symbol of undying love and beauty in Romanticism.[27]

La Roche's adherence to social convention and androcentric perspective, in particular her emphasis on love and marriage as the determining factor of women's happiness and usefulness, is undercut through the narratives of both *Sternheim* and *Rosalia's Letters*. Although the disruptive instances are greatly reduced in her second work, each novel transmits ambivalent messages to her female readers. In *The Story of Miss von Sternheim*, Sophie's disastrous false marriage to Lord Derby and her dialogue on the pros and cons of matrimony with the Widow von C** counteract the idyllic scenes of domestic bliss that open and close the novel. La Roche's depiction of widows and single women leading contented, productive lives offsets her emphasis on Sophie's marriage to Seymour as the destined end of her aimless wandering. Only the subplots provide the dissenting perspective in *Rosalia's Letters*. The illness and tragic death of Henriette Effen warn of the destructiveness of boundless sentimental love.[28] Madame Guden's resoluteness and creative use of her time and money to provide herself with a productive life and loving friends offer an alternative to Rosalia's protected, predetermined existence within the private sphere.

Rosalia's Letters is neither a didactic fictional correspondence with a weak narrative structure, as Eva Becker has argued, nor is it La Roche's most skillfully crafted novel, as maintained by Christine Touaillon.[29] There are elements in this neglected work that justify its reevaluation by literary critics, however, such as its more open narrative structure, which encompasses the experiences of men and especially women at various social levels. The emphasis on community is reflected in Rosalia's integration of group conversations into her letters, while the stories related in the correspondence stress cooperation, tolerance, and compassion as essential human characteristics.

Indeed, Sophie La Roche creates a kind of utopia for the women in both *Sternheim* and *Rosalia's Letters* that mirrors the contradictory elements of these texts. On the one hand La Roche projects a world in which her fictional females are loved and respected, active and useful, surrounded by friends and admiring neighbors.[30] On the other hand, the fictional community is still a patriarchal, male-dominated world, and in her second novel, it is increasingly withdrawn from the larger commercial world of paid work.

While Goethe's epistolary novel, *The Sorrows of Young Werther,* had in 1774 initiated a trend away from the didactic novel, it is telling that La Roche intensified her commitment to pedagogical letter fiction in her second novel. La Roche internalized the prevailing justification of women authors as public mothers and teachers of female middle-class readers, particularly in *Rosalia's Letters* and her subsequent works. Sophie La Roche's emotional and financial dependence on men until her husband's death in 1788 as well as her insecurity as a late-developing woman writer further reinforced her desire to please and her willingness to adapt to roles projected upon her. Despite her pride and ambition, her correspondence attests to an increasing need for reassurance and sensitivity to criticism.[31] These personal qualities, in addition to growing dependence on the earnings from her books, prevented La Roche from taking risks and contributed to her conformity to popular gender ideology.

In spite of the significance of her literary periodical for women, *Pomona,* in 1783 and 1784, La Roche's first two novels are her most accomplished works. Steadfastly committed to her mission as moral educator of Germany's daughters, she became ever more conventional in her writing. In her pedagogical *Letters to Lina,* published in three volumes from 1783 to 1797, La Roche projects an increasingly rigid dichotomy between, on the one hand, female patience, complaisance, and education defined according to men's needs, and male activity, scholarship, and authority on the other.[32]

La Roche's contributions as a female author in eighteenth-century Germany should not be underestimated, however. Her ambivalent representations of women in *Sternheim* and *Rosalia's Letters* demonstrate an attempt to combine an affirmation of the kindness, compassion, and sensitivity cultivated in her own sex with the idea that the Enlightenment emphasis on education, community, and self-improvement is applicable to the development of both sexes. Her celebration of feminine virtues was made problematic in the 1770s by their justification solely as qualities relegated to the private sphere and unsuitable outside the bourgeois family. She therefore accepted at least in part the prevailing ideology that proclaimed complementary masculine and feminine character traits as "natural" indicators of woman's inevitable identity as pleasing, self-denying wife and mother. The androcentric definition of the female sex, which appeared only sporadically in *Sternheim,* determined her portrayal of Rosalia in the second novel. An analysis of La Roche's first two epistolary novels demonstrates the degree to which the author internalized the new ideals of bourgeois femininity and domestic intimacy, and indicates the pervasiveness of the nurture/nature shift in gender theories that emerged in the late eighteenth century.

NOTES

1. Erich Schmidt, *Richardson, Rousseau and Goethe* (Jena: Eduard Frommann, 1875), 62.

2. Karin Hausen, "Die Polarisierung der 'Geschlechtscharaktere'—Eine Spiegelung der Dissoziation von Erwerbs—und Familienleben," in *Sozialgeschichte der Familie in der Neuzeit Europas,* ed. Werner Conze (Stuttgart: Klett, 1976), 363–93.

3. Compare Heidi Rosenbaum, *Formen der Familie* (Frankfurt a. M.: Suhrkamp, 1982), 251–309; Dieter Schwab, "Familie," in *Geschichtliche Grundbegriffe: Historisches Lexikon zur politisch-sozialen Sprache in Deutschland,* ed. Otto Brunner, Werner Conze, and R. Koselleck (Stuttgart: Klett, 1975), 253–301; Otto Brunner, "Das 'ganze Haus' und die alteuropäische 'Ökonomik,'" in *Neue Wege der Verfassungs- und Sozialgeschichte,* 2d enlarged ed. (Göttingen: Vandenhoech & Ruprecht, 1968), 103 ff.

4. See Gerda Tornieporth, *Studien zur Frauenbildung* (Weinheim & Basel: Beltz, 1977), 11–73; Dagmar Grenz, *Mädchenliteratur von den moralisch-belehrenden Schriften im 18. Jahrhundert bis zur Herausbildung der Backfischliteratur im 19. Jahrhundert* (Stuttgart: J. B. Metzler, 1981), 6–112; Rosenbaum, *Formen der Familie,* 261–309; Peter Petschauer, "From *Hausmütter* to

Hausfrau: Ideals and Realities in Late Eighteenth-Century Germany," *Eighteenth Century Life* 8 (1982–83): 72–79.

5. Compare Barbara Duden, "Das schöne Eigentum: Zur Herausbildung des bürgerlichen Frauenbildes an der Wende vom 18. zum 19. Jahrhundert," *Kursbuch* 47 (1977): 125–40; Silvia Bovenschen, *Die imaginierte Weiblichkeit* (Frankfurt a. M.: Suhrkamp, 1979); Sigrid Weigel, "Die geopferte Heldin und das Opfer als Heldin," in *Die verborgene Frau,* ed. Inge Stephan and Sigrid Weigel (Berlin: Argument, 1983), 138–52; Rita Jo Horsley, "A Critical Appraisal of Goethe's *Iphigenie,"* in *Beyond the Eternal Feminine,* ed. Susan L. Cocalis and Kay Goodman (Stuttgart: Akademischer Verlag Hans-Dieter Heinz, 1982), 47–74. This idea is also developed in my book, *Woman as Bourgeois Ideal: A Study of Sophie von La Roche's Geschichte des Fräuleins von Sternheim and Goethe's Die Leiden des jungen Werthers* (New York, Bern: Peter Lang, 1988).

6. See Natalie Halperin, *Die deutschen Schriftstellerinnen in der zweiten Hälfte des 18. Jahrhunderts* (Quakenbrück: C. Trute, 1935), 18–26.

7. Julie Bondeli, Sophie Albrecht, Elisa von der Recke, Friderika Baldinger, Philippine Engelhard, Marianne Ehrmann, Sophie von La Roche, Friederike Helene Unger, and Karoline von Wolzogen exemplify this trend.

8. Compare Gerhard Sauder, "Gefahren empfindsamer Vollkommenheit für Leserinnen und die Furcht vor Romanen in einer Damenbibliothek," in *Leser und Lesen im 18. Jahrhundert,* ed. Rainier Gruenter (Heidelberg: Winter 1977), 83–85; Wolfgang Martens, *Botschaft der Tugend* (Stuttgart: Metzler, 1968), 531–32, 540–42; Helga Meise, *Die Unschuld und die Schrift* (Berlin/Marburg: Guttandin & Hoppe, 1983), 66–82.

9. Recent studies of La Roche's life and works include: Ruth-Ellen Joeres, "'That girl is an entirely different character!' Yes, but is she a feminist? Observations on Sophie von La Roche's *Geschichte des Fräuleins von Sternheim,"* in *German Women in the Eighteenth and Nineteenth Centuries,* ed. Ruth-Ellen B. Joeres and Mary Jo Maynes (Bloomington: Indiana University Press, 1986), 137–56; Barbara Becker-Cantarino, "Nachwort," in Sophie von La Roche, *Geschichte des Fräuleins von Sternheim* (Stuttgart: Reclam, 1983), 381–415; Jeannine Blackwell, "Bildungsroman mit Dame," (Ph.D. diss., Indiana University, 1982), 109–29; Helen Kastinger Riley, "Tugend im Umbruch: Sophie Laroches *Geschichte des Fräuleins von Sternheim einmal anders,"* in *Die weibliche Muse* (Columbia, S.C.: Camden House, 1986), 27–52; Bernd Heidenreich, *Sophie von La Roche—eine Werkbiographie* (Frankfurt a. M., Bern, New York: Peter Lang, 1986); Günter Häntzschel, "Nachwort," in Sophie von La Roche, *Geschichte des Fräuleins von Sternheim* (Munich: Winkler, 1976), 301–36; Michael Maurer, "Das Gute und das Schöne: Sophie von La Roche (1730–1807) wiederentdecken?" *Euphorion* 79 (1985): 111–38; Peter Petschauer, "Sophie von La Roche, Novelist Between Reason and Emotion," *Germanic Review* 61 (Spring 1982): 70–77; Petra Sachs, "Sophie von La Roche: Ein 'Frauenbild,'" in *Frauenjahrbuch 1,* ed. Hildegard Kuhn-Oechsle and Elizabeth Renz (Weingarten: Drumlin, 1983), 101–49, and Winkle, *Woman as Bourgeois Ideal,* 45–92.

10. The most comprehensive study of the "women's novel" in eighteenth-century Germany is still Christine Touaillon, *Der deutsche Frauenroman des 18. Jahrhunderts* (Vienna, Leipzig: Wilhelm Braumüller, 1919).

11. See Brüggemann, "Einführung," in *Geschichte des Fräuleins von Sternheim,* Sammlung literarischer Kunst- und Kulturdenkmäler in Entwicklungsreihen, Reihe Ausklärung, vol. 15 (Leipzig: Philipp Reclam, 1938), 12; Siegfried Sudhof, "Sophie Laroche," in *Deutsche Dichter des 18. Jahrhunderts: Ihr Leben und Werk,* ed. Benno von Wiese (Berlin: Erich Schmidt, 1977), 303–4.

12. Compare Touaillon, 112–16; Ridderhoff, "Einleitung," in *Geschichte des Fräuleins von Sternheim;* Sophie von La Roche, Deutsche Literaturdenkmale, no. 138, ed. Kuno Ridderhoff (Berlin: Behr, 1907), 34–35; Wilhelm Spickernagel, *Die Geschichte des Fräuleins von Sternheim von Sophie von La Roche und Goethes "Werther"* (Greifswald: Hans Adler, 1911), 33–35; Heidenreich, *Sophie von La Roche,* 14–15.

13. See Wulf Koepke, "The epistolary novel: from self-assertion to alienation," *Studies on Voltaire and the Eighteenth Century* 192 (1980): 1277–79.

14. See Kuno Ridderhoff, *Sophie von La Roche, die Schülerin Richardsons and Rousseaus* (Einbeck: J. Schroedter, 1895); and Schmidt, *Richardson, Rousseau und Goethe,* 46–63; Touaillon, *Der deutsche Frauenroman,* 106–11.

15. *Leiden* means "to suffer" in German.

16. Compare Joeres, "That girl," 137–56; Becker-Cantarino, "Nachwort," 407–15; Blackwell, *Bildungsroman mit Dame,* 120–29.

17. Claudine Herrmann asserts the improbability of a woman's ability to determine her own world within an androcentric culture and society in "The Virile System," in *New French Feminisms,* ed. Elaine Marks and Isabelle de Courtivron (New York: Schocken Books, 1981), 88.

18. La Roche, *Geschichte,* 178, translation mine. All further references to this work appear in the text.

19. Petschauer, "Sophie von La Roche," 73–74.

20. Joeres, "That girl," 153.

21. Compare Touaillon, *Der deutsche Frauenroman* 120–22; Becker-Cantarino, "'Muse' und 'Kunstrichter,'" *MLN* 99 (1984): 582; and J. M. R. Lenz, "To Sophie La Roche," June 1775, *Briefe von und an J. M. R. Lenz,* ed. Karl Freye & W. Stammler (Leipzig: Kurt Wolff, 1918), 1:121.

22. See Burghardt Dedner, "Sophie La Roche: 'Die Geschichte des Fräuleins von Sternheim' and 'Rosaliens Briefe': Die Umdeutung der Tradition im Bereich 'realistischen' Erzählens," in *Topos, Ideal und Realitätspostulat: Studien zur Darstellung des Landlebens im Roman des 18. Jahrhunderts* (Tübingen: Max Niemeyer, 1969), 78; Heidenreich, *Sophie von La Roche,* 69.

23. See La Roche, "Vorwort," in *Melusinens Sommerabende,* ed. C. M. Wieland (Weimar, 1806), 31–35; Heidenreich, *Sophie von La Roche,* 67–73; Touaillon, *Der deutsche Frauenroman,* 125.

24. Compare Touaillon, *Der deutsche Frauenroman,* 201–2.

25. Sophie La Roche, *Rosaliens Briefe an ihre Freundin Mariane von St**,* 3 vols., rev. ed. (Altenburg: Richter, 1797), translation mine. All further references to this work appear in the text.

26. Sophie La Roche herself experienced the extent of her husband's rule over her daily routine. Every morning he left books with marked passages for her to read and weave into conversations with Count Stadion, her husband's guardian and employer. When her children were born, she was refused permission to

nurse them, for fear her even temper would suffer. See La Roche, "Vorwort," 50–51, 54.

27. Compare Horsley, "A Critical Appraisal," 47–74; Weigel, "Die geopferte Heldin," 138–47; Winkle, *Woman as Bourgeois Ideal*, 127–36; Barbara Becker-Cantarino, "Priesterin und Lichtbringerin," in *Die Frau als Heldin und Autorin. Neue kritische Ansätze zur deutschen Literatur*, ed. Wolfgang Paulsen, Amherster Kolloquium zur deutschen Literatur 10 (Bern, Munich: Francke, 1979), 111–24.

28. See La Roche, *Rosaliens Briefe*, 1:65–133.

29. Eva Becker, *Der deutsche Roman um 1780* (Stuttgart: J. B. Metzler, 1964), 65; Touaillon, *Der deutsche Frauenroman*, 145.

30. See Heidenreich, *Sophie von La Roche*, 89–91.

31. Compare Michael Maurer, ed., *Ich bin mehr Herz als Kopf: Sophie von La Roche in Briefen*, (Munich: C. H. Beck, 1983).

32. See La Roche, *Briefe an Lina als Mädchen*, 2d enl. ed., vol. 1 (Leipzig: Gräff, 1788); Grenz, *Mädchenliteratur*, 70–74; Heidenreich, *Sophie von La Roche*, 151–57.

6

Narrative Cross-Dressing and the Critique of Authorship in the Novels of Richardson

JAMES CARSON

RESTORATION and early eighteenth-century authors as various as Wycherley, Congreve, and Ned Ward conventionally took upon themselves the debased role of the female prostitute, thereby objectifying their own anxieties and disarming in advance criticism of their ungentlemanly activities: "The condition of an *Author,* is much like that of a *Strumpet,* both exposing our *Reputations* to supply our *Necessities,* till at last we contract such an ill habit, thro' our Practices, that we are equally troubl'd with an *itch* to be always *Doing.*"[1] The analogy between author and prostitute, exemplified here by Ward in 1700, appears frequently in conjunction with the practice of *female impersonation.* Eve Sedgwick has recently interpreted "female impersonation" in the epilogue to *The Country Wife* as a confirmation of the assumption "that women go on the stage to market their bodies to men, as much as to embody the conceptions of male playwrights."[2] We may question Sedgwick's view that Wycherley's feminine identification is as triumphant as Horner's simulated castration, for Horner, the witty hero of *The Country Wife,* sees his own feminized condition as superior to that of the poets. He himself employs the prostitution metaphor derisively against poets, who "like Whores are only hated by each other."[3] The anxieties about authorship inherent in this conventional analogy mitigate somewhat the confident phallocentrism that such critics as Nancy Miller and Robert Markley have found, for example, in John Cleland's adoption of the narrative voice of a prostitute in *Fanny Hill.*[4] Cleland participates in an English tradition of cross-gender narration in which male authors lead us to question their own adoption of the female voice by showing us within their novels the dangerous, potentially tragic results of cross-gender imitation.

The prostitution metaphor for male authorship suggests that some qualification is needed for the interpretation of literary tradition in terms of the traffic-in-women paradigm, in which women serve either as the degraded objects through which men can engage in homosocial relations or as mirrors and echoes for the narcissistic male. Eve Sedgwick herself admits that the traffic-in-women paradigm "fails to do justice to women's own powers, bonds, and struggles."[5] Nor does the classic feminist anthropological study of this paradigm permit us to ignore the role of female resistance within a system in which men, indeed, have largely suppressed female sexuality. Gayle Rubin argues that in cultures that practice the exchange of women, "much of the drama . . . consists in female attempts to evade the sexual control of their kinsmen."[6] I intend to argue that women's powers pervade even the phallocentric representations that seek to degrade or cancel women. According to Nancy Miller, male power and male bonds are the predominant issues in Sade's impersonation of Juliette. "She *testifies* simply to the power not of the female imagination, but to the power of the female in the male imagination. To the extent that she is a heroine, she is *that which* allows men to write, to and of each other."[7] The questioning of the status of the subject by Sade and others might permit us to give a slightly different emphasis to Miller's terms. The male imagination does not have absolute control over the fantasized figure of the female. It is not so much that men are allowed to write in a certain way as that they are constrained to write thus. One of the constraints on discourse is "the *power* of the female" within, but not completely in the control of, the male imagination. The male anxieties about authorship revealed through authorial self-criticism are not merely evidence for a theory about the dissolution of the subject, a theory that could easily coexist with male dominance over and violence against women. Rather, the practical power relations between the sexes are determined precisely by the answers to such questions as what an author is and what moral, intellectual, or social qualifications are necessary to fill the authorial function.

Samuel Richardson's novels invite an examination of both the authorial function and the male author's use of the female voice, though Richardson characteristically assumes the voice of virgin rather than whore. His fictional works embody a conflict between potential communal authorship by his readers and correspondents and his own attempts to assert control. But what Richardson found most pleasurable in writing both fictional and actual letters was less the assertion of his authorial self than a sympathetic dissolution of the self.

A narrative technique in which a male author adopts the female voice was for Richardson a radical example of sympathetic identification— sympathy across the bounds of gender—and a way of drawing upon the female socializing function to support his own efforts at moral reform. Richardson believed that the epistolary form was especially well suited for the sympathetic communication of feeling. The letter, for Richardson and for his exemplary characters—Clarissa Harlowe, Harriet Byron, Charles Grandison—involved enunciation in the first person, not for the purpose of self-affirmation, but rather for that of self-denial, in making another's case one's own. However, Richardson recognized that sympathy could never be complete, however much one tried to divest oneself of self. Cross-gender identification is especially difficult, given the differences in men's and women's education and perhaps essential nature and given the inescapable contamination of sympathy by gender hierarchy, sexual desire, and duplicitous disguise. My claim is that Richardson objectified his recognition of the imperfection of his cross-gender sympathies by having his villains adopt female dress and the female voice in the service of their lust and will to dominate. Richardson emphasized his kinship with his villains, especially Lovelace, so as to engage in criticism of the inevitable hierarchical perspective of his authorship, since it was in part this hierarchy that rendered sympathy imperfect. At the same time, however, Richardson used the figure of the villain as author to show how authority, even if one were to seek absolute dominance and the reduction of the other to an echo or mirror of the self, could be no more complete than sympathy. Interpretations of the male adoption of the female narrative voice in terms of the traffic-in-women model generally subscribe to the notion of a monolithic patriarchal power. I take the example of Richardson in order to argue against the traffic-in-women model, drawing my evidence from Richardson's letters and all three of his epistolary novels: *Pamela, Clarissa,* and *Sir Charles Grandison.*

In his well-known account of the value of familiar letters, Samuel Richardson placed correspondence above even "personal conversation" as a means "of displaying the force of friendship." Richardson accounted for this preference by observing that "The pen . . . makes distance, presence," a presence, moreover, less subject to interruption than actual physical presence. "For the pen is jealous of company. It expects, as I may say, to engross the writer's whole self." These remarks occur in the context of introducing one of Richardson's many female correspondents to the delights of familiar letter writing. The pen engrosses the whole self, so that the writer's mind can be delivered to another, in an individual style, "generally beyond the power of disguise."[8] But this loss of the self to the pen still occurs, for Richardson, where there indeed seems to be some disguise; that is, when he writes in the person of fictional characters, who claim to be delivering their whole heart in letters to their confidants. Writing epistolary fiction permits Richardson to divest himself of self: "I am all the while absorbed in the character. It is not fair to say—I, identically I, am any-where, while I keep within the character" (*Letters* 286; 14 Feb. 1754). Indeed, Richardson took delight in such sympathetic identification with his fictional characters; for, after the end of his career as a novelist, he regretted being confined to his own character: "O that I could carry myself out of myself, into *other* Characters, as in Times past!"[9] Uninterrupted dedication to the pen and undisguised (though perhaps fictional) self-expression foster the pleasures of getting outside of one's self.

But one of the primary purposes of Richardson's novels is to maintain that such self-alienation is not so much pleasurable as it is ethically valuable. The letter for Richardson is, in one respect, one of several Protestant equivalents for the Roman Catholic confession. A faithful narrative of one's actions in letters to a mentor, as with Charles Grandison's letters to Dr. Bartlett, helps the writer avoid dubious actions. Letter writing, for all of Richardson's exemplary characters, is a form of self-examination and moral accounting, a delivering over of one's whole self to the confidant for correction. In much of Richardson's own familiar correspondence, however, what he offers up for correction is not identically himself but rather his epistolary fiction. For example, he asks Aaron Hill's daughters "to honour me with their Censure and Correction, in such places (I know their Delicacy!) where my Clarissa wants Delicacy and Female Grace" (*Letters* 101; 18 Nov. 1748). Richardson's voluminous correspondence with young women grows out of his desire for confirmation and approval of his sympathetic identification with fictional female characters. His novels are thus opened up to the voices of actual women, even if their objections and corrections generally prompt him to introduce into his works defenses of his original conception rather than a revision of it. The novels are part of the same textual network as Richardson's personal correspondence.

But the main burden of Richardson's epistolary fiction is to argue for the ethical value of precisely his own authorial activity—learning to lose one's self in the situations of others. What makes Charles Grandison so perfect, for example, is that he "can put himself in every one's situation; and can forget his own interest."[10] Imaginative identification is the central term in Richardson's ethics: Briefly, "a feeling heart" produces sympathetic identification, which in turn promotes moral action, "since the heart that is able to partake of the distress of another, cannot wilfully give it" (*Grandison* 2:258). What was an ethical issue for Richardson has become an aesthetic one for his modern biographers. Eaves and Kimpel argue that it is essential for an epistolary novelist to "live" his characters (246), and that when Richardson is unsuccessful (in their view, in *Sir Charles Grandison* and *Pamela,* Part 2), "we see merely a dummy through whose mouth someone else is droning platitudes" (110). Setting aside the aesthetic question, I suggest that, for Richardson, a person or character who relates to another as ventriloquist to dummy is acting in a morally reprehensible fashion. To the extent that his own authorial activities betray something of this relationship, Richardson engages in a critique of his own authorship.

Richardson's authorship must be ventriloquial to some extent, since, as he himself recognizes, sympathetic identification cannot be complete. Responding to Charlotte Grandison's Hobbesian view that compassion is ultimately based on self-interest, Harriet Byron reasserts philanthropic motives but, at the same time, admits the limits of sympathy: "A compassionate heart, said I, is a blessing, though a painful one: And yet there would be no supporting life, if we felt quite as poignantly for others as we do for ourselves" (*Grandison* 1:335). In addition to the general constraints imposed by the very mechanism of sympathy, Richardson also recognizes that religion, class, and gender all limit and influence one's ability to put oneself in the place of another. The familiar correspondences based on the mutual communication of feeling are likewise threatened by the gender and class constraints on sympathy. These constraints for Richardson cut both ways. On the one hand, he was painfully aware that, as a middle-class printer, his manner of life and place of residence might be regarded as "low" by some of the fashionable ladies whom he corresponded with and visited, and that he might be regarded as ill-qualified to depict fashionable society in his fiction. On the other hand, Richardson knew that his gender situated him higher in the epistolary hierarchy.

Corresponding with members of the opposite sex was much more dangerous for women than for men, since male designs would almost invariably interfere with mutual expression from the heart. Lovelace, in the devious use he makes of his correspondence with Clarissa, is the best example of Richardson's designing males. Richardson believed that men

like Lovelace would not permit a correspondence to end until they could
go no further. At the outset of his correspondence with more than one
woman, Richardson shows himself aware of the potential of male designs. In requesting a letter from Lady Bradshaigh upon her receipt of
the fifth volume of *Clarissa,* Richardson offers her a playful warning:
"Yet you must take care how you favour me too—Men are naturally
Incroachers" (*Letters* 97; 26 Oct. 1748). Elsewhere Richardson denies
that he shares the designing and encroaching masculine nature. He is a
mere "undesigning scribbler," nothing "less than paternal in [his] views"
(*Letters* 66; [1746?]). What he perhaps did not see is that his desire to
play the paternal role in relationships with a number of young women
might well be another kind of male design, quite consistent with patriarchal control. Richardson's cross-gender identification was doomed
to imperfection, then, both in ways that he recognized and in ways that
he probably did not.

The necessary incompleteness of sympathetic identification, especially across gender lines, means that we probably cannot praise Richardson for devising an epistolary form that is "an image of freedom"
since the characters are permitted to "speak for themselves."[11] While it
is thus imprecise to accept the possibility of the utopian liberty of a truly
polyphonic novel, Richardson's fiction remains open, as we have seen, to
dialogue. While it is probably the case that dialogic traces can be discovered in every novel and, in fact, in every piece of writing, Richardson's familiar letters and his epistolary fiction do highlight the presence
of dialogue. What John Carroll observes about Richardson's familiar
letters is equally true of many of the letter writers in Richardson's fictional works: "In following his correspondents' leads he often quotes
their observations at length before replying to them and thus turns the
letters into dialogues."[12] The emphasis on dialogue in Richardson's novels, and in epistolary fiction generally, justifies a brief consideration of
Mikhail Bakhtin's perspective on the novel. Indeed, the concept of dialogism permits a reconsideration of an author's ventriloquism of his
characters, which in turn suggests that the traffic-in-women model supplies an inadequate interpretation of the male author's adoption of the
female voice.

I would like to approach Bakhtin's dialogism obliquely through his
notion of the carnivalesque. For Bakhtin, grotesque and carnivalesque
phenomena are never merely destructive but are always partly re-
generative.[13] Of particular relevance to the question of the male adoption of the female voice is the carnivalesque phenomenon of men dress-
ing in women's clothes. If we view the activities of male novelists as
analogous to popular social struggles—specifically, if we regard female

impersonation in fiction as parallel to cross-dressing in popular protest—
then we would have to qualify the traffic-in-women model.

The motives behind the male appropriation of female dress in popular ritual and social protest are perhaps best explained in Natalie Davis's
essay "Women on Top." Davis describes the varied and sometimes subversive meanings of the female persona:

> On the one hand, the disguise freed men from full responsibility for
> their deeds and perhaps, too, from fear of outrageous revenge upon
> their manhood. After all, it was mere women who were acting in this
> disorderly way. On the other hand, the males drew upon the sexual
> power and energy of the unruly woman and on her license (which they
> had long assumed at carnival and games)—to promote fertility, to
> defend the community's interests and standards, and to tell the truth
> about unjust rule.[14]

Davis's claim that men adopted female dress in the first place to avoid
responsibility for their acts can be readily applied to the activity of writing fiction in the eighteenth century. Authors practiced various strategies
of authorial disavowal in order to avoid the vanity of publishing and the
guilt of fictionalizing.[15] Female impersonation might be added to the
number of such strategies. Second, the fertility symbolism of woman and
her clothing has a close relationship to an important opposition informing the novel of sensibility: sterile artistic production versus fertile natural reproduction. Female impersonation can be regarded as an attempt to
collapse this opposition by attaching the sign of fertility to artistic production. As we shall see, maternal nurturing can be regarded as a metaphor for intertextual transmission in Richardson's novels. Third, the
woman's license in popular protest "to tell the truth about unjust rule" is
a similar phenomenon to the subversive potential of female authority in
the novel: the female persona situates an author outside "the elite social
group" and makes it possible to question the political and social
orthodoxy and to examine with relative impunity the contradictions
within the dominant order.[16]

Richardson identified with women in part because, given his position
outside the social elite, he had been similarly denied educational oppor-
tunities. The observations that the wise Mrs. Shirley (the grandmother
of Harriet Byron, the heroine of *Sir Charles Grandison*) applies to
merchants and military officers, Richardson would have extended to
printers.

> In the general course of the things of this world, women have not
> opportunities of sounding the depths of science, or of acquainting
> themselves with polite literature: But this want of opportunity is not

> entirely confined to *them*. There are professions among the men no
> more favourable to these studies, than the common avocations of
> women. (*Grandison* 3:243)

A middle-class male author in the eighteenth century might have strong
motives, then, for identifying with women, even if this identification did
not necessarily prompt him to question the political orthodoxy. But in
addition to the survival of the popular notion that women (or other
excluded social classes) had the right to criticize unjust rule—a notion
quite opposed to the negative values of passivity and a degraded, mar-
ketable sexuality that the traffic-in-women model argues were imposed
on women—the figure of woman was endowed with another positive
symbolic value in eighteenth-century moral philosophy: that of socializing the more brutal sex and hence leading to the greater refinement of
society and the progress of civilization. Indeed, Charles Grandison follows up Mrs. Shirley's remarks by observing that women's knowledge is
to be valued not only for the joy it gives to the possessor, but also
because it may serve to "improve a man of sense, sweeten his manners,
and render him a much more sociable, a much more amiable creature"
(3:250). Woman's socializing function, for Richardson, amounts to more
than merely providing a domestic refuge from the active world of commerce; it is a creative capacity, as Richardson wittily observes when he
seeks help from his female correspondents in drawing the character of
the good man for *Sir Charles Grandison:* "The young ladies must help to
make such a one. It is more in the power of young ladies than they seem
to imagine, to make fine men" (*Letters* 164; 20 July 1750). Although
Richardson designs the character of Lovelace in part to show male resistance to being "new modelld" (Lady Bradshaigh's term; *Letters* 95; 26
Oct. 1748) by women, his conception of the creative socializing power of
women counts as a kind of inversion of the Pygmalion scenario. The
traffic-in-women interpretation of female impersonation would not lead
us to expect either Richardson's emphasis on the formative social role of
women or the critique to which he subjected the male Pygmalion figure.

The notion of the carnivalesque suggests, then, other reasons for
disputing the characterization of female impersonation as an effective
male narcissistic strategy. The concept of totalizing male power would
seem to be shared by those who view literary history in terms of an
oedipal struggle and those who believe that the narrative mode of female
impersonation serves to eradicate women discursively. Using Mikhail
Bakhtin's terms, I argue that instead of male authors' securing the power
of monologue, a dialogue is established between authors and their
(female) characters or narrators. In this view, taking on another dress or

another voice is neither a means of individual appropriation nor a way for men to increase sexual oppression. Carnivalesque cross-dressing negates neither the costume nor "proper" sexual identity, but the consequent assertion of androgyny does not represent an access of power or knowledge to the individual, for the limits of the individual body have been transgressed. Only when the body is individualized, according to Bakhtin, does it become "self-sufficient and [speak] in its name alone."[17] The dual body, on the contrary, speaks dialogically.

The problem with drawing upon Bakhtin's notion of the carnivalesque in order to situate the novel culturally is that his work has lent itself to a utopianism that provides an inadequate interpretation of social phenomena.[18] This utopianism resembles that of those Richardson critics who appear to argue for a perfectly polyphonic novelistic form in which the author "lives" his characters so fully that they speak unproblematically for themselves: such criticism, it seems to me, ignores Richardson's own recognition of the imperfections of sympathy.

Bakhtin posits an ideal, original community of the people, which was realized temporarily during carnival. David Carroll, however, reads Bakhtin against himself and disrupts the supposed unity of the carnival crowd by means of Bakhtin's notion of the dialogic. Thus, heterogeneity or the presence of many voices is affirmed for the people as it is for the author. Carroll disputes Michael Holquist's view that Bakhtin acted as a ventriloquist toward members of his circle (P. N. Medvedev and V. N. Volosinov) in works published under their names. Carroll offers an interpretation of literary ventriloquism, which has great value for an understanding of literary influence and quotation, as well as for reconsidering the relationship between authors and their narrators or characters.

> If the ventriloquist's dummies do not have the first or the last word
> (neither does the author-ventriloquist), they continually transform,
> interrupt, and redirect the intentions and words of the ventriloquist; and
> as we know from watching accomplished ventriloquists work, their art is
> in the way they lose their own voice in other voices, the way their voice
> is continually thrown or disseminated outside of itself from the start.
> The true ventriloquist continually risks losing his power and mastery
> over all his voices, even "his own," for his "true voice" and the message
> it is supposed to convey cannot be separated from the dialogue created
> among his various and conflicting voices.[19]

This concept of a ventriloquism traversed by dialogue enables us to avoid, on the one hand, the idealism of perfect polyphony and complete authorial sympathy and, on the other, the monologism of the traffic-in-women interpretation of female impersonation.

As we can see in Richardson's epistolary fiction, male authors, instead of simply reinscribing the domination of the male voice or the phallus, may provide a critique of the masculine appropriation of women. Evidence for such a critique appears in the analogy between the writing of fiction and the adoption of disguises, an analogy that is especially clear when fictional works are presented from the point of view of first-person narrators and letter-writing characters, and especially significant when the resulting memoirs and letters are justified on the basis of their putative factuality. In the eighteenth-century English novel, delight in the mask is invariably chastened by criticism of deceit. The moral condemnation of fiction and disguise may be especially virulent when it retains some vestiges of the Puritan critique of transvestism on the Elizabethan and Jacobean stage.[20] A mask indicative of radical otherness, such as a gender difference between author and narrator, may also serve to highlight the conflict of perspectives within an individual utterance, thus creating "the space for critical and self-critical distance in language."[21]

In Richardson's novels, the male villain serves as a figure of the author—a strategy of authorial self-criticism that Richardson bequeaths to such works as *Les Liaisons dangereuses* and to the Gothic novel, with its satanic, and sometimes protean, villains. In these works, the villain becomes the author's surrogate in the testing of the heroine. At critical moments in the heroine's trials, the villain adopts female dress or a woman's voice in the service of seduction. But the "mean" strategy of, for example, Mr. B.'s appearing "in a Gown and Petticoat,"[22] in one of his attempts on Pamela's virtue, increases his resemblance to the bourgeois author who adopts the persona of a servant girl; Mr. B.'s crossdressing reflects back on Richardson's cross-gender narration. In the second part of *Pamela,* Richardson continues his critique of the masculine appropriation of woman, when a male character adopts a female epistolary persona. The vulgar lawyer Turner, having aspired to the hand of a countess, busies himself upon rejection in destroying both the lady's character and the incipient liaison between her and Mr. B. One of his strategies is to write a badly spelt letter "in a woman's hand," signed "Thomasine Fuller,"[23] in which he informs Pamela that her husband is traveling to Tunbridge in order to set up housekeeping with the countess. The middle-class lawyer amidst the gentry and aristocracy is an appropriate figure for the author whose capacity for portraying the language of high life had been questioned. That "Thomasine Fuller" speaks and spells in such an uncultivated manner points to Richardson's awareness that it is exactly this kind of male appropriation of the female voice that he wishes to exorcise from his text, as he raises the style in the revisions of *Pamela* for later editions.

In *Clarissa,* with more tragic results, Lovelace performs an oral female impersonation, summoning a servant in a female voice as a preface to having the widow Bevis impersonate Clarissa herself.[24] His impersonations and his direction of female actresses serve as part of a successful strategy for luring Clarissa back from her refuge at Hampstead to the London brothel of Mrs. Sinclair. Lovelace has more frequent recourse to another mode of female impersonation: he uses his knowledge of the female mind and his skill at *"manual imitation"* (2:468) to compose both sides of Clarissa Harlowe's and Anna Howe's correspondence once he begins intercepting their letters. Lovelace, then, engages in the same activities as Richardson himself, taking the subject of female friendship and writing letters as a woman.

Richardson thus objectified certain self-doubts about his right to invade the province of women and depict female friendship. He addresses yet another female subject, that of maternal breast-feeding, in a somewhat similar fashion, since he shows how his libertine characters imperiously extend male prerogative into this sphere. In *Clarissa,* the rakish hero's fantasy "of seeing a twin Lovelace at each" of Clarissa's charming breasts, "drawing from it his first sustenance," is followed immediately by his proposal to allow maternal breast-feeding "for physical reasons, [to be] continued for one month and no more!" (2:477). In order to explain these "physical reasons," Richardson appends a footnote referring to his earlier novel *Pamela.* Appropriately, a fantasy of lactation prompts a transgression of the boundaries of Richardson's *Clarissa* and establishes an intertextual link with his earlier work. Intertextuality operates not in terms of oedipal self-assertion but analogously to lactation, on a maternal rather than a paternal model. By its place in Richardson's footnote (and by its subsequent reference to the psychoanalytic oral phase), lactation names a principle that challenges the separability and autonomy of individual novels. It may seem paradoxical to regard a footnote as transgressing the boundaries of *Clarissa,* since Richardson's footnotes have usually been seen as part of the textual apparatus he creates in an attempt to control interpretation, to transform the textual locus of interpretive conflict into the self-identical book.[25] However, such regulative efforts are not placed above the fray, for Richardson's footnotes adulterate the margins of his book along with those of *Clarissa's* most pedantic letter writer—Elias Brand. Richardson's novel, that is, incorporates a critique of the very method he adopts in an attempt to extend authorial control.

Recent critics have agreed that in the second part of *Pamela* Richardson uses the female voice in an unpleasant and relentless paean to patriarchy.[26] Yet even here there are moments when the voice of the master ventriloquist seems to be lost in that of the female automaton, as in the debate between Pamela and her husband, Mr. B., on the pros and cons of maternal breast-feeding. Characteristically, Richardson presents the better reasoned arguments (resembling those presented later in the decade from William Cadogan's "Philosophic Knowledge of Nature"[27]) in the female voice. Mr. B.'s arguments appear to derive from puerile selfishness and jealousy: his concern for any detrimental effects of breast-feeding on Pamela's "personal graces" and "easy, genteel form"; as well as his reluctance to have his "rest broken in upon" by "the child's necessities" (2:233–34) or to have conjugal sexuality curtailed by the duties of nursing ("according to Galen, who was followed by sixteenth and seventeenth-century doctors, husbands ought not to sleep with nursing wives since 'carnal copulation . . . troubleth the blood, and so in consequence the milk' ").[28] Mr. B. further declares that "even a son and heir, so jealous am I of your affections, shall not be my rival in them" (2:234).

Not only are Mr. B.'s arguments presented as selfish and unscientific, but Pamela protests later in the novel that maternal breast-feeding might have prevented her son from contracting smallpox: "I fear the nurse's constitution is too hale and too rich for the dear baby! Had *I* been permitted—" (2:340). The interrupted sentence encodes the signs of Pamela's self-censorship. Richardson permits his heroine greater liberty of speech than Mr. B. does liberty of action. Even in his most patriarchal work, Richardson cannot deny his heroine the partial expression of feelings which, precisely because they stop short of questioning the duty of self-denial, affirm her moral superiority. While Richardson approves of Pamela's submissiveness, he later arrives at a quite modern reinterpretation of his first novel when he suggests that Pamela cannot be entirely happy with Mr. B., for the squire does not constitute an adequate reward for the servant's virtue: "It is apparent by the whole Tenor of Mr. B.'s Behaviour to Pamela after Marriage, that nothing but such an implicit Obedience, and slavish Submission, as Pamela shewed to all his Injunctions and Dictates, could have made her *tolerably* happy, even with a *Reformed* Rake" (*Letters* 124; 21 Jan. 1748/9). Even in the novel itself there is a poignant moment when Richardson suggests that Pamela's sacrifice in the dispute over breast-feeding seems to her a relinquishing of the maternal role: "And the result is, we have heard of a good sort of woman, that is to be my poor *baby's mother,* when it comes" (2:240). Nor does Pamela's muted protest against her perpetual state of pregnancy

(2:440) seem entirely consistent with the standard view of this patriarchal work.

The intertextual link of lactation takes the reader into Richardson's final novel as well, for in *Sir Charles Grandison* Lady G. (née Charlotte Grandison) is surprised by her husband "[i]n an act that confessed the mother, the *whole* mother!—Little Harriet at my breast" (3:402). Charlotte G. plays the same assertive role in *Grandison* that Anna Howe played in *Clarissa*. What cousin Morden says of independent women like Anna Howe—that sex or motherhood "*domesticates*" them (*Clarissa* 4:470)—is repeated by Harriet Byron (when elevated to the position of Lady Grandison) about her friend and sister-in-law: "She will be matronized now. The *mother* must make her a *wife*" (3:388). Morden and Harriet would seem to have been proven right, when Charlotte trades her bantering simile of brides as "heifers led to sacrifice" (3:236) and her playful allusions to infanticide (3:358) for the maternal scene that Lord G. views with a more sentimental form of Lovelacean rapture. But Richardson does not permit the genuinely engaging power of the independent woman to be so easily subdued into the *wife* and *mother* of Harriet. Even the newly domesticated Charlotte still sticks at the word *obey* in the marriage vows (3:419). Moreover, while the troubled marriage of Lord and Lady G. is transformed into a happy union, it is not a union in which the wife is subsumed in the person of her husband. Richardson sought, as it were, to answer in advance Ray Strachey's witticism: "my wife and I are one, and I am he."[29] When Charlotte G. uses the first person, it is, on the contrary, the feminine *I* that is inclusive. Late in the novel Charlotte writes of her arrival at Grandison Hall, "I arrived here on Monday afternoon," and then adds, "My Lord and I are one now: If therefore I say, *I* arrived, it is the same as saying, *he* did" (3:417–18). Instead of adopting the epistolary voice of a woman to eradicate her, Richardson imagines that the *I* of a woman of superior talents might include the *he* of her aristocratic, somewhat silly, though properly sentimental husband.

While there is significant resistance to male power in *Grandison* and *Pamela,* it is *Clarissa* that offers the most powerful critique in the eighteenth-century English novel of male ventriloquial appropriation of women. Such ventriloquism is shown to depend on the rakish maxim that women have no souls. Lovelace sees himself as a Pygmalion figure. On a visit to Yorkshire, Richardson's rake meets the two nieces of Colonel Ambrose: "I thought them passive-faced, and spiritless. . . . I believe I could, with a little pains, have given them life and soul, and to every feature of their faces sparkling information—but my Clarissa!—O Belford, my Clarissa has made me eyeless and senseless to every other beauty!" (3:392). If we recall Freud's interpretation of the loss of eyes in

"The 'Uncanny,'" Lovelace's "eyeless" condition suggests the dread of castration, which, as we shall see, characterizes his aesthetic femininity. The central incident of the novel—the rape of a woman reduced to a deathlike state by opiates—stands as an inversion of the rake's fantasy of animation. The Pygmalion fantasy is answered and frustrated by an elided representation of quasi-necrophilia, an act which Richardson condemned as unmanly and inhuman.

Richardson is critical of the rakish Pygmalion who imagines himself able to animate women because he believes that they have no souls, but the male novelist who impersonates and animates female characters bears a close resemblance to this kind of rake. The threat of this resemblance leads Richardson to reinterpret the Pgymalion figure as one characterized by sentimental affection rather than misogynistic lust. In defending, in a letter to Lady Bradshaigh, his representation of Clarissa's distresses and death, Richardson depicts himself as Pygmalion in the guise of the man of feeling: "Nor can I go thro' some of the Scenes myself without being sensibly touched (Did I not say, that I was another Pygmalion?)" (*Letters* 90; 26 Oct. 1748). When Richardson imagines himself to be the animator of a woman, he imagines her to have a soul capable of experiencing exquisite pain, by which he will be deeply affected in his role as spectator. Richardson's dialogue with Lady Bradshaigh turns on the question of the possibility of sympathetic authorship for, in his ethical system, a feeling heart cannot willfully give distress to another. Since Richardson must give distress, his exercise of authorship is questioned on the basis of his own principles. He is, then, critical both of the Pygmalion figure who believes that women have no souls, and the Pygmalion figure who gives pain to a woman who, like Clarissa, is all soul. At the same time he shows the inevitable slippages from the absolute control sought by one who would reduce another person to a creature without will or soul.

Lovelace makes "puppets" of those whose independence is compromised by their passions or need: most of his "implements" are either women or members of the lower orders. But distinguishing the voice from the echo, and the puppet master from the puppet, is no simple matter in this novel. Is Lovelace the instrument of James Harlowe's sordid ambition, or is James the instrument of Lovelace's lust (2:320)? Lovelace is careful to maintain his independence by avoiding "pecuniary obligations" (2:67), yet he loses his independence to the very instruments of his vice: the bawd Mrs. Sinclair begins "to catechize and upbraid me, with as much insolence as if I owed her money" (3:275). The arts, arguments, and ridicule of Sinclair and the other prostitutes prevent the wavering Lovelace from abandoning his libertine plots; in fact, they carry these plots to barbarous lengths that escape his intentions (3:425). Lovelace imagines himself to be a playwright and an emperor, but whether literary or political, his power is undermined repeatedly.

If the relationship between master and slave has potential for inversion in *Clarissa,* so too the distinction between the sexes is confounded.[30] Male souls inform women's bodies, and men adopt the female voice. The male villain's part in this gender confusion once again reflects back on the author who sympathetically takes the woman's part. After the rape, Lovelace concocts new schemes to subdue Clarissa through sexual assault. He relates one of these to Belford in the form of a dream. Clarissa would be allowed to escape from Mrs. Sinclair's house and would be offered sanctuary by a matronly lady. Since anything is possible in dreams, this matron would be metamorphosed into Mother H., "an old acquaintance of Mother Sinclair" (3:250). Because of the unexpected arrival of company, Clarissa would have to share the matron's bed. Mother H. would then arise during the night to get a cordial.

> Having thus risen, and stepped to her closet, methought she let fall the wax taper in her return; and then [O metamorphosis still stranger than the former! What unaccountable things are dreams!] coming to bed again in the dark, the young lady, to her infinite astonishment, grief, and surprise, found Mother H. turned into a young person of the other sex. (3:250)

The most nightmarish part of Clarissa's rape was the assault by a "mannish" woman (3:211), Mrs. Sinclair. Lovelace proposes another nightmare, in which Clarissa will witness the metamorphosis of a woman into a young man, of Mother H. into Lovelace himself.

Lovelace's dream metamorphosis from a woman into a man offers further insights into his character. Lovelace has a feminine nature. He has what he considers the feminine qualities of tyranny in love (3:65) and willfulness (2:386). His original bashfulness has made it possible for him to acquire, "like Tiresias," an uncommonly deep knowledge of women (2:55). Lovelace's claims to femininity are in part a satire on women, in part an insight into his own character, and in part theatricality in service of seduction. If this rapist, who boasts of his exploits to other men, thereby sustains phallocentrism, his hold on power is shown to be increasingly tenuous. Lovelace tells how his aristocratic uncle enjoys the tales of his rogueries, "encoring him, as formerly he used to do the Italian eunuchs" (3:389). Disgusted by Lovelace's extravagant reaction to Clarissa's death, his fellow rake Mowbray reflects "How love unmans and softens!" (4:344). Lovelace's violence against women seems prompted by his own fears of impotence. Richardson's novel in fact celebrates the foiling of the phallus, as unbending (if serpentine) masculinity is metamorphosed into female circularity, through the "principal device" on Clarissa's coffin: the serpent with its tail in its mouth.[31]

In his bashfulness, his knowledge of the female heart, his adoption of the female voice, and his execution of plots that require him to create characters and their roles, Lovelace resembles the author Richardson. I am certainly not drawing the parallel between the two as a defense of the fictional rapist but rather in order to show that the author of *Clarissa* is implicated in the crimes of the rake. Rather than simply reinscribing the domination of the male voice or the phallus, this novel presents a critique of men's knowledge of women, of a man who impersonates women in speech or writing, and of a man who takes female friendship as the subject of a series of letters. Richardson indicates the immorality and ineffectuality of Lovelace's attempts to traffic in women, thereby creating the space of self-criticism which grants subversive potential to his own adoption of the female epistolary voice. Richardson's recognition of his own compromised position in a structure of male power did not simply result from self-denying benevolence but was produced in part by the responses and expectations of an audience that prominently included women. Indeed, I have not intended to show that Richardson was an eighteenth-century feminist but rather that the power of actual women, both as members of his audience and as an inescapable part of his mental universe, permeated the very fabric of his writing.

Richardson's adoption of the female voice in his epistolary novels does not simply, or even primarily, serve to reinforce patriarchy by reducing woman to a mirror or conduit for homosocial desire. The metaphor of the mirror or echo, like that of the prostitute, serves as a means for male novelists to express their anxieties about their own authorial activities. Such authors have not transcended the patriarchal attitudes of their society in thus defining themselves against female figures. Nor are they capable of such complete sympathy that they could transcend the contradictions in a "feminist" appropriation of the female voice. But the figure of woman is not a mere construct or fantasy of the male imagination. What counted as the female voice or what was signified by female dress was determined by the conflicts and compromises, albeit in relations of unequal power, of eighteenth-century men and women.

NOTES

1. Edward Ward, *A Trip to Jamaica: With a True Character of the People and Island,* 7th ed. (London, 1700), in *Five Travel Scripts Commonly Attributed to Edward Ward* (New York: published for the Facsimile Text Society by Columbia

University Press, 1933); Deborah Laycock brought this passage to my attention. Catherine Gallagher has examined the prostitute metaphor for female authorship in "George Eliot and *Daniel Deronda:* The Prostitute and the Jewish Question," in *Sex, Politics, and Science in the Nineteenth-Century Novel,* ed. Ruth Bernard Yeazell (Baltimore: Johns Hopkins University Press, 1986), 39–62.

   2. Eve Kosofsky Sedgwick, *Between Men: English Literature and Male Homosocial Desire* (New York: Columbia University Press, 1985), 64–65.

   3. William Wycherley, *The Country Wife,* in *The Complete Plays of William Wycherley,* ed. Gerald Weales (New York: Norton, 1966), 297.

   4. See Robert Markley, "Language, Power, and Sexuality in Cleland's *Fanny Hill,*" *Philological Quarterly* 63 (1984): 343–56; and Nancy K. Miller, "I's in Drag: The Sex of Recollection," *Eighteenth Century* 22 (1981): 47–57. Other recent critics, on the contrary, have discovered self-criticism or an unsettling of fixed gender identities in male transvestism or ventriloquism; see Susan J. Wolfson, " 'Their She Condition': Cross-Dressing and the Politics of Gender in *Don Juan,*" *ELH* 54 (1987): 585–617, and Mary Jacobus, *Reading Woman: Essays in Feminist Criticism* (New York: Columbia University Press, 1986), 3–24.

   5. Sedgwick, *Between Men,* 18.

   6. Gayle Rubin, "The Traffic in Women: Notes on the 'Political Economy' of Sex," in *Toward an Anthropology of Women,* ed. Rayna R. Reiter (New York: Monthly Review Press, 1975), 182.

   7. Nancy K. Miller, *The Heroine's Text: Readings in the French and English Novel, 1722–1782* (New York: Columbia University Press, 1980), 153.

   8. "To Sophia Westcomb" (1746?), *Selected Letters of Samuel Richardson,* ed. John Carroll (Oxford: Clarendon Press, 1964), 64–66.

   9. Quoted in T. C. Duncan Eaves and Ben D. Kimpel, *Samuel Richardson: A Biography* (Oxford: Clarendon Press, 1971), 425.

   10. Samuel Richardson, *The History of Sir Charles Grandison,* ed. Jocelyn Harris, The World's Classics (Oxford: Oxford University Press, 1986), pt. 2, 576.

   11. Margaret Anne Doody, *A Natural Passion: A Study of the Novels of Samuel Richardson* (Oxford: Clarendon Press, 1974), 11.

   12. Carroll, ed., *Selected Letters,* 33.

   13. Mikhail Bakhtin, *Rabelais and His World,* trans. Hélène Iswolsky (Cambridge: M.I.T. Press, 1968).

   14. Natalie Zemon Davis, "Women on Top," in *Society and Culture in Early Modern France* (Stanford: Stanford University Press, 1975), 149–50.

   15. See Lennard J. Davis, *Factual Fictions: The Origins of the English Novel* (New York: Columbia University Press, 1983), esp. ch. 10.

   16. Nancy Armstrong, "The Rise of Feminine Authority in the Novel," *Novel* 15 (1982): 129.

   17. Bakhtin, *Rabelais and His World,* 12. See also Terry Castle, *Masquerade and Civilization: The Carnivalesque in Eighteenth Century English Culture and Fiction* (Stanford: Stanford University Press, 1986). Following Bakhtin, Castle argues that the mask signified identification with otherness or introduced a difference within the self. But radical alterity is restricted in Castle's account, since

she believes that the traffic-in-women paradigm accurately describes eighteenth-century English society (255).

18. Such idealism leads Barbara Babcock-Abrahams to privilege the oral over the written and to posit direct, unmediated contact with the world; see "The Novel and the Carnival World," *Modern Language Notes* 89 (1974): 923. Michael André Bernstein rejects this brand of utopianism, denying that a fall from a universal participatory carnival occurred with the rise of the bourgeoisie ("When the Carnival Turns Bitter: Preliminary Reflections upon the Abject Hero," *Critical Inquiry* 10 [1983]: 82).

19. David Carroll, "The Alterity of Discourse: Form, History, and the Question of the Political in M. M. Bakhtin," *Diacritics* 13:2 (1983): 73–74.

20. See J. W. Binns, "Women or Transvestites on the Elizabethan Stage?: An Oxford Controversy," *Sixteenth Century Journal* 2 (1974): 95–120.

21. Dominick LaCapra, "Bakhtin, Marxism, and the Carnivalesque," in *Rethinking Intellectual History: Texts, Contexts, Language* (Ithaca: Cornell University Press, 1983), 312.

22. Samuel Richardson, *Pamela,* ed. T. C. Duncan Eaves and Ben D. Kimpel (Boston: Houghton Mifflin, 1971), 175.

23. Samuel Richardson, *Pamela* (London: Dent, 1931), 2:307; I have used this edition for all quotations from the second part of *Pamela.*

24. Samuel Richardson, *Clarissa,* 4 vols. (London: Dent, 1962), 3:159.

25. See William Beatty Warner, *Reading "Clarissa": The Struggle of Interpretation* (New Haven: Yale University Press, 1979), 188; but see also Warner's brilliant reading of a particular Richardsonian footnote "as the navel of the text" (238).

26. See Terry Eagleton, *The Rape of Clarissa: Writing, Sexuality and Class Struggle in Samuel Richardson* (Oxford: Basil Blackwell, 1982), 36; and Terry Castle, *Clarissa's Ciphers: Meaning & Disruption in Richardson's "Clarissa"* (Ithaca: Cornell University Press, 1982), 169.

27. William Cadogan, *An Essay upon Nursing, and the Management of Children, from Their Birth to Three Years of Age* [London: Printed for J. Roberts, 1748]; rpt. in Morwenna Rendle-Short and John Rendle-Short, *The Father of Child Care: Life of William Cadogan (1711–1797)* (Bristol: John Wright & Sons, 1966), 3.

28. Lawrence Stone, *The Family, Sex, and Marriage in England 1500–1800,* abridged edition (New York: Harper & Row, 1979), 270.

29. From *The Cause,* as quoted in Irene Tayler and Gina Luria, "Gender and Genre: Women in Romantic Literature," in *What Manner of Woman: Essays on English and American Life and Literature,* ed. Marlene Springer (New York: New York University Press, 1977) 98.

30. Judith Wilt relates Lovelace's Tiresian androgyny to his blindness, his impotence, and his status as puppet; see "He Could Go No Farther: A Modest Proposal about Lovelace and Clarissa," *PMLA* 92 (1977): 21, 32n.10. I would dissent from Wilt's argument insofar as it places Richardson firmly in a misogynistic tradition of representing woman as Sin-Death. For another account of Lovelace's gender transformations and loss of mastery, see Tassie Gwilliam,

"'Like Tiresias': Metamorphosis and Gender in *Clarissa*," *Novel* 19 (1986): 101–17.

31. I owe this interpretation of the device on Clarissa's coffin to Rachel M. Brownstein, "An Exemplar to Her Sex," in *Becoming a Heroine: Reading about Women in Novels* (New York: Viking, 1982), 75.

7

Letters from the Harem:
Veiled Figures of Writing
in Montesquieu's Lettres persanes

SUZANNE RODIN PUCCI

> *What if, therefore, the crucial thing to do were rather, or especially, to*
> *conclude that the other exists—and the self in the other—from the fact*
> *of thinking? What if I thought only after the other has been inserted,*
> *introjected into me? Either as thought or as a mirror in which I reflect*
> *and am reflected?*
>
> Luce Irigaray, *Speculum of the Other Woman*

 CAN THERE BE a better place to view female passion than in the often torrid and suggestive letters of the harem wives in Montesquieu's eighteenth-century novel, the *Lettres persanes?* Written exclusively to their absent husband and lord Usbek—who, in self-imposed exile, is set adrift in the exotic culture and intellectual climate of the West—these letters allow the European reader to dream of those sacred and secret places where, protected, shielded, imprisoned, the intriguing and sensuous women of the Orient are cultivated like rare flowers for the exclusive adornment and pleasure of their master. Schooled to remain ignorant of all that lies outside the harem's well-guarded walls and bolted doors, the women of the harem seem knowledgeable only in the gratification of man's desire. From the novel's outset and from the very first letter from the harem, female passion is inscribed within the confines of a spatial, political, and epistolary structure whose discursive and virtual subject is determined by a male perspective.

Montesquieu's novel presents the world of eighteenth-century France through letters written for the most part by Usbek and Rica, two

114

Persian travelers on a prolonged visit to Europe. While these so-called Persians document their experiences and their often astonished reactions to the strange customs, practices, and beliefs obtaining in the West, their letters also provide the reader a fleeting glimpse of the exotic Orient, whose mystery is embodied in the representation of the harem, a realm of seemingly radical political, and especially erotic, alterity. But the dreams of the voyeur take on for Usbek the shape of a nightmare. Obsessive fears regarding his harem women's fidelity and what he deems their constantly threatened virtue are not abated by the army of eunuchs who govern them in his absence; nor are these fears mediated by Usbek's evolving tolerance throughout the *Persian Letters* in the domains of political, religious, and philosophical thought culled from firsthand experience during his sojourn in the West and particularly in Paris, the capital of the French Enlightenment. In his protracted absence from Ispahan and the seraglio, the erotic vision provided by letters from his harem wives, to be enjoyed or ignored by Usbek at will, is irrevocably transformed into personal tragedy with the ultimately overt infidelities and revolt of his harem and with the suicide of one of his wives.

Studies such as those of Alain Grosrichard, Aram Vartanian, Alan Singermann, and Michel Delon focus on the importance of the harem in the *Lettres persanes,* whose erotics of polygamy is demonstrated to retain characteristics integral to the representation of oriental despotism in Montesquieu's text—a structure that at the same time resembles that of eighteenth-century western institutions, particularly that of the absolute monarchy.[1] From 1711 to 1720, the scrupulously dated letters that fly back and forth from Usbek and Rica to their diverse correspondents of family, friends, and acquaintances at home and abroad reflect an experience of the French capital and of the western world that continuously dislocates and distances each social, political, religious, and philosophical practice from its conventional signified. The exotic in the text frequently displays, in effect, a disquieting reversibility into an uncanny similarity with familiar French eighteenth-century institutions of government and religion, and with western models of male and female sexuality.

Even the eunuch, that distorted portrait of male power and sexual prowess, whose monstrous appearance serves as a shadow necessary to flesh out the aggressive image of the master's power and potency, strangely resembles, as we will soon see, more familiar figures of erotic desire.[2] Even (and especially) this supremely exotic representation of absence and lack, as I have discussed in another essay, functions as a literal signified of castration that is inscribed at all levels of this very dense text as a signifier of the separation between a man and his culture; between virtue and its various appearances or masks; between a man's own passions, loves, beliefs, and the exteriority of those truths as they exist beyond the frame of the individual letter; beyond the purview of *his* own epistolary self-expression and cultural, intellectual, erotic vision.[3]

His own, because the diverse epistolary subjects in this novel are almost exclusively male. No female voice disturbs the hegemony of the male perspective of Usbek and Rica or their various correspondents in Persia and abroad, apart from those few letters addressed to Usbek from the cloistered harem women, numbering a mere eleven out of 161. It is therefore not surprising that, despite some excellent studies on the importance of the harem as a metaphor and as a signifying structure central to the relation of western eroticism and politics in the *Lettres persanes*, there should be virtually no attention paid to those letters of passion written by women. They are usually treated as evidence of the larger political-erotic structures within which the female discourse of passion is enlisted in the imperial service of their lord and master Usbek and, simultaneously, in a male voyeuristic fantasy.

Precisely those elements that constitute the westerner's fascination with the women of the harem preclude or, better, occlude notice of and subsequent focus on the instance of women's writing. The conventions of letter writing and of the letter novel that position the individual within a text as an active writing subject who assumes the linguistic perspective of the first person—the enunciating "I" of autobiographical and/or reciprocal discourse—do not coincide with the representation of the seraglio.[4] These "oriental" images in the *Persian Letters* appear to retain the obscure female objects of desire within the secret precinct of their inhibiting and provocative confinement. How might the westerner's gaze fasten on this forbidden place of multiple pleasures from the individual perspective of a harem woman as the active subject of enunciation? And how would the collective entity of the harem relate to epistolary codes if not to subvert those claims inherent in this genre of literary discourse and in fact extolled by Montesquieu in the preface of the 1754 edition of the *Lettres persanes?* Here, Montesquieu signals the relevance of epistolary form to individualized, autobiographical expression and perspective: "Moreover, novels of this sort are usually successful because one takes account oneself of one's own present situation; which allows one to feel passions more than all the stories that could be written about them" (*Lettres persanes* 43).[5]

The project of this essay, to examine the particular language of women's passion and oppression in the letters from the harem, reveals the paradoxical status of epistolarity as it operates throughout Montesquieu's novel. Moreover, the narrative and rhetorical devices of women's epistolary writing are significant to the complex notion of the exotic as it is demonstrated repeatedly to transgress the boundaries of the individual writing subject in the *Lettres persanes*. To anticipate our argument for a moment, representation of female passion in this novel derives from the nature of a writing subject whose very inscription within the rhetoric of male desire constitutes a prevalent textual strategy that ultimately undermines a distinction between a concept of knowledge and the exotic.

In the first letter from the harem (the third in the novel), Zachi, one of the wives, writes Usbek to lament his absence, and recounts an outing in the country that offers a respite from the confinement of the seraglio and from her obsessive reminiscence of past lovemaking with her now absent husband. The so-called pleasure trip into the countryside is presented by Zachi as a momentary escape from those high walls and carefully prescribed barriers, which are also denoted in this letter as the demarcations that enclose the intimate space of former lovemaking. The word *harem*, from the arabic *haram* or *harim*, signifies a place of interdiction as well as of holiness.[6] As both a prison and a sacred altar of love, the harem consistently ties the demonstration of female sentiment and passion to the thematic of confinement and prohibition.

In effect, the enclosure of the harem opens only long enough for the master's treasures to place themselves in the even more confining parameters of the boxlike conveyance that carries them on their outing: "We placed ourselves following the custom, in boxes" (3:53). The illusion of partial liberty is immediately dispelled not only by mention of the type of conveyance used to transport the sultan's women, but by the reflexive verb, which insists on the willing participation of the women in their own captivity.

More importantly, the epistolary attribute of individual self-expression advocated by Montesquieu, as we have just seen, is already attenuated by a plural female subject. In the short paragraph that introduces the perspective of a harem woman for the first time in the novel, the pronoun "I" is missing and, in its place, the subject of female discourse is presented as a plural entity. The pronoun "we" is repeated eight times in the initial two sentences of this letter in the capacity of both subject and object of painstaking preparation wherewith the women take the initiative of "placing themselves" within their well-guarded prisons of transport.

Continuing her letter, Zachi assumes the first-person singular pronoun, ostensibly to relate private, intimate feelings of passion to her husband and correspondent. Nevertheless, from the outset, Zachi's expression of intimacy is conveyed by a representation of a collective harem experience, that is, in a scene in which Zachi's perspective is doubled by the constant presence of the other women. Though Zachi's memories of her first encounter with Usbek are briefly mentioned ("At moments I saw myself in that place where, for the first time in my life, I received you in my arms," [3:53]), they are overshadowed by her detailed reconstruction of a collective experience in which Usbek had selected her alone as the most beautiful woman of his harem. Zachi chooses to elaborate the scene of that "famous quarrel of the wives." For it is before the eyes of Usbek and her female counterparts that Zachi will see herself being desired, and where she recalls Usbek's exclusive desire through the "I"'s (eyes) of the other.

That supposedly most intimate and individual experience of passion finds expression in the necessary plurality of witnesses, all of whom await to see themselves in the "I"/"eye" of Usbek's desire. All the women, again the collective "we," present themselves to Usbek's view in a scene whose emphasis on male scopic pleasure is mirrored in the I's of the other harem women and in Zachi's own epistolary emphasis. The women's exhaustive preparations as they dress to elicit their husband's desire ("We presented ourselves to you [nous nous présentâmes devant toi], after having exhausted all that the imagination could provide in decoration and ornament," [53–54]) are related by Zachi in terms of their reflection in Usbek's visual pleasure: "You saw with pleasure the miracles of our art." And from art to nature's marvels, a subsequent scene of unveiling is recounted by Zachi, who recreates "her" experience from the exclusive visual perspective of Usbek: "We had to present ourselves for your view in the simplicity of nature" (54). Female charms, which are displayed "for your view," find an echo in Zachi's prose as she reflects Usbek's scopic pleasure and his visual perspective through her own insistence on the verbs of sight and locates herself as the visual object of his desire: "I saw myself slowly becoming [je me vis devenir insensiblement] the mistress of your heart" (3:54).

The subject of female passion is located elsewhere—in the desire, in the gaze of the *other*. And as the emphasis on sight becomes more pronounced, the multiple instances of the verb "to see" are concurrent with an insistance on the plurality of the female subject. Even as she becomes the unique visual focus of Usbek's desire, the same voyeuristic structure is sustained in the reflecting mirrors of Zachi's "I"'s, in the plural "we" of the other women's desire. Though the triumph was hers alone, though the ensuing sentences evoke the utter privacy of Usbek's and Zachi's subsequent shared moments from which the other women are now banished, Zachi rhetorically recalls them to the trysting place to witness, to *view*, the intimate, exclusive rewards of her personal victory. And in an emphasis on her singularly authentic feelings for Usbek, she once again conjures up this most private sentiment to be ascertained in the eyes of the others. "If they had *seen* my transports, they would have felt the difference between my love and theirs: they would have *seen* that if they could rival my charms, they couldn't rival my sensibility" (54, my emphasis).

The locus of erotic pleasure—the eyes of the harem women—relay the phallocentric structure of Usbek's passion in their own reflections of the voyeur's gaze. Zachi communicates to Usbek, not through the reciprocity of epistolary dialogue, but through the representation of a scene or stage of passion where woman views herself as the object of the desire of the other. The figure of the voyeur is clearly mirrored in the reflections of women's "own" display of passion. In effect, the harem women's frequent use of the reflexive and/or reciprocal form of the verb does not seem to produce a folding back of the female epistolary subject on herself, as in a *prise de conscience,* or a heightened sense of self-awareness. Rather, the active writing subject turns back on herself *through* and *as* the other. The reflexive verb does not signal self-reflexivity but introduces instead a split in a writing subject which is exteriorized or externalized as object of the other's gaze, of the other's law. This structure that veils sexual difference inscribes women's passion within that of male scopic pleasure. Yet within this economy, where women substitute for each other in a reciprocal reflection of male sexual desire, a homosexual eroticism, which will become more explicit later on in the harem letters, is already intimated.

The apparent split that separates and veils the female writing subject from herself—as object of Usbek's point of view—is accompanied by a lack of epistolary exchange between Zachi, as well as every other female writing subject, and their unique correspondent. The third, fourth, and seventh letters of this text are avowals of passion from three different wives, each mirroring the statements of the other and each going without response from the addressee. For Usbek never answers the letters from his harem in the capacity of a lover, though such reciprocity is inherent in the epistolary communication of passion. On the contrary, he relates to his wives' text of passion from a position specifically outside the I–you relation of interlocutors. The first time and, with almost no exception, every time he addresses one of his wives, it is to speak in the name of his authority that governs the harem, with the finality of his law. In his first words directed to a harem wife, the same Zachi, Usbek conveys his displeasure at her infringement of a harem law: "You have offended me, Zachi; and I feel in my heart emotions that you would fear, if my remoteness didn't allow you the time to change your conduct" (10:84). Zachi's letter of passion to Usbek goes unanswered while, seventeen letters and nine months later, Usbek responds to a eunuch's report *on*

Zachi. His communication to this favorite wife is a chastisement containing the threat of further punishment. Usbek's letter to Zachi, which
appears long after he has already exchanged several letters with other,
male correspondents, intensifies, through its startlingly diverse subject
matter as well as its estranged position, the gap between the sender and
the receiver of these epistolary messages. The chain of letters that constitutes the text of this novel manifests repeated ruptures in the communication of female passion, which is broken off in its separation and difference from a persistently deferred and jarringly incongruous response.

Though he does not enter into epistolary dialogue in response to his
women's desire, Usbek writes *about* his sentiments to others. Positioned
after the third harem letter, Usbek's letter to his friend Nessir stands in
the place of amorous dialogue. Overwhelmed by a feeling of exile from
the friends, family, and customs left behind, Usbek suffers most acutely
the distance from his wives. "It is not that I love them, Nessir. In this
respect, I find myself in a state *devoid of feeling,* [dans une *insensibilité*],
leaving me with no desires at all. In the well-populated seraglio where I
lived, I anticipated love and destroyed it by loving. But from my very
coldness there grows a secret jealousy that devours me" (57, my emphasis). *Sensibilité,* the same term used by Zachi to mark her privileged
sentiments for Usbek, is here given inverse value in the opposing context of Usbek's confession to another.

Moreover, this letter situates Usbek outside the enclosure of the
harem erotically and sentimentally, as well as geographically, outside
the scene of the women's representation of his "own" desire. Within the
structure of epistolary reciprocity and exchange, the harem wives occupy
with respect to Usbek a position of the third person in discourse, that is,
following Emile Benveniste's term, the *non-personne.*[7] Usbek does not
enter into a reciprocal relation with the represented object of his desire,
either with respect to linguistic or sexual intercourse, but relegates himself to a position on the outskirts of the stage or staging of passion.
Usbek's geographical, erotic, and interlocutory distance from the harem
resembles in effect the exotic difference and distance of the reader from
this supposedly other culture.

The representation of desire is inscribed within the epistolary frames
of portraits presented to Usbek, the nonreciprocal and nondialogical
beneficiary, the absent subject in these portraits figuring his "own" desire. Implicated in his harem wives' repetitive tableaux as a viewing
entity, as a gaze internalized in the woman's depiction of (her) his pleasure, Usbek subsequently reviews these moments from the distance afforded by the frames of epistolary correspondence and by a temporal,
geographical discrepancy. As receiver of these letters, Usbek is provided

a place to view while being absent. At this juncture, Usbek and the reader become one and the same, for the position of the reader with respect to the world of the harem is articulated as a primary function of Usbek's own geographical, epistolary, and erotic distance. While she exposes herself to Usbek's exclusive gaze, the harem woman presents her portrait as well to the reader, allowing him secret entry to the interdicted seraglio, allowing him to see (himself) without being seen.[8] Usbek's geographical, erotic, and interlocutory distance from the harem provides a textual model of the voyeur that structures and is structured by the reader's difference and distance from this exotic, supposedly other culture.[9]

Detached, separated from the harem where he sees himself seeing, so the voyeur as foreigner in the western world is constituted on the model of this self-referential, self-reflecting "I"/eye that articulates Usbek's epistemological and philosophical as well as his erotic perspective. Usbek's analysis of particularly western religious, political, philosophical, and social practice and theory engages a distancing of the autoreferential subject who has removed, separated, severed himself from the field of inquiry that his perspective has simultaneously evoked. If women see themselves through and as the other, offering themselves as the reflexive, reflecting pronouns, the object pronouns in Usbek's act of seeing himself see, his numerous philosophical speculations, as we will examine further on, are also drawn on the model of this "objective," self-objectifying experience. Usbek relates an endeavor predicated on the similarity, the identity between himself as subject of discourse and desire, and as legislator of justice, virtue, and truth. Usbek's speculations thus are formally linked to the perspective of the exotic and coincide with the ubiquitous presence of the (western) voyeur.

In fact, the westerner is linked to the representation of desire and knowledge in the *Lettres persanes* in yet other far-reaching ways. This fascination with oriental polygamy casts in erotic terms an opposition between the one and the many, a principle that subtends western political, philosophical, and metaphysical structures. Though the West had renounced polygamy, a fundamental ambivalence as to man's constitutive right to possess many females persists in the early Christian fathers (for example, in Saint Augustine's *De Bono Conjugali*)[10] and survives into more modern times in such treatises as the one cited by Usbek himself: *La Polygamie triomphante* (35:111) written by a Protestant, Johan Leyser, and published in 1682.

Alain Grosrichard reviews the importance of polygamy as a concept fundamental to the philosophical distinction between man and woman. "In their plurality, women can not attain the One—the All that is the master" (178). From the metaphysical assumptions made by Saint Augustine and earlier by Aristotle, the male is awarded the right to several wives and not the other way around, just as the master possesses several slaves, as a multitude of souls is rightly submitted to one god, as, following Spinoza, substance is qualitatively different from and superior to its modes. Only *he* is recognized as capable of actualizing all the potential of the human essence (178–79). Grosrichard insists that the conceptual apparatus of classical metaphysics promotes the notion of man as a male sexual being. "It is less the other sex in which the male takes pleasure than in its multiplicity which, compared to his own unicity, his uniqueness, characterizes the inferior" (178).

Usbek's anxiety concerning his harem wives is predicated not on sensibility, as we have seen, but precisely on his anguished fear of their infidelity. For, if women's desire in the harem letters always reflects the desire of the transcendent other, this indivisible, unique, and unalterable other, Usbek, is dependent on the innumerable reflections in the seemingly infinite number of "I"'s of the harem women. Usbek's gnawing jealousy then is a function of his need for these multiple portraits of passion, which must be continuously forthcoming even and particularly when they represent women's sorrow and frustration. Zachi's distress must be depicted by the laws of his desire. "I emit sighs which go unheard; my tears flow and *you do not take pleasure in them*" (3:55, my emphasis). Her sorrow is offered for Usbek's appropriation in the convention of voyeuristic pleasure. As visible products of emotion, tears are the external signifiers that remain faithful and transparent to the interior female sentiment of desire as well as to the frustrated anguish of subjection. Most of the letters from the harem entail an exposition of this theme of longing, sorrow, and lament. To please, to continue the role as object of pleasure that shores up and makes possible Usbek's all-seeing omnipotence as discursive, self-reflexive subject, the harem woman must present her desire in the form of a visual portrait of frustration and anger. Usbek's cruelty, of which all the women write, is integral to their portraits of desire and imperative to the male self-representation, to his fiction of female desire and virtue.

These portraits mark an interesting deviation from another female epistolary model, Mariane in the *Lettres portugaises*. Confined to her Portuguese convent, she repeatedly and obsessively addresses her frustrated passion, like the harem women, to the void of an absent lover who, unlike Usbek, remains anonymous, unseen, and unheard throughout the text. As Peggy Kamuf has demonstrated, the absence of her lover becomes ultimately unimportant to Mariane's relentless but gradually self-aware discourse of desire.[11] Letter writing leads Mariane out of the circle where "the articulation of the question of the other's desire no longer operates a closure" (59). Within this textual dichotomy, we should note the harem wives' and Mariane's contrasting and complementary use of the reflexive verb and of self-reflexivity. Mariane takes account of the split operating within the discursive "I" of the letter, which leads, as Kamuf says, "to a self-awareness that she is producing rather than merely registering the events of a subjectivity" (61). The complaints and laments of the letters from the harem, on the other hand, are *dictated* by Usbek's absence as an integral part of this structure, which veils individual female sentiment and eroticism, appropriating it as the faithful portrait of fidelity in which the harem woman sees and writes herself as and through the other.[12] The text of female passion is designed by and for Usbek to offer a direct correspondence between the signifiers and signified of fidelity, virtue, and desire.

Each letter from the harem resembles the others in this respect, conjuring up always former pleasures and present suffering according to the "I" of the voyeur, according to conventions necessary to one man's pleasure and security, to one discourse of desire, always similar to itself. Unmarked by individual characteristics, the supposedly most intimate sentiments of female passion do not retain distinct voices but, like a series of echoes and unending reflections, mirror each other throughout the *Lettres persanes.*

Veils, which earlier were set in place by the harem women to be removed under Usbek's exclusive gaze, must continue to cover over and mask sexual difference. Yet those passionate epistolary avowals and complaints proffered in Usbek's absence and lack also constitute the linguistic conventions that serve to veil female erotic desire from Usbek's all-seeing gaze. This veiling of the "I"'s, drawn faithfully according to Usbek's perspective, shields female virtue and fidelity from the view of any other but also operates in the twists and folds of this textual fabric to mask deviant female erotic activity and transgression.

The very plurality and quasi-anonymity in the epistolarity of female passion, where each letter offers a representation for and according to the dominating perspective of male scopic pleasure, takes on textual value in an opposing context. The lack of differentiation in the female epistolary subject is accompanied by a growing lack of distinction between male and female object of desire, between castrated eunuch and phallic male, between an exclusive, single pleasure defined by Usbek's desire and a plural desire. As the female epistolary subjects proliferate in names that echo and reflect one another—Zachi, Zélis, Zélide, Zéphis—so a plural eroticism in the women's homosexual tendencies and other perversions of phallic desire are simultaneously veiled and unveiled in an increasingly unsettling rhetorical rhythm of female epistolarity.

Zéphis has been accused by her guardian eunuch of taking sexual pleasure with her female slave Zélide. Writing to Usbek to express outrage and to reaffirm her exclusive love, Zéphis refuses to justify herself. "No, I have too much respect for myself to condescend to justifications: I want no other guarantee of my conduct than you yourself, than your love, than mine, and if I have to tell you, dear Usbek, than my tears" (4:55). Instead, she conjures up the image of tears as the synecdoche for her portrait that faithfully resembles the law of Usbek's desire. By evoking those tears to be inscribed within the conventional visual representation of female subjection and passion for her absent husband, she allows no space for another image, no discrepancy between the representation and its referent, between the signifiers and signified of virtue. And as these women remain imprisoned within the confines of the harem and within the narrow limits of a masculine, phallocentric discourse of eroticism, so Usbek remains bound until the last letter of the novel to his wives' repetitive, undifferentiated representation of his "own" desire. But a detour from this linear discourse is perceptible in these multiple reflections of the harem wives.

Zéphis is not the only wife accused of taking pleasure with her female slave. The first letter of Usbek to a wife, Zachi, chastises her for having spent time alone with a white eunuch. But in the same letter, Usbek also alludes to Zachi's suspect relations with her female slave Zélide, the same name of the slave mentioned in Zéphis' letter. Though it is Zéphis who had complained in her letter to Usbek of "this black monster," the head eunuch, for depriving her of Zélide, Usbek responds to the supposed complaints of Zachi, for which there is no text in the novel. "But what did your first slave do? He/she [*Elle*] told you that the familiarities you were taking with the young Zélide were against propriety! There's the reason for your hatred" (20:86).

Is this the same female slave, the same Zélide involved earlier with Zéphis? Or an "oversight" perhaps on the part of Usbek or Montesquieu? But what's the difference? To retain the same slave's name with respect to the conduct of two harem wives, whose own names are themselves so similar, intensifies the structure of replaceability of each harem woman for another. Yet this play of minimal differences between one woman, one name, and another, between slave, wife, and mistress, conflating female activity and identity according to a unique male perspective, serves simultaneously to minimize the discrepancies between one kind of erotic activity and another. The overdetermined similarity of female proper names is clustered in the text around multiple and indiscriminate erotic objects whose sexual characteristics lose their specificity in terms of gender difference. The eunuch in this passage also acquires the feminine gender in the term "slave" and in Usbek's subsequent reference to his wife's "first slave" with the pronoun "she." From a neutered or neutral status, the eunuch functions as both male and female, not quite one or the other, assuming attributes of each sex.[13]

In a subsequent letter, Zélis writes to request Usbek's advice as to whether she should allow her slave (again the same?) Zélide to marry a white eunuch, proclaiming revulsion, which is also fascination with this deviance, this other, of erotic pleasure.

> I've heard you say a thousand times that eunuchs experience with women a kind of unknown voluptuousness; that nature compensates for her losses; that she has resources which remedy the defect in their condition . . . and that in this state, one acquires a kind of third sense so that one exchanges, so to speak, one pleasure for another. (53:144)

Borrowing Usbek's own words and perspective, Zélis evokes supplements to the unique pleasure of phallocentric love, which compensate for the absence, the lack in the eunuch, and which also evoke the lack inherent in Usbek's relation to his wives during his continuing absence. Indeed, these very circumstances are strangely similar to life in the harem under normal circumstances.[14] Zélis, like her almost identical slave, must be content with "the vain shadow" of marriage and a man. Her cry of disbelief that such a union could bring any happiness resembles an all too familiar, familial situation echoing throughout the letters from the harem, and emphasizes dreams of lost pleasure and of present frustration. As Zélis in the same letter protests in sympathy for her underprivileged slave: "What! to be always the prey of semblance and deceptions [*images et fantômes*]? To live only to imagine? to find oneself always near pleasure and never in pleasure?" (144).

And the eunuch, like the women, also addresses his frustrated complaints to Usbek's lack and absence. While standing in to echo the male law of women's necessary plurality, the eunuch repeats both the woman's plaint and Usbek's fear.

> The more women we have under our eyes, the less trouble they give us. A greater need to please, less opportunity to band together, more examples of submissive obedience—all of this forges chains for them. . . . But all of that, magnificent lord, is nothing without the presence of the master. What can we do, with this *vain phantom* of an authority that is never entirely communicated? We represent only weakly half of your own self. (226, my emphasis)

Here, as earlier, the eunuch as a representation of male authority resembles the shadows and phantomlike model of Usbek's own sexual representation as determined in the harem letters. He/she literalizes this model and, like the harem women, has internalized it as his/her own lack. The eunuch, as an empty sign, assumes both male and female gender markings and provides the space around which such gender distinctions are effaced and undifferentiated sexual acts proliferate.

The shadows, the phantasms of erotic images that are represented by women's letters in and to their husband's absence, must remedy the loss of an actual encounter; they also function to supplement the singularity and nonreciprocity of scopic pleasure, which remains the property of Usbek's *imaginaire*. The letter, like the referent of the experience itself, becomes a stage of representation that displaces and substitutes for passionate exchange, for a dialogical model—a version or, better, a perversion of both sexual and epistolary intercourse. A lack of reciprocity between the writing subjects constitutes the visual stage of the "vain shadows and phantoms" of male sexual potency and of female passion. While Zélis repudiates the very image in which she is embedded, she is also evoking under the tutelage of Usbek's own words and perspective those compensations of "unknown voluptuousness" that indeed we see in the reported crimes increasingly taking place in the harem.

In effect, as a forerunner of this simultaneous critique and avowal, Zachi had already been accused in a previous letter of being found alone with a white eunuch, a behavior strictly prohibited by the laws of the harem. At the same time, then, that letters of female passion can be dedicated only to Usbek, insistent in their representation of one singular, dominant passion and erotic object, these letters reveal the simultaneous concealment of devious and deviant erotic desire and practice. But the ultimate subversion of Usbek's law and order finds a direct voice in the last letter of Montesquieu's text, that of Roxane.

Silent throughout the letters, this most virtuous of the harem women is first heard of through a description of her as an edifying example offered by Usbek in a rare letter to one of his other wives (letter 20). Usbek also writes one letter to Roxane (letter 26), his sole letter of passion to a woman in the novel and one that, specifically, does not reply to any avowal of Roxane's desire. In his letter, which evokes the stage of passion reminiscent of those letters of Zachi and the other harem wives, Usbek recalls Roxane as a paragon of virtue in her resistance to his sexual advances; her flight from his gaze and his caresses is rapturously represented within the conventional framework of woman's passivity as object of male desire. Indeed, Usbek outlines a scene of rape. In fact, Roxane's very silence, her almost complete lack of letter writing and therefore lack of pretext to epistolary and sexual reciprocity offer an incontestable model of female passion and virtue, which the other harem letters only approximate, simulate, and, as we have seen, also subvert.

Roxane's silence is, like the language of the harem letters, designed to coincide with Usbek's limited vision, his blindness. When she speaks, it is to dispel this phantasm of Usbek's *imaginaire*. She reveals her reticence to be hatred; her modesty, disgust, and seemingly total obedience to be a mask for her love of another, a veil for her active role in transforming the harem into a place of "delights and pleasures" (161:350). As the head eunuch reports: "You suspected Zélis, and were completely sure of Roxane: but her savage virtue was a cruel deception. It was the veil of her betrayal" (159:348).

This reversal, which entails, says Roxane to Usbek, "a language which is new to you," constitutes the last letter from the harem and the final words of Montesquieu's text (letter 161). Roxane's letter redefines female passion, nature, and virtue according to their difference from and discrepancy with the meanings Usbek has attributed to them throughout his discourse on and to women. The eunuch in fact remarks on a generalized change throughout the harem in the female demeanor with respect to sexual (in)difference. "No longer is there to be found on the countenance of your women that *male*, stern virtue that reigned there previously" (151:341, my emphasis). This new perspective, which confirms the duplicity operating throughout the harem letters, affirms, as Luce Irigaray has said concerning the difference brought by women to male discourse and desire, "an other economy that upsets the linearity of a project, undermines the goal-object of a desire, diffuses the polarization toward a single pleasure, disconcerts fidelity to a single discourse."[15]

Yet, how new to Usbek is this plural economy, this "new language" rendered explicit by Roxane? In the course of his travels in the West, Usbek's letters, as every critic concurs, manifest a decided evolution toward enlightened concepts of justice, religious tolerance, nature, and virtue; and his discussions and the principles he derives from them encompass not only the West but nearly every continent, while remaining unswervingly, rigidly faithful to the same oppressive and singular discourse of erotic and political despotism.[16] But do these contrasting facets of Usbek's discourse that produce the text's bitter irony necessarily constitute the radical contradiction to which most readers ascribe? For Usbek's self-reflexive discourse of erotic desire and despotism, integral to the definition of the voyeur, is also constitutive of his intellectual and philosophical project.

In his definition of the concept of justice, for example, Usbek introduces a metadiscourse that discerns an absolute, inflexible principle. "Justice is a relationship of appropriateness which truly exists between two things, and this relationship is always the same, no matter who considers it, whether it be God, whether an angel, or, finally, whether it be man" (83:203). Justice is "eternal" and does not depend on human conventions of any kind, even when man's practice and understanding remain flawed. "And when it [justice] does depend on them [human conventions], it would be a terrible truth that would be necessary to hide from oneself" (204). By definition, according to this letter, justice is always similar to itself, not contingent on empirical situations nor on conventions of any kind, even when man's practice and understanding subvert these principles.

Usbek's discussion in this letter swings back and forth between the truth of preestablished principles and the truth that justice in its implementation indeed depends on a local context, on a culturally specific definition, on individual practice and self-interest. In effect, Usbek's logic is enunciated in the semantics of self-reflexivity that serve to establish the principles of absolute justice as well as to counter them. It is preferable to separate oneself from one's own knowledge, from the truth of man's inability to follow these absolute principles, than to incur the danger of recognizing others' and one's own difference from this judgment. Furthermore, the measure of man's incapacity to follow the eternal, self-identical postulates of justice is, following Usbek, the measure in which man makes "a return to oneself" in favor of self-interest (204). The very terms of separation of self from self articulate the notion of justice, distinguishing judgment from self-interest on the one hand and precluding self-knowledge on the other. In other words, at stake in Usbek's metadiscourse is precisely the definition of a subject as different from the thinking, legislating, and enunciating cogito. The perspective and distance necessary for maintaining these criteria of justice are eliminated by a "return to oneself"—a hiding from oneself of the truth of the dissimilar, plural nature of justice and of the plural, dissimilar nature of oneself.

So even as he refuses to know what he knows, Usbek repeatedly departs from the straight and narrow of a singularly coherent and self-identical logic on which he claims to erect his philosophical discourse. The letters from the harem are written from a perspective in which the subjects define themselves from the outset as multiple and identical signifiers of the discourse and desire of the other. Yet these plural voices become increasingly related in the text to the proliferation in the harem of multiple and dissimilar pleasures, of duplicitous desires that pervert the goal of a unique, unequivocal signified and discourse. The letters from the harem become the plural, shifting signifiers, the multiple and doubled voices that can no longer be bound and tied to one desire, to one signified. Rather, they proliferate in the discrepancy that separates Usbek from himself. Usbek relates an endeavor predicated on the ultimate identity between himself as subject of discourse and desire and as

transcendent legislator of justice, virtue, and truth—even when this ne-
cessitates and even engenders his separation from the world and from
himself.

Roxane's letter discloses the women's subversive textual and sexual
activity that has throughout the *Lettres persanes* defined a space lying
outside and beyond each individual epistolary perspective in the letters
of Usbek and others as well. And it is the distance opening between that
individual writing viewpoint and what lies, precisely, beyond it that creates the space of the exotic in Montesquieu's novel, and that also troubles the reader's transparent self-reflection. For the discrepancy, the
irreducible difference and distance in the sign between signifier and
signified in the *Persian Letters,* conveys a notion of the exotic as a fantasy
of political, cultural, and sexual alterity, while introducing exile, self-
estrangement, separation of self from self as the unsettling basis of
knowledge.

Usbek's departure from his native Persia is occasioned by two separate though related causes. He first gives as his reason for leaving a
necessary search for knowledge: "We didn't believe that the boundaries
of Persia should be those of our knowledge" (1:51). But we subsequently
learn that Usbek's departure was precipitated by political problems at
court due to his outspoken introduction there of a new discourse of
virtue. In unmasking vice, in identifying the masks worn by the courtiers
as so many deceptive images of virtue, Usbek recounts, "I spoke a language until then unknown" (8:60). Usbek transgresses not only the geographical and cultural boundaries encircling his country, but from within
he dissolves the bonds cementing sacred, conventional practices to the
concepts of virtue. The first indications of Usbek's desire to know and of
his almost simultaneous need to *exile himself* from the familiar territory
of his own culture, laws, etc., is associated in this text with a transgression of the laws of signification. Usbek's "unknown language" at the very
beginning of the novel, like Roxane's "new language" at the novel's
close, detaches the multiple signifying masks or veils from the accepted
"truths" to which they are bound. It is this self-exile, a kind of death in
the ensuing painful separation of self from oneself, like Roxane's suicide,
that literally opens the space of knowledge and of new horizons in the
gap where the multiple signifiers are severed and are liberated from their
signified. In this space, a plural shifting discourse is dangerous and disruptive to the singular law and sanctity of Usbek's desire, as well as to the
established conventions in what becomes in the course of these letters
the scarcely more familiar realm of the absolute monarchy, the church,
and the social, economic, and political entity of Paris.

But Roxane's suicide partakes of the same irreconcilable paradox we have identified in conjunction with Usbek's discourse of knowledge and desire. On the one hand, it marks a violent separation between the conventional signifiers and signified of Usbek's justice, virtue, and nature. Roxane says, "I have reformed your laws following those of nature" (161:351), thereby inscribing her own and Usbek's discourse in the same movement of difference that Usbek had already opened at the novel's outset. On the other hand, is Roxane's act not the absolute because irrevocable gesture that precludes forever an otherwise shifting, plural self-identity? Her admission of previous duplicity and contradictory behavior is simultaneously remedied in an act that consummates and annihilates her self-assertion. Roxane's discourse in this last letter also bears resemblance then to Usbek's own singular and exclusive self-reflective speculation.

It is no coincidence that Usbek, earlier in the novel, had decried the severe punishment meted out in the Christian West to those who take their own lives. "It seems to me, Ibben, that such laws are quite unjust. When I am overwhelmed with grief, misfortune, scorn, why should they want to prevent me from putting an end to my troubles, and why cruelly deprive me of a remedy that lies in my own hands?" (76:191–92). The obvious irony that it is Usbek's harem wife who avails herself of this right to self-assertion and liberation should not prevent us from also seeing the similarity with Usbek's own perspective. For he sanctions suicide in the same way that he decrees the absolute, self-identical principles of justice and a self-identical discourse. To give birth to oneself as in Descartes's self-constructing cogito, where the self legislates and legitimates its own existence through its distance from the world, resembles after all the act of putting an end to oneself. In a certain sense, the act of suicide represents Usbek's intellectual/erotic discourse that insistently separates him from the world he is seeing himself see.[17] Suicide for Usbek as for Roxane is the reverse but companion side of a discourse and perspective that traverse the *Lettres persanes* as always already the "I" of the other.

The act of violent self-estrangement and self-exile integral to creating a notion of the exotic becomes the basis for a "new language" of knowledge and at moments becomes indistinguishable from the discourse of self-identity. Knowledge, in other words, derives in this text from the strategies of the voyeur and of the exotic. As the act of violent self-exile is linked to its apparent opposite, to the supreme affirmation of self-legislating identity, so these opposing valorizations of suicide should be understood in conjunction with the paradox of knowledge as a meta-discourse constructed on the principle of an enunciating "I" whose reflection is irrevocably deferred in the difference that defines the "I" in/as the other.

Montesquieu's text speaks its most overtly violent language in the last letter of Roxane's transgression. That most audacious statement must be read therefore in conjunction with Usbek's discoveries and own transgression as well as with his blindness. The multiple figures of the exotic—the eunuch, the ancient sect of the Guebres, the mythical tribe of the Troglodytes, as well as Rica and Usbek himself—are, like the text of women's letters from the harem, the detours that exteriorize the perspective of the reader and transgress the boundaries of the sayable in eighteenth-century Paris but that do so in the discourse and in the vision of the other.[18] As the initially anonymous author of these "Persians'" letters, Montesquieu avoids censorship by relying on plural discourse and by taking up the veil that separates him from these discrepancies of a singular logic and discourse that this text persistently reveals. Commenting on the numerous errors to be found in subsequent published editions of the novel, Montesquieu remarks in the idiom of his own text, "These errors, in subsequent editions, have multiplied innumerably because this work was abandoned by the author from its birth" (420).

In certain respects then this text recuperates or, rather, generates from the very impotence and lacks it reveals, the same singular law of the father, of self-reflexive and transparent specularity that appears to dominate the epistolarity of female eroticism. Yet inasmuch as this simultaneous veiling and unveiling of the signifying system resembles the plural economy of women's discourse and eroticism, inasmuch as the epistolary self-reflexive "I" is always and repeatedly becomes the "I" and the eyes of the other, it is perhaps appropriate to say that Montesquieu, author of those letters from the harem and of this "new language," is, indeed, throughout the *Lettres persanes,* writing like a woman.

NOTES

I wish to thank the SUNY/Buffalo Office of Sponsored Programs for a 1987 grant, which enabled me to complete this essay.

1. Alain Grosrichard, *La Structure du sérail: La Fiction du despotisme asiatique dans l'occident classique* (Paris: Seuil, 1979); Aram Vartanian, "Eroticism and Politics in the *Lettres persanes*," *Romanic Review* 60 (1969): 23–33; Michel Delon, "Un Monde d'eunuques," *Europe* 55 (1977): 79–88; Alain Singerman, "Reflexions sur une métaphore: le sérail dans les *Lettres persanes*," *Studies on Voltaire and the Eighteenth Century* 185 (1980): 181–98.

2. Grosrichard speaks of the eunuch as well as other "negative" figures who inhabit the seraglio and who, following the western perspective, constitute its structure in the following terms: "All (the blind, the children, mutes, dwarfs, women, eunuchs) count only inasmuch as they exhibit in the negative, what the despot does and what he has" (204).

3. See my essay, "Orientalism and Representations of Exteriority in Montes-quieu's *Lettres persanes,*" *Eighteenth Century: Theory and Interpretation* 23:3 (Fall 1985): 263–79.

4. For a good discussion of the first person in epistolary discourse, see Janet Altman, *Epistolarity: Approches to a Form* (Columbus: Ohio State University Press, 1982), esp. ch. 4.

5. I have consulted primarily J. Robert Loy for the English translation of the *Persian Letters* (New York: Meridian, 1961); however, I take responsibility for the many changes introduced in order to achieve a more literal rendering of Montesquieu's text. All references in my essay to Montesquieu's text indicate the number of the particular letter discussed but give page reference to the French edition of the *Lettres persanes,* ed. J. Starobinski (Paris: Gallimard, 1973).

6. The western notion of the harem as a forbidden place of closure and confinement can be traced even in the etymological development of the term *sérail,* in English *seraglio.* "From the Italian (with a double r, by attraction to *serrare,* to close, to lock up, *serraglio,* closure), from the turco-persian *serâï,* palace." *Nouveau Dictionnaire Etymologique* (Paris: Larousse, 1971).

7. Emile Benveniste, *Problèmes de linguistique générale* (Paris: Gallimard, 1966), 1:226–36.

8. Thus, epistolary frames that situate Usbek and the reader in the perspec-tive of the voyeur serve the same ends as framing devices of pictorial representa-tions of women. The western tradition of painting, as John Berger was perhaps one of the first to point out, serves the interest of a dominant male voyeurism in the portrayal of women, particularly in the example of the female nude (John Berger, *Ways of Seeing* [London: Penguin, 1972], chs. 2 and 3). The epistolary frame, like the pictorial, situates the male viewer outside and beyond the frames that simultaneously enclose women and expose them to view—where she gives herself to be seen as object to an absent but dominant and transcendent male viewing perspective. See, for example, Sharon Willis's analysis in "Lettre sur des taches aveugles: à l'usage de celles qui voient" (*L'Esprit Créateur* 24:1 [Spring 1984]: 85–98) of the multiple pictorial representations of the biblical motif, Suzanne and the elders, in relation to Diderot's commentary on these paintings. She underscores Diderot's appreciation of Tintoretto's pictorial structure in which Suzanne, while attempting to hide behind robes from the depicted old men's lascivious glances, simultaneously exposes herself to the gaze of the male viewer situated beyond the frames of the canvas (85–92).

9. The interdiction of the seraglio in the *Lettres persanes* serves to exaggerate demarcations that articulate the closure necessary for constructing the voyeur's perspective. In fact, the western tradition of the voyeur has recently been ex-plored in its "oriental" context by Malek Alloulah, *The Colonial Harem,* trans. Myrna and Wlad Godzich (Minneapolis: University of Minnesota Press, 1986). The French colonial presence in Algeria produced photographs taken by the French of Algerian women positioned in the role of harem women. Following Alloulah, these were strictly simulated scenes, the women having been paid to assume the pose of harem captives (18–20). Sent back home to French viewers as

postcards, these images constructed a notion of the harem from the exclusive perspective of the western male photographer's eye and lens; the image portrays and betrays the closure of an interdicted place where the photographer/voyeur, though the constructor as well as fabricator of these scenes, is not implicated visually anywhere in them. As Alloulah states, "Exoticism is always established as the gaze of the other" (19*n*.11).

10. Saint Augustine, "De Bono Conjugali," *Oeuvres*, trans., intro. Gustave Combes (Paris: Desclees de Brouwer, 1948), 2:69–71.

11. Peggy Kamuf, *Fictions of Feminine Desire* (Lincoln: University of Nebraska Press, 1982), ch. 2.

12. The postcard of the harem, following Alloulah, functions as an "illustration" of colonialist discourse whereas the discourse of the harem letters functions as an exotic portrait. "But the postcard is also one of the illustrated forms of colonialist discourse, its chatty and self-satisfied imagery. In and of itself, it does not speak . . . : *it is spoken.* Its meaning resides elsewhere; it comes from outside itself" (120, emphasis added).

13. Following Grosrichard, the eunuch is "always much more or much less than a eunuch" (194). (S)he is also related by this author to the theory of the sign in classical discourse as "the power of the signifier as such" (193).

14. Usbek himself speaks of life in the harem under normal circumstances in the relation between polygamy and depopulation. Man is presented as not only surfeited with pleasure, but sexually inactive, exhausted (*épuisé*), and ultimately incapable of propagating (114:260).

15. Luce Irigaray, *This Sex Which is not One,* trans. G. C. Gill (Ithaca: Cornell University Press, 1985), 30.

16. Tzvetan Todorov, "Réflexions sur les *Lettres persanes*," *Romanic Review* 74 (1983): 306–15, speaks of this tendency towards "an immersion in the others that renders Montesquieu lucid about himself" (308). Yet, though Usbek in several instances does consider, as Todorov says, "all countries and all continents" (308), this seems due as much to a universalizing, singular perspective, a lucidity which remains blind, as to a definition of self conceived on plurality and differences.

17. As I have related the perspective of the voyeur and a visual stage or scene of women's epistolary voice to Usbek's philosophical project, so Jean-Joseph Goux ("Descartes et la perspective," *L'Esprit Créateur* 25:1 [Spring 1985]: 10–20) has introduced the relation of architectural and pictorial to philosophical perspective, specifically with respect to Descartes and the cogito. The perspective of *un seul* ("only one") appeared initially (then was eliminated) in Descartes's *Discours de la méthode* as a kind of prologue to and grounding for the articulation of the cogito (13–16). A discussion of the architectural unity of a city, conceived on a single plan and visual perspective as opposed to a city developed in time and through its many accretions (Goux uses the term *bricolage*), enhances the perspective of *un seul* and *precedes* as a model the introduction of a necessarily self-legitimating cogito. Goux also extends his discussion of Descartes's perspective in architecture and philosophy to include pictorial per-

spective as it evolved from the Greeks in the western tradition (18–20). See also Goux, "Société et sujet," *Les Iconoclastes* (Paris: Seuil, 1978), 129–43.

18. For further discussion of these figures of the exotic in Montesquieu's novel such as the ancient sect of the Guebres and the mythic Troglodytes, see my "Orientalism and Representations of Exteriority," 267–73.

8

Fanny's Fanny:
Epistolarity, Eroticism,
and the Transsexual Text

JULIA EPSTEIN

JOHN CLELAND'S erotic novel, *Memoirs of a Woman of Pleasure*, was published in two parts in 1748 and 1749 and is generally referred to as *Fanny Hill*. Its historical significance as the first work of "pornography" to be composed originally in English—translations from Italian and French are another matter—has frequently been noted by scholars who seek for this text an appropriate classification within the taxonomies of popular culture.[1] Less frequently have critics recognized that Cleland linguistically and structurally blends his poeticized underground discourse of sexually explicit description with the eighteenth-century's conventionally accepted literary tropes and framing devices. The moment-by-moment operation of this blending lies in Cleland's famous mechanically euphemized and power-charged language of the male genital "engine." Indeed, Cleland's text is best known for its elaborate genital terminology and its flamboyant sexual metaphors; nowhere in the text do anatomical terms of any sort appear. But Cleland's circumlocutions and coded euphemisms—he uses expressions such as "master of the revels" and "scepter-member," "soft laboratory of love" and "luscious mouth of nature"—work together with the narrative strategies he skillfully deploys to represent and then to mask the sexual ambiguities that inhabit the center of his work. The work's narrative strategies in fact depend upon an ingenious manipulation of epistolary form in order to marry epistolarity and sexuality and thereby to cross this exhaustive catalogue of sexual activity with a conventional romance plot. It is therefore necessary to read the *Memoirs of a Woman of Pleasure* not as an aberrant and ingenious underground text, but as an accomplished mainstream exemplar of the newly defined genre of the novel, a text so comfortable with its formal niche that it is free to undercut its own generic conventions. The "woman of pleasure" writes letters in such a way that her service as a sexual sign is exploited for erotic purposes at the same time that it provides a means by which the eighteenth-century novel can inscribe and subvert social structures of power. An examination of how Cleland masterminds his female narrator's use of the letter and the ways in which he inflects his own voice into hers may point the way to a reading of the novel as a critique of the cultural constructions of sexuality in the mid-eighteenth century.

I

At the end of Cleland's erotic romance, the heroine, Fanny Hill, is reunited with her first and true lover Charles, a curly-haired, vermillion-lipped Adonis who is described as being long both of eyelash and of intimate parts. Fanny had eloped with Charles from Mrs. Brown's bordello early in the novel and blissfully given up her virginity to him. But his father tricks him into leaving her several months later and four years pass before the reunion and the fall into domesticity that trigger the novel's dénouement. Between Fanny's early sexual initiation and the reunion of these true lovers, she samples a comprehensive array of human sexual experience: from voyeurism to lesbianism, from masturbation to heterosexual intercourse, from flagellation to fetishism to group orgies, Fanny's "animal spirits" are titillated and satisfied. Cleland's text, however, does not focus, as one might suppose from its plot, on the aroused female body. It offers instead a celebration of male genitalia, of the aroused male, and of idealized and invincible male sexual prowess: the phallus is everywhere and is everywhere worshiped. Woven through Fanny's sexual adventures is the always primary return to Cleland's fantasy of overpowering conventional heterosexuality. Indeed, Fanny herself becomes a metonymic site for female sexual responsiveness. Numerous commentators have pointed out that the narrator's name, Fanny Hill, literally means *mons veneris,* and the *Memoirs of a Woman of Pleasure* has come to be known "simply" as *Fanny Hill* in part as acknowledgment of this metonymy.[2] It is interesting, therefore, that when at the end of the novel Fanny returns to bed with her long-lost lover, the arena of discourse in her letters moves away for the first time from simple celebratory sexual description. This time her sexual response is mediated through moralized love, and the resulting description of the novel's last sexual act bears a curiously split rhetoric of eroticism that relies on its epistolary form.

Two letters to an older female friend constitute Fanny's *Memoirs*.[3] As Fanny and Charles prepare to consummate their reunion, Fanny apologizes to her correspondent:

> And here, decency forgive me! if, once more I violate thy laws, and keeping the curtains undrawn, sacrifice thee for the last time, to that confidence, without reserve, with which I engaged to recount to you the most striking circumstances of my youthful disorders. (181)[4]

The curtains are never drawn in this text. Indeed, when others draw them, Fanny can always find a convenient peephole, even if it means standing on the furniture. Nevertheless, this final account of sexual pleasure differs fundamentally from those that have preceded it because it is interrupted in two ways. First, the sign of Charles's prodigious sexual desire launches Fanny not into mock-heroic encomia on the male sex organ, as has been her wont in previous encounters, but rather into a reverential philosophy of pleasure. "The feel of that favourite piece of manhood has, in the very nature of it, something inimitably pathetic," Fanny remarks (182–83). "And now," she continues, becoming meditatively oblivious to her impassioned lover,

> it felt to me something so subduing, so active, so solid and agreeable that I know not what name to give its singular impression; but the sentiment of consciousness of its belonging to my supremely beloved youth, gave me so pleasing an agitation, and work'd so strongly on my soul, that it sent all its sensitive spirits to that organ of bliss in me. (183)

Never difficult to arouse (and never before at a loss for words to name her arousal), Fanny has nevertheless not until now laced her sexual accounts with abstract ideas about the soul. To this point, the *Memoirs* offers physiology aplenty, but not much *philosophie dans le boudoir*. Here she is drowned, she says, by "two distinct ideas" and lies "overwhelm'd, absorpt, lost in an abyss of joy, and dying of nothing but immoderate delight" (183).

When Fanny soars into this philosophical flight, she leaves Charles behind with his "manhood . . . at its mightiest point of stiffness," and he becomes impatient with her "extatic distraction" (183). With a bit of prompting, she returns to earth and to bed, but only for the narrative to arrive at a second interruption. Fanny's Richardsonian "writing to the moment" skills at sexual description shift rhetorical gears here. Her previous accounts have all been rendered in the past tense, but now absolute presence takes over, then explodes: "I see! I feel!" she exclaims, "the delicious velvet tip!—he enters might and main with—" and then she stops. Writing interruptus: "oh!—my pen drops from me here. . . . Description too deserts me, and delivers over a task, above its strength of Wing, to the imagination" (183).

The key question to ask of the *Memoirs of a Woman of Pleasure* is not why Fanny's pen should now fail her for the first time, in the prelude to what becomes the narrator's "tail-piece of morality" (it might more accurately have been called a "codpiece" to make its simultaneously veiling and emphatic functions explicit). Rather, we should ask why the pen has not failed her before. In fact, the crucial question to ask of the eighteenth-century epistolary novel, particularly in its "writing to the moment" mode, is a question that must insist on breaking down and breaking through the transparent conventions of letter writing and their attendant narrative subterfuges: Why are these people writing? Literary convention has recognized and overlooked the fact that this writing, as an activity, is frequently implausible. On one apparently interminable day shortly before he rapes Clarissa, for example, readers are expected to believe that Lovelace produces some 14,000 words, an extravagant epistolary output. But letter writing represents more than its own simple productive or expressive activity in eighteenth-century epistolary novels. Letters structure and control these narratives and inscribe in their texts the duplicitously self-conscious self-awareness of their writers. At the same time they also inevitably weave sexuality and the body into their textual tapestries. The fundamental activity of a letter is to circulate, and a circulating letter can always be "purloined."[5] While letters require the impulse of literal physical absence, they replace it with a surrogate presence. Richardson expressed this function in a 1746 letter to Sophia Westcomb, to whom he extols the virtues of familiar correspondence: "And shall a modest lady then refuse to write?" he asks her. "Shall a virtuous and innocent heart be afraid of leaving its Impulses *embody'd,* as I may say?"[6]

Sexuality and textuality combine in this view, as Terry Eagleton has suggested in observing that Pamela wears her letters around her waist, prompting Mr. B. to threaten to strip her to gain access to them. Lovelace, similarly, expends much energy tracking down and trying to intercept Clarissa's letters and sabotaging her ability to correspond with Anna

Howe. "Letters concede yet withhold physical intimacy," Eagleton writes in *The Rape of Clarissa,* "in a kind of prolonged teasing, a courtship which is never consummated," and he goes on to assert that "the letter comes to signify nothing quite so much as female sexuality itself, that folded, secret place which is always open to violent intrusion."[7] If women and sexual parts are objects of exchange in the erotic economy of the *Memoirs,* then letters circulate as verbal icons of sexual desire. The suspended impatience of epistolary anticipation, delay, and receipt stand in textually for sexual tension and its release.

In the retrospective epistolarity of Fanny Hill's *Memoirs,* letter writing mirrors and projects not just abstract sexuality, but *concrete* sexual pleasure itself. Fanny's erotic discourse mimics the rhythms of an echoing and repetitive sexuality watched, teased, touched, inflamed, engorged, flooded, suspended in unconsciousness, and finally liberated. "Writing it down" means literally that: propelled by desire, writing reenacts, releases, and retracts sexual tension. At first glance, it is paradoxical that this is the male sexual geometry of tumescence and detumescence. Nancy K. Miller has argued that Fanny's *Memoirs* represents "female impersonation" (what Miller calls "the 'I' in drag") and Janet Todd calls it "a transvestite work."[8] But more is going on here than these terms of external disguise allow, terms that could as well be applied to Defoe's *Moll Flanders* and *Roxana* and to Richardson's *Pamela* and *Clarissa,* which all present male authors speaking in female voices. In addition, Cleland creates a female voice that thinly disguises a masquerading homoerotic male voice. In that sense, we may suggest that Fanny herself is transsexualized; it is "the pen" that "drops" when her desire bursts its bounds. Fanny's effort to write about sexual desire in its morally sanctioned form—that is, within legal heterosexual marriage—ultimately fails her, and her epistolary project draws to a close as she recognizes the superiority of the penis over the pen and begins to question (without invalidating) her earlier indulgence of pleasure for its own (and its financial) sake over pleasure in its conjugal context. Language, of course, in any context, is inadequate to express sexual pleasure. But, as Robert Markley has pointed out, Cleland's novel is about, among other things, the difficulty of capturing the erotic in writing, and the erotic enterprise itself insists that writing about (and reading about) sex is itself a form of sexual pleasure.[9]

When Fanny uses epistolary form, then, as a medium for her accounts of sexual *Bildung* and what one critic has called "erotic topography,"[10] she is not just mediating eroticism through the filter of linguistic exchange. In a textual gesture that reflects and repeats Fanny's own lesbian initiation with Phoebe in the novel's opening, she is also appropriating and recapitulating the erotic in order to seduce her female correspondent. The second letter opens with Fanny "passing . . . from a private devotee to pleasure, into a public one" (92) and learning to do "millinary work, which was the cover of a traffic in more precious commodities" and to ally "pleasure with interest" and "a necessary outward decency, with unbounded secret liberty" (93). Fanny's initiation into the house of Mrs. Cole derives, as it had at Mrs. Brown's house in the first letter, through other women. The first sexual descriptions of the second letter occur as each woman "entertain[s] the company with that critical period of her personal history, in which she first exchanged the maiden state for womanhood" (96). This group storytelling—another repetition of the novel's insistence on losses of virginity and initiations of various sorts—provides a metavoyeurism that imitates the novel's narrative framing. Male writer Cleland creates a narrative directed at libertine male readers, in which Fanny produces a lascivious story for her female addressee, in which Emily and Harriet and Louisa recount how they were first overpowered by sexual desire. By renegotiating sexual desire in this way from the physical ground of the story to the linguistic ground of the narrative, Cleland moves Fanny beyond surrogate lovemaking in her letters. The *lettre* becomes *l'être;* "letter" becomes "being": Writing a letter signifies sexual desire, and it also plays out that desire.

II

Fanny Hill's may have been the first epistolary voice in literature to use letter writing in this way, but hers has certainly not been the last. It is instructive to look at several examples of the tradition Cleland's novel inaugurated, beginning with a twentieth-century text and working backwards to the eighteenth century. First, the "Lotus-Eaters" episode of James Joyce's *Ulysses,* a work that, like *Fanny Hill,* has had its legal difficulties. In that episode about narcotics of various sorts—tea, tobacco, soap, opium and flowers of memory and oblivion—Leopold Bloom (using the reasonable alias "Henry Flower") receives a letter from Martha Clifford, a woman he has not met but with whom he has been carrying on an epistolary affair. Her letter responds to one we have not seen, and enclosed in it is a "yellow flower with flattened petals."[11] Martha writes:

> Dear Henry, when will we meet? I think of you so often you have no idea. I have never felt myself so much drawn to a man as you. I feel so bad about. Please write me a long letter and tell me more. Remember if you do not I will punish you. So now you know what I will do to you,

you naughty boy, if you do not wrote. O how I long to meet you.
Henry dear, do not deny my request before my patience are exhausted.
Then I will tell you all. (chapter 5, lines 249–254)

Bloom reflects on the encoded scenario he uncovers in this letter and its
enclosure:

> He tore the flower gravely from its pinhold smelt its almost no smell
> and placed it in his heart pocket. Language of flowers. They like it be-
> cause no-one can hear. Or a poison bouquet to strike him down. Then
> walking slowly forward he read the letter again, murmuring here and
> there a word. Angry tulips with you darling manflower punish your
> cactus if you don't please poor forgetmenot how I long violets to dear
> roses when we soon anemone meet all naughty nightstalk wife Martha's
> perfume. Having read it all he took it from the newspaper and put it
> back in his sidepocket.
>   Weak joy opened his lips. Changed since the first letter. Wonder did
> she wrote it herself. Doing the indignant: a girl of good family like me,
> respectable character. Could meet one Sunday after the rosary. Thank
> you: not having any. Usual love scrimmage. Then running round cor-
> ners. Bad as a row with Molly. Cigar has a cooling effect. Narcotic. Go
> further next time. Naughty boy: punish: afraid of words, of course.
> Brutal, why not? Try it anyhow. A bit at a time.
>   Fingering still the letter in his pocket he drew the pin out of it.
> Common pin, eh? He threw it on the road. Out of her clothes some-
> where: pinned together. Queer the number of pins they always have.
> No roses without thorns. (chapter 5, lines 260–78)

Bloom hardly needs actually to meet Martha. Reading and "fingering"
her letter permit him mentally to project an entire (and quite unsatisfac-
tory) sexual encounter. Indeed, the letter so thoroughly and poignantly
encodes all that it promises—the obstacles, the futility—that Bloom
becomes jaded with the prospect; "running round corners" follows directly from pseudonymous correspondence.

   In an only slightly more satisfying exchange, again in letters dependent upon sexual desire and its frustration, Gustave Flaubert contemplates "your little slippers" in an 1846 letter to his mistress Louise Colet,
whose bed he had recently left. His writing itself catalogues the traces of
his lover still left to him: "I have just arranged all the things you have
given me: your two letters in the embroidered bag; I am going to reread
them when I've sealed mine." The rhythm of this letter's opening paragraph mimics its erotic subject matter. Flaubert begins by invoking their
recent lovemaking ("It's been twelve hours"); the prose then crescen-
does into an exclamatory series ("What a memory! and what desire!").
He goes on to describe a fear of sexual failure in the fear that his words

will not arouse Louise: "It seems to me that I write badly; you are going to read this coldly; I don't say anything of what I want to say." Flaubert worries that he may not be able to recapture in his letters their erotic mutuality: "It's that my phrases heave against each other like sighs; to understand them, it is necessary to fill in what separates them; you will do that won't you? Will you dream of each letter, of each mark of writing?"

In this correspondence, Flaubert attempts to validate letter writing as an adequate erotic substitution. His letter tries in vain to dissipate the distance between the correspondents: "Hardly had I left you, and in proportion to the distance between us, my mind wandered back to you. It ran faster than the smoke of the locomotive that fled behind us (there is fire in the comparison—pardon the sting)." And he ends with a literal attempt to mail kisses: "Come on, a kiss, quick, you know how, . . . and another one, oh another! another and then, afterwards, under your chin, in that place I love on your skin so soft, on your breast where I lay my heart."[12] This attempt becomes almost a chorus in the Colet letters, though Flaubert's mistress apparently found it crude, telling him, "It's the fleeting memory of a moment of physical happiness" (October 29, 1849)—the word resists becoming flesh. But he persists despite her complaints: "I have hardly any room," he writes, "but all the same I send you through these hurried lines a long and tender kiss, as though from behind bars" (August 30, 1846). Flaubert elsewhere justifies this surrogate use of letter writing by asserting that writing is an activity as intimate as smoking or sleeping, "a nearly animal function, so much is it personal and intimate" (August 16, 1847).[13]

Perhaps the best known use of letter writing as erotic substitution, however, is Valmont's in Laclos's *Liaisons dangereuses*. Valmont is far more explicit than Flaubert, less petulant and brooding, and certainly less desperately beset with sexual frustration. His famous forty-eighth letter to la Présidente de Tourvel is written on what is at least as extraordinary a writing desk as Clarissa's coffin: he uses the back of the prostitute with whom he is in bed. The letter constitutes, therefore, an extended series of double entendres that juxtapose a projected lovemaking scene with a very real one. Louise Colet was always afraid that Flaubert might show her letters to others; Valmont actually shows his epistle to Emilie, whose proffered back he finds a convenient desk, and he sends the letter through the intermediary of Madame de Merteuil in order that it be duplicitously postmarked from Paris. In the cover letter he encloses to Madame de Merteuil, Valmont remarks, "I have been using her for a desk upon which to write to my fair devotee—to whom I find it amusing I should send a letter written in bed, in the arms, almost, of a trollop (broken off, too, while I committed a downright infidelity). . . . Emilie, who read it, split her sides laughing: I hope you will laugh too" (109–10).[14] Moments of ironic and manipulative cruelty proliferate in the letter to the duped Madame de Tourvel, whose pathos consists precisely in the fact that she cannot share with the others and with us the illicit linguistic pleasure literally embedded in this text. And readers are delighted despite their better selves at Valmont's audacity. His letter begins:

> I come, Madame, after a stormy night during which I never closed an eye, after suffering without cease now the turmoil of a consuming passion, now the utter exhaustion of every faculty of my being, I come to you to seek the peace I need, but which as yet I cannot hope to enjoy. Indeed my situation, as I write, makes me more than ever aware of the irresistible power of love. I have scarcely enough command of myself to put my ideas into order. I foresee already that I shall not be able to finish this letter without breaking off. (110–11)

Valmont goes on, shamelessly.

> Never have I taken more pleasure in writing to you; the very table on which I write, never before put to such use, has become in my eyes an altar consecrated to love. (111)

In fact, the importance of this letter in the erotic economy of the *Liaisons dangereuses* may inhabit just the notion of a "sacred altar" of love, because the narrative radically questions the very possibility of such a concept. Writing itself becomes the sacred amorous activity. Valmont's studied, multiply audience-conscious prose turns inside out its stale romantic clichés, unlike Flaubert's increasingly frenzied effort at linguistic love-making. Here we have more eroticism with less expense of spirit and no waste of shame. Flaubert's eroticism is mediated by the letter; Valmont's letter is mediated by the erotic. Flaubert fails dismally; in contrast, Valmont's oscillation between the sacred and the profane represents a magnificent triumph of mediated sexuality—his desecration of the "sacred altar" becomes its apotheosis in the eighteenth-century epistolary novel.

These admittedly ill-assorted examples demonstrate that letters, whether fictive or actual, not only can contain and project sexuality, but can themselves represent sexual acts. John Cleland was fully aware of this epistolary potential when he composed *Memoirs of a Woman of Pleasure*. As Janet Todd has suggested in her *Women's Friendship in Literature*, Fanny's letters to another woman constitute an erotic encounter in which the heroine's correspondent comes to "know" Fanny as Fanny has been "known" by her various sexual partners.[15] These lesbian erotics implicated in the letter exchange bear a certain parallel to the homosocial erotics of Cleland's relation to his male reader: Fanny and her creator both offer male sexuality as the coin for their textual transactions. Both seduce by offering an "other" and a "same" to their readers. But Fanny's lesbian textuality is more innocent because more overt: she writes explicitly to share, to explain, to justify, to titillate. Fanny invokes the "unresolved intimacies" between herself and her friend, and distinguishes between "private closets" and public rooms as sites for the nudity she will present. From the outset she promises her correspondent "Truth! stark naked truth," and insists, "I will not so much as take the pains to bestow the strip of a gauze-wrapper on it" (1).

If the truth is naked, then so is its teller. She opens the first letter by announcing, "I sit down to give you an undeniable proof of my considering your desires as indispensible orders," and goes on to introduce "the loose part of my life, wrote with the same liberty that I led it" (1). And as the second letter opens and Fanny apologizes for the cloying repetitions her subject matter—with its "*joys, ardours, transports, extasies,* and the rest"—invites, she also entrusts herself to her addressee's "imagination" for "supplements" to her descriptions "where [they] flag or fail . . . where they are dull, or worn with too frequent handling" (91). When she is "got snug into port" (187) at the novel's end, a metaphor used salaciously in other sections of the narrative, her marriage signifies an end to these letters. Conventional domesticity and monogamy are not fit subjects for epistolary discourse, and domestic legitimation circumscribes the arena for exposing the phallic deity to which Fanny's letters owe obeisance.

III

Most of Cleland's fame rests on his ingenious manipulations of corporeal euphemism and on the energy with which sexuality discloses itself throughout the *Memoirs of a Woman of Pleasure.* As I have been trying to show, much of this sexual charge resides in the novel's knowing control over the erotics of epistolary exchange itself. It is also important to notice, however, the unraveling of sexual and sexualized speech that begins to occur as the plot approaches its domestic resolution and returns its emphasis to the novelistic conventions of what Frances Burney was later to call "a young lady's entrance into the world." Fanny Hill's philosophical loss for words when she is carnally reunited with Charles is prepared by several earlier sequences that involve observing rather than participating in sexual acts and that return the novel to the voyeuristic initiations of its opening letter. It is important to trace how Cleland progressively and carefully transforms Fanny from her position of speaking subject to that of silent object.

Long alleged to be a later interpolation by another hand but recently restored to its rightful place in Cleland's text, the controversial homosexual scene in the *Memoirs* makes clear the ways in which Fanny's participation as other than narrative voice is unnecessary for sexual consummation.[16] This scene appropriately occurs near the end of the second letter, when Fanny's *Memoirs* are drawing to a close. She is seized by "a spirit of curiosity" to learn the identity of the two handsome young gentlemen in the next room in an inn, and she searches the partition with discerning zeal until she detects a spot for "espial-room sufficient" (157). Fanny refers to homosexual activity with outrage at the men's "project of preposterous pleasure" (157) and her discovery of "what they were" (158), then proceeds to detail this sexual act just as she has detailed every other act in the novel. Only after she has witnessed and testified to the entire scene from her perch on a chair does she pretend to moral indignation.

> All this, so criminal a scene, I had the patience to see to an end, purely that I might gather more facts, and certainty against them in my full design to do their deserts instant justice, and accordingly, when they had readjusted themselves, and were preparing to go out, burning as I was with rage, and indignation, I jump'd down from my chair, in order to raise the house upon them, with such an unlucky impetuosity, that some nail or ruggedness in the floor caught my foot, and flung me on my face with such violence, that I fell senseless on the ground, and must have lain there some time e'er any one came to my relief, so that they, alarm'd, I suppose, by the noise of my fall, had more than the necessary time to make a safe retreat, which they affected, as I learnt, with a precipitation no body could account for, till, when come to my self, and compos'd enough to speak, I acquainted those of the house with the transaction I had been evidence to. (159)

This passage, which is followed by a transcribed diatribe on "these unsex'd male-misses" by Mrs. Cole, bears close scrutiny for its inconsistencies. Fanny's "patience" to "gather more facts" keeps her at her post long after she has ascertained "what they were" and time enough for the handsome young men to have "readjusted themselves." Even "rage" and "indignation" brought about by "so criminal a scene" cannot tear her away from watching the dalliance of "an engine, that certainly deserv'd to be put to a better use" (158). When she does leap to bring "instant justice," she not only makes enough noise to provide ample warning, but is knocked senseless in the process. Only after having told her reader the encounter in detail does she tell of losing her capacity to speak until after the men are safely out of danger; even when she regains consciousness, she is not immediately "compos'd enough to speak" (159). This foretells the speechlessness with which she will be reunited with Charles, though here it follows rather than precedes a sexual act in the textual order. Having catalogued all possible erotic maneuvers and all marks of bodily desire, Fanny's task of speaking is effectively finished. This scene, one of the final sexual consummations in the novel, represents a perfective moment: not one phallus, but two. As metonymic woman, Fanny is so sexually unnecessary in this scene that her fumbling voyeurism actually helps the lovers to safety.[17]

The only kind of sensual pleasure onto which Fanny inscribes any moral judgment is this sexual act between two men; it represents a primary locus of sexual anxiety in a narrative that otherwise boasts of sexual ease. This anxiety and the speechlessness into which it leads had been prepared in an earlier sequence in which Fanny, in an aberrant gesture, takes up for a brief moment with a sailor she meets on the street. In a sequence filled with nautical metaphors, she describes a "blind" sexual act from behind that almost misses its mark; indeed, this passage may bear the first use of the phrase "any port in a storm." "Feeling pretty sensibly that it was going by the right door," says Fanny, "and knocking desperately at the wrong one," she steers the sailor to the port of her choice; anal intercourse is the only sexual act she refuses to perform (141). The "fanny," in other words, is the one bodily site the memorialist protects, and it is a site that signals transgression and decomposition in addition to homoeroticism.[18]

The homosexual sequence—a critical return to Fanny's preliminary "scopophilic" initiation[19]—is followed immediately by Louisa's encounter with the idiot changeling, "Good-natur'd Dick," a simpleton who can only stammer to express himself, "so that there was no understanding even those sounds that his half-a-dozen, at most, animal ideas prompted him to utter" (160). In this scene, Fanny describes sex with "a mere natural" (161) in terms of speechlessness and the "no meaning" (165) countenance of Louisa's exploited bed partner, a procedure that escalates from and underlines the importance of her fall into temporary muteness after observing two men make love. This fall out of language at the end of the novel begins with a simultaneously homophilic and homophobic voyeurism and culminates in Fanny's inability to consummate linguistically her desire for Charles in this letter, and it highlights the tight formal structure and intricate framing devices of the *Memoirs of a Woman of Pleasure*. At its (soft) core, the novel is "about" the linguistic potential of sexual desire. How can desire be replicated in language? Surrounding that Adamic core—the naming of body parts, each one bigger and more potent than the last—is a political frame, a frame of sexuality as a cultural construction. Each letter opens with a scene of women alone, enacting and talking sex. Each letter travels from one woman to another, so that the text would seem at first blush to be fundamentally feminocentric. But John Cleland speaks this woman's voice, the voice of a woman whose very name codes her as a speaking sexual part, a *bijou indiscret*. And Cleland writes as a man for a male audience in a culture that claimed to condemn homoeroticism even while it approved mergers of wit and desire among men.

Following the tradition of *La Puttana errante, L'Ecole des filles* or *The School of Venus,* and *Vénus dans le cloître, ou la religieuse en chemise,* Cleland's novel uses a conventional plot of domestic romance grafted onto the basic formula of a dialogue between an experienced woman and an innocent female interlocutor.[20] However, Cleland not only grafts a domestic romance onto this form in the courtship, brief days of bliss, obstacles and interruptions, and joyous reunion of the two principal lovers, he also plays on the "plot" of sexuality itself within language. For Cleland as later for Freud, sexuality is distinctive in that it entails un-pleasurable tension as well as pleasure and resolution, and Cleland re-enacts the needs, impatience, and resolving release of sexual desire in his narrative framing.[21] The reader never forgets (though Fanny seems to) that Charles is the true lover, that bigger and better genital instruments cannot replace him, even while Fanny underlines the desirability of vir-ginity, of innocence, and of defloration in her stories. This catalogue of sexual acts is, after all, a novel that obeys all the rules of fictional nar-rative established in the 1740s, a crucial decade for the early modern history of the novel.

Cleland's work has often been read and interpreted as a special case of the novel, when in fact it bears a greater resemblance to *Pamela* or to *Tom Jones* than it does to Aretino's *Postures* or to *My Secret Life.* Cleland's very insistence on the established trappings of narrative fiction suggests his desire to place his work within the mainstream of the developing novel genre. He employs a number of conventions of erotica: apparently private transactions violated within the text by voyeuristic participation and description and without by public readership; an objectification of women as objects of exchange employed in the service of the subjec-tification of men; authorial power literally inscribed as erotic power, the penis homologically and metaphorically related to the pen. These con-ventions of erotica are then subordinated to the conventions of the romance plot and its ideologies. Romance ideologies surface in the dé-nouement of domestic monogamy with Charles and in what Susanne Kappeler calls the "cultural archeplot of power" as it is figured in heterosexual desire.[22] Fanny's usefulness is not so much, then, as a physical container or enabler of male heterosexual power as it is as a figure available for exchange in a transaction based on male homosocial desire as that desire reifies sociosexual ideologies.[23]

In Defoe's *Roxana,* a novel with many parallels to the *Memoirs of a Woman of Pleasure,* the memorialist heroine-narrator uses the term "conversation" as a euphemism for carnal knowledge, and among the meanings Samuel Johnson's 1755 *Dictionary* assigns to the verb "to converse" are "to cohabit with" and "to have commerce with the opposite sex."[24] Language and sexuality converge in this usage. Both Roxana's increasingly schizophrenic confession and Fanny Hill's increasingly self-satisfied narration present "conversations" with their readers, in both senses in Fanny's case.[25] Both, ironically, also contain (or perhaps I should say fail to contain) heroines who are erased by the very narratives they produce, Roxana by guilt and madness and Fanny by a kind of subsuming sexuality or sexual absorption. Fanny Hill's epistolary memoir takes its very life from the possibility of a rhetoric of exchange, but then obliterates that exchange's other half. By its structure, the *Memoirs of a Woman of Pleasure* always implicates its readers in a voyeuristic sexual relationship with its narrator. But this implication is ultimately fraudulent, because it resides only in the novel's epistolary framework—it is a mere tease. Fanny's masquerading narrative uses the female voice—and the encoded lesbian erotics implied by the letters—as a disguise: its framed sexuality supposedly privileges but actually erases the female. Fanny's story thrives on the ability of epistolary discourse to make this narrative an emblem of Fanny's fabricated sexual responsiveness. Nevertheless, underneath the letters lies a triumphant glorification of the male body, a panegyric to Cleland's fantastic idealization of masculine power. Cleland in fact imposes a homoerotic phallocentrism on the pleasures his text narrates, with its apparently heterosexual subject matter and its apparently lesbian formal presentation. By using letters literally to *embody* Fanny's eternal feminine receptivity, the text thereby dispossesses and expels her.[26]

The *Memoirs of a Woman of Pleasure* erases the subjectivity of its heroine-narrator because Fanny Hill's subjectivity is appropriated by male self-celebration. An analysis of the novel's structural use of the framing devices embraced by its epistolary form reveals the concentric circles of voices that cloak Cleland's ultimately male-to-male speech and make the text and its narrator transsexual. My reading of Cleland's narrative strategies points to the work's fundamental sexual ambiguities in both its voice and its themes. By subsuming the vocal concentric circles of gender proteanism and transformation into the formal structure of a novel in accordance with the fiction-making conventions of the 1740s, Cleland not only offers a critique of gender categories and social arrangements, but opens in addition new ways for the novel to practice critique, and thereby asserts the nature of the genre to operate as a social form. These formalist considerations need to be understood in relation to the novelistic conventions of the mid-eighteenth century. In accordance with the already established epistolary tradition for what can become of heroines, Fanny must either marry or die. Later in the century, women novelists such as Frances Burney, Mary Wollstonecraft, Elizabeth Inchbald, and Mary Hays began to question this teleological imperative. Cleland might have preempted these writers by offering a radical alternative in the *Memoirs;* he could have permitted Fanny a contented and lucrative life first as a prostitute and then as a successful manager of her own small business, a bawdy house. Though Fanny's ultimate transformation into the bourgeois wife removes her from the scene of prostitution enacted through most of the novel, Cleland's text can also be read for its analysis of the prostitute as a threat to bourgeois class categories. Class, indeed, is inscribed onto Fanny's body because her body represents a conjunction of sex and money.[27] Entrepreneurial talents, inherited perhaps from Moll Flanders, are among the considerable skills Fanny Hill possesses.

But Cleland chooses instead to return his heroine to the conventions and constraints of social respectability in the novel. He parrots these conventions to a fault in his work's domestic resolution. In so doing, Cleland is able to get away not just with the explicit sexual description that has made his work a legal cause célèbre for more than two centuries, but with a complex critique of the politics of sexual ambiguity in the eighteenth century.[28] The woman allegedly at the center of these sexual adventures pays for her entrepreneurial independence and hedonistic attachment to the phallus with a final bow to subordination in monogamous marriage and with the ultimate absorption of her metonymic female sexuality by the phallus she has housed and worshiped. The woman's voice emerges transsexually from Cleland's male pen as a mask for the work's fundamentally homoerotic economy. Cleland exploits Fanny as a sexual receptacle, but in so doing he also critiques both conventional novel plots and the sociosexual ideologies they embrace. He achieves thereby far more than the vocal and corporal acrobatics achieved in the erotic texts of Laclos, Flaubert, and Joyce.

NOTES

1. The term "pornography" literally means writing about prostitutes, and Cleland's novel arguably fits that strict definition. The novel is also arguably what Steven Marcus calls "pornotopia," a work that measures time and space by

fantasy or idealized sexual encounters with no clear connection to social reality, in *The Other Victorians: A Study of Sexuality and Pornography in Mid-Nineteenth-Century England* (1966; 2d ed., New York: Norton, 1974), 268–71. While the *Memoirs of a Woman of Pleasure* has usually been discussed with the focus on its deployment of sexual acts, it also uses the conventions of the eighteenth-century romance plot and the formal structures of eighteenth-century novelistic narrative in ways that make it misleading to classify it primarily according to its energetic sexual description. I find the term "pornography" problematic in relation to Cleland's text for this reason, and I therefore refer to it as "erotic fiction," a more politically neutral term. Other commentators have approached this issue differently. Michael Shinagel cites Boswell's remark about "that most licentious and inflaming book" and calls the novel pornography in *"Memoirs of a Woman of Pleasure:* Pornography and the Mid-Eighteenth-Century English Novel," in *Studies in Change and Revolution,* ed. Paul J. Korshin (Menston, England: Scolar Press, 1972): 211–36. Lawrence Stone refers to the novel (he calls its author "James Cleland") as "a lively piece of cheerful and literate hard-core pornography" in *The Family, Sex and Marriage in England 1500–1800,* abridged ed. (New York: Harper & Row, 1979), 335. Maurice Charney discusses the work under the simple title "sexual fiction" in *Sexual Fiction* (London: Methuen, 1981), 71–89. Michael Ragussis has called the work "an apparently random picaresque of sexual adventures" whose goal is to provide a comprehensive "classificatory system" of sexual acts in *Acts of Naming: The Family Plot in Fiction* (New York: Oxford University Press, 1986), 191–98. For an interesting discussion of the history of pornography, see Walter Kendrick, *The Secret Museum: Pornography in Modern Culture* (New York: Viking, 1987), especially chs. 1 and 2. Recently, the cultural valences of the term "pornography" have been shifting. Susanne Kappeler's *The Pornography of Representation* (Minneapolis: University of Minnesota Press, 1986) analyzes the ways in which pornography is a form of representation and a construct of particular discourses rather than a given concrete entity or special case of sexuality. Susan Suleiman offers a discussion of pornography as "transgressive" in relation to Bataille in "Pornography, Transgression, and the Avant-Garde: Bataille's *Story of the Eye,"* in *The Poetics of Gender,* ed. Nancy K. Miller (New York: Columbia University Press, 1986): 117–36. The representational and political issues engaged by recent debates about pornography are relevant to my argument even though I avoid the term itself, because I want to demonstrate that Cleland plays with literary convention and expectation in order to question and to subvert cultural categories.

2. Searching for an origin for this slang use of "fanny" to refer to part of a woman's anatomy leads to an etymological abyss. Partridge, for example, suggests Cleland's novel itself as a possible source.

3. In the later revision entitled *Memoirs of Fanny Hill,* edited to appease the censors, the work is altered from two letters to eleven, though without much attention given to epistolary verisimilitude. My analysis concerns the original *Memoirs of a Woman of Pleasure.* For an analysis of the later version and a discussion of the work's interesting publication history, see Peter Sabor, "The Censor Censured: Expurgating *Memoirs of a Woman of Pleasure," Eighteenth-Century Life* 9

(1985): Special Issue: "Unauthorized Sexual Behavior during the Enlightenment," ed. Robert P. Maccubbin, 192–201. William H. Epstein also details the elaborate publication history of the *Memoirs* in his biography *John Cleland: Images of a Life* (New York: Columbia University Press, 1974).

4. I am using the recent Oxford World's Classics edition, ed. Peter Sabor (Oxford: Oxford University Press, 1985). All page references are to this edition and are given parenthetically in the text.

5. Poe's famous story plays with this circulation of the letter in brilliant ways, and the debate between Jacques Lacan and Jacques Derrida on "The Purloined Letter" derives from this play. See Lacan, "Seminar on the Purloined Letter," trans. Jeffrey Mehlman, *Yale French Studies* 48 (1973): 38–72; Derrida, "The Purveyor of Truth," trans. W. Domingo, J. Hulbert, M. Ron, and M.-R. Logan, *Yale French Studies* 52 (1975): 31–113; and Barbara Johnson, "The Frame of Reference: Poe, Lacan, Derrida," in *Literature and Psychoanalysis: The Question of Reading: Otherwise,* ed. Shoshana Felman (Baltimore: Johns Hopkins University Press, 1982): 457–505. All these materials have been collected in John P. Muller and William J. Richardson, eds., *The Purloined Poe: Lacan, Derrida, & Psychoanalytic Reading* (Baltimore: Johns Hopkins University Press, 1987). I am indebted to Antonio Cussen for pointing out this connection to me.

6. This letter and the previous one to Sophia Westcomb outline in detail Richardson's theory of correspondence as "the converse of the pen" and as "presence." *The Correspondence of Samuel Richardson,* ed. Anna Laetitia Barbauld, 6 vol. (London: Richard Phillips, 1804), 3:248. This edition has been reprinted in facsimile (New York: AMS Press, Inc., 1966). Bruce Redford takes his title from these letters in *The Converse of the Pen: Acts of Intimacy in the Eighteenth-Century Familiar Letter* (Chicago: University of Chicago Press, 1986).

7. Terry Eagleton, *The Rape of Clarissa: Writing, Sexuality and Class Struggle in Samuel Richardson* (Minneapolis: University of Minnesota Press, 1982), 45, 54.

8. Nancy K. Miller, "I's in Drag: The Sex of Recollection," *The Eighteenth Century: Theory and Interpretation* 22 (1981): 49; and Janet Todd, *Women's Friendship in Literature* (New York: Columbia University Press, 1980), 70.

9. Robert Markley, "Language, Power, and Sexuality in Cleland's *Fanny Hill,*" *Philological Quarterly* 63 (1984): 342–56.

10. See Douglas Brooks-Davies, "The Mythology of Love: Venerean (and related) Iconography in Pope, Fielding, Cleland, and Sterne," in *Sexuality in Eighteenth-Century Britain,* ed. Paul-Gabriel Boucé (Manchester: Manchester University Press, 1982), 184; and John Hollander, "The Old Last Act: Some Observations on *Fanny Hill,*" *Encounter* 21 (October 1963): 76.

11. James Joyce, *Ulysses: The Corrected Text,* ed. Hans Walter Gabler with Wolfhard Steppe and Claus Melchior (New York: Vintage, 1986), chapter 5, l. 239, p. 63. All references are to this edition, and episode and line numbers are given in the text. I am indebted to Michael O'Shea for this reference.

12. The previous quotations derive from *Oeuvres complètes de Gustave Flaubert: Correspondance,* première série (1830–1846), (Paris: Louis Conard, 1926), 211–13. English translations are my own.

13. From Flaubert, *Correspondance,* ed. Jean Bruneau (Paris: Pléiade, 1973). English translations are my own.

14. Choderlos de Laclos, *Les Liaisons dangereuses* (Paris: Livre de poche, 1972), 130–31. All page references are to this edition. English translations come from the 1961 translation by P. W. K. Stone (New York: Penguin Books, 1977), with page numbers given parenthetically in the text.

15. Todd, *Women's Friendship in Literature,* 73.

16. In his introduction to *Memoirs of a Woman of Pleasure* Peter Sabor discusses Fanny's response to the homosexual scene. David Foxon was the first to argue that this scene is not a later interpolation in *Libertine Literature in England, 1660–1745* (New Hyde Park, N.Y.: University Books, 1965).

17. For important discussions of homosexuality and outlaw sexualities in the eighteenth century, see Randolph Trumbach, "London's Sodomites: Homosexual Behavior and Western Culture in the Eighteenth Century," *Journal of Social History* 11 (1977): 1–33; Trumbach, "Sodomitical Subcultures, Sodomitical Roles, and the Gender Revolution of the Eighteenth Century: The Recent Historiography," and G. S. Rousseau, "The Pursuit of Homosexuality in the Eighteenth Century: 'Utterly Confused Category' and/or Rich Repository?" *Eighteenth-Century Life* 9 (1985): 109–21 and 132–68; and, most recently, *Sexual Underworlds of the Enlightenment,* ed. G. S. Rousseau and Roy Porter (Chapel Hill: University of North Carolina Press, 1988). The semantic issue is complicated here, because the word "homosexual" did not come into common use until the end of the nineteenth century. Trumbach discusses sodomitical categories in the seventeenth and eighteenth centuries and their relation to gender roles in "Modern Prostitution and Gender in *Fanny Hill:* Libertine and Domesticated Fantasy," in *Sexual Underworlds,* 69–85. I have not resolved the lexical difficulties, but rather have variously used the terms "homosexual," "homoerotic," and "homosocial" in this essay; editor Robert P. Maccubbin and Rousseau remark on the lexical difficulties in that volume. See also Roy Roussel, *Conversation of the Sexes: Seduction and Equality in the 17th and 18th Centuries* (Oxford: Oxford University Press, 1986); and Walter Perrie, "Homosexuality and Literature," in *The Sexual Dimension in Literature,* ed. Alan Bold (London: Vision Press, 1982): 163–82.

18. Swift's excremental poetry bears the marks of a resident fear of defecation and decay at this site; its transgressive possibilities are discussed by Peter Stallybrass and Allon White in *The Politics and Poetics of Transgression* (Ithaca: Cornell University Press, 1986). I am indebted to Aryeh Kosman and Kimberly Benston on these points.

19. Terry Harpold discussed this scene and Fanny's "scopophilia" in a paper delivered at the Conference on Feminism and Psychoanalysis at Illinois State University, May 1, 1986.

20. See Kendrick, *The Secret Museum,* and Paul-Gabriel Boucé, "The Secret Nexus: Sex and Literature in Eighteenth-Century Britain," in *The Sexual Dimension in Literature,* 70–89.

21. For a discussion of this double characteristic of sexuality, see Leo Bersani, "Sexuality and Esthetics," in his *The Freudian Body: Psychoanalysis and Art* (New York: Columbia University Press, 1986): 29–50.

22. This phrase is used by Kappeler, *The Pornography of Representation*, 104.

23. An explanation of the term "homosocial desire" and a full-length discussion of the triangulation it has entailed can be found in Eve Kosofsky Sedgwick, *Between Men: English Literature and Male Homosocial Desire* (New York: Columbia University Press, 1985).

24. Samuel Johnson, *A Dictionary of the English Language* (1755; repr. 1 vol. New York: Arno Press, 1979).

25. See Janet E. Aikins, "Roxana: The Unfortunate Mistress of Conversation," *Studies in English Literature* 25 (1985): 529–56, for an analysis of the importance of writing and language for Roxana's disastrous self-realization.

26. Nancy Armstrong demonstrates in *Desire and Domestic Fiction: A Political History of the Novel* (Oxford: Oxford University Press, 1987) the ways in which the construction of a female subjectivity through the appropriation and deployment of female voices in the domestic novel gives shape and force to the novel's subversive political power. This may be the reason Cleland resists domestication in this text until the very end.

27. In a discussion of the reception of Manet's 1865 painting *Olympia*, T. J. Clark offers a useful analysis of the category of prostitute in bourgeois society as "one that authority tries to keep in being on the edge of social space, as a kind of barrier against nature—against the body's constant threat to reappear in civilized society and assert its claims." The sensitivity of bourgeois society to prostitution comes, Clark argues, from the fact that the prostitute raises "a matter of bodies turning into what they are usually not, in this case money." (T. J. Clark, *The Painting of Modern Life: Paris in the Art of Manet and His Followers* [New York: Knopf, 1985], 102). Trumbach compares Cleland's fantasy of the prostitute's life with the legal realities in "Modern Prostitution and Gender in *Fanny Hill*." I have not begun to offer a materialist or class analysis of the *Memoirs of a Woman of Pleasure*, but such an analysis remains to be done and would integrate the book's function in the mid-century marketplace into its readings.

28. For broader discussions of the history of sexuality, see Michel Foucault, *The History of Sexuality, Volume One: An Introduction*, trans. Robert Hurley (New York: Pantheon, 1978); and Jeffrey Weeks, *Sex, Politics and Society* (London: Longman, 1981); and Weeks, *Sexuality* (Chichester: Ellis Horwood, 1986). Useful analyses that touch on some of the issues outlined here occur in George Van Den Abbeele, "Sade, Foucault, and the Scene of Enlightenment Lucidity," *Stanford French Review* 11 (1987): 7–16, where the essayist offers a critique of Foucault's denial of sexual difference, and in Cora Kaplan, "Wild Nights: Pleasure/Sexuality/Feminism," in her *Sea Changes: Essays on Culture and Feminism* (London: Verso, 1986): 31–56, where Kaplan elaborates on Foucault's and Weeks's pluralistic notions of class and gender sexualities.

9

In Search of a Female Voice:
Les Liaisons dangereuses

SUSAN K. JACKSON

*Women of sincerity, it is you whom we are questioning. . . . You will
not answer us; but dare to examine your hearts and judge for yourselves.*
Choderlos de Laclos, *On the Education of Women*[1]

COUNTLESS ANALYSES of *Les Liaisons dangereuses* origi-
nate in the statement or assumption that they are dealing
with a "masterpiece." If the exceptional paucity of Laclos's
oeuvres complètes allows his only novel to be read, as if by
default, as his *chef d'oeuvre,* the metaphorical possibilities of this biographical phenomenon have not been lost on literary historians who single out
the *Liaisons* as a masterpiece unrivaled in the lifetime of epistolary fiction. Christopher Hampton puts it wittily in "A Note on Laclos," which
prefaces his recent adaptation of the novel for the commercial stage: "In
many respects, Pierre-A.-F. Choderlos de Laclos (1741–1803) is the
perfect author: he wrote, at around the age of forty, one piece of fiction,
which was not merely a masterpiece, but the supreme example of its
genre, the epistolary novel; and then troubled the public no further."[2]
Whatever the competition, the *Liaisons* can be said to dwarf it. Likewise,
in a further extension of the metaphor, Merteuil and Valmont, the
novel's own two "masters" of deceit, are credited with reducing their
victims (and their own avatars in French letters) to the status of more or
less insipid secondary characters. The word would seem to have gone out

154

that any writing relative to the *Liaisons* had better produce yet another successful exercise of *libido dominandi*—a cover blurb does not fail to herald Hampton's adaptation as "masterful"—or else. Irving Wohlfarth's deconstructive survey of Laclos criticism details this obsession with what he calls "control," and uses the critics' own favorite term, "irony," to condemn it to futility; but he leaves unexplored some of its dangerous implications.[3]

For one thing, a tradition of celebrating and striving after mastery, of canonizing masters and masterpieces, necessarily complicates discussion of the *Liaisons* in terms of the female voice. Where the stakes are literary stature, dwarfing is a matter of drowning out. By the term "masterpiece," we designate, as Nancy J. Vickers reminds us, "the single part of a whole (a genre, an author's *corpus*) that silences, by the strength of its voice, all other parts."[4] In the case of the epistolary genre, the parts which the *Liaisons* as masterpiece would silence are in a disproportionately high number of instances novels written for, about, and by women. A certain view of literary history thus confirms the gender specificity of a certain model of literary achievement. Even as he gives a hearing to many women's letter novels previously consigned to oblivion, even as he makes a refrain of insistence on "the feminine vocation of the genre," Laurent Versini prepares to champion more fervently than any other critic I have read the *Liaisons*'s privileged status as the genre's *terminus ad quem*. More compelling than any single argument is the reenactment of an implicit teleology by which all roads lead to the *Liaisons* not only in the monumental *Laclos et la tradition* but in Versini's general study *Le Roman épistolaire*. It is as though the *Liaisons* accomplished, with respect to women's letter novels, what the Présidente de Tourvel at one point in the novel contemplates doing to her own letters: rereading them and, in the process, erasing them (with her tears). In the aftermath of what Versini calls the "crowning" and "liquidation" of a genre by its masterpiece, the female voice must to some extent strain to be heard, and readers strain once again to hear it.[5]

The several essays in this volume devoted to female practitioners of epistolary fiction address that challenge more straightforwardly than can this one, since I have chosen to attend primarily to authorial voices (and only in passing to those of fictional characters like Merteuil and Tourvel), and to label as "female" only voices emanating from biological women. I do not mean to suggest that accidents of birth exclude anyone a priori from "feminine" or "feminist" discourse; depending on one's understanding of those two terms, a case can be made that Laclos engages in both. But to the extent that his text yields evidence of dissatisfaction with those possibilities, the most narrowly defined female voice becomes important in absentia. Laclos had no way of foreseeing that posterity would give him credit for besting women at their own game of epistolarity, or for collaborating with gentlemen-in-waiting like Richardson and Rousseau to make the game worth playing, and watching. And yet, the nearly unanimous adulation that his contemporary public accorded Laclos on other grounds already deflected attention from what the chorus of post-Romantic criticism has all but suppressed: a certain uneasiness in and about the author's voice, a sense that she or he who speaks as the other may not be playing fair.

Expressions of this uneasiness frame the novel, surfacing noticeably at the outset and at the opposite extreme. In anticipation of reading the postface provided by Laclos's correspondence on the *Liaisons* with Mme Riccoboni, I would look first to the liminal letter addressed by young Cécile Volanges to Sophie Carnay, a fellow pensioner and best chum recently left behind in the convent. An informal survey has confirmed my suspicion that readers tend to remember this letter for two reasons: as the locus of an amusing *quiproquo* (Cécile recounts having mistaken her mother's shoemaker for her own partner in an arranged marriage, the presumed pretext of her leaving the convent), and as an exemplum of Laclos's consummate ventriloquism; within the context of a closed aristocratic society, schoolgirlish babbling stands at the furthest imaginable remove from the "personal" style of a savvy general and man of the world. In fact, what will in hindsight have rendered these features salient is the shocking contrast in style and substance provided by the immediately ensuing letter, from Merteuil to Valmont. Well-wrought phrases running the gamut of tones from command to cajolery and calculated by the marquise to win the vicomte's support for her diabolical plot to cuckold a former lover—and, incidentally, to deflower "the Volanges girl" (6)—have the honor of underwriting a binarism essential to the thematics of mastery. The apparent closure of Cécile's letter, which resolves its own problem of mistaken identity, is exposed as illusory by the creation of much graver problems of which she has no inkling. Rather than for their own sake, her error must be remembered as foreshadowing the fatal misprision to come, her "discovery" that the shoemaker is not her intended as a sign of Merteuil's immense epistemological advantage. Merteuil possesses knowledge of vital interest to Cécile, Cécile knowledge of no interest whatsoever to Merteuil.

There would seem to be no resisting a coupling that victimizes, overpowers, indeed masters both the character of Cécile and her letter, silencing as eminently forgettable whatever parts of that letter the *telos* of mastery does not absolutely need to appropriate. That which will only have forestalled letter 2's confrontation between the queen (Merteuil) and king (Valmont) of the gods is tantamount to the prattle of Echo and, so, punishable by forfeiture of the right to an autonomous voice. Inevitably caught in the cross fire, letter 1 becomes the first civilian casualty in a war of words between the sexes. In the face of such unmistakable rewards for reading the situation right as the putative editor's thoughtful suppression of later scribbling from and to Cécile, it will take an almost perverse counterreading, if not an outright reversal of figure and ground, to dissociate ourselves from the enterprise of mastery, uncouple letters 1 and 2, and begin again at the beginning.

"You see, my dear, that I have kept my word and that bonnets and pom-poms do not take up all my time—there will always be some left over for you" (3). The initial sentence of letter 1 uses grammatical (*ma bonne amie*) and cultural ("bonnets and pom-poms") codes to overdetermine the mutual femaleness of correspondents already named as Cécile Volanges and Sophie Carnay. Beyond that, it serves primarily to fill the pair's time—past, present, and future—with instances of linguistic exchange. The first clause declares the double present of Sophie's reading ("You see") and Cécile's writing ("I keep my word"), the latter depicted as fulfilling a past promise to write, which the rest of the sentence implicitly renews and extends into the future. What the letter puts, redundantly, into words is an assurance of its own existence and a presumption of safe arrival at its destination. The missive is the message, the minimal epistolary gesture that establishes as more important than anything else Cécile and Sophie might say or hear the fact of their being in relation to language.

It requires no foreknowledge of the many uses to which Merteuil and Valmont will put the epistolary act to imagine that the present letter will somehow move beyond this linking of female correspondents to their correspondence. In fact, halfway through her first paragraph, Cécile interjects a further reminder that she is writing into a sentence whose accent nevertheless falls on extralinguistic acts of acquisition: "I have my own maid; I have a room and a study at my disposal and I am writing to you at a very pretty writing-table whose key was given to me so that I can shut up anything I want in it" (3). By the same paragraph's end, however, Cécile complains of having run out of things to say: "It is not yet five o'clock; I do not see Mamma until seven; plenty of time, if I had anything to say to you!" (3). Lest we leap too hastily to solemn conclusions about the "utter bankruptcy of spiritual existence in the waning hours of the Ancien Régime," Cécile does manage to pen another paragraph *before* the shoemaker's unexpected arrival provides genuinely new material.

In the interval, letter 1 carries on with none other than the two activities launched by what comes to look more and more like a topic sentence: naming females, naming them in such a way that there can be no doubt as to their sex; and matching them with verbs of speech, animating them almost exclusively as supports for language. This all-female cast comprises, in order of appearance: the haughty (*la superbe*) Tanville, identified by an editor's note as "pupil in the same convent"; the aforementioned maid or *femme de chambre;* Mamma, named four times and referred to by numerous subject and object pronouns; Mother Perpetue; numbers of sewing women; and the good (*la bonne*) Josephine, "attendant of the convent turning-box," according to a second note (3–4). As practiced here, name-dropping can easily be explained as feeding the illusion of an authentic correspondence oblivious to the ignorance of third-party readers. (The *incidence* of name-dropping is abnormally high only in light of as yet unestablished norms of masterful plotting, including the economical deployment of limited personnel and the elimination of extras.) Nor, given prevailing mores, does the cast's uniform femaleness, whatever pains are taken to proclaim and preserve it, come as any surprise. A series of implicit pairings (Mother Perpetue/Mamma, the good Josephine/the maid, and so forth) continually tests the difference between one interior, the convent, from which males were excluded by law, and another, the aristocratic drawing room, where idled warriors were increasingly welcomed but still viewed to some extent as foreign invaders. Limited to the womanly ritual of assembling a trousseau, wedding preparations apparently in progress function to perpetuate the conventual order, to suspend "real" difference indefinitely, in favor of such relative differences as Cécile is positioned to perceive. "I have seen more clothes in this single day than in the four years we spent together" (3).

Neither literary nor sociological conventions account, however, for the systematic way in which letter 1 goes about assigning speaking parts to its incidental females. Cécile anticipates showing off her finery to Tanville ("I intend to ask for her"); weighs the pros and cons of her new life ("Mamma asks my opinion in everything. . . . Mother Perpetue is not here to scold me. . . . my Sophie is not here to talk and laugh with me"); and wonders whether rumors of her engagement can be chalked up to further drivel (*un radotage de plus*) on the part of the good Josephine (3–4). Amidst this flurry of asking, consulting, scolding, chatting, laughing, and rambling, only the voices of the sewing women who parade through the Volanges's household in silence go unrecorded. Not that the others are charged with delivering anything much in the way of specific lines; on the contrary, if Madame de Volanges's utterances to her daughter consist essentially of telling her that she will tell her later when they will talk, this potentially infinite deferral of content recalls promises to write made in the absence of anything to write about. Intransitive verbs (chat, laugh, ramble), verbs that take interlocutors rather than locutions as their objects (ask for, consult, scold), make for a high volume of female voices, but tend toward dissociating the faculty of speech from the production of meaning.

Even Cécile seems inclined to dismiss the female voices she faithfully records as so much background noise. When it comes to something as important as her long-term future, it is no longer "she," her mother, who is accused of keeping Cécile in the dark, but the neuter *on* (one). Rendered by the passive voice in Aldington's translation, the pronoun occurs twice in the original. "So far nothing has been said [*on ne m'a encore parlé de rien*] and except for the preparations I see being made and the numbers of sewing-women who all come for me I should think there is no intention of marrying me [*je croirais qu'on ne songe pas à me marier*] and that it was one more delusion [*un radotage de plus*] on the part of the good Josephine" (3–4). Not only is the feminine pronoun precluded from standing in for the voice of truth and authority, but pronouncements withheld by *on* derive value from explicit contrast with feminine drivel, such that *on* becomes a barely disguised synonym for *il* (he). The voice of authority must be *his*. But whose? For want of an available male referent, for want of an *il/on* to tell her the truth in no uncertain terms, Cécile can only piece together syllogisms out of the repetitive, inconclusive propositions of her female entourage. "Mamma has told me so often that a young lady should remain at the convent until she is married that Josephine must be right, since Mamma has taken me away" (4).

It is at this juncture, the absence of male voices having been rendered conspicuous and problematical, that the chance arrival of a carriage interrupts the letter-writing process. Needless to say, ensuing developments carry to parodic extremes the sexual naïveté of a stock literary figure, the conventually educated ingénue. But Cécile's progress from hypothesis to belief to certainty that the carriage has delivered none other than her fiancé can also be read as confirming our own hypotheses about male and female voices. "Suppose it were *he* [*le Monsieur*]?" (4)—any man could be *the* man, the deus ex machina equipped by nature to rescue language from the impasse of inconclusiveness. What matters is maleness; whatever his proper name, the visitor announced as Mr. C. fulfills the essential criterion for belief that "it *is* he [*c'est lui*]," he who will declare (himself). The belief needs verifying, however, insofar as the maid's announcement terminates, not in a positive identification, but in appropriately ambiguous laughter (4). What clinches the case, inspiring Cécile to such heretofore unscaled heights of inarticulateness as "a piercing cry," is the verbal and body language emitted by "the gentleman" himself. No "remark" could be more "plain" than his compliment: "'Madame,' said he to my mother, as he bowed to me, 'This is a charming young lady and I feel more than ever the value of your favour'"—unless, of course, he should subsequently assume the unmistakable posture of a smitten supplicant: "I had scarcely sat down when this man was at my knees!" As though to underscore the fact that at long last the bass rumblings of a male voice have made themselves heard, Cécile's search for a situation of comparable horror leads her back to "the day of the thunderstorm" (4).

Jupiter has spoken, or would have if he did not turn out to be a shoemaker speaking only in the discharge of his duties, leaving Cécile as ignorant as had the silence of his fellow tradespeople the sewing women. Not that Mamma seizes this golden opportunity to appropriate the voice of truth; she responds typically to Cécile's predicament with a burst of laughter and an order: "Sit down and give Monsieur your foot," which stops short of revealing the truth even of the present situation. The matter of fact that "'Monsieur' was a shoemaker" is reported without attribution to any speaker, male or female. *On* has yet to be heard from; the letter's complimentary closing repairs the rift between past and present and makes it clear that nothing has changed. "Good-bye, dear Sophie. I love you as if I were still at the convent" (4).

As for the future. Cécile ventures only to say: "I think that when I am married I shall never employ this shoemaker" (4). His impeccable conduct notwithstanding, the shoemaker has been scapegoated. Mister has become Mister Wrong, victimized by the inescapable fact of his maleness, put out of a job for the unforgivable impropriety of speaking with a bass voice (and thus leading Cécile down the primrose path through sexual to intellectual shame). Poor fellow! What *was* his name anyway, or, more puzzling still, what possible reason could there be for referring to Cécile's mysterious visitor only as *M. C****? It makes no sense to ascribe the suppression by asterisks to Cécile: though she may not have caught the name on first hearing, a point is made of the fact that she got a second chance. Willful suppression on her part would be more unlikely still: C.'s anonymity hardly needs protecting from the likes of Sophie, with whom Cécile obviously shares everything, including an ignorance of men, which makes Sophie a poor candidate for guessing games. In fact, the longstanding conventions of protective anonymity and guessing games (*romans à clé*) frame a message—these unnamed individuals are/were real—belonging primarily not to the discourse between characters, but to that between novelists and their external readers. Readers like us, novelists like the one we have come to call "Laclos," but whose initials appear on the original title page of the *Liaisons* as "M. C.....de

L. . . ," and who, until late in his life, "was referred to and referred to himself as Choderlos or Choderlos de Laclos."[6] What if the mysterious recurrence of the initial "C" so few pages later were charged with writing a cameo part for the novelist qua novelist in and out of his novel? The possibility of such a provisional incarnation of the authorial voice would be less appealing if we felt obliged to silence all possible objections with a masterful proof of conscious intentions, less intriguing if the letter in which M. C*** makes his lone appearance did not so consistently and coherently problematize the issue of voice and sensitize the unhurried exegete to the questions of who is speaking and how.

Read as an aside to the external reader, the shoemaker's dismissal as persona non grata formalizes the implications for the novelist of his decision to write an epistolary novel: exclusion from speaking in his own name either as a character or as a global narrator, self-conscious retreat into marginal craftsmanship (the editor as shoemaker). The basis for his dismissal, Cécile's error, in turn warns us readers against mistaking the voice of any character, no matter how eloquent the speaker or how desperate our need, for the authorial *on,* which the entirety of letter 1 solicits in vain. The joke of the author's plight is on us: *on* will, for the duration of this or any epistolary novel, remain elusive, resisting all attempts at localizing in this or that scriptor's body what emanates instead from an overall corpus. Even the authorial voice that we might claim to read between the lines (of a double entendre like C.'s compliment, for example) does not really speak for itself; it depends, for the production of meaning, on the sometimes unwitting collusion of a reader's (in)experience, expectations, and values. Like C.'s, Laclos's power to disconcert resides, paradoxically, in the alienation of his discourse, in the act of speaking, never in his own name, but always through roles *and* through his readers. "The very nature of epistolary fiction supposes the novelist's protean talent to transmute his voice into that of another."[7]

But what are we to make, for purposes of our analogy, of the fact that C. wields his power inadvertently and derives from its exercise not exultation but acute embarrassment? Why does this version of mastery look so much like misery? The cameo does more than provide an occasion for rehearsing generalities about the authorial voice in epistolary fiction; it *particularizes* the voice at work everywhere and nowhere in *this* novel and, in so doing, reminds us that no voice can avoid forever being traced to a particular individual. Whether that individual has the right or responsibility to claim it as his or her own remains a question for philosophers and moralists. It is a matter of common sense that some*body* wrote, published, and made his reputation from *Les Liaisons dangereuses,* that somebody being not some asexual, perfectly protean God, but Choder-

los de Laclos, "Monsieur . . . he . . . a gentleman in black . . . this man"
(4).

The limits of biology are most succinctly rendered by C.'s compliment: " 'Madame, . . . This is a charming young lady and I feel more than
ever the value of your favour.' " The male author can speak in terms of
utmost respect *to* women and *about* them; he can prostrate himself, literally and metaphorically, at their knees. Like shoemaking, novel making
provides him access to the secret gyneceum or no man's land from which
those of his sex are normally banned; he can make his life's work of
pleasing his female clientele and setting them off to their best advantage.
What more eloquent gesture of good faith than that his liminal letter
should make a mockery, at the novelist's own expense, of the authority
too automatically and universally ascribed to the male voice? A show of
embarrassment at the interchangeability of *il* and *on* does not, of course,
explain away the unproductive noisiness of the letter's various *elles*. But
the argument could be made—and Laclos will make it in the fragments
on the education of women—that the fault lies with the phallologo-
centric social order, which encourages women to buy into this mystique
of the male voice (417–18). What more is Laclos to do in the present
context than to validate the female voice in its virtuality, even as he
hesitates, however briefly, to put words into *her* mouth? And yet, even in
the guise of self-appointed spokesman *for* women, even through his
many experiments in speaking as women might, Laclos cannot, short and
simple, speak as a woman. Neither abdicating the authority of *on* nor
appropriating it with the best of intentions brings him all the way out of
himself. Letter 1 stages the cruel joke played by nature on whoever
knows sexual difference to make a difference. However tenuous in the
writing of a letter novel—as Merteuil reminds Valmont, letters are read
where the writer's body is not (59)—the inescapable liaison of voice and
body gives rise to a certain anxiety of authorship.

Symbolic compensation for this anxiety takes many forms in *Les Liaisons dangereuses,* among them the quantitative and qualitative advantages
enjoyed by the novel's female correspondents. Not only do their voices
continue to outnumber those of their male counterparts, but they have a
virtual monopoly, for example, on thoughtful discussion of sexual difference. (This unequal distribution of the best lines and tirades becomes
all the more striking when they are spoken aloud in the theater.) Truths
told at length by Merteuil and Rosemonde sustain the illusion of a female
presence where none exists behind the scenes. In his final curtain call as
editor, M. C. . . . . de L. . . does more than a little to dispel that illusion.
The sequel he has in mind for the *Liaisons* would necessarily be scripted
or at least received as a pair of discrete third-person narratives *about* the

novel's two surviving heroines: "For the moment, we cannot give the reader the continuation of Mademoiselle de Volanges's adventures nor inform him of the sinister events which completed the misfortunes or the punishment of Madame de Merteuil" (368). With this bracketing of epistolarity, a monopoly on discourse reverts to the male editor and his generic *lecteur*. And rightly so: no Mademoiselle or Madame, neither Juno nor Echo, will really have spoken anywhere in the *Liaisons*. Of course, the possibility that letters have been arbitrarily withheld from us perpetuates the fantasy of *libido dominandi*. But the more likely possibility, that no further letters exist (to whom could either Cécile or Merteuil have written? Surely not to each other) would, if admitted directly, put too emphatic an end to the concurrent fantasy of coauthorship, of authentically polyphonic composition. What the editor says and fails to say at the last begs the question: Could Laclos have a personal investment not only in Merteuil's plot to master her male rival but in her earlier dream gone astray of collaborating with a member of the opposite sex in the writing of a novel?

A sequel of sorts does exist, which testifies better than anything Laclos himself could have written to the survival of his preoccupation with the female voice. To the 1787 edition of the novel, the last Laclos supervised personally and the one he claimed to prefer,[8] was appended an exchange of eight letters between Laclos and the popular novelist Madame Marie-Jeanne Riccoboni. A bookseller's foreword facetiously advertises these letters as neatly summarizing for readers too lazy or unsure of themselves to form their own opinions all possible arguments for and against the *Liaisons,* and opines that this authentic correspondence might have ranked among the all-time great literary polemics had the correspondents not refrained from trading insults (730).

Indeed, what is disappointing about the exchange as literary criticism—aside from the fact that the theoretical assumptions jointly espoused seem so far in arrears of Laclos's practice—is the amount of space reserved, especially by him, for the formulation of elaborate, even extravagant compliments. At one point, Riccoboni bids him back off from what is verging on gallantry, with a reminder of her advanced age: How can someone who first talked about her with his grandmother expect her to take seriously claims that he would experience the termination of their correspondence as "deprivation" (692)? His hastening to endorse and justify the wording stands as only one example among many of what our reading makes understandable as delight at having been addressed by a living, breathing female (694). Riccoboni's first sally having arrived as much by chance, from as far out of the blue as C.'s carriage, Laclos seems to relish his lack of authorial control over the correspondence as such, to thrill in the tenuousness of the liaison that connects his with this other autonomous voice. Will Riccoboni write back even after, putting that tenuousness to the test, he gratuitously "confesses" that she has every right not to continue (690)? When she catches him in the contradiction of attaching his address (692), as when mere politeness dictates that she thank him for enclosing a copy of *Les Liaisons* (689), he is happy enough to admit to the transparency of subterfuges which, in each instance, guarantee him at least one more reply (694). How palpably different from the absence of real female voices in the *Liaisons* is that silence rendered eloquent by his "threat" to send along another installment unless he hears from her forthwith (696).

However much they must have unnerved an addressee more or less fated to read the possibility of Valmont's mocking overtones into the discourse of his creator, we third-party readers have the luxury of appreciating that these otherwise banal and suspect compliments also bespeak a certain gratitude for making the dream of epistolarity come true. In combination with repeated direct assurances of the high value he attaches to Riccoboni's approval or *suffrage* (692, 696, 697)—the French term also translates as "vote," as does *voix*, the term for "voice"—peripheral expressions of thanks for her expressions of thanks (689), for her very willingness to engage in debate (697), draw attention to a truly honest difference (of opinion). Whereas Riccoboni starts out by referring to herself in the first person singular and to Laclos in the third person respectful as "the son of M. de Chauderlos" (686), his response uses a pair of third persons not only to redress tactfully the implied inequality of extralinguistic stature but to linger over the realization that discourse is really in progress between a male and a female of equal status *in* that discourse. "M. Laclos sincerely thanks Mme Riccoboni. . . . M. Laclos begins by congratulating Mme Riccoboni," and so forth (687). Even *after* the correspondence has been appended to *his Liaisons*, Laclos nurtures an illusion of perfect parity by placing responsibility for what looks suspiciously like reappropriation of the female voice squarely on the shoulders of *on*, some other authority (*Lettres inédites*, 295).

A hidden agenda incompatible with master planning on Laclos's part is further served by Riccoboni's spontaneously setting an agenda for debate which centers on the character of Merteuil. To be sure, the presence of a female interlocutor who happens to be a widely respected author and former collaborator provides grounds enough for Laclos's assuming in his own name and with all due seriousness C.'s reverential (if seductive) posture before this particularly prized client.[9] But deflection of his compliments onto a wider public requires Riccoboni's easily won admission that the portrayal of the she-devil Merteuil offends her personally *as a woman*. It is she whose hints that others of her sex are similarly offended give way to warnings about incurring the wrath of women without exception, she who goes so far as to put herself at risk of having her eyes scratched out for her relative indulgence (689, 693). Laclos thus finds himself "forced" to rehearse, in the face of seemingly insurmountable evidence to the contrary, his impeccable credentials as a man who loves and respects the other as other. He manifests a desire to do just that by declaring Merteuil's nationality to be contingent to her essential character (691), thereby dismissing as equally contingent Riccoboni's further claims to have responded viscerally as a "Frenchwoman" and "zealous patriot" (689). Nor does he pay more than lip service to the easy but unconvincing argument according to which Merteuil's demonic version of womanhood would be offset by the positive images projected by, for example, Tourvel and Rosemonde (687–88). He must already have sensed that Riccoboni would refuse to honor the argument with a single word of rebuttal when he referred her for "proof" to one in particular (130) of Rosemonde's letters. By contrast, his reader's memory required no such refreshing about the otherwise memorable marquise. In fact, his reference to the Rosemonde letter remains the only specific allusion in this correspondence between connoisseurs to the text of the novel—and, remarkable as it may seem, given our present-day fascination with form—the only clue as to the novel's epistolarity. Laclos's half-hearted attempt to locate and amplify artificially the voice of female virtue attests to the virtually unlimited silencing powers of what was already presumed to be a unique masterpiece of characterization, Merteuil.

It is in the guise of yet another victim, as the master ironically silenced by his own masterpiece, that Laclos now dusts off C.'s black suit. Painstakingly, ingeniously, exhaustively, even defensively, as Ronald Rosbottom has suggested (*Choderlos de Laclos*, 48), he sets about answering the eighteenth century's favorite charges of untruth and immoralism in characterization, as Riccoboni has made them pertain to his own attitudes toward women. In no way the projection of some vengeful misogynist, the character of Merteuil has its source in external, observable, everyday reality (687, 691). Were it less true to life, it would scarcely have touched a collective nerve or created such a furor; who, after all, thought to attack poor Don Quixote for tilting at windmills, or leapt to the defense of the windmills themselves (690)? On the other hand, though the models are many and the character a composite, it represents not the essence of womanhood as Laclos himself understands it, but rather a deplorable perversion of that essence by a seditious fringe element. The virtuous majority should applaud rather than lambaste him for exposing and combatting the traitress in their midst (690–91). And so forth.

Much more could be written about and against these arguments than Riccoboni, with a much smaller stake than Laclos's in "winning" a debate that she could only assume to be private, chose to write. Rather than abandon so early on the issue or Merteuil's troubling attractiveness as a role model, she might, for example, have demanded to know where exactly in the novel Laclos "combats" vice and makes its "horror" so unmistakably repugnant as to discourage all thoughts of imitation (687–88, 690). By way of contrast, another contemporary female reader, Isabelle de Charrière, scoffs at the inconsequentiality of whatever punishments the novel's dénouement metes out, and reads the "moral" of the story as follows: give me the pleasures and power of a Merteuil, and I'll know enough not to write incriminating letters or catch smallpox, which I've already had.[10]

In the course of the correspondence, Riccoboni's role is thus gradually reduced to that of prompter for the long-winded laments of one who fancies himself to be womankind's misunderstood lover. Louder and more plaintive still, and more germane to our discussion of the female voice, are those passages where Laclos blames the characterization of Merteuil on what once again emerges as a crucial limitation, his very biological maleness. How unfair that women in society should heap further abuse on those whom nature has already "condemned," leaving them no choice but to write as men (688). This claim begs to be buttressed and it is, however sketchily, by an explanation of what Laclos perceives to be the fundamental difference between characteristically male or masculine writing and that feminine writing declared off limits to those of his sex. The former is or would be, at its best, essentially voiceless. Perfectly analogous with the plastic arts—the metaphor recurs ad nauseum—masculine writing can aspire to no other perfection than adequate representation of external models. Far from coming naturally to its practitioners, this version of mimesis demands harder, less pleasant work (*un travail plus sévère*) than feminine writing, and brings few rewards. Failure to let the facts, all the facts, speak for themselves means falling short of masculine writing's only accessible goal, "rendering nature exactly and faithfully" (688). Hard-won artistic success in turn means falling victim to the kind of misunderstanding that would not have arisen had Laclos spoken for himself in the only way available to him as a male artist, by "silencing at least a part of what he has seen" (687). Limited in this enterprise of unrelieved grimness to approaching psychological realism as a limit from the underside of less than full disclosure of perceived reality, the male novelist can set his sights only on the Pyrrhic victories of characters like Merteuil. He stands to be damned by his female readership if he tells all he knows, damned as an artist if he holds anything back.

The eye is indeed covetous which looks up to "feminine" writing—and here the novels of Laclos's correspondent provide an exemplary case in point—as uniquely "charming" and charmed (688). What makes the difference is women's exclusive birthright to a faculty that Laclos—after Valmont (66)!—calls "precious sensibility" (688). Supplementing or even replacing "observation" and "painting," this sensibility corresponds in its functioning to our notion of voice. By "embellishing" and "adding to," the increment of voice propels female writing beyond the austere masculine ideal of voicelessness into the far side of more than external reality, the "real" ideal. Unlike eyes, which must be trained to see clearly, and hands disciplined to paint without trembling, voice emanates spontaneously, as is, "smiling" and "facile," from within the female body (695, 688). Considerations of technique have nothing at all to do with the designation of the best female writers as those "born" to the greatest quantity of sensibility (695). To compliment a woman's work thus amounts to congratulating the woman herself on the extent of her femaleness. As if on cue, Riccoboni takes personally the praise that Laclos showers on her novels and takes *them* not at all seriously; "trifles emitted by my pen," she calls them (689).

But the liaison between the female writer and her writing turns out to be more complex and more consubstantial still. Invoking the painting metaphor in what looks like a desperate attempt at reestablishing some common ground, lest his two poles spin off wildly in opposite directions, Laclos locates the "models" for Riccoboni's characters "in the heart of the painter" (688). That female voice credited with embellishing "everything it touches" would thus touch nothing beyond the speaker herself, except that even "she" must inevitably be lost in the very process of embellishing, which yields no other truth than that of its own inexhaustible energy. The best woman writer "pours out" only a portion of her innate sensibility onto the self-"portrait she traces" (695). Tending always towards auto-referentiality, the female voice thus constitutes itself as the unique, forever elusive object of female discourse. Echoes of Echo, shades of Cécile's vociferous coterie: their having "nothing to say" renders more faithfully and fundamentally even than Tourvel's characteristic solipsism or Merteuil's fatal attraction to autobiography an essential conflation of means and ends into the single self-sustaining, self-proclaiming entity of voice. For all the limitless possibilities held out by Laclos's positively charged rhetoric and by an enabling pseudologic of supplementarity, serious limits are being placed on the domain of women's letters.

Laclos's rhetoric further dissimulates the obvious proximity of embellishment to willful dissimulation. His implicit model of feminine writing is borrowed, not from any fine art, but from the everyday art of cosmetology, a subject discussed at some length in two chapters of *De l'éducation des femmes* (436–48). The woman who paints herself with words has everything in common with the seductress who uses cosmetics to "make herself up," including ready means to the end of pleasing men. How much more transparent is the motive when courtship of the opposite sex entails simply letting one's own voice be heard, rather than, as he has had to do, allowing a Merteuil to speak for herself. Laclos thus makes it against women's best interests to challenge his version of the female voice, and makes virtually irresistible the temptation to venture self-consciously even further into the realm of the ideal, of "objects as they should be," than the untrained voice—if indeed it exists—would naturally lead (688).

Riccoboni's tacit compliance with this theoretical demonstration also leaves unchallenged the fundamental inequality for which, try as he might, Laclos's effusions cannot overcompensate. Just as predictably as he (and Riccoboni) come back time and again to the painting metaphor, that metaphor breaks down when asked to perform the literally inappropriate task of rendering the operations of the female voice. For it is masculine, voiceless writing à la Laclos that conforms on every count to the literary values of the mainstream moralist tradition in French letters, feminine writing that derives and differs from that which controls the difference. More is less, voice the sign and the stigma of failure to conform. The so-called "son of M. Chauderlos" can lay claim as well to an impeccable literary bloodline passing from the illustrious Molière through Crébillon fils and Richardson (687, 690–91) and get no argument or alternative genealogy from a woman as imbued as he with the prescriptions of the patriarchy. How telling that, in his article on Fanny Burney's *Cecilia,* Laclos should linger admiringly over the circumstances of Burney's coming to writing out of a desire to please not some lover of her own generation, as might have been feared, but rather her adored and adoring father. Laclos's further recollection that Burney revealed to no one the secret of work on her first novel until it was fully finished remystifies the *process* of female writing more honestly than do the forced metaphors of his letters to Riccoboni (502). So too does a latent analogy between Burney's clandestine operations and those of the solitary natural childbirth exalted in the essay on female education (408).

There is another reason for reading, as a companion piece to the Riccoboni letters, the essay on *Cecilia,* which, in its theoretical introduction, attenuates to the point of blurring distinctions between the writings of the two sexes. Successful novels, his *and* hers, depend, according to the essayist, on the novelist's possessing a threshold level of talent whose three component parts—the familiar observation, sensibility, and painting—may coexist in varying proportions. Women tend toward sensibility but have no corner on this precious commodity (501); nor are women in general and Burney in particular precluded from the accurate depiction of mores (521).[11] It would appear, then, that we have Riccoboni's intervention to thank for transforming this relative difference into an absolute one. A hardening of the lines that works, at least rhetorically, to the advantage of women, giving them a voice of their own, even voice itself, pays homage to that intervention; Laclos seeks to reproduce, in the arena of public letters, the rhetorical frame of separate but equal participation in epistolary exchange.

To be sure, the male novelist has everything to gain from a separation that effectively eliminates the possibility of "bisexual" women writers. Aram Vartanian has convincingly read the demise of Merteuil as Laclos's way of dealing with the threat of female bisexuality.[12] I would only add to his arguments the reminder that Merteuil, she who would be king *and* queen, is paired at both extremes of the novel with Cécile, whose attraction to and for members of both sexes places her sexual preference literally in doubt. Assuming control over the future adventures of both heroines may well be the response of the "editor" to the specter of Jupiter's absence from the decisive confrontation where Juno and Echo manage to settle the question of voice between themselves.

Nor does the expenditure of energy involved in masterminding (a semblance of) parity by overvaluing the feminine go unrewarded. If Laclos backs Riccoboni into a corner of silence from which only an ingrate would come out swinging, he also gets a chance to wallow in that victim's role whose persistent attractiveness to him I hope to have suggested. However patronizing (and unconvincing) the appropriation of that role by one of the really empowered, it places into question the more or less universal assumption of Laclos's exclusive identification with the dominant protagonists of the *Liaisons*. I would argue that the novel's virtuosity depends less on superficial ventriloquism than on the wide-ranging possibilities of the novelist's own inner voice, on his feeling equally at home in the three registers of mastery, co-mastery, *and* victimization. What passes for the unremitting practice of mastery might more inclusively be rethought as a preoccupation with mastery as a problematics.

Sensitivity to that problematics, the ability to consider it from vantage points other than that of the master, would seem to account for Laclos's intuition of the threat posed to Riccoboni's novels by a masterpiece such as his own. His rhetorical question, posed by way of reassurance—"What could one write that could ever destroy the charm of those delicious works which you alone call trifles?" (690)—admits of a three-word response, *Les Liaisons dangereuses,* which appears already obvious to him. So too the prophecy in his declaration that a posterity with no taste for Riccoboni's novels would forfeit his esteem can be read as betraying a vague awareness of the sexual politics of canon formation (690). It would be going way too far to fantasize a Laclos indifferent to his own present "glory" (698) or to the prospect of being installed, at whatever cost to others, in a central niche of the canon. He would no doubt have been horrified to learn that the public's attention could be so really "fickle" (697) as to delay the proceedings for more than a century.

Indeed, he has it both ways, controlling and publishing in his own name a correspondence that reveals him to be always in control of everything *except* Riccoboni's vote of approval, which her terminal letter refuses in the name of personal integrity to surrender: "To say what I do not think seems to me a betrayal" (698). Co-opting at the stage of publication a voice that he will earlier have failed to co-opt, Laclos commemorates and undermines whatever need for equality the correspondence may temporarily have served. Still, however much he uses and abuses Riccoboni's letters for his own purposes, he does rescue them from silence; he makes a public spectacle of pursuing earnest exchange, of turning a deaf ear on the self-deprecation of a would-be "unknown cenobite" who, in an uncanny coincidence, relegates her own voice to (Cécile's) convent and (Echo's) cave (698, 692). Most invitingly, in his several incarnations, Laclos—alias C***, alias M. C. . . . . de L. . . , alias son of Chauderlos—never fails to remind us that, when he speaks, (only) a man will have spoken. We could do worse than accept his open invitation to read "*Ernestine, Fanny, Catesby,* etc., etc., etc." (688), there to learn what Echo has to say, and with what unexpected force, otherwise than in the service of Jupiter, even as we continue to listen for regions of silence *in* the masterpiece.[13] On two separate occasions, Laclos proposes to Riccoboni a model of right reading that would consist in seeing the body or essential through the drapery or contingent (688, 691). In writing back, we continue to wonder aloud how bodies make a difference, and whether that difference might have something to do with disagreement as to where the drapery leaves off and the body begins.

NOTES

1. In citing *De l'éducation des femmes,* the correspondence with Riccoboni, and the essay on *Cecilia,* I have used the text of Laclos's *Oeuvres complètes* edited for the Bibliothèque de la Pléiade by Maurice Allem (Paris: Gallimard, 1951); En-

glish translations are mine. In the case of *Les Liaisons dangereuses,* I cite (and page numbers refer to) Richard Aldington's English translation, *Dangerous Acquaintances* (New York: New Directions, 1957). The original French wording is given wherever essential to my reading.

2. *Les Liaisons dangereuses, from the Novel by Pierre-Ambroise-François Choderlos de Laclos* (London: Faber and Faber, 1985), 7.

3. Irving Wohlfarth, "The Irony of Criticism and the Criticism of Irony: A Study of Laclos Criticism," *Studies in Voltaire and the Eighteenth Century* 120 (1974): 269–317.

4. In Nancy J. Vickers, "The Mistress in the Masterpiece," in *The Poetics of Gender,* ed. Nancy K. Miller (New York: Columbia University Press, 1986), 19.

5. *Laclos et la tradition: Essai sur les sources et la technique des "Liaisons dangereuses"* (Paris: Klincksieck, 1968); *Le Roman épistolaire* (Paris: Presses Universitaires de France, 1979), 11, 60, 182, 149–67; *Dangerous Acquaintances,* 271.

6. Ronald C. Rosbottom, *Choderlos de Laclos* (Boston: Twayne Publishers, 1978), 18.

7. Lloyd R. Free, ed., *Laclos: Critical Approaches to "Les Liaisons dangereuses"* (Madrid: Porrúa, 1978), 42.

8. In a letter to his son. See Louis de Chauvigny, ed., *Lettres inédites de Choderlos de Laclos* (Paris: Mercure de France, 1904), 295.

9. Laclos had penned the libretto for a disastrous operatic adaptation of Riccoboni's novel *Ernestine.*

10. Isabelle de Charrière, *Suite des Trois Femmes,* in her *Oeuvres complètes,* 9 (Amsterdam: G. A. van Oorschot, 1981), 135.

11. Since completing this essay, I have read what Nancy K. Miller writes along similar lines about Laclos's piece on *Cecilia:* "Although we find here the classic move of putting the woman in her place that Delon et al. repeat, what interests me in Laclos's poetics of the novel is its explicitly bi-sexual approach to comparative literature." See Nancy K. Miller, "Authorized Versions," *French Review* 61:3 (1988): 411.

12. In Aram Vartanian, "The Marquise de Merteuil: A Case of Mistaken Identity," *L'Esprit créateur* 3 (1963): 172–80.

13. How much we would miss were we to take Laclos's word alone for the uniform essence of Riccoboni's corpus is already implicit in their contemporary Mme de Genlis's reading of Fanni Butlerd as "a vehement, passionate woman" who "utterly lacks decency and charm." See Joan Hinde Stewart, intro. to *Lettres de Mistriss Fanni Butlerd,* by Madame Riccoboni (Geneva: Droz, 1979), xix.

10

Graffigny's Epistemology and the Emergence of Third-World Ideology

JANET GURKIN ALTMAN

The way you know who discover America, Nettie say, is think bout cucumbers. That what Columbus sound like. I learned all about Columbus in first grade, but look like he the first thing I forgot. She say Columbus come here in boats call the Neater, the Peter, and The Santomareater. Indians so nice to him he force a bunch of 'em back home with him to wait on the queen.

Alice Walker, *The Color Purple* (1982)

Inventing a New History: The Third-World Epistolarian as Intellectual Heroine

"Historically," as Roland Barthes wrote in *Fragments d'un discours amoureux,* "the discourse of absence has been the province of Woman: Woman is sedentary, Man is a traveler and hunter."[1] Numerous epistolary fictions, beginning with Ovid, have reinforced this classical convention whereby it is Man who travels and Woman who writes from a fixed address (to Him, about Him, about His absence); Man who discovers, explores, and philosophizes, while Woman awaits his messages (about the World); Man who conquers, seduces, and abandons, while Woman responds to His actions of conquest, seduction, and abandonment. Indeed, the fundamental narrative economy of an important strain of epistolary literature is predicated on an interest in documenting Man's acts (as conquest, seduction, abandonment) obliquely and uniquely through His effects on Woman. Ovid's *Letters from Heroines (Heroides),* the *Lettres portugaises,* and the numerous fictions composed solely of a woman's letters to her lover typically document a man's advances and retreats all the more intriguingly by focusing exclusively on a woman's reaction to them.[2] Ovidian heroines draft the epitaphs for their own tombstones as a testimony to their heroes' power; each presents her corpse only as a body killed by the hero and her grave as a memorial to the hero who "slept here."[3] Woman's writing thereby functions as yet another monument to Man's passage, by turning upon the moments when Man passes through her life.

Letters from "heroines"—insofar as they follow the influential paradigm of Ovid's *Heroides* (for example, Dido to Aeneas, Medea to Jason, Briseis to Achilles, Ariadne to Theseus) or later European models like Héloïse, Pamela, and Clarissa—constitute a literature of *reaction* to *actions* undertaken by the conquering heroes with whom their names are linked. The heroines of countless epistolary fictions are locked into erotic dramas that turn primarily around the agency and power of entrepreneurs on whom their destiny depends. Indeed, fundamental to the *story* that these narratives recount is a conception of *history* as manifest destiny, a history where the heroine's body figures as one among many territories traversed and claimed by heroes bent upon building larger empires. When Laclos's Merteuil displays her talents as a female Don Juan in *Les Liaisons dangereuses,* she temporarily reverses the sex roles, but she does not invent any new plots: Merteuil remains within the classic formulae that stage the sexual encounter as conquest by a master.

Western literature has made a heavy investment in *ars amatoria* and erotic narratives based on conquest scenarios. Epistolary fictions have privileged heroines whose letters trace the birth and progression of desire as the ceding of territory to a conqueror. In this area even epistolary heroes, from Saint-Preux and Werther on, have followed suit, investing the soliloquy of passion with new tropes and contexts, as passionate men assume the posture of submission to an authority that overtakes them. For the classical hero(ine) of this scenario, the dénouement typically offers either alliance with the superpower (Pamela's fortune) or despair leading to suicide (Clarissa's lot). Survival as a nonaligned entity capable of nurturing an independent culture is rarely an option.

Occasionally, however, epistolary fictions have overtly challenged the privilege accorded to male conqueror figures in western narratives, not by reversing sex roles and casting woman as conqueror, but by inventing plots that refuse to present history as driven by acts of conquest. One such fiction—Alice Walker's *The Color Purple*—is composed entirely of letters addressed by two black sisters to God or to each other. The younger sister (Nettie) escapes rape, receives an education, and travels to New York, England, and Africa as a missionary living with the Olinka tribe; she writes as a traveler with a shifting global perspective.

The other sister (Celie) is forced to abandon her formal education after a rape; Celie remains in the rural South and writes about her immediate neighbors as they evolve during a thirty-year period.

As epistolary heroines, Nettie and Celie offer a striking contrast to their Ovidian and Richardsonian predecessors. Whereas Pamela, Clarissa, and countless other classical epistolary heroines organize their narratives around the question of "what he did to me," "what will he do next?" or "what I am doing as a consequence of his action," Nettie and Celie's narratives are not driven by the acts of powerful men. Although men exercise power fairly violently in their universe, the sisters lavish their attention as writers upon moments of mold-breaking ferment, healing, and creativity that constitute the possibility of daily living, survival, and pleasure. In the novel these moments occur primarily between black women, but they ultimately transform the relations between the sexes, classes, and races. As Celie and Nettie together learn more about the complex historical relations among Africa, America, and Europe, they write a new history, in which Celie's inability to "know" who "discovered" America wryly exposes the inadequacy of the old history.

One of the compelling aspects of Walker's novel is the way in which Celie's restricted point of view engages reader identification with her position. Because we are limited to her letters and language, we see the world as Celie sees it, we discover it and explore it with her (instead of with Columbus), and we (re)name it with her. In other words, Celie's epistolary epistemology leads us to know the world as she comes to know it, not as she "failed" to know it in school. I would like to turn now to a novel from the French Enlightenment that deployed a comparable epistolary epistemology in a highly original way, at a time when both epistolary novels and epistemological fictions were about to experience their greatest heyday in France.

Purple Like Me: Entering the Peruvian Body of Knowledge

I never saw a Purple cow, I never hope to see one.
But I can tell you anyhow, I'd rather see than be one.

Since we are always predisposed to favor ourselves, we recognize merit in other nations only insofar as their customs imitate ours, only insofar as their language approximates ours. How can a person be Persian?

Françoise de Graffigny, preface to
Les Lettres d'une Péruvienne (1747)[4]

In 1747 a woman who had come to Paris from Lorraine published what was to be her only novel, the *Lettres d'une Péruvienne (Letters of a Peruvian Woman)*. Although it was published at a time when novels were still considered an inferior literary genre in France, the *Lettres d'une Péruvienne* immediately garnered critical esteem in the major literary journals.[5] This unusual novel even inspired some probing reflections by the *philosophes'* favorite political economist and statesman, Turgot. Sixty consecutive editions and translations kept the novel widely read in Enlightenment Europe for the next ninety years.[6] Between 1835 and 1967, however, there were no new editions of this novel. Although the *Lettres d'une Péruvienne* is now available in the Garnier-Flammarion series of literary classics, and it has recently been reprinted in English translation,[7] thus far it has attracted relatively little critical attention.[8]

The novel merits careful consideration, however, as a maverick enterprise in the history of epistolary fictions and in the history of the novel in general, for it constitutes one of the first challenges that was delivered from within European culture to a patriarchal European's ethnocentric perspective on world history. This essay is not the place to compare Graffigny's narrative strategies to those of Enlightenment historians, but we might note that Voltaire's narrator of world history in *Essai sur les moeurs* always recounts events from the European explorer/conqueror's point of view, enumerating the economic gains for Europe and condemning only the massacres, which waste "useful" lives. Moreover, although Voltaire critiques the conquest of Peru, he devotes a great deal of time to narrating that conquest from the European point of view, and he assumes that the subordination of "naturally stupid" Indians to smarter Europeans is historically inevitable and irreversible.[9] The originality of Graffigny's novel, on the other hand, derives from a subtle combination of narrative strategies that urge the reader to relive history as a Peruvian Indian woman might have experienced it from the time of the Spanish conquest, when she undertakes her own ideological resistance to European-imposed authority, until the time when she and other "Peruvians" (i.e., non-Europeans, nonwhites, and women) regain economic and political independence from "European" control.

Yet Graffigny's fiction of a "free Peru" is not written as a utopia. It is written as a psychological novel that seemingly slips into a tradition of epistolary fictions from its period. For this reason, Graffigny's novel has often been dismissed by post-Enlightenment criticism as an undistinguished "imitation" of two better-known novels. In twentieth-century literary histories, the *Lettres d'une Péruvienne* is typically listed as one among many imitations of Montesquieu, and is described as having simply grafted the technique of his *Lettres persanes* (letters from a foreign traveler) upon the technique of the *Lettres portugaises* (letters to a lover). In another article, I have questioned the adequacy of this imitation theory, by reviewing three paradigms that twentieth-century literary criticism has applied in evaluating the *Lettres d'une Péruvienne*.[10] Since the novel: (1) does not employ the amorous discourse of classical heroines' passionate love monologues (from Ovid to Crébillon), or (2) display the encyclopedic range of topics covered by the usual *philosophe* travelers, and (3) since its Peruvian heroine does not characterologically fit the norms established by Montesquieu, Rousseau, and Voltaire for cultural outsiders, thus far critics have generally dismissed Graffigny's novel as unoriginal on the ground that it *adds nothing* and *fails to live up* to these well-known models in Enlightenment fiction. Such a critique, however, implicitly conceives originality only as incrementation that reinforces an established norm.

The seductive norms just outlined have guided evaluation of the novel, but they do not describe Graffigny's choices. Although Graffigny is seen as having fallen short of canonical models for the amorous heroine, the *philosophe,* and the cultural outsider in Enlightenment fiction, in fact her rhetorical strategies constitute a deliberate and innovative deviation from standard literary representations of these types. Most simply put, Graffigny's primary innovation is to have *culturally situated her heroine Zilia within Peruvian history,* a history conceived as *ongoing and unfinished,* a history that she presents as *now residual within European history.* By this formulation I do not mean, of course, that Zilia refers to a person known in Peruvian history as it has come down to us. I mean instead that Graffigny imagines a character who has been formed by that history (including the history of conquest) in psychologically complex and culturally specific ways. As such, Zilia cannot be compared to the noble savage stereotypes that abound in French Enlightenment writing, who are either Hurons or Iroquois only titularly, or who are deliberately situated outside of history in a state of nature. Nor can Zilia be equated with fictional foreign travelers like Montesquieu's Persians and Voltaire's Huron Ingénu, who have already received sophisticated European educations before they arrive in France, who seem to have mastered (or were born knowing) the language of every country they visit, and who travel throughout Europe as free agents. By contrast, Graffigny represents her captive Peruvian heroine as a member of a different culture that has been despoiled by Europeans and come under European carceral control. As such, Graffigny's heroine faces foreign language acquisition and cultural assimilation as identity-altering processes, and she must constantly negotiate her place in a society that has no room for her language and culture.

Although some critical attention has been paid to Graffigny's deviation from the standard dénouement for sentimental novels (by her refusal to marry off her heroine at the end),[11] I would like to focus less on the ending than on the inaugural gestures of the novel. The novel's beginnings, from its two prefaces through its twelfth letter, are hardly ever commented upon, yet they deploy one of the most original writing strategies in French Enlightenment fiction. More importantly, they set the stage, I would argue, for a much more subtle and complex reading of the dénouement than we have yet contemplated, because we have insisted on reading the novel as a sentimental rather than a philosophical fiction. What is at stake in the disposition of Zilia's body, mind, and heart, as Graffigny writes it, is not simply whether or not a female will marry. The place of the female in Graffigny's fiction is also the place of "Peru"—i.e., the space (to be) occupied by peoples who have experienced colonization and cultural expropriation.

Positioning Zilia: The Work of the Prefaces

Let us therefore look more closely at the novel, beginning with its 1747 preface, which first broaches the question of *how readers are to position themselves and their known world* (understood as "Western European culture") in relation to the novel's captive Peruvian heroine, Zilia, and therefore—by extension—what place they will accord to her within history and philosophy *as a person formed by a different culture*. In order to stress just how unusual Graffigny's prefatorial gesture is for the France of 1747, I shall first take a detour through a later preface, one written by Etienne de Condillac in 1754, a warning to the reader that could in many respects have served as a preface to the *Lettres d'une Péruvienne*.

> I therefore warn the reader that it is very important to put yourself exactly in the place of the statue that we are going to observe. You must start to exist with her, have only one sense when she has only one; develop only the ideas that she develops, acquire only the habits that she acquires: *in a word, you must be only what she is.* She will judge things the way we do only when she has all of our senses and all of our experience; and we will judge things the way she does only when we imagine ourselves deprived of everything that she lacks. *I think that the readers who put themselves exactly in her position will have no difficulty understanding this work; the others will raise countless objections.*[12]

Condillac is well known for his role in adapting Locke's theory of human understanding to his own theory that all human thought is nothing but transformed body sensations. The work from which I have just quoted, his *Traité des sensations,* was published seven years after the *Lettres d'une Péruvienne.* In it Condillac creates a fictional character, a statue initially stripped of all her sensing faculties, in order to follow closely the progress of her perceptions of her self and the outside world as each new sense (from smell to touch) is added incrementally. In his prefatory "Important Notice to the Reader," Condillac stresses the rigorously limited subjective point of view that the reader of the *Traité des sensations* must be willing to espouse in order to follow the development of the statue's understanding. Condillac's preface repeatedly emphasizes the need for his readers to identify with the statue's world view at each point in her development. He stresses how crucial it is for readers to put themselves "in the statue's place," in order to avoid substituting their own views for hers.

If I have dealt at length with Condillac's preface, it is not in order to suggest that Condillac was imitating Françoise de Graffigny. The success of Graffigny's similar focalization strategy in the *Lettres d'une Péruvienne* may, of course, have encouraged Condillac's decision to write his *Traité* as a narrative of mental activity, rigorously limited to the perceptual consciousness of a single sensing body that happens to be female.[13] I cite Condillac's *Traité* and its preface, however, because they offer a clear example of an intellectual interest that was beginning to take hold of French philosophic writing around 1750—the effort to focus on the combined role of both the body's physical sensations and its experiential limits in the formation of ideas, knowledge, and judgments concerning the self and the perceived world. It has been traditional to attribute the widespread dissemination in France of this sensation-based psychology of the self and its perceptions to Diderot, Rousseau, Condillac, and the Encyclopedists and to date the beginning of its triumph in France as 1750.[14] Graffigny implements this psychology of perceptual understanding in a most thoroughgoing way in her 1747 novel, and it would therefore be problematic to assume, as many critics have, that she was simply borrowing from *philosophes* who in fact wrote after she did.

Obviously, however, Françoise de Graffigny was part of the same milieu as the Encyclopedist philosophers and she espoused most of their causes. She read many of the same English philosophers and felt a particular affinity for Locke's work. Unlike the well-known French *philosophes,* however, she wrote her philosophy of human understanding as a novel of psychological development, and it is therefore her rhetorical strategies as a novelist that we must scrutinize. Let us return to that preface in which she begins to reveal her method.

Like Condillac in 1754, Graffigny constitutes her 1747 preface as a warning to the reader (*Avertissement*), in which she anticipates the difficulties that her readership may have in suspending its own world view in order to see the world as her Peruvian heroine sees it. The preface that we are advised to read before embarking upon the novel subtly articulates the crucial issue that will in fact ultimately determine critical reception of her work; therefore we must pay close attention to it. It begins as follows:

> *Truth* that deviates from *verisimilitude* ordinarily loses credit in the eye of reason, but not irremediably. However, if truth also goes against *cultural bias {préjugé}*, it rarely finds favor in that court of appeal.
>
> Imagine therefore how concerned the editor of the following work must be, in publishing the letters of a young Peruvian woman whose *style and thoughts* correspond so little to our biased notion of her *nation's* mediocrity.
>
> *Enriched by the precious spoils of Peru,* we should minimally regard the inhabitants of that part of the world as a magnificent people. And the idea of magnificence often inspires the feeling of respect.
>
> But since we are always predisposed to favor ourselves, we recognize merit in other nations only insofar as their customs imitate ours, only insofar as their language approximates ours. How can a person be Persian?
>
> We have contempt for Indians, *we scarcely grant a thinking soul* to those unfortunate peoples. And yet their *history* is available to everyone; it is full of monuments that show the wisdom of their minds and the solidity of their *philosophy*.[15]

Graffigny's initial distinction between documentable truth (*vérité*) and fictional plausibility (the *vraisemblable*) is a commonplace for French novel prefaces of the eighteenth century, where an appeal is often made to the "documented" authenticity of a "real life" in all of its singularity in order to excuse the narrative's deviation from conventional fictional codes (i.e., usually moral norms). However, Graffigny's insistence on pointing out the role of cultural bias (*préjugé*) in defining what is considered acceptable "truth" in storytelling constitutes an unusual effort to move beyond this well established prefatorial cliché for novels. Moreover, as a French Enlightenment writer Graffigny is also making a fairly audacious move for 1747 in openly asserting that even *reason's* judgment does not escape cultural bias, although she is quite in line with militant Enlightenment rhetoric in asserting reason's status as the highest available court of appeal for debating differences of opinion (paragraph 1).

In fact, Graffigny cannot and does not rest her own argument for the "truth" of her story on either the documentable, historical authenticity of her narrative,[16] or on its conformity to conventional codes of verisimilitude that govern novel writing, since she has chosen to narrate a story (the experience of a captive Peruvian Indian woman) for which there are very few precedents in either historical or fictional narratives. Graffigny has chosen this story, however, because her interest lies precisely in the very question of how the lacunae of a society's historical and fictional accounts effectively represent cultural alterity, if only by default, as a *failure* to conform to the known culture's norms.

Thus Graffigny insists throughout the preface on the challenge that her heroine's style and thoughts will offer to the conventional representations of Peruvian culture *as lack* by European culture. The particular bone of contention, as Graffigny articulates it in the five paragraphs quoted above and in the continuation of the preface, is whether or not a people who have been conquered and despoiled by Europeans, whose customs and language cannot be assimilated to European culture, and who have left comparatively fewer of the written documents and monuments that Europeans rely upon to write history, can be considered by Europeans to *have* a history and a philosophy and can be respected as "thinking souls" (paragraph 5). Alluding to the work of those few historians and literary writers who in her view have contributed to a more enlightened representation of Indian peoples (Garcilaso de la Vega, Voltaire, Montaigne), Graffigny offers her narrative to those readers who attempt to live beyond the frontiers (*bornes*) of prejudice's "empire" (paragraphs 5–7).

The "Historical Introduction" that Graffigny added as a further preface to her 1752 definitive edition of the *Lettres d'une Péruvienne* cannot simply be overlooked, as many readers have chosen to do, as the work of another writer, Antoine Bret (the friend of Graffigny who is thought to have written it). The account of Peruvian history offered by this second preface stands between us and the novel as yet another text rhetorically positioning the narrative to follow. No less than the first preface, it points to a "place" for Zilia, located in this instance within Peruvian history. Drawing heavily upon Garcilaso de la Vega's descriptions of Peruvian culture and history up until the time of the Spanish conquest, the "Historical Introduction" introduces an element on which the novel will subtly capitalize—the figure of the woman legislator who shares the throne with her brother-spouse. In the "Historical Introduction," the Peruvian transition from the state of "barbarism" to Inca civilization is attributed to the joint reign of Mancocapac and his wife, Coya-Mama-Otello-Huaco. Son and daughter of the Sun and the Moon, father and mother of Inca civilization, they were sent to earth to create legislation that would organize an enlightened urban and agrarian society; the Inca rulers who succeeded them inherited their responsibilities. This Inca throne, shared by enlightened male and female legislators, is effectively the "place," we shall learn through letters 1 and 2, that the novel's heroine Zilia would have inherited had she remained within Peruvian history.

But even as Zilia enters the novel she is being torn away from Peruvian history, both literally and figuratively. Zilia's first letter situates her as an interrupted Peruvian historian turned epistolarian through an abrupt fall into someone else's history. If we read closely and do not skip Graffigny's footnotes, we realize that the activity that Zilia was engaged in at the precise moment of the Spanish invasion of her temple was "transmitting for posterity the memorable acts of . . . Incas" (letter 1, n. 2). At the dawning of her wedding day Zilia had risen early in order to execute a project conceived the night before—to employ the quipus (knotted cords) normally used for bookkeeping in Inca civilization to create a permanent record of her and her fiancé's "history." Letter 1 makes it clear that the narrative she had begun to knot in the silence of the temple was abruptly interrupted by the Spanish invasion of the temple. We shall never have an opportunity to read her interrupted Peruvian history, for Zilia will subsequently have to resort to reknotting the same quipus as letters to her fiancé, Inca Prince Aza.

In the letters that constitute the novel, Zilia must abandon her Peruvian history in order to write journalistic communiqués relating her capture and her new surroundings, since she is immediately shipped off as captive property to Europe.[17] Her abandoned history remains visible only indirectly as a palimpsest persisting beneath the epistolary narrative that she subsequently knots into quipus: it will be readable only in the form of occasional flashbacks and references to the abandoned culture and in the persistence of an identity formed by that culture. Uprooted from her culture, separated from the fiancé with whom she was to share leadership responsibility for Inca civilization, witness only to the destruction of her civilization, Zilia the chronic writer will forever be deprived of the means to write an Inca chronicle.

What Zilia will write instead is a discourse with the two Others who attract her and who anchor the two cultures with which she must henceforth deal: Peruvian and French. Letters 1 through 36 are addressed to her captive Peruvian fiancé, Aza, from whom she remains separated until letter 37, while letters 37 through 41 are sent to Déterville, her French captor-turned-wooer. Graffigny's narrative economy rigorously limits Zilia's discourse to the form of soliloquy, for within Graffigny's plot Zilia receives almost no responses to her letters: Aza's forwarding address is unknown until letter 25, and by letter 37 he has arrived in person to cut off further dialogue. Déterville races home from Malta before the letters that close the novel reach him. Only one response from Aza and three letters from Déterville are mentioned in the uninterrupted stream of Zilia's letters that compose the novel. Because we read only Zilia's letters, we are rigorously limited to Zilia's stream of mental activity.

Superficially, therefore, insofar as one aspect of Graffigny's narrative technique is concerned, Zilia's letters can be compared to the slow-traveling letters written by the Portuguese nun or by Montesquieu's Persian ruler, Usbek, to interlocutors in a distant country from whom they have been painfully separated and who are comparably slow to respond. Indeed, this may be one of the resemblances—beyond the fortuitous alliteration of P's in the three titles (Portuguese, Persian, Peruvian letters)—that have led literary historians to assume that Graffigny was simply imitating the *Lettres portugaises* and the *Lettres persanes*. However, Zilia's dialogue with the distant and slow-to-respond Other departs significantly from both the "Portuguese" and the "Persian" traditions of novel writing that Graffigny is so regularly considered as having merely copied. For Zilia's discourse *with* the bodily Other(s) abroad (Peruvian fiancé left behind, French wooer who has departed for Malta) is also a discourse *of* the linguistic Other(s) that are layered within her. Hers is the discourse of the bilingual self that speaks the mother tongue ("Peruvian") even while translating into the language of the more recently acquired culture (French). To both Aza and Déterville, Zilia speaks of a "France" in which "Peruvians" can live, provided they retain their critical ability to operate dialectically within both cultures. Zilia's doubled discourse of the self is neither schizophrenic (as Usbek's Persian and French identities have been seen to be)[18] or hysteric (as the Portuguese nun's language has been so subtly analyzed to be).[19] For Zilia's doubled discourse actively keeps her differing cultural voices together in delicate balance, in a universe that more than once threatens her poise.

Strikingly absent from Graffigny's novel, in which a female writes to an absent male, is the rigid delimitation and opposition of male and female spaces, identities, and spheres of activity that so frequently structure more familiar narratives of desire (including the *Lettres persanes* and the *Lettres portugaises*) as battles in which one sex must triumph over the other. Whether Zilia writes to her captive Peruvian fiancé or to her French captor-turned-wooer, she systematically refuses the language of conquest, possession, and triumph that hierarchizes relationships in a self-perpetuating master-slave dichotomy. Emblematic is Zilia's bemused comment on French gallantry early in the novel. Trying to puzzle out why Déterville has fallen to his knees beside her, she speculates: "Could it be that this Nation . . . *worships* women? . . . But if they adored me, would they add to my misfortunes the *awful constraint* in which they *confine* me?" (letter 5). Later in the novel she will investigate at greater length the contradiction between simultaneous veneration and scorn that appears to govern French society's attitudes toward women (letters 33 and 34). For the time being, however, in her earliest encounter with the problem, Zilia simply concludes that these French "savages" must be in the same developmental stage that Peruvians were in before the arrival of their enlightened male and female legislators, the state of barbarism when they superstitiously "*deified* everything that *struck* them with *fear* or *pleasure*" (letter 5). Zilia's aphoristic formulation does not call attention to itself, in the way that a maxim by La Rochefoucauld would. Yet rarely has the master-slave model for human relationships been so concisely and mockingly described—as the persistence of a superstitious attitude toward beings who initially "strike" us with fear or pleasure.

From the above formulation we can further observe that as early as letter 5 Zilia is actively questioning a "worship" that leads to forced confinement of "gods" and their magic properties. Zilia herself will resolutely resist the language of deification by insisting on behaving as an equal partner with her interlocutors. Although Zilia is nominally a captive throughout most of the novel, her language of assumed equality and reciprocity, as well as the type of resistance plot that Graffigny chooses for her, enables Zilia to escape from the master-slave (or subject-object) model that governs so many other narratives of desire. Zilia is thereby freed to use her various environments of captivity and confinement to develop her self-consciousness, critical understanding, and political freedom in significantly different terms from the model offered by the conventional captive heroines of Enlightenment fictions. For Zilia will never cease to view herself as a citizen critically engaged in the life of a "nation," even during the long periods when she finds herself a woman without a country. A closer look at the way that Zilia experiences her confined environments will bring Zilia's new, subtly politicized, language of self-positioning more closely into focus.

From Peruvian Cloister to French Coach (Letters 1–12): Re-placing the Self on the Map of the World

Graffigny's narrative begins right away in letter 1 with the act in a confined space that so many other eighteenth-century novels suspensefully defer: the profanation of the resisting virgin in her sacred temple cloister. When we first encounter Zilia just after the Spanish conquest, the bloody violence has been done, yet the crimes that inspire Zilia's horror and outrage are described as political and social crimes. They are never described as sexual rape; indeed, the question of whether or not there has been sexual rape in this temple is not raised at all by the narrative. Instead, Graffigny's representation opts for a more epic vision of the destruction of an entire civilization, for which Zilia's royal and sacred body (like Hector's similarly dragged body in the *Iliad*) is a crucial metonymy.

> As soon as I tried to leave, I felt an impediment: Oh, dear Aza, the memory still makes me shake! those blasphemers dared to put their sacrilegious hands on the daughter of the Sun.
>   Torn from the sacred dwelling, *dragged ignominiously* outside the temple, I saw for the first time the threshold of the celestial door that I was supposed to cross only in royal dress. *Instead of* the flowers that would have been strewn in my path, I saw avenues covered with blood and dying people; *instead of* sharing the honor of a throne with you, I am a slave of tyranny, locked up in a dark [*obscure*] prison: *the place that I occupy in the universe is limited to the extent of my being.* A straw mat soaked with my tears is all that greets a body fatigued by anguish. (letter 1)

Economically written in the tight classical tradition of the *Heroides,* Zilia's first letter turns in numerous ways on the simple figure of dramatic reversal of expectation: anticipating her bridegroom when the temple doors are thrust open on her wedding day, Zilia encounters instead the looting Spanish soldiers. Expecting to leave her Inca cloister in order to ascend to the throne, Zilia is instead dragged past the bloody bodies of her people and deposited on the straw mat of a prison.

Like many of Ovid's heroines, Zilia repeatedly spirals back in her narrative discourse to the moment that reversed her fate, what she calls the "terrible moment that should have been effaced from the chain of time" (letter 1). However, unlike Ovid's heroines, who tend to view their fate as sealed by that past moment (*illa dies*),[20] Zilia invents a language devoted less to the past chronology of the self than to the space that the momentarily stunned self now occupies. The language of spatial replacement in which she re-articulates her experience of dramatic reversal (blood in lieu of flowers, prison mat in lieu of throne) is linguistically simple and terse, but the existential drama of resituating herself within the obscure new "universe" in which she suddenly finds herself is more complex and time-consuming. Indeed, it will occupy the whole novel.

In one sense, the "place" in which Zilia first finds her self at the end of her first letter will not vary throughout the novel, and for a good reason: Zilia's sudden and tersely stated recognition in the passage just quoted, that *"the place that I occupy in the universe is limited to the extent of my being,"* is a philosophically basic but interpretively open proposition. Strategically speaking, however, this discovery is the founding statement for the entire narrative, whose burden will be to invest and reinvest Zilia's perceptions of her being and of her universe with experiential contexts and referents.

Thus, contextually speaking, Zilia's first discovery of her being in letter 1 is reduced to the dimensions of her fatigued, despoiled, and uprooted body. Her universe is a minimally furnished dark prison that she cannot locate on her internal map. Like Clarissa, who finds herself similarly despoiled and disoriented at a much later point in Richardson's novel, Zilia's first move is to make epistolary contact with the outside world. The resemblance between Clarissa and Zilia stops here, however, for Graffigny imagines a heroine who is more politically bonded to that outside world than Clarissa. Zilia is therefore less hateful of a self[21] that has been only momentarily despoiled in Graffigny's narrative (as opposed to endlessly degraded, disinherited, and invaded by the outside world in Richardson's). Thus Zilia more quickly succeeds in renewing contact with another being whose confirmed existence will give renewed meaning and orientation to hers. Between letter 1 and letter 2 she succeeds in exchanging letters with Aza.

Zilia's first letter and Aza's implied response to it will be the only lovers' letters that immediately reach their addressees in the novel, but they are sufficient to inspire Zilia's sustained and sustaining discourse with her absent Other until she and Aza finally get together between letters 36 and 37. For letter 2 reestablishes Zilia's identity as Aza's intended spouse and co-ruler in two important ways: not only through Aza's epistolary confirmation of the bond but also through Zilia's flashback narrative, in which she relates their two-year courtship and the rigorous education by which she was prepared to share the throne as Aza's equal. In letter 2 Zilia uses her education and knowledge to warn Aza against the "error" of taking the Spaniards for the gods that they appear and claim to be. The "extent of Zilia's being" reinstated by the end of letter 2 is therefore her epistolary being-with-Aza, and her "universe" is the "free" Peruvian kingdom that she urges him to maintain together with her in an exiled government of two, rather than to collaborate with the Spanish conquerors.

In her first prison, therefore, Zilia is still within a state that she can call Peru. This first confined space, immediately recognizable to her as a prison near Aza, permits both communication with her coruling lover and the hope of reinstating a kingdom within Peruvian borders. However, by letter 3 Zilia has once again been torn away from the confined environment in which she had so quickly reoriented herself, and she is transferred to another closed space. Her disorientation in this new environment, which moves incessantly and nauseatingly, is even more radical. And Zilia's despair upon realizing that this new prison will not permit her to correspond with Aza, combined with her physical discomfort, brings her close to death.

It is certainly easy for us as readers to recognize that the "hard-to-reach house"[22] that feels as if it is prodigiously "rocking in suspension and detached from the earth" is a boat. Perhaps precisely because it is so easy for us to understand what we think Zilia is being so naïve about in her descriptions, twentieth-century readers have concluded that Graffigny is being quite unoriginal in the passages where she has Zilia describe European objects that are new to her. After all, as the argument against Graffigny's originality seems to go, all the *ingénus* in Enlightenment literature rely on periphrasis: indeed, we might not recognize them for *ingénus* if they didn't use such periphrasis. We've all heard the one about the boat, the one about the mirror, the one about the telescope, and they don't make us laugh any more. The foreign travelers who regale us with their descriptions of European objects in Voltaire, the Théâtre de la Foire, and Montesquieu are much funnier—or so the objection seems to go.

But what we may be temporarily forgetting if we hastily dismiss Zilia's naïve descriptions of European objects as unoriginal is that Graffigny is not writing comedy or satire. She is not simply using a circumlocution that is different from the proper language in order to let us laugh at the child who hasn't learned our language yet. Indeed, Zilia will later question the pleasure that French parents seem to take in maintaining and displaying naïveté as a form of entertainment (in letter 34), although Graffigny never goes so far as Rousseau in imposing a seriousness that rejects comedy and satire. Graffigny's chosen rhetoric for Zilia remains quizzical, rather than accusatory and homiletic (as in Rousseau) or satirical (as in Voltaire, Montesquieu, and the Théâtre de la Foire).

Still, as some readers object, why is Graffigny so "uninventive" as to have Zilia confront European objects that we have already seen non-Europeans confront in Enlightenment literature? And why does she "bore" us by having Zilia describe these objects at such length? When we accuse Graffigny of being unoriginal or boring in her insistent use of Enlightenment *ingénu topoi*, however, I would argue that we have forgotten the broader narrative context and figural economy within which Graffigny inscribes Zilia's naïve descriptions of her environment. For within Graffigny's overarching rhetorical strategy in the early letters, the description of each new foreign object encountered—the boat, the telescope, the coach, the mirror, and so forth—is a deliberate rewriting of Zilia's previous encounters with similar objects and environments. In each of the passages in question, Zilia's descriptions constitute her intellectual effort to resituate her body within a universe transformed by mysterious technologies that alter her previous understandings of both herself and that universe.

Thus I would argue that Zilia's account of her being and her universe in each of the early letters constitutes some of the most *phenomenal* writing in the novel, in both accepted senses of the word. Zilia offers rather extraordinary phenomenological descriptions of those activities around her that she cannot puzzle out. As a historian concerned to record every detail that could be useful for Peruvian annals,[23] in these passages Zilia shows a concern to distinguish between description of event and interpretation; she is reluctant to risk what might be an overhasty interpretation of events that she realizes she is experiencing in a fragmented way. In the following passage, the italized locutions suggest the way in which Zilia's language lucidly *acknowledges* the *limits* of her *knowledge*.

> A *fairly long* period of time had elapsed, I was almost over my illness, when I was torn from my sleep one morning by a noise worse than Yalpa's: our dwelling received a shock from it *like the one* that the earth will receive when the moon falls and reduces the universe to dust. Human cries increased this din and made it all the more terrible; my senses, seized with a secret horror, *communicated to my mind only the idea* of a total destruction of nature. *I believed* the peril was universal; I trembled for your life. My fears reached the final peak of *excess* at the sight of a troop of furious men with bloody faces and clothes, who noisily crashed into my room. I was unable to bear this horrible spectacle; strength and knowledge/consciousness [*la connaissance*] abandoned me: I *still do not know the consequences* of this terrible event. When I came to my senses, I found myself in a rather clean bed, surrounded by several savages who were no longer the cruel Spaniards, but who were *no less known to me*. (letter 3)

Even as she attempts to assimilate to a Peruvian cosmology what she is witnessing, and even as she reacts emotionally to catastrophes that closely resemble the apocalyptic destruction predicted by her religion, Zilia questions the adequacy of both the Peruvian cosmology and of her own limited viewpoint to explain what she is experiencing or to establish a chronology.

Moreover, as sophisticated readers, even we cannot know at this point (in letter 3) that Zilia is simply offering a naïve account of the takeover of her Spanish boat by soldiers who have transferred her to a French boat. We have no greater ground for identifying a nation called "France" than she has. At this point in the narrative Graffigny has made certain that we will not profit from a knowledge that we might consider superior to Zilia's. Therefore it is hard for us to call this passage a "tale told by an idiot," either in Shakespeare's pejorative sense (absurd noise "signifying nothing") or in the Faulknerian sense (another version of a story that we've already heard). This passage, where Graffigny limits our knowledge to Zilia's prudent activity of detection and intellection, makes a clear point about all of Zilia's naïve descriptions: they are plausibly the work of a Peruvian historian-turned-journalist, who is trying to be intellectually responsible in distinguishing between what she can report on adequately and what she knows that she cannot describe. As such, Zilia's environmental descriptions are quite unique in the history of the eighteenth-century French novel.

In the early part of the novel (letters 1–12), each letter recounts a new discovery that (1) shakes Zilia's sense of where she is in relation to her known world and (2) makes her radically question the adequacy of her past education to describe the new world that she is experiencing. Most of Zilia's discoveries are catalyzed by encounters with objects developed by European technology, which her own culture had given her no ground for understanding. Thus in letter 6, in which her new captors finally give her the "freedom" she had strained after to get up from her sickbed, she immediately heads for the window to learn more about where she is. The view of the sea stretching around her enables her to understand better and therefore to fear less the cause of her physical nausea, as she infers that she is in "one of those floating houses that the Spanish used to reach our unfortunate provinces, *which had been only imperfectly described to me.*"

This reasoned conclusion, in which Zilia further questions the adequacy of her past informants, only partially relieves her, however, for it provokes a more terrifying, although equally reasoned hypothesis—the fear that she is no longer on Aza's map or in his history. "I am certain that they are putting distance between you and me; I am no longer breathing the same air, I no longer inhabit the same element; you will never know where I am, whether I love you, whether I exist; *the destruction of my being will not even appear an event important enough to be reported to you*" (letter 6). Cast adrift in a world that does not appear to be part of Peru or the Peruvian cosmos, Zilia's sense of the "extent of her being" within the universe reaches its nadir of nothingness; even her death will be a non-event, taking place on no one's map, in no one's history. In the intensity of her pre-Kierkegaardian sickness unto death, her pre-Sartrean nausea, Zilia attempts to throw herself overboard.[24]

Letter 7 announces Zilia's survival, thanks to her vigilant bodyguards, in terms still strikingly close to Sartre's formulation of the psychosomatic feeling of superfluity, of being *de trop.* "I am afraid that *my body is taking up too much space;* I would like to remove it from the light." Zilia's philosophic and physical disquietude is only increased by the fact that she is the constant object of stares by people whose language she does not understand. Her feeling of isolation is further augmented by the contrast between her own melancholy and her captors' inexplicably sudden festive behavior upon contemplating the sky in strange ways and with instruments that she cannot fathom. Letters 6 and 7 taken together, then, constitute the most intense reduction of being that Zilia will experience. On the boat she is convinced that she has been irreparably severed from her known universe, and she has no cognitive or affective ground for bonding with the new universe surrounding her. She describes her unrelieved anxiety as "a sea of uncertainties" (letter 10), with a simple metaphor that has nonetheless accrued considerable contextual value.

Letter 8 introduces Zilia to another instrument of European technology, the telescope. Zilia rejoices in the "assistance" that "this marvelous machine" gives to her eyes; her joy at the sheer pleasure of enhancing her body's vision is amplified by the related pleasure of having something to see with this instrument—land. Land for her spells both a retrospective understanding of what everyone else on the ship was so happy about, and the hope that she can get to Aza. Zilia is anxious to determine whether she is about to land in one of those distant parts of Peru that she has heard about, where people speak a different language from hers. Since her cosmology has taught her that all lands under the sun are Inca, and since the sun is shining on this land, she has no ground yet to conclude that she is not on Inca territory. Indeed, the deferential treatment that she has received from her French captors encourages Zilia's hope that they may be part of her nation and planning to escort her back to Aza. Zilia carefully observes the topography in order to describe it for Aza, finding that it conforms thus far to some of the descriptions of distant Peruvian territory that she has heard in the past. Thus Graffigny, like Alice Walker, wryly rewrites the Columbus story, this time with a Peruvian heroine as the explorer who is unable to distinguish between continents but who is inclined to claim the territory all the same.

Zilia's euphoric style that begins to take over in letter 8 is an important phenomenon. I would argue that it is only partially determined by the marriage plot (getting Zilia married to Aza or to Déterville), which almost all critics have seen as the narrative's only driving force. Indeed, the letters we have looked at thus far (1–8) have already suggested a quite different principle of narrative organization from the marriage plot. For although Zilia's writing is certainly motivated by her hope of reunion with her fiancé, even her flashback descriptions of their amorous encounters indicate that it was her mind as well as her body that were riveted by Aza. Letter 2 leaves no doubt that the erotic pleasures Zilia and Aza enjoyed together were mental as well as physical, enhanced by "conversations" (*entretiens*) when they were together, and by quipu letters when they were separated. Letter 2 not only describes their first encounter as a simultaneous exchange of glances *at equal height* of *equal physical desire* ("I dared to lift my glance to your height, and my eyes met yours. . . . our souls . . . met and were fused in a single instant"). That letter also describes, in similarly erotic terms, the pleasure of knotting and unknotting the quipus that pass between them, as Zilia receives Aza's letter: "The treasures of Love are open to me: I draw from them a delicious inebriating joy. In unknotting the secrets of your heart, my own bathes in a perfumed sea."

At this point, physical and mental pleasures are inseparable for Zilia. She describes both as animated by the same principle of "fire" and "light" that she considers to constitute her and Aza's similarly composed selves as representatives of the Sun: "If we were able to doubt our origin, my dear Aza, that shaft of light would challenge our uncertainty. What other principle than fire could have transmitted to us this intense understanding of each other's hearts [*cette vive intelligence des coeurs*], communicated, diffused, and felt with such inexplicable speed?" However, Zilia will come to enjoy the pleasure of writing (described as a very physical one for as long as she uses quipus) for its own sake, increasingly independent of its umbilical connection with Aza. Part of the work of the novel is to turn Zilia's gravitation away from Aza as the Peruvian Sun and center of her existence toward the Sun of the European Enlightenment as Graffigny imagines it, a decentered and diffused Sun that may not be so different from the Inca Sun as Zilia experienced it, after all.

Thus we should not ignore the importance of Zilia's simple but insistent apostrophe, in which she constantly addresses Aza as the "dear light of [her] life." We are far from the banality of the courtly or religious cliché that predicates love on a blinding, debilitating stroke of lightning, and which grounds knowledge on a single, transcendently illuminating vision. In fact, Aza never was the source of enlightenment for Zilia. His occasionally fiery but always warming glance simply provided the stimulating, challenging, and supportive environment in which she arduously acquired an education from the same tutors who tutored him. "Without the desire to deserve your respect, your trust, by qualities that strengthen love, qualities that become voluptuous through love, I would only be an object for your eyes" (letter 2). Zilia describes her ongoing education as having been a source of daily exhilarating pleasure for both her and Aza in their conversations. And it is her desire to continue to grow, learn, and communicate her knowledge that will nourish Zilia's will to live throughout the novel. Her own letters of "enlightenment" to Aza must be understood in this broader erotic context.

Beginning with letter 8, then, a euphoric style takes over and energizes Zilia's writing with the knowledge that her thoughts can *go somewhere:* by letter 9 she herself describes her emergence from a state of lethargic, unmarked, unmappable nothingness (*néant*) in which she could not think, keep track of time, or describe any distinguishing aspects of her environment to a state in which she "savors the pleasure . . . of recovering the faculty of thinking." Zilia officially attributes her joy solely to the renewed hope of seeing Aza, but the juxtapositions of her letter reveal another source of pleasure: "Two days ago, I started to understand some words of the *Cacique*'s [Déterville's] language." Her exhilaration at being able to communicate, even inadequately, with another human being is only slightly dampened by the fact that this new language is giving her no linguistic reinforcement for her hope that "France" (where she now knows her boat is about to land) is part of "Peru."

In fact, as Zilia works through the dilemma that her quest for knowledge is posing—the recognition that knowledge may bring unpleasant revelations—she reveals the deep commitment of her body to this enterprise of learning to speak the Other's language.

> I had resolved to stop thinking; but how can you stop the movement of a soul that has been deprived of all communication, that acts only upon itself, and whose reflections are stimulated by such crucial questions? I can't stop, my dear Aza, I seek knowledge [*des lumières*] with a devouring energy, and I constantly find myself in the deepest ignorance [*obscurité*]. . . . Could it be that the ability to understand a foreign language is the same thing as the ability to understand a soul? (letter 8)

The basic euphoria that takes over in letter 9 thus coincides with Zilia's first successful attempts at communicating in the language used by those around her, a language that pleasurably augments the "extent of her being" and increases her understanding of where both she and others are on the map of the universe.

In the following letter, Zilia descends from her boat into another

closed space, a room in an inn, where she will encounter another strange
European object, the mirror. Zilia's mirror stage was one of the most
appealing scenes to the eighteenth-century public, one that Goldoni
privileged in his dramatization of Graffigny's work. Twentieth-century
critics call it unoriginal, citing the fact that Prévost had already had a
woman naïvely encounter this marvel in *Histoire d'une Grecque moderne*
(1741). Prévost, however, presents a beautiful Sicilian woman who has
been locked up to expiate her grandmother's and mother's sexual sins by
preserving her own chastity. Since her guardians have denied her the use
of a mirror, she first discovers her sexual charms when a merchant gives
her a mirror, and she is immediately seduced by a knight who learns
about her through the merchant. All of this takes place in two pages of
text.

In Graffigny, on the other hand, the mirror experience is not elided
with a sexual access plot. Nor is it the inevitable catalyst whereby women
assume an overdetermined (hereditary and environmental) identity as
prostitutes, as in Prévost. In Graffigny the mirror encounter is instead
carefully woven into the experience of culturally identifying self and
other that is absorbing Zilia's psychic life at this point in the narrative.
Zilia ecstatically takes her mirror image for another Peruvian woman and
rejoices at the thought that she has in fact landed in Peru. When she
discovers the literally "hard" truth of the mirror as she attempts to
embrace its cold surface, her meditations turn upon the reflection that
she perceives of Déterville touching her in order to teach her about the
mirror, "so close" when her eyes turn directly toward him and yet "so
distant" as reflected in the mirror. This experience in turn spawns further
questions concerning the relation between her culture, in its presumed
ignorance, and a culture whose technologies and knowledge can make
fools of Indians. The mirror letter (letter 11), however, ends on an
upbeat note as Zilia rejoices in a new contact with a real other woman
(described as her first female contact since leaving the temple), a girl
whom Déterville hires as a servant-companion for Zilia. Zilia suspends
judgment, pending further information, concerning her fear that this girl
is not Peruvian.

The early letters of the novel move Zilia from one confined environment to another, at the rhythm of one new setting per letter (with the
exception of the boat setting in letters 3 through 9, where each letter
introduces a new perspective on the unmappable boat environment).
Letter 11 exposes Zilia to yet another confined space—a French salon,
presumably in the seaside town where she and Déterville have landed.
Here she is examined as a curiosity and taught to behave according to
French codes. Zilia describes the salon environment in considerable

ironic detail, always in comparison to her previously known world of confined environments, distinguishing this one as "a larger room" than she has been in before. She cleverly picks up on Déterville's indications for performing in this room, although she finds them silly. She cooperates in this instance simply because she does not want to "embarrass a nation that has learned so little about Peruvian customs."

The next letter (12) offers Zilia one of the most euphoric experiences of the novel—a ride in a coach. Her account bears comparison to Proust's descriptions of the way that travel in coaches, cars, and trains alters perception.[25] At first Zilia assimilates the movement of this "machine or hut, I don't know what to call it" to the boat. Her first reaction is therefore intense fear of nausea, but as soon as she has understood the principles of the coach's movement she begins to relish the accelerated view of "the beauties of the universe" that this machine gives her. The coach ride from the seashore to Paris exposes Zilia for the first time to the natural world that she had never been allowed to see in her Peruvian temple. Zilia critiques that Peruvian confinement. Yet even as she relishes the expanded sense of self that traveling and contact with natural wonders afford her, Zilia questions the very feeling of omnipotence that she describes.

> Nature must have endowed her creations with an unknown attraction that the most skillful art work cannot imitate. . . . The immense country landscapes, which are constantly changing and renewing themselves before my eyes, carry my soul toward their shifting horizons with the same swiftness as I feel in the coach that is speeding us through this countryside.
>
> The eyes scan, embrace, and effortlessly settle upon an infinite variety of attractive objects. *One believes* that the only limit to one's view are the limits of the entire world. *This error flatters us:* it gives us *a satisfying idea of our own grandeur* and *seems to make us resemble the Creator of so many marvels.* . . . we enjoy the universe *as if* we alone possessed it; we do not see anything in it that does not belong to us. (letter 12)

This letter, which continues with sensuous descriptions of a walk in the woods and the stages of reverie induced by sunset, is typically cited as pre-Rousseauist and pre-Romantic in its attitudes toward nature. Yet what has thus far escaped notice is that even while relishing the delicious sensations inspired by contact with nature, and even while communicating contagiously the "voluptuous feeling" that the view from a coach or a high mountain gives her, Zilia questions the *illusion of omnipotence* that can be induced by this pleasure. As a sensually excited body, Zilia writes to share her pleasure with Aza, but she questions any effort to translate the illusion of omnipotence provoked by this pleasure into the idea that one is godlike or owns the world. Thus Graffigny effectively inscribes a critique of certain aspects of Romanticism within her own seemingly Romantic writing. This critique in turn is part of Zilia's broader questioning of the right claimed by individuals, predicated upon their feeling or the appearance of omnipotence, to establish exclusive territorial claims over universes where other people also live.

Thus, by the end of letter 12, the epistemological foundations are laid for the remainder of Graffigny's novel, in which—letter by letter and with lucid increments—still further issues are introduced. Zilia becomes increasingly knowledgeable and therefore increasingly wary concerning the limits of her and others' knowledge. The drama of cultural assimilation also intensifies, as Zilia critiques her Peruvian education while nonetheless using it as a yardstick to trace the even greater disparities that she perceives in France between the education of men and the education of women, between social classes, and between appearances and realities in the linguistic and economic ostentation of luxury. Insofar as Zilia's critiques of French society are concerned, I believe that it would be difficult to sustain the argument advanced by Gianni Nicoletti and others, that Zilia is "destroyed" by the "inauthenticity" of French culture, which does not measure up to her Peruvian ideals. Those who pursue the latter argument attempt to subsume Graffigny's ideology within what they perceive to be Rousseau's system of oppositions. Zilia is, on the contrary, exhilarated by French intellectual, artistic, and technological developments and she forms close bonds with people who she ultimately decides, in all lucidity, are members of her own nation after all. In Graffigny's ultimate dénouement, Zilia figures as the self-determined Peruvian-now-resident within France, representing her culture to Europe as equal partner in a reciprocal exchange of ideas.

Graffigny's novel simply questions the assumption that Enlightenment should travel in one direction only—outward from European minds. Through Zilia, Graffigny advances the notion that there might be a Peruvian enlightenment—a language, history, and philosophy worth preserving, studying, and disseminating to western Europe. The Peruvian that Graffigny imagines considers that "barbarism" and "savage" are simply what one culture calls the other culture's prejudices, and Zilia reserves those epithets in her own writing only for people not yet capable of conceiving other cultures as equal to their own. What Zilia's writing accomplishes, at least in the fiction, is nothing less than the abolishment of the ideology of cultural inequality, as she and her interlocutors practice respect for cultural difference and become each other's teachers.

In the title of this essay, I implied that Graffigny's novel offers an epistemology from which an ideology emerges. In a strict sense, of course, Graffigny is not contributing to epistemological inquiry, because she is not writing as a philosopher. However, Graffigny was writing at a time when the labels *philosophe* and *philosophique* were being appropriated for special uses in France, as they were extended to writers and forms of writing that were outside the traditional institutions of philosophy. I know of no better way to describe Graffigny's novelistic strategy than to call it an epistemological fiction. Graffigny's narrative proceeds as a thinking being's rigorous investigation of the nature, grounds, limits, and validity of the knowledge that she has been given by one culture, fueled by her encounters with another culture. Eschewing the assumption that one culture's body of knowledge is superior to another's, Graffigny's intellectual heroine is willing to conclude only that all cultures can benefit from cross-cultural education. Her premise and conclusion constitute an ideology, if by ideology we mean a set of ideas and representations that can influence a group or national culture, shaping especially their political and social procedure. The ideology that emerges from Graffigny's fiction, furthermore, differs perceptibly from the ideology governing many other Enlightenment narratives. In order to make this final point about Graffigny's *difference,* I shall compare her epistemological fiction to a similar textual strategy as deployed by Buffon.

Buffon vs. Graffigny: The Restoration of First-World Ideology

In 1749, two years after Graffigny's novel was published, Buffon incorporated what he called a *récit philosophique* (short philosophic tale) in his *Histoire naturelle* in order to illustrate how the first man, on the day he was created, might have formed ideas and judgments based on his body sensations. Introducing the tale, Buffon stresses how important it is to let the man speak for himself, in the first person, in order to reconstruct "the history of man's first thoughts" and to "make the facts more concrete." Like Graffigny, Buffon limits his narrative to a first-person account of ideas in process, ideas that the narrator articulates and progressively corrects or questions.

Buffon's narrative is part of the section of *Histoire naturelle* that he devoted to "The Senses in General," and it follows an arithmetic model that would be used by more than one *philosophe*. Buffon imagines what perception would be like as Adam[26] adds each of the five senses incrementally, in this case from sight to taste. Adam's primary concern, as

Buffon elaborates it, is to augment his personal "pleasure" by including as much of the universe as possible within his own self. His intense pleasure upon opening his eyes at the moment of creation derives from his perception that all the objects that he sees "were in me and were part of me" (114). When he closes his eyes, he grieves the resulting loss of his self, but he is soon consoled by the sounds that he hears, since they induce the pleasurable sensation that "this harmony was me." Upon reopening his eyes, Adam recovers the "joy of finding myself once again in *possession* of so many brilliant objects." Blinking produces yet another thrill in Adam, the idea that he has a demiurgic power to destroy and recreate the world: "*I had the power to destroy and to reproduce* at will that beautiful part of myself." The addition of the sense of smell gives Adam "an interior expansion" that further augments his "love for myself" (115).

Adam soon discovers, however, what he calls the "limits of my existence" (115) through the combined additions of movement and touch. For Adam, this discovery of limits, this realization that there are bodies outside his own, constitutes the most unpleasant experience of his life. When he bumps into a tree that turns out to be a "foreign body" (*corps étranger*) different from his own, he feels "horror" as he discovers "for the first time that there was something outside of myself" (117). Adam is so humiliated by the discovery of a being that resists incorporation into his own body, and so fatigued by his unsuccessful attempts to use his latest sense (touch) to reach the sun, that he sinks to the ground beneath a tree.

The sense of touch, according to Buffon, is the "sense that rectifies all the other senses" and permits man to acquire "complete and real knowledge" (114). This proposition, which Buffon had stated before embarking upon his narrative, is presumably what his fable is designed to illustrate. Yet Buffon's fable exceeds his proposition, for the narrative continues beyond the incremental knowledge offered by touch. In fact, in Buffon's narrative, touch is not the crowning sense that completes Adam's epistemological quest and provides him with "real knowledge." For when Adam acquires touch he has not yet acquired taste. This fifth sense is acquired only after Adam uses touch to seize a fruit that he suddenly notices near his hand, which is ripe for the plucking. Even before tasting the fruit Adam is delirious with pleasure, for by holding the fruit in his hand he has recovered some of his sense of power over the world: "I imagined that I had made a conquest, and I glorified myself for *my ability to contain within my hand another whole being*; its weight, although not great, seemed to me *an animated resistance that I took pleasure in defeating*" (117). Pleasure for Adam, it would seem, consists in locating beings that are "lightweight" enough to enable him to "defeat" their "animated resistance."

The being that Adam is about to conquer is also a very tasty being, as he soon discovers. Its tastiness, however, functions uniquely to prove a crucial bit of knowledge for Adam: that his own body "possesses . . . a superior inner sense of smell" (117). Adam's pleasure augments as he brings the fruit closer and closer to his mouth and inhales its perfume from his mouth in a slowly played out scene of *dégustation*. Adam reaches the ecstasy of a climax only when he consumes the fruit: "finally I tasted." This is indeed the crowning moment for Adam: "up until then I had had only pleasures, [*plaisirs*], taste gave me the feeling of voluptuousness [*volupté*]; the intimacy of this pleasure [*jouissance*] gave birth to the idea of possession; I believed that the substance of the fruit had become my own, and that I was the master of transforming beings" (118). Adam's pleasures and pains—always defined in terms of his *power to incorporate* other beings within his own body—determine the formation of his ideas, and Buffon's narrative makes it clear that the most important idea that Adam's experience gives birth to is the idea of possession of other beings.

The encounter with Eve that terminates the fable is merely an extension of Adam's crucial discovery of the kind of power and mastery that he can rely upon to affirm his existence in the world. Adam experiences Eve as a double of himself, who is "better than I" because he can "animate" her with his own hand (i.e., she is like the fruit that he held earlier) and because he can make her reproduce yet another image of himself that allays his fear of death. Like the fruit, Eve enables Adam to assert his power to transform beings and extend his dominion over the world.

With his Adam narrative, as in other parts of the *Histoire naturelle,* Buffon recounts the traditional conquest scenario with a new twist. For what Buffon outlines is a narrative of manifest destiny in which "civilized" (i.e., technologically refined) masters are educated for a single, driving purpose: to conquer nature, triumph over all savage opposition, and populate the world with images of themselves. This scenario is fairly apparent in the sections of *Histoire naturelle* that Buffon devotes to "Wild Animals" (1756), "Negroes" (1749), and "Savages and Society" (1749), where he argues that civilization must ultimately triumph over all wildlife, that Negroes are by nature mentally deficient but work harder on plantations if they are treated kindly by their masters, and that savages— in spite of what some travelers' reports say—have no ideas, language, customs, laws, or "master" that would compel Europeans to recognize them as a "nation" or even as a "society." Indeed, in "Savages and Society" (1749) Buffon rejects as absurd the notion that savages have any ideas or possess a language other than cries. He is convinced that "it must be easier for a savage to understand and to speak the language of all other savages than it is for a man living in a civilized nation to learn the language of another equally civilized nation" (144–45). Buffon therefore concludes, with the authority of a person confident in his knowledge, that it is "useless to investigate the customs and manners of these so-called nations" (145).[27]

Graffigny's psychology, epistemology, and ideology were obviously based in different assumptions—that human pleasure, even of the most intensely erotic kind, might be physiologically experienced without possessing and incorporating another being as part of oneself; that the discovery of "foreign bodies" independent of one's own produces horror only if those foreign bodies try to confine and possess your body. Buffon speaks from the only kind of experience he can imagine and articulates his scenario as a universal truth predicated on the philosopher's access to the original model for human behavior: the thoughts of the "first" man. Buffon's model is predicated on the assumption that man's nature precedes his culture, that thought is independent of language, and that epistemological inquiry can therefore proceed without consideration for the individual languages and cultural histories in which human thought is generated. Graffigny, on the other hand, advances the notion that thinking beings, at whatever stage of their consciousness, are already implicated in languages, histories, and cultures that position their subjectivity and dispose them to what she calls "prejudgments."

Whereas Buffon's intellectual hero immediately represses the idea that his body has limits and hastens to replace it with the idea of possession and mastery of other bodies, Graffigny's intellectual heroine is quite comfortable with the idea of sharing the universe with other sovereign beings. Buffon imagines an Adam engineered to "defeat" any body that resists incorporation into his own, an Adam who quickly learns to pluck as many fruits as he can from the tree that bruised him. Zilia draws a different conclusion from being bruised by a foreign body, precisely because she accepts the idea of limits to her sovereignty that the encounter with alterity imposes.

Both Adam's and Zilia's narratives are driven by the initial discovery that "my universe is limited to the extent of my being." Adam acts in order to expand the extent of his being by claiming dominion over as much of the universe as he can. Zilia, on the other hand, works to acquire the language that will enable her to communicate with beings who she recognizes inhabit other universes. Buffon's scenario for producing First World masters is a familiar narrative, but the Third World alternative (the insistence on self-determination and a historical accounting that undoes the ideology of conquest) has also been with us for a while. Thanks to the publication of voices that the First World has heard less frequently, we can listen to a history of Third World enlightenment (be it fact or fable) that has been articulated quite differently.

NOTES

1. Roland Barthes, *Fragments d'un discours amoureux* (Paris: Seuil, 1977). All translations in this essay are my own.

2. For a subtle description of seventeenth- and eighteenth-century French letter novels of this type, see Susan Lee Carrell, *Le Soliloque de la passion féminine ou le dialogue illusoire* (Paris: J.-M. Place, 1982). See also J. Altman, "'Portuguese' Writing and Women's Consciousness," *Degré Second: Studies in French Literature* 7 (1983): 163–75.

3. See, for example, Ovid, *Heroides* 2, verses 145–48; 7, verses 194–96.

4. Here, as in all quotations in this essay, the emphasis is mine.

5. See, for example, reviews by Raynal in *Nouvelles littéraires manuscrites* (1747), bound in *Correspondance littéraire, philosophique et critique par Grimm, Diderot, Raynal, Meister, etc.* (Paris: Garnier, 1877) 1:132 (letter 14); by Pierre Clément in *Les Années littéraires* (The Hague: De Groot, 1748) 1:18–23; and Fréron in *L'Année littéraire* (Geneva, 1749–55 [Paris: Duchesne]) 1:73–103.

6. For a detailed bibliography covering most of the known re-editions and translations, see Gianni Nicoletti's critical edition of the *Lettres d'une Péruvienne* (Bari: Adriatica Editrice, 1967), 49–67, which includes Turgot's essay on the novel (459–74). Turgot's essay also appears in his *Oeuvres* (Paris: Delance, 1810), 9:260–87, where it constitutes the only attention paid to a novel by a political economist whose other literary writings centered on Virgil, Horace, Pope, and German poetry. Although Turgot's essay has been almost totally ignored by literary critics, I consider it a crucial barometer for rereading Graffigny's novel as a philosophic as well as a literary enterprise.

7. The Garnier-Flammarion edition (Paris, 1983), which was prepared by Bernard Bray and Isabelle Landy-Houillon, offers fine introductions by both editors. The English edition that is currently available, *Letters Written by a Peruvian Princess* (New York and London: Garland, 1974), is a facsimile reprint of the London edition of 1748, made from a copy in the Yale University Library.

8. We owe a considerable debt to English Showalter for rediscovering Françoise de Graffigny in the early 1960s and devoting so much careful research to her literary career, correspondence, and relations with other Enlightenment writers. Each of Showalter's books and articles on Graffigny is a model study of literary relations. Thanks to the work of Showalter, Gianni Nicoletti, Jürgen von Stackelberg, Bernard Bray, and Isabelle Landy-Houillon, we have two recent editions of the novel, an edition of Graffigny's correspondence en route, and a growing body of criticism on her life, relations, and sequels to her novel. However, very few articles have been devoted to reading her novel.

9. "Nature has made Europeans so superior in everything to the peoples of the New World that the dispersed Peruvians were stupidly waiting to find out which faction among their destroyers would claim them!" Voltaire, *Essai sur les moeurs* (Paris: Editions sociales, 1975), 265. In *Anthropologie et histoire au siècle des Lumières* (Paris: Flammarion, 1977), Michèle Duchet has painstakingly exposed the racial and ethnic biases at work in Buffon, Voltaire, Rousseau, and other writers who attempted to write a history of the relations between "civilized" and "primitive" cultures.

10. See "Making Room for 'Peru': Graffigny's Novel Reconsidered," forthcoming in *Dilemmes du roman,* ed. Joan DeJean, Catherine Lafarge, Philip R. Stewart, et al. (Stanford: Anma Libri [Stanford French and Italian Studies]).

11. See English Showalter, "Les *Lettres d'une Péruvienne:* Composition, publication, suites," *Archives et Bibliothèques de Belgique* 54:1–4 (1985): 26–28, and Elizabeth J. MacArthur, "Devious Narratives: Refusal of Closure in Two Eighteenth-Century Epistolary Novels," *Eighteenth-Century Studies* 21 (1987): 7–10.

12. Condillac, "Important Notice to the Reader," *Traité des sensations* (1754).

13. When the *Traité des sensations* was published in 1754, Grimm accused Condillac of stealing his idea for the statue from Diderot's *Lettre sur les sourds et muets* (1751); others claimed that Condillac copied Buffon's account of Adam's awakening in his *Histoire naturelle* (1749). Condillac retorted that Mlle Ferrand had suggested this strategy (see Jean Piveteau's edition of Condillac, *Oeuvres philosophiques* [Paris: Presses Universitaires de France, 1954], 309). Charles Bonnet would later use a similar strategy in his *Oeuvres d'histoire naturelle et de philosophie* (1779–83), claiming that he had arrived at the idea independently of Condillac. Isabel F. Knight briefly reviews these plagiarism quarrels in her careful study *The Geometric Spirit: The Abbé de Condillac and the French Enlightenment* (New Haven and London: Yale University Press, 1968), concluding that "it seems evident that [Condillac] had merely picked up an idea that was current coin at the time" (83).

14. See, for example, Jacques Chouillet, *L'Esthétique des Lumières* (Paris: Presses Universitaires de France, 1974), 84–85, for a summary of this account. See Ira Wade's chapter, "Paths to the Self," in *The Structure and Form of the French Enlightenment* (Princeton: Princeton University Press, 1977), 1:583–651, for an extended discussion of Condillac's, Rousseau's, and Diderot's contributions to theories of the self based on the experience of body sensations. Almost all the works that Chouillet and Wade cite as indices of this theoretical shift fall into the 1750 to 1772 period, i.e., the period of intense philosophical reflection that accompanied the writing and publication of the *Encyclopédie.*

15. Graffigny, *Lettres d'une Péruvienne,* in *Lettres portugaises, Lettres d'une Péruvienne et autres romans d'amour par lettres,* ed. B. Bray and I. Landy-Houillon (Paris: Garnier Flammarion, 1983), 249.

16. Traditionally, literary critics have assumed that Graffigny made a chronological blunder by having a Peruvian who was captured during the Spanish conquest in the sixteenth century arrive in a France of the eighteenth century. In this case the blunder is so egregious that we might want to stop taking it as proof of the author's lack of historical knowledge or novelistic craft. On the contrary, Graffigny may have purposefully created such a rupture in her fiction. Showalter's research on Graffigny's correspondence during the composition of the *Lettres d'une Péruvienne* shows that Graffigny was indeed aware of this discrepancy, and that she was criticized by her friend Devaux for it. She, however, maintained her conviction that this sort of license with chronology was quite acceptable in fiction. Although Graffigny apparently did not elaborate on her ground for maintaining the discrepancy, her chronological telescoping clearly enables her to

imbricate and interrelate two distinct historical experiences: (1) the Peruvian experience of the Spanish conquest, and (2) the way that a Peruvian who recalls that conquest might experience the technological, artistic, and economic advances of the France of the mid-eighteenth century.

17. Thus far none of the readers of the *Lettres d'une Péruvienne* has considered the possible analogy between Zilia's situation and the experience of Africans wrenched from their culture and transported across the sea under even more brutal conditions. It is doubtless readers' insistence on assimilating Zilia to the standard foreign travelers in French Enlightenment literature (chiefly Voltaire's Ingénu and Montesquieu's Persians) that has precluded consideration of any other paradigms for understanding her narrative. No readers, for example, have noticed that the foreign travelers to whom they are constantly comparing Zilia (Voltaire's Huron Indian and Montesquieu's Persians), *choose* to visit France, travel as free agents, and have already received a European education before leaving their native countries.

18. See Roger Laufer's chapter on the *Lettres persanes* in his *Style rococo, style des "Lumières"* (Paris: Corti, 1963).

19. See Peggy Kamuf's chapter, "Writing on the Balcony," in *Fictions of Feminine Desire: Disclosures of Heloise* (Omaha: Nebraska University Press, 1982), 44–66.

20. Cf. Oenone to Paris in *Heroides* 5, v. 33: "Illa dies fatum miserae mihi dixit" (That day spoke doom for wretched me), or Dido to Aeneas in *Heroides* 7, v. 93: "Illa dies nocuit" (That dreadful day was my ruin).

21. "What a tale have I to unfold! But still upon *self*, this vile, this hated *self!* I will shake it off, if possible; and why should I not, since I think, except one wretch, I hate nothing so much?" Samuel Richardson, *Clarissa Harlow* (London: J. M. Dent, 1932), 4:138–39.

22. Zilia's description is actually a two-paragraph report on "a house which, I could perceive, in spite of the darkness, it was extremely difficult to reach." Critics have tended to condense her lengthy description into the simple locution, "moving house." On that basis they have no difficulty claiming that "moving house" is a banal description of a boat. The expression "moving house," however, occurs nowhere in the two paragraphs: it is instead a considerably impoverished reduction of two paragraphs of intellection and description, designed to give Aza maximum information on Zilia's whereabouts.

23. I use the word "annals" quite deliberately here, keeping in mind the productive distinction that Hayden White has drawn between "annals," "chronicle," and "history" writing as discursive practices within the history of historiography. See his essay, "The Value of Narrativity in the Representation of Reality," *Critical Inquiry* 7 (1980): 5–27. We need to bear in mind that in the early letters Zilia still thinks that she is in Peru, has hopes of maintaining a Peruvian kingdom, and therefore tries to situate what is happening to her within Peruvian geography and history.

24. In French Enlightenment novels, suicide is typically either a topic for philosophical debate (as in the *Lettres persanes* and *La Nouvelle Héloïse*) or a threat used by libertine seducers to cow resisting women (as in *Les Liaisons dangereuses*).

Graffigny's handling of the suicide issue as a subjectively experienced existential crisis, gradually provoked by a perceived reduction of "being" to "nothingness," constitutes to my knowledge a quite new language for the eighteenth-century French novel.

25. Indeed, Graffigny's descriptive method, as well as her choice of environments for description, finds many analogues in Proust, where a comparably confined narrator carefully positions his body in relation to a variety of closed environments that alter his previous perceptions of his subjective positioning in the world. Like Proust's narrator, Zilia observes those environments in various states of psychic consciousness—from awakening, to reverie, to locomotion.

26. Buffon does not actually call his first man Adam, but his narrative follows the basic narrative of Genesis, insofar as the creation of Eve is concerned. All paginations for my quotations are taken from Buffon, *Histoire naturelle,* ed. Jean Varloot (Paris: Gallimard/Folio, 1984). The translations and the emphasis are mine.

27. In the *Supplément* to *Histoire naturelle* (1778), Buffon insists once again that the indigenous peoples of Africa and America are "of little value." Arguing that they merit only "contempt," he offers the following proof: "You can easily judge how little value these men have by how few impressions their hands have left on their land: be it through stupidity or laziness, these half-brutes . . . are deadweight on our globe, drawing nourishment from the earth without fertilizing it" (275). Buffon seems unaware of the knowledge of plant and animal life that native Americans possessed and had already communicated to Europeans.

11

Writing to the Divine Marquis:
Epistolary Strategies of Madame de Sade
and Milli Rousset

JULIE C. HAYES

TO READ the letters of the Marquis de Sade couples the ambiguous pleasure of reading someone else's mail with the pleasurable ambiguities of exploring a scandalous writer's verbal delirium. Several generations of critics have proclaimed Sade's letters as interesting as his novels, if not more so.[1] For the most part, unfortunately, these admirers have had very little to say about the reception of those letters by the persons to whom they were sent, or about the responses they elicited. Two women were the privileged audience for Sade's epistolary excesses: his wife, Renée-Pélagie de Montreuil de Sade, and an old friend, Marie-Dorothée de Rousset. They received the most brilliant and the most disturbing of the letters; they reacted with alternating pleasure and dismay. Says Rousset:

> If ever I have his letters published, I assure you that they will create a greater stir than the memoirs of the celebrated Beaumarchais; *he writes like an angel.*[2]

> To copy all of the marquis's letters for you would take too long, and you would see too much madness, along with the deepest possible darkness. (Bourdin 136)

The chief difficulty for Rousset and the marquise is to discover how to reply to a discourse that might be either "angelic" or delirious and that would in any event become increasingly aggressive and domineering. For although the women are free and Sade is in prison, it is they who are intimidated and victimized in the epistolary exchange. Their response to the aggression varies, as does their success in limiting it. Read together, the trio's letters constitute a model of reading and counterreading, production and distortion of meaning, attack and defense. One cannot exclude their "real weight" (to borrow Mireille Bossis's term[3]) as an important part of their force. The letters are the record, the physical remains, of suffering.

It is a curious fact that even as Sade's name became a synonym for perversion and his books were banned, his letters were preserved and transmitted from generation to generation by people who neither cared nor dared to read them. Many have now been published, as Rousset foresaw, but there is no single inclusive edition.[4] The reader must pick up one book after another, flip pages and search for the date, the reference, or the quotation that would indicate which letter might be the answer to another.

I will concentrate in this essay on the period from late 1778 to mid-1779. Here is the situation: having already spent more than a year in Vincennes, Sade has been reimprisoned there under his mother-in-law's *lettre de cachet*. His wife, powerless to help, may not visit him and must rely on periodic letters; she sends biweekly packages of food, clothing, and books. Mademoiselle or "Milli" Rousset (dubbed "the Saint") was present at Sade's arrest in his château La Coste; she comes to Paris in November 1778, where she lodges with the marquise. The two women console one another, attend to Sade's many requests, and attempt to interest important people in his case. Each writes to the marquis and each receives letters from him. They read and add teasing postscripts to each other's letters.

Rousset plays at coquetry and Mme de Sade gives an arch rendering of a jealous spouse. They are very close. "Mademoiselle de Rousset has become another me," says the marquise (Bourdin 134). Gradually the picture darkens. Rousset and Sade cease corresponding in May 1779, and her relations with the marquise have also cooled: "There are times when I am tempted to drop everything. Madame de Sade is not exactly lively, you know. We live in angelic monotony" (letter to Gaufridy, 29 May 1779, Bourdin 144). She remains in Paris, but her efforts in Sade's behalf lead her only to learn that "there are serious, very serious reasons indeed" for his imprisonment (Bourdin 160). She returns south in 1780, looks after La Coste, and dies there at age forty, in 1784.

Mme de Sade's first visit with her husband, in 1781, unleashes a furious series of letters accusing her of sexual infidelity. Transferred to the Bastille in 1784, Sade would be released by the revolutionary government in the spring of 1790. Friendship and jealousy, freedom and confinement, physical and mental illness all have a part in shaping the letters from those years.

Current debates on "self-consciousness" in the epistolary genre point up several important aspects of the Sade correspondence. There can be little doubt that, Rousset's occasional thoughts of publication aside, each letter would qualify as what Roger Duchêne called a "true letter . . . the spontaneous direct expression of lived reality written for the benefit of a privileged other."[5] These true letters tend nevertheless to skew the terms. Concrete "lived reality" is clearly enough in evidence:

> List of what I'm sending you:
>   6 "Enfant-Jésus" butter pastries; a catalog of books; 12 frosted cakes; 24 large macaroons; 26 pears (I packed them unripe, so they won't spoil in transport. I ate some similar ones that I found quite good.) (Mme de Sade to her husband, 14 Sept. 1779, Daumas and Lely 2:216)

but one quickly recognizes in reading other letters that "reality" inspires little writing beyond the lists of requests fulfilled. Sade's lived reality, as we shall see, often strays into one that is private and well-nigh inaccessible. "Spontaneity" is also a touchy issue. In the early stages of the correspondence, the most self-conscious of the letter writers are the two women. It is they who take into consideration problems regarding their reader(s); it is they who become sensitized to the danger posed by readers' interferences and aberrant interpretations. The primary topic of conversation is soon the correspondence itself—the main events recorded, the reception, and the reading of letters.

> Here's what's decided, I won't send you anyone's letters: but don't you want me to tell you what people might write to you? For example, your son is to write you to give an account of his studies. I won't send his letter, but will copy out the principal parts, and you could answer with a little note that would make him happy, instead of if you continued not answering, which would seem strange to his tutor. (Mme de Sade to her husband, 30 July 1779, Daumas and Lely 2:211–12)

Few outside events are narrated: the letters refer to themselves and constantly pose the same questions of who will read what and how the readings might determine the course of the personal relationships involved. The correspondence stages a struggle to see who can control the exchange, whether Mme de Sade and Milli Rousset will have their say or the marquis will impose his own meaning.

The women face numerous obstacles in getting their messages across, in terms of both the material conditions of the correspondence and its overall rhetoric. Materially and rhetorically, the correspondence is both unduly "open" and desperately "closed." Sade may well be the intended recipient of his wife's and friend's letters, but all communication is passed with the knowledge that it will be read by others—the prison censors. Writing to Gaufridy, Rousset reports a remark she inserted in a letter to Sade (" 'It's clear to me that your detention is only a game' ") and comments, "If that sentence passes, he'll respond to it. Even if the censors erase it, they'll have read it; that's all I want" (Bourdin 139). All the letters are marked by the same unnerving, uncontrollable openness; it is highly likely that each will be read by the trio of writers and by prison officials who can delay, deform, or even (in the case of Sade's more abusive ravings [Bourdin 158–59]) withhold them altogether.

> We are in a frightful disorder, my dear Saint, with our letters. The 27th, I had one from the 12th, in other words two weeks late. What can be the reason? I know nothing. The worst I see, is that our letters being thus disconnected from one another, my responses must seem quite stupid to you, and have nothing to do with what I would answer, if I had seen your latest letter. (Rousset to Sade, 30 April 1779, Daumas and Lely 1:339)

The women's letters are often censored as well, much to Sade's frustration: "And so, it's to be erasures, cross-outs, and all possible kinds of scribbling that succeed to the doodles!" (letter to his wife, 4? Oct., 1778, Lely 12:161). Since the marquis is intent on seeing meaning in every scratch, Rousset takes care to note when it is she, and not the censors, who has crossed something out.

> It was I who just erased that word. I was going to tease you about exclamation marks, question marks, and periods. You would have imagined it had some meaning or some riddle. So . . . *nescio vos.* (10 Jan. 1779, Daumas and Lely 1:325)

Despite their helpless availability to foreign eyes, the letters also bespeak closure—not only the marquis's confinement, but also the angelic monotony of the women's existence, their convent residence, and the cycle of endless errands and fruitless petitions. The letters are opened, but the discourse is closed. It is closed in the first place, because it relates to private events in a small world and, in the second place, because the correspondents collude in an attempt to subvert the outside pressure and evade the authorities by coding certain messages. The coding takes many forms. Mme de Sade refers to Rousset in the masculine and to Sade himself as "Oreste" in 1778 (Daumas and Lely 2:156, 167). In an early letter, Rousset briefs Sade on what "signal" to give indicating reception of an object or message (Daumas and Lely 1:318). For a time, Mme de Sade includes passages in sympathetic or "disappearing" ink (*lettres blanches*) whose writing would appear at the application of heat. Significantly, the "white letters" rarely contain anything that could not have been included in ordinary letters. Take, for example, the following note, given in its entirety.

> My promptitude, tender friend, in giving news of myself should impel you to break your silence, which pains me greatly. My only consolation would be to receive news from you that would prove your friendship. Why this obstination in refusing me? Whatever the reason, my attachment to you will remain as vibrant and constant as ever.
> (invisible ink)
> Explain yourself, my good friend, I conjure you. Tell me clearly just what you have against me. . . . However much I examine myself, I can't fathom the cause of your silence and your change with regard to me. (3 Oct. 1777, Daumas and Lely 2:110)

The hidden text reveals no "secret" in the conventional sense, but instead it should be read as an attempt to seize that which has been appropriated by outsiders, to authenticate the message by reestablishing a personal, privileged relationship. Mme de Sade's overuse of her stratagem led to its quick discovery (Daumas and Lely 2:114) and considerably limited the number of white letters she was able to pass after 1777.

Milli Rousset's earliest use of Provençal phrases in her letters resembles the marquise's technique. Her direct address to the censors, for whom she provides translations, alerts them to the fact that although she is willing to cooperate with them, she possesses a means of communication that is beyond them.

> *Aco es une marchandise melado tout pas vaou.* You can see, Sirs, that *it's all worth very little.* Since my readers doubtless do not understand patois, you can translate it from the underlined sentence; it means: "It's a mixed bag of goods, it's all worth very little." You can see, Sirs, that I do not cheat. I even gallicized the patois, so that you might understand it more easily. (18 Jan. 1779, Daumas and Lely 1:329)

The marquise's and Rousset's decisions to encrypt their language, to bury their meaning, however innocent it may be, stem from the desire to preserve a semblance of privacy. Mme de Sade, with her heartfelt tone and her sympathetic ink, seeks sympathy through sentiment; hers is the emotional heroine's voice. Milli Rousset is teasing, proud of her superiority over the "Messieurs" who intrude on her letter. Following a second Provençal/French passage in the 18 January letter, she remarks to Sade,

"The translation is not for you, since you understand it. I owe this attention to those who don't understand" (Daumas and Lely 1:331). The translations render the encoding transparent, but in no way dilute its effect: the mere "use" of Provençal allows Rousset to assert her privileged relationship with Sade as countryman and friend.

The invitation to decode has a serious side effect. For even if the marquise and Rousset have little to communicate besides their love and sympathy, they cannot prevent the marquis from wanting to read a far more crucial message, the date of his liberation. Sade begins to decode every word, every date, every pun, every mark. *Nescio vos,* says Rousset, ("You're crazy"), but there is little either she or the marquise can do to preserve their intended meanings. The closure of epistolary intimacy is gradually transformed into the hermetic confine of psychosis.

Sade begins by laboriously weighing the nuances of each letter he receives; soon his letters are but explications of other texts, exploded into a thicket of ramifications.

> What signifies *"Your children have gone away for the next two years; I promised them that on their return they would rejoin us, you and me, wherever we might be; they departed satisfied that they would see you in two years?"* . . . In God's name, if you've any pity left in your heart, . . . make that sentence clear to me and explain if what you meant thereby was that *I won't leave here for another two years?* (Letter to Mme de Sade, Lely 12:168–69; reply to Daumas and Lely 2:150)

Turns of phrase and objects received could easily be construed as signals, but before long Sade had discovered an even more seductive interpretive grid for reaching the frantically desired truth. Sade kept all letters (numbered in order of reception), reread them, counted the words, lines, and letters, and began endless variations on the figures that recurred in the operations, even devising interpretive puns: *cesse,* ("cease") for *seize* (sixteen), *vint,* ("came") for *vingt* (twenty), etc. Occasionally it would occur to him that his "cipher system" (*système chiffral*) was madness, but "what can I do here other than calculate and beget chimeras?" (Lely 12:170–71). As the years passed, the letters took on a certain elegant exoticism; Sade became a writer. As frightening as such texts must have been for their recipients, they have become objects of fascination since they began to be published early in this century. The signals' and ciphers' relationship to what a recent critic called Sade's debit and credit of pleasure[6] has proved engrossing for modern readers, but for Sade's correspondents they constituted an obstacle to communication far more dangerous than any intervention by prison officials. Sade refuses any and all surface meanings and presupposes a signification from elsewhere, even when that "elsewhere" is unknown.

For after all these signals can have but two possible objects: either that I should understand them or that I shouldn't. If it's the first, make them clearer, give me at least a hint, a reference-point; if it's the latter, why are you doing it? (4 March 1783 [?], Lely 12:281)

And, while it is certain that Sade suffers profoundly from his incertitude, fear, and consequent attacks of ciphers, it is no less evident that, from his position of total weakness, he has succeeded in fashioning an instrument for insulting and inflicting severe pain upon his readers. "For the signaler must by nature be very illiterate, very ignorant, very drab, very foolish, very clumsy, very pedantic, very imbecilic, and very flat" (Lely 12:174). How, then, can one write to the "divine" marquis? How to communicate despite the delays and "scribblings" imposed by foreign hands, and especially despite the savage reversals imposed by the recipient himself?

In examining how Sade's correspondents faced the problem, I will first examine the letters of Mme de Sade. The *Mélanges* provide 243 letters written between 1777 and 1789, which testify to what must have been a remarkable attachment, but which tell us little about the woman who wrote them and almost nothing about the world she lived in. During the tense month of June 1789, for example, the marquise asks her husband to be polite to his guards, explains the arrangements for the next exchange of letters, and mentions a problem with hemorrhoids. Hers is an extremely private sphere; she instills an intimate quality to her letters by insisting on small talk, shopping lists, and expressions of affection. Her husband is her "tender friend" (*mon tendre ami, mon compère, mon bon et tendre petit*), and she invariably addresses him with the familiar *tu* (Sade usually replies with the aristocratic *vous*). Even her most dramatic invention, the "white letters," has a homey side: milk is her sympathetic ink.

Renée-Pélagie de Montreuil de Sade is confident in her husband's imminent release and she refuses to relinquish her optimistic future tense: "when you're out" (*quand tu seras dehors*). Whatever doubts she might harbor in the guise of negations and hypotheses, she never abandons her confidence in the world. "If we weren't sure of the good will of those in whose hands everything rests, it would be unbearable; but it is impossible for us to doubt them any more than our own existence, and certainly nothing is more real" (30 Dec. 1777, Daumas and Lely 2:123). She believes in the power of the emotions and in language's capacity to contain her meaning, if only Sade would read her as she intends.

I conjure you, my good friend, to see nothing in the sentences I write you other than a sincere desire to console you and to assure you of all the lively tenderness I bear you. . . . Begin by persuading yourself that I adore you. Read them with your heart, not with your head. (ca. 20 Dec. 1778, Daumas and Lely 2:171–72)

The marquise's emphasis on truth, transparency, and meaning has the undesirable effect of encouraging Sade to persist in experimenting with his ciphers, since they too are postulated on meaningfulness. Indeed, the marquise seems no more willing than her husband to envisage the possibility that his detention may be prolonged indefinitely: "Yes, I believe that your term has been set, but I am convinced that out of cruelty they don't want to tell me" (Daumas and Lely 2:186). Optimism is as dangerous as were the innocent codes and white letters, since it only confirms Sade's idea that there is something to be learned by combing through and interpreting all letters and events. As long as the marquise claims her words are meaningful, he will seek out the meaning *he* desires.

Another aspect of Mme de Sade's writing that seems to act as an inducement to (de)ciphering is its kinship with the *système chiffral* in terms of the "platitude" or "idiocy" (*bêtise*) Sade attributes to both. Sade rages at the weaknesses of his wife's prose in the same terms with which he takes offense at the cipher system. "Platitude!" he writes in her margins; "liven up your style," he prompts in one letter (Daumas and Lely 1:114); and in another, "I advise you to change your *slavish* and *crawling* style" (3:112). He greets her none-too-felicitous phrase, "the sad perspective in which we have been plunged until today" (2:273), with the annotation, "I should very much like for someone to explain to me how it is possible to be plunged in a perspective. They've a great deal of wit and they certainly speak good French, the people who write these letters!" Mme de Sade's affection for various stock phrases—"So don't as they say put the hammer to your head. . . . Patience! To everything there is a time. . . . It's easier said than done. . . . Time passes slowly when one suffers"—leads her to fill her language with homely objects, as comforting to her in their familiarity, perhaps, as Sade's ciphers are disorienting, but as irritating to him as his ciphers are to her. Again, such writing is an inducement to the decoder. The clichés have lost meaning through overuse; they sit in the sentences like foreign entities waiting to be invested by a new meaning, a new use—not unlike the elements Sade interprets as "signals."

Aware that her message is not getting through, the marquise tends to fall back on the hope that, once her husband has been freed and they are again face to face, she will be able to convince him of her sincerity. In the meantime (despite the half-expressed admission of defeat implied by such a hope), she deploys her strategies for dealing with the situation.

Denying the problem has strategic usefulness. Mme de Sade claims (understandably enough) to know nothing about the signals and ciphers; she protests their imposition. "*All* that I write, you turn it around; *all* that I do, you misconstrue, and, unfortunately, despite *all* my precautions, I can't prevent you from imputing the most absurd and baroque ideas to me" (Daumas and Lely 2:212). In a subtler form of denial, she often refuses to take notice of the ciphers, answering the most insane letters as if nothing untoward has been said. If she mentions them, she attributes them to a passing phase, a momentary indisposition on Sade's part (*un mouvement de noir*). Just as the numerical obsession is Sade's defense against an uncertain fate, Mme de Sade's denials are hers. So is her insistence on the concrete, the list. "You misinterpret everything I say. So I'm going to take the same approach as you, and limit myself to asking for news of your health, inquiring what you want" (12 April 1779, Daumas and Lely 2:188).

More pragmatically, she sometimes appeals to her husband's self-interest by noting that his epistolary abuses can only prolong his detention, impede delivery of letters, and prevent her from visiting him (Daumas and Lely 2:265–66, 306, 308, 340, etc). All too frequently, however, she finds herself drawn into involved justifications of herself, her words, or her actions (2:155, 158, 289, 296, etc). Her insistence on the meaning of her words (*her* meaning) produces, as we have seen, the undesired effect—her pleas for Sade to cease "interpreting" are typically covered with word counts, puns, and opinions.

Mme de Sade is perplexed and deeply hurt by the imputations and reconstructions of her acts and words, but she appears incapable of stopping the process. Too many features of her writing subvert her determination to deny the ciphers' validity; her very desire to console and cheer her *ami*—the reiterated "when you come out"—creates intolerable tensions for him. "If I have so long a time remaining in this infamous place, why then do you seek with every sentence to hint at imminent happiness?" (Sade to Mme de Sade, Daumas and Lely 3:19).[7] The conversation continued for twelve years with little change—protestations of sincerity and proofs of devotion on her part, oblivious interpretations and elegant rebuttals on his.

Milli Rousset's correspondence with Sade cannot be compared with the marquise's for either length or intensity, but her response to the signals and ciphers was significantly different. By the time of her arrival in Paris, Sade was an experienced decoder; like the marquise, Rousset's first reaction is painful surprise. She is also highly irritated. "Your wretched letter has spread its misery to me," she writes in December (Daumas and Lely 1:321), but two days later she recovers from her dark mood to write again.

> But if I truly care for you, I cannot keep from saying certain little
> truths that others will hide from you. You know that I'm more than a
> little frank; I don't seek out polite turns of phrase to tell someone I

love, "You're wrong." Ahem! You remember? (Daumas and Lely
1:321–22)

The denial of "turns of phrase" may be an attempt to ward off future
deciphering, but the passage also gives a clear idea of Rousset's idea of
herself. For several months, she will try to "tell" Sade what others will
not, to answer the ciphers in a way no one else has attempted. The
correspondence becomes a contest. "Oh yes, we women all have our
weak side, but so do you! Which of us will be clever enough to subjugate
the other?" (18 Jan. 1779, Daumas and Lely 1:329). The project was
worthwhile, but Sade would prove incorrigible; Rousset would find herself enmeshed in denials and justifications. By May she had had enough:
"Look, Sir, let us write no longer. It's not worth saying such harsh things
to one another, it embitters one's heart" (Daumas and Lely 1:355). Before the rupture, however, the correspondence had succeeded, on occasion, in its aim: preserving a link and a memory of past friendship,
despite many obstacles. And, for Rousset, preserving self.

Rousset's most consistent approach to the *chiffres* is a refusal to take
them seriously. Without denying their existence, she takes them in
stride, even pokes fun at them. "Be prepared for works full of eloquence, beautiful handwriting, periods and commas everywhere!" (30
Dec. 1778, Daumas and Lely 1:324).

Mme de Sade enters into the game:

I shall pray to Heaven that we may spend our next Easter together in
the parish of *Mazan* in Provence.[8]
   Here's the marshmallow creme. Your letters will be sent. The Saint
wants me to write the word *Mazan,* because she says that it will make
your head spin and make you write twelve pages on the subject, given
that you'll see all sorts of things in it. (3 April 1779, Daumas and Lely
2:186)

Rousset couches all references to the ciphers in terms that tease and
minimize their importance. "I see by your calculation of 365 days that
incertitude over your term is making your head whirl like a windmill"
(30 April 1779, Daumas and Lely 1:343).

Rousset concentrates her forces elsewhere. In her elaborate flirtation
game with Sade, the contest of letters takes place within the context of a
battle of the sexes and opens, appropriately, during a discussion of
Clarissa.

The women you have had loved and cherished your passions and your
money. With Saint Rousset there's no such hold! How will you take
her? You'll swear delicate sentiments and a few extras. Oh! but I
already know that one well, and others besides. Believe me, turn back
from the joust, it isn't too late! (18 Jan. 1779, Daumas and Lely 1:330)

Several years before Merteuil, Rousset offers her Valmont the prospect of "winning her"—if he will behave. Mme de Sade too plays a part. Rousset having mentioned that "Madame reads everything" in an earlier letter, and Madame herself having already added footnotes to several of Rousset's letters, the stage is set. Rousset makes a passionate declaration in Provençal (*Moun cher de Sade, delicé de moun ame*); Madame reacts appropriately: "But what do you think of her Saintliness? She makes enormous efforts to say sweet things to you. Might she be cutting the grass from under my feet? Easy now, my good people, I'll oppose it with all my forces." The Saint provides the dénouement.

> Faith, there's some jealousy in her. What do you say to that? Will you still offer yourself to be my suitor? If your very tender and faithful better half won't permit it, there's no way to find a way. What shall we do? Shall we deceive her? But we both have too much delicacy. (24 April 1779, Daumas and Lely 1:338–39)

I quote the letter at some length because it gives an apt rendering of Rousset's playfulness and of her complicity with the marquise. In a number of surviving letters, Sade responds in kind; he and Rousset exchange billets-doux and letters in various comic styles. Sade having failed to forego his penchant for aggressive decoding, however, she announces disgustedly (in Provençal) that she will no longer send him anything other than *de cansouns ou de sounettes* (14 April 1779, Daumas and Lely 1:334).

"Songs and sonnets" play a vital role in the exchange. Rousset's idea to limit the scope of the letters echoes the marquise's, but differs importantly. Mme de Sade's maneuvers amount to a flight from the problem, a flight from language—"If I could tell you what you want to hear, my dear friend, I would not resort to signs" is one of her more revealing phrases—whereas Rousset's tactic is to engage language directly through analyses of her opponent's style. If the ciphers are a cry from the depths, Rousset's replies represent an attempt to bring her friend back to the surface, to master the ciphers by parodying them, and to engage in less dangerous linguistic codes—highly mannered love letters, comic New Year's greetings, versification schemes, language lessons.

> It is as though I see you searching for your words, which you then render with all possible grace. The same slight awkwardness reigns in your style and your Provençal; you would never believe the pleasure it gives me. I seem to see a young man who wants to speak an unfamiliar language, who uses different gestures, different postures, to show the ideas of his imagination and the sensations of his heart through the expressivity of his person. If you had been able to transform yourself into a little boy, I'd take you in my arms, I'd have devoured you with caresses. (24 April 1779, Daumas and Lely 1:335)

She extols the delicate points of phrasing in Provençal; she requests Italian lessons; she critiques Sade's poetry and sends verses of her own. Love and linguistics go hand in hand. Limiting speech to discourse on "your words" allows a paradoxically enlarged perspective, an enactment of friendship, as the slide from the marquis's use of patois to the small boy "devoured with caresses" suggests. Rousset writes herself, imagines her role, in the midst of a faintly rhyming, archly transparent ("all this is an allusion, as you are well aware") *explication de texte.*

> The next couplet proves better still what was said beforehand: a woman who is your friend, whatever you may think, is all you need; forget your former loves forever, *ta fremo vaou,* your wife should suffice. (30 April 1779, Daumas and Lely 1:343)

The exchange ostensibly comes to an end when Sade refuses to hold up what she sees as his part of the bargain, that is, reforming himself. His failure to follow her scenario robs her of a triumph and convinces her to break off relations. Certain letters, however, suggest an additional source of tension. On one occasion, Rousset includes an anecdote recounting the difficulties provoked by a good friend's wife, who, it seems, is jealous of Rousset's "wit." Reportedly begging the friend to convince his wife "that I'm no more than a dumb animal" (*une bête*), Rousset asks the same of Sade. "I have not lost hope that you might present me with a bale of hay" (Daumas and Lely 1:349). In the anecdote, her request reestablishes complicity with her friend ("we laughed like crazy over it"); in the correspondence, its effect is immediately transposed to the relationship with Sade, who consoles her ("Is it really only today that you learned how people fear wit?") and shows himself willing to begin a new game, playing *bête*. "Hey now, my little beast, here's someone bringing my oats; I have to leave you to go eat; I'll be back to you for dessert, you'll be my little compote" (Daumas and Lely 1:68). That letter would, however, cross the one in which Rousset calls for epistolary silence: "Let us no longer write."

It is difficult to do justice to Rousset's vivacity and her mercurial changes of style—within one letter, she passes from the melancholy remembrance of a springtime past in hers and Sade's youth, to one of his Provençal poems, to a teasing close: "I love you and bite your little finger!" (Daumas and Lely 1:346). More difficult still to suggest through a few quotations is her technique for transposing her coquetry—"a sly little manner that slays men without their noticing" (1:324–25)—into her text, so that the letter becomes itself an extended flirtation with a previous text, through self-conscious commentary or interplay interspersed with requests for more (poems, lessons) and promises of advice or poems in return. Such letters alert the reader to the communication that takes place on a level seemingly belied by the "inconsequential" topic at hand. Rousset's letter of 7 May 1779 and Sade's reply are exemplary in this regard. The code of nuance, rhythm, and tone proves here more efficacious than even Provençal.

In the letter in which she requests to be known as a *bête*, Rousset defends her "poor miserable style" and reminds Sade of his privileged place among her acquaintances. "I've always been reproached for being laconic. With you, I run on. I gallantly fill my four pages for the sheer pleasure of chatting with you! If you yawn, I don't see it." Her professions of innocence and ignorance notwithstanding, she includes veiled allusions to another understanding altogether.

> Eh! well . . . the . . . it's something you did not want to say and that I perhaps once heard you whisper. . . . Desire, etc., you divine, Monsieur le marquis, puts me in a strange situation. To penetrate the honor of your genius one mustn't be totally stupid, since you put my wit to strange sorts of contortions. (Daumas and Lely 1:346–47)

Sade's response is enthusiastic.

> Yes, my dear Saint, yes, you fill your four pages gallantly and *voluptuously.* . . . But Madame your friend [Mme de Sade] hasn't the same talent. . . .
>
> On to gayer topics. *The desire to divine you in order to penetrate . . .* and the whole mad sentence that follows is charming, my little Saint. . . .
>
> But a really delicious transition, one that's worth the best phrases in Bossuet and Fléchier: it's: "*Ah! that Rousset, she's a good dumb creature. . . . Would you care now for a little lesson in Provençal?*" What gaiety, what madness, what sweetness in that transition! (Daumas and Lely 1:63–65)

If only briefly, Rousset has succeeded in her project—maintaining complicity without losing her voice, despite censors and ciphers. And perhaps despite Mme de Sade. But the letters from early May are the last. Recognizing the game's ultimate futility, she elects to quit.[9]

Three accomplices, united against a *système carcéral*, attempt to preserve their amical and conjugal ties, only to have the *système chiffral* disrupt their solidarity. Contact with the system brings many unspoken tensions, reveals what each member of the trio elects to ignore: Sade is blind to concerns from the "outside," particularly financial matters; Mme de Sade seems unwilling to conceive of either life on the inside or the snares of mental illness; Rousset, despite her empathy with the practical and emotional dilemmas of her friends, excludes that which is inescapable for the others—the body, sexuality. Sade's language to her often borders on the lewd; she teases, but continues to picture him "transformed into a little boy" while her epistolary games keep the man at bay. Much is left unsaid about the relationship between the two women, beginning in devotion and identification, ending in silence, marked only by Rousset's anecdote about her "friend's wife" and by Mme de Sade's stray remarks regretting her lack of proficiency in Provençal. The letters testify to friendship's mortality.

The comparison between Rousset and Mme de Sade is inevitable, but unequal. The marquise can neither vary nor escape the repetitive cycle of epistolary victimization, but she is implicated in the correspondence in a way Rousset is not. Underlying her letters to her husband, inaccessible to any outside reader, remains the physical substratum of shared experience, sexual and emotional. Nevertheless, the strategies she attempts to mount against Sade's aggressive misreadings are entirely ineffectual. She continues to be blind to the effect of much of her own writing (as in her "when you are out"); her attempt to change the subject by focusing on "news of your health and what you want" only excludes her and reinforces his domination. The role she writes for herself is silence. "*What business is it of yours, Saintly as you are,*" she reports having said to Rousset, "*to scold him, and to keep him from scolding me? And {if} I want him to beat me, what is it to you?*" (14 Jan. 1779, Daumas and Lely 2:176).[10] Far from explaining the biographical data, the marquise's letters remind us of their unknowability.

After Milli Rousset's death, the marquise receives many letters and plays many roles. Sade sends her letters of abuse, letters of tenderness, and, increasingly, plays, short stories, a novel (*Aline et Valcour*). Mme de Sade replies to all, comments on the manuscripts, sends more books. Over time, the ciphers dissipate, but when Sade is at last liberated, she refuses to see him and obtains a divorce.

Sade later claimed that the years of the cipher system had forever marked his development as a writer (Lely 15:26). The system makes it abundantly obvious how fragile communication can become, how tenuous is our hold upon what we take to be our meaning. Both Mme de Sade and Milli Rousset realized what was at stake. Both were forced to develop defenses, to explore ways of possible entry into the system. The marquise seemed bound by either social or erotic constraints, or both. "Your desires are my laws" (Daumas and Lely 2:154, 175). She would like to escape from language, since words are so treacherous, only to have it flung at her that every *thing*, every notebook, shirt, or biscuit, is a sign and can be invested with an alien meaning. Rousset, for her part, wrapped herself in language, concentrating on its playful potential, hoping to master it. She nearly succeeded. Once the ciphers had begun their work, however, there was no compelling reason for them to stop, to allow us to think that anyone—Rousset, the marquise, or Sade himself—might be entirely master of her or his discourse.

NOTES

1. "With the energy of his unreason and release of the epistolary style, swollen with anger and bursting with verve, the marquis deserves to be read and ceases to bore." Paul Bourdin, ed., introduction to *Correspondance inédite du marquis de Sade, de ses proches et de ses familiers* (Paris: Librairie de France, 1929), xliii. While not one to consider the novels "boring," Gilbert Lely saw in the letters "the language of the future" (G. Lely, ed., *Vie du marquis de Sade, in Oeuvres complètes du marquis de Sade* [Paris: Cercle du livre précieux, 1966], 2:243). Lely's sentiment is echoed by Jean-Jacques Brochier, who describes the letters in terms of their "distortion" and their "combustion" of language, in "Sade et le langage," Lely, *Oeuvres complètes* 15:518.

2. Undated fragment cited by Lely, *Oeuvres complètes* 2:239.

3. Mireille Bossis, "Methodological Journeys Through Correspondences," *Yale French Studies* 71 (1986): 63–75.

4. The largest groups of letters are those that were kept by the Sade family, by the family of Sade's lawyer Gaufridy, and in the Bastille archives. Many have probably been lost or dispersed in private collections. Vol. 12 of the *Oeuvres complètes* is devoted to Sade's letters; the *Lettres et mélanges littéraires,* ed. George Daumas and G. Lely (Paris: Editions Borderie, 1980), contains letters by Sade, his wife, and Rousset (and numerous other documents). Bourdin's edition, containing letters to Gaufridy, presents the widest range of correspondents, but unfortunately gives abridged versions of most letters.

5. Roger Duchêne, "Réalité vécue et réussite littéraire: le statut particulier de la lettre," *Revue d'histoire littéraire de la France* 71 (1971): 194. Duchêne's debate with Bray on literariness and self-consciousness in familiar letters is well known. For discussion and critique of the debate and some of its implications, see, among others, Louise K. Horowitz, "The Correspondence of Madame de Sévigné: Letters or Belles-Lettres?" *French Forum* 6 (1981): 13–27; and English Showalter, Jr., "Authorial Self-Consciousness and the Familiar Letter: The Case of Madame de Graffigny," *Yale French Studies* 71 (1986): 113–30. Both these essays have the merit of exploring ways in which the "true letter" can also partake of the myth-making, self-consciousness, and awareness of literary models or eventual public that Duchêne sees as the exclusive province of the *auteur épistolaire.*

6. Marcelin Pleynet, "Sade, des chiffres, des lettres, du renfermement," *Tel quel* 86 (1980): 26–37. Among the many critics interested in sounding Sade's affection for the *chiffral* have been Roland Barthes, *Sade, Fourier, Loyola* (Paris: Seuil, 1971), 182–83; Philippe Sollers, "Lettre de Sade," *Obliques* 12–13 (1977): 213–17; Jane Gallop, "The Immoral Teachers," *Yale French Studies* 63

(1982): 117–28; Joan DeJean, *Literary Fortifications: Rousseau, Laclos, Sade* (Princeton: Princeton University Press, 1984), 302–6; J. Hayes, "Sophistry and Displacement: The Poetics of Sade's Ciphers," *Studies on Voltaire* 242 (1986): 335–43. For the biographer's perspective, see Lely, *Oeuvres complètes* 2:31–35, and "Notice sur les signaux," Daumas and Lely 1:43–46.

7. Even Milli Rousset seems to have found the marquise somewhat irritating on this score. She writes to Gaufridy, "She's so totally unconscious of it that she daily says to me with absolute *sang froid:* 'When Monsieur de S. is out, we'll do this, we'll say that, etc.' Each project crazier than the last!" (15 Nov. 1780, Bourdin 160).

8. One of Sade's titles—and preferred aliases—was comte de Mazan.

9. In order to save it as well. Sade and Rousset corresponded again in 1782–83; he sent her what have become some of his best-known letters, among them the so-called "Etrennes philosophiques," Lely, *Oeuvres complètes,* 14:33–37 (for her answer, see Daumas and Lely 1:359–62); an "English" fantasy inviting her to dine "at milady Folleville's" (Lely 12:385–87); and the poetic meditation on the bells of Vincennes (Lely 12:387–89).

10. The marquise has been "impenetrable" (her mother's word) from her day to ours. Cf. her mother's comments (Bourdin 80, 93, etc.); the governor of the Bastille (Daumas and Lely 1:441–42); Rousset's report on "public" reaction (Bourdin 160). Sometimes romanticized (as in J. Delpèche's flowery *La Passion de la marquise de Sade* [Paris: Planète, 1970]), she is also described by modern biographers in terms of erotic fascination or complicity (Lely 2:12; Bourdin xxxii–xxxiv; Jean-Jacques Pauvert, *Sade vivant,* vol. 1: *Une Innocence sauvage 1740–1777* [Paris: Laffont, 1986], 96–108, 353ff.). It is interesting to note that, while Rousset has escaped having a sexual motive imputed to her actions in this century, such was not the case during her life: "The public is determined to link me up with Monsieur de Sade" (Bourdin 147; see also Daumas and Lely 1: 364–65).

III

Gender and epistolarity
in a modern key

12

Special Delivery:
Twenty-first Century Epistolarity
in The Handmaid's Tale

LINDA KAUFFMAN

A woman's life is all like the act of giving birth; a solitary, painful,
furtive act.

— The Three Marias: New Portuguese Letters

SET IN CAMBRIDGE before the year 2000, Margaret Atwood's *The Handmaid's Tale* (1986) depicts the aftermath of
a paramilitary coup by right-wing fundamentalists who establish a theocracy in the United States, renamed the Republic
of Gilead. Born about 1965, the heroine is old enough to remember her
feminist mother's activism, but young enough to be recruited into surrogate motherhood in the new regime. Toxic wastes, nuclear accidents, and
epidemics like AIDS have so decimated the population that reproduction
is compulsory: the surrogates, called handmaids, dressed in red habits
and veils, are assigned to aging childless couples among the regime's
elite. The narrator is stripped of her previous identity and given the
name "Offred," a patronymic composed of the possessive preposition
and the first name (in her case, Fred) of the Commander whom she
services.

The novel seems at first to have little in common with epistolary
literature, since letter writing will presumably become extinct in the age
of telecommunications and technological wizardry. But Atwood transports the dominant motifs of epistolarity into the twenty-first century,

transforming the heroine's "letter" into a tape recording from the 1990s, purposely recorded randomly from memory. The medium changes, but the mode remains the same. The novel's re-presentation of speech is a reconstruction several times removed, for Offred's discourse is muted, mediated, and modified by the interventions of time and technology, and by masculine writing appended to her own speech. Her tapes are unearthed and reconstructed in 2195 by a male archivist whose written transcript is the narrative we read. The representational status of writing and the voice of authority are thus decentered by Atwood's juxtaposition of two entirely different texts, one masculine and one feminine. Atwood apocalyptically foresees the failure of humanism, liberalism, individualism, feminism, and capitalism; disintegration and calamity follow. Postmodernism is therefore stamped on the text as indelibly as the postmark of epistolarity is. My aim in this essay is first to examine the novel's formal relations to epistolary traditions, particularly in terms of masculine writing versus feminine speech. I shall then explain how the novel functions as an anatomy of ideology, in order to show that apocalyptic politics are as vital as poetics in the special delivery of the postmodern epistolary mode.

Masculine Writing/Feminine Speech: Atwood's Epistolary Predecessors

The Handmaid's Tale has been compared thematically to *The Scarlet Letter* and to "fearsome future" novels like *1984*,[1] but its origins can be traced to the *locus classicus* of epistolarity, the *Heroides*, for, like Ovid's heroines, Offred narrates from exile, a ceaseless reiteration of her desire and her despair. She is multiply exiled: in obliterating the world she used to know, the Gileadean regime transforms her into "a refugee from the past."[2] When she flees Gilead, she is literally exiled; she makes her tapes while being hidden by the underground resistance movement. Thus, as with Ovid's Briseis, Dido, Penelope, and Medea, both Offred's psyche and the nation are in a state of siege among warring factions; in narrating, Offred situates herself in a landscape that is simultaneously psychic, physical, and political.[3] Whereas in earlier epochs the heroine addressed a reader (real or imagined), Offred addresses an imaginary listener. But like all earlier epistolary heroines, she reveals her pain and compulsively repeats it, as when she confesses:

> It hurts me to tell it over, over again. Once was enough: wasn't once enough for me at the time? But I keep on going with this sad and hungry and sordid, this limping and mutilated story, because after all I want

you to hear it. . . . By telling you anything at all I'm at least believing in you, I believe you're there, I believe you into being. Because I'm telling you this story I will your existence. I tell, therefore you are. (268)

What Offred wills is nothing less than a future for the human race, since, at the moment when she actually speaks, its destruction seems imminent. By positing a listener, she affirms her faith in its survival. Far from being a solitary testament of individual feeling, a purely interior discourse of the heart, Offred's obsessions of necessity center on history, politics, and apocalypse. Apocalypse generally connotes catastrophe: terrorism, mass torture, nuclear accidents, deadly new strains of contamination. But apocalypse also signifies revelation of what was, is, and will be; in this sense, Offred is a "handmaid" metaphorically as well as literally; she is the handmaid of history, who prophetically reveals the monstrous shape of things to come for a listener she can only imagine, but whom she wills into being by telling.

The epistolary gesture always entails the invention of a confidant who is absent at the moment of narrating, and it is therefore an act of dissimulation as well as of confidence. Offred's narrative embodies both impulses: she dissimulates by disguising all the names and by scrambling the order of her tapes, and she confides by repaying tenacious listeners with her remarkable revelations. As Janet Altman points out, "The epistolary confidant is most fundamentally an archivist"; Offred's listener is literally an archivist.[4] Just as the heroine's narrative provides a glimpse into a past that the archivist barely comprehends, his own historical notes provide a glimpse into a future that neither the heroine nor the reader could have foreseen, for by 2195 the entire map of the world has been transformed in terms of territory, language, culture, religion, and politics.

The text thus articulates the problems of transmission and reception, an articulation for which epistolarity is justly renowned, and in which the female voice is particularly problematic. As Bernard Duyfhuizen explains, "If a novel in letters is to exist, the act of transmission must include its inverse: the act of retaining or collecting. . . . One part of the narrative of transmission . . . is the story of the collection—how the letters become available to an "Editor."[5] That is precisely the story that the historical notes tell. Only after the reader finishes Offred's discourse and turns to those notes do the novel's epistolary origins become apparent: the fiction of found tapes is the next century's equivalent to the fiction of found letters. Professor Pieixoto, Cambridge University's director of twentieth- and twenty-first-century archives, recounts his discovery of Offred's tapes to the 12th Symposium on Gileadean Studies in 2195. More than thirty tapes are found in what used to be Bangor,

Maine; they were purposely recorded at random intervals on different musical cassettes to camouflage their chronology, coherence, and significance. Pieixoto determines that the tapes are authentic rather than forged, and draws deductions about the handmaid's culture. The very sequence of the sentences we read results from Piexioto's guesswork; he arranges Offred's "blocks of speech" in a plausible order. He is aided by voice-print experts and technicians who reconstruct a machine long obsolete: the tape recorder. The narrative we read is thus a reconstruction, an approximation, subject to numerous interventions, all of which undermine the voice(s) of authority and the validity of interpretation.

Perhaps the most celebrated predecessor in the tradition of the fiction of found letters is *Lettres portugaises,* published in France in 1669 by Claude Barbin, who added an *avis au lecteur* asserting that the letters were written by a Portuguese nun, Mariane, after her seduction and abandonment by a French chevalier. Barbin recounts his difficulties in "translating" the letters and "verifies" their authenticity, but he may have perpetrated one of the greatest literary hoaxes of all time, for many now believe that Racine's friend Gabriel-Joseph de Lavergne de Guilleragues authored the letters.[6] Both editor and author, well aware of the public's distaste for fiction, accurately predicted the scandalous appeal the "history" of the nun's passion would have for the public. Like Barbin, Atwood's archivist insists on the authenticity of his discovery, and repudiates those forgeries "for which publishers have paid large sums, wishing to trade no doubt on the sensationalism of such stories." One of his moralistic editorial intrusions follows: "It appears that certain periods of history quickly become, both for other societies and for those that follow them, the stuff of not especially edifying legend and the occasion for a good deal of hypocritical self-congratulation" (302). But the archivist commits the very crimes he condemns, for he has little sensitivity to Offred's predicament or her pain. His tone is jocular; Offred's narrative comes to be entitled "The Handmaid's Tale" as a bawdy joke among his colleagues: "the word *tail* . . . being, to some extent, the bone, as it were, of contention, in that phase of Gileadean society" (301). In this pun, the issues of genre (tale) and gender (tail) are joined. Professor Pieixoto does not know how to describe the document as a genre; in terms of gender, he is condescending, ascribing the aleatory construction of the discourse, its lack of style, to the poor education of North American females in the 1980s, and apologizing for the quality of Offred's mind. He wishes her record contained more data about the Gileadean regime and yearns for some of the Commander's computer printouts. He ignores the fact that it is precisely because she is female that she is denied access to the kind of information he desires. Pieixoto and his cohorts are merely the most recent of a long series of epistolary editors who appropriate the female voice for their own purposes—fame, fortune, power, self-aggrandizement, and self-congratulation.

His obsession with literal facts is particularly chilling since Gilead, like Puritan America, is founded on a literal interpretation of the Bible, specifically Genesis 30:1–3, where Rachel tells Jacob, "Behold my maid Bilhah, go in unto her; and she shall bear upon my knees, that I may also have children by her." These words result in a monthly "flesh triangle": Offred lies on her back between the knees of Serena Joy, the Commander's wife, while the Commander attempts to inseminate Offred. If and when she delivers a healthy baby, its appropriation and the handmaid's dismissal will follow—an ugly perversion of the spirit of the biblical dictum. How does one respond to such perversions? "One detaches onself. One describes," says Offred (95).

As so often in epistolary narration, Offred gives us the sense not just of narrating to the moment, but of narrating under compulsion: "I don't want to be telling this story," she confesses (273). Just as traditional epistolary heroines draw attention to the blots on the paper, the tear-stains on the page, and the self-reflexivity of their acts of writing, Offred repeatedly reminds us that

> this is a reconstruction. All of it is a reconstruction. It's a reconstruction now, in my head. . . . When I get out of here, if I'm ever able to set this down, in any form, even in the form of one voice to another, it will be a reconstruction then too, at yet another remove. It's impossible to say a thing exactly the way it was, because what you say can never be exact, you always have to leave something out, there are too many parts, sides, crosscurrents, nuances; too many gestures, which could mean this or that, too many shapes which can never be fully described, too many flavors, in the air or on the tongue, half-colors, too many. (134)

She emphasizes synesthesia, the poetic mixture of sensory impressions, because it is the texture of life that language cannot capture; that texture is too ineffably rich and temporally fleeting. She is, moreover, suspicious of all attempts to label, to sum up, to encapsulate, to define: Gilead has shown her too well the repression that results from literally enforcing one way, one truth, one interpretation. The compulsion to describe what cannot be put into words is one of the hallmarks of epistolarity; as the Portuguese nun reflects, "It seems to me that I am doing the greatest possible wrong to the feelings of my heart in trying to make them clear in writing to you."[7] Offred is similarly overwhelmed by the incapacity of language to encompass experience or feeling; it is always approximate, as she says in describing her affair with Nick: "I'm not sure how it happened; not exactly. All I can hope for is a reconstruction: the way love feels is always only approximate" (263). What is lacking in the archivist's commentary about Offred's discourse is precisely any sensitivity to taste, texture, touch, sound, sight—to the particularity of material existence in a specific historical moment.

That particularity is one of the hallmarks of epistolary writing-to-the-moment, but it has frequently led epistolary theorists to identify the epistle exclusively with individual feeling, as if such feelings could be isolated from social issues or politics. That is one of the myths Atwood dismantles. Epistolarity is in fact intrinsically political, whether one thinks of Ovid's exile, or Clarissa's rebellion against patriarchal bourgeois ideology, or the three Marias' prosecution for obscenity. Exiled, imprisoned, cloistered, or "shut up," epistolary heroines are deeply subversive because for them writing itself is an act of revolt. As the three Marias proclaim, "When woman rebels against man, nothing remains unchanged."[8] Transgression lies in the telling. *The Handmaid's Tale,* then, differs in degree rather than kind from its epistolary predecessors: what remains implicit in a text like *Lettres portugaises,* for example, is merely more explicit in Atwood's novel: sex and politics are indistinguishable as transfer points of power and oppression in a society under siege. The Portuguese nun's seduction is metonymic: she is enthralled by (and in thrall to) a Frenchman stationed in Portugal to expand the empire of the Sun King; once the conquest of woman and colony is accomplished, the chevalier sails home. In Gilead, similarly, woman's body becomes the territory to master; female sexuality is harnessed for the "higher good" of the body politic, and viable ovaries become a "national resource" (65).

The appropriation of the female body and voice is therefore closely allied with other political acts of appropriation and conquest. One begins the process of mastery by stealing the language, a theft that is a recurrent theme in Atwood's poetry as well as her fiction. In the "Circe/Mud" poems in *You Are Happy* (1974), for example, Circe is initially mistress of the island and namer of all things on it, but Odysseus vanquishes her by possessing her body and stealing her words: she spends her days "with my head pressed to the earth, to stones, / to shrubs, collecting the few muted syllables left over." She resists speaking in the "received language," as if aware that mythology always reproduces the same stories— of seduction, betrayal, conquest, power. She tries to subvert the glorious epic of omnipotent patriarchs by referring to Odysseus's "stupid boat, / your killer's hands." Yet she is helplessly doomed to silence, for she recognizes that he is the narrator of his odyssey, and she knows that "It's the story that counts." Despite her magical powers and prophetic capacities, she beseeches him to answer her questions: "When you leave will you give me back the words? Don't evade, don't pretend you won't leave after all: you leave in the story and the story is ruthless."[9] She knows that since he is master of the myth, his story will depict her as evil, and that she cannot change its contours or course. Atwood thus draws on Ovid's *Metamorphoses* as well as the *Heroides;* like Circe, Offred expresses the same powerlessness, the same awareness that she has no control over the outcome of what she narrates: "I would like to believe this is a story I'm telling. . . . If it's a story . . . then I have control over the ending. Then there will be an ending, to the story, and real life will come after it" (39). The catastrophic events she witnesses are so unreal that Offred tries to believe they are fictional, but she cannot sustain that delusion for long. Her circumstances are too desperate and the regime is too ruthless.

The archivist fails to appreciate the profound implications of Offred's act, for he does not comprehend the effort of will and the leap of faith it requires for her to imagine a listener. Nor does he fully understand her objectives, for the particularity of her predicament is closely allied to the collective fate of women in her society, and one of her aims is to record their individual voices as well as her own. Traditionally, the epistle brings the absent beloved before the writing heroine; the motif of *je crois te parler* enables her to "hold him in her hands," to believe that she is speaking to him. That is a complex process for Offred, because she must first re-create herself, since the regime has turned her into a "missing person . . . disembodied . . . deserted . . . like a room where things once happened and now nothing does" (103–4). She first has to reclaim herself, retrieve her voice; once she does so, she turns to reinscribe the voices of other women. Poignantly, in this context, *je crois te parler* amounts to raising the dead, for Offred tries to bring into being a nonexistent archive of women so as to memorialize, for history, the women she will never see again: her daughter, her mother, her friends, her co-conspirators. She re-presents the speech of Moira, for example, the gutsy college roommate who ends up as a prostitute in the Commander's private club. Offred consciously tries to mime Moira's iconoclastic, witty speech: "I've tried to make it sound as much like her as I can. It's a way of keeping her alive" (243–44). As a result, the entire narrative is a polyphony of distinctive female voices, but the archivist is deaf to these nuances. His scholarly, detached approach to the tapes reflects the assumptions of scientific research, technology, and objectivity; it assumes the status of truth. But his "truth" is not the same as women's. In Gilead, as in all previous periods of history, women's history is repressed; Gilead is merely the most recent regime to suppress their voices by prohibiting them from reading, writing, or speaking. The conditions of existence under which Offred labors do not permit the luxury of the archivist's so-called objectivity. As Pierre Macherey observes,

> The act of knowing is not like listening to a discourse already constituted, a mere fiction which we have simply to translate. It is rather the elaboration of a new discourse, the articulation of a silence. . . . What can be said *of* the work can never be confused with what the work itself is saying, because two distinct kinds of discourse which differ in both form and content are being superimposed.[10]

Atwood juxtaposes the handmaid's discourse with "what can be said" by the archivist, who errs in presuming that knowledge is an act of mere translation, once he assembles the proper technological equipment. The traditional definitions of "feminine" speech versus "masculine" writing are thus reaccentuated in Atwood's novel: the feminine is subjective, disordered, associative, illogical; the masculine is objective, orderly, controlled, logical. Such dichotomies have been reiterated by theorists of epistolarity through the ages, and have been used to decide whether the letter writer's sex can be determined solely by internal stylistic evidence; with such texts as *Lettres portugaises,* for example, the question continues to be intensely controversial.[11] Since on a tape recording it is easier to hear whether the speaker is male or female, the question will be less ambiguous in epistolary productions of the twenty-first century.

Ovid's heroines and the Portuguese nun are clearly Offred's ancestors, but her relationship with her missing husband, Luke, most closely resembles Héloïse's with Abelard. Years after Abelard's castration and her conventual incarceration, Héloïse still refuses to face the fact that their separation is permanent; instead she sustains her illusions and her passion in her letters. Offred is equally defiant and illogical; she cannot reconcile herself to the fact that she and Luke will never be free, never make love again, that he may not even be alive. She imagines three alternative fates for him: that he was killed when they were captured; that he is a political prisoner; that he escaped and is working in the resistance movement. She confesses, "The things I believe can't all be true, though one of them must be. But I believe in all of them, all three versions of Luke, at one and the same time. This contradictory way of believing seems to me, right now, the only way I can believe anything" (106). In contrast to Pieixoto's literalness, Offred strives to sustain a spiritual belief. "In reduced circumstances you have to believe all kinds of things. I believe in thought transference now . . . I never used to" (105). Thus, irrationality, which in former times would be seen as merely personal—and feminine—is here transformed into an explicitly political act, for Offred's survival is at stake in sustaining herself in order to witness to posterity about the fate of other political prisoners. Given the horror of her predicament, her danger, and its apocalyptic proportions, irrational faith is her only defense, for to be able to imagine one listener, she has to imagine the survival of thousands capable of vanquishing Gilead; these are the conditions of her survival and hence her narration. She explicitly relates her discourse to letters when she says:

> A story is like a letter. Dear *You,* I'll say. Just *you,* without a name. Attaching a name attaches *you* to the world of fact, which is riskier, more hazardous; who knows what the chances are out there of survival, yours? . . . *You* can mean more than one. *You* can mean thousands. . . . I'm not in any immediate danger, I'll say to you. I'll pretend you can hear me. (40)

Letters have long functioned to defamiliarize the distance between fiction and reality by drawing attention to the fictiveness of the narrative act, as Offred does here. But here, *je crois te parler* is linked not solely to sustaining sexual passion, but to the survival of the human race.

The same transformation of the personal to the political through the act of forbidden discourse applies to forbidden reading, which has long been a feminine transgression in fiction, as with the forbidden letters Clarissa receives from Lovelace. But in Gilead, it is not just personal letters that are forbidden; all reading is forbidden to women. The Commander indulges Offred's craving by offering her a secret supply of banned books and magazines: Charles Dickens, Raymond Chandler, *Ms.* magazine, *Mademoiselle, Vogue, Esquire, Reader's Digest.* She reads voraciously, trying to absorb as much material as quickly as possible in stolen moments. These materials help her remember a time before Gilead redefined even the language, developing such terms as "un-women," "unbaby," and "gender traitors" to reshape reality. That is why Offred's surreptitious Scrabble games with the Commander are so subversive: it is her method of stealing the language back again, a proleptic hint of the tape recordings she will eventually make. Language is what she steals, and through language, knowledge and power.

The epistolary novel is the site of numerous transgressions, the formal codes of which are all familiar: adultery in *Les Liaisons dangereuses;* prostitution in *Clarissa;* suicide in *The Sorrows of Young Werther,* forbidden reading in all of these. Atwood transforms these familiar codes while leaving their traces legible: since the previous handmaid killed herself when her trysts with the Commander were discovered, suicide is never far from Offred's mind. She is, moreover, defined by the regime as an adulteress since she married a divorced man. Furthermore, she deceives Serena with the Commander and later deceives the Commander with

Nick. Finally, when the Commander takes her to Jezebel's, the private men's club and brothel, she plays the prostitute. But the formal codes are here transformed into political crimes, for reading is not merely "an imaginary or metaphorical transgression."[12] Instead it is a literal crime, punishable by the amputation of a hand. The Gileadean regime punishes those who commit the "crime" of "unchastity" by amputating an arm and the crime of adultery by execution (275). In Gilead, these codes reflect an ideology devoted to the repression of human desire in general and female sexuality in particular.

What caused such sudden and severe societal repression? Offred learns from the Commander that the revolution came about because men felt irrelevant. "There was nothing for them to do with women . . . the sex was too easy. Anyone could just buy it. There was nothing to work for, nothing to fight for. . . . You know what they were complaining about the most? Inability to feel. Men were turning off on sex, even" (210). This revealing statement implies that male potency derives from and depends on the oppression of others. Only by wrapping women in veils and habits, by persecuting "deviants," by suspending civil liberties, do such men derive a sense of meaningful existence. As the three Marias observe, "The basic repression, the one which . . . lies at the very core of the history of the human species, creating the model and giving rise to the myths underlying other repressions, is that of the woman by the man."[13] At one point, Offred prophetically envisions a male listener to her tape and addresses him directly. After declaring that it is impossible to describe anything accurately, in all its fullness, she makes a crucial distinction between masculine and feminine responses to her discourse:

> If you happen to be a man, sometime in the future, and you've made it this far, please remember: you will never be subject to the temptation or feeling you must forgive, a man, as a woman. It's difficult to resist, believe me. But remember that forgiveness too is a power. To beg for it is a power, and to withhold or bestow it is a power, perhaps the greatest. (133-34)

This puzzling statement is perhaps made clearer by relating it to Offred's attitude toward the Commander. She weighs individual responsibility, emotional involvement, and the power of forgiveness as she tries to find the words to describe his monthly violation of her.

> He is fucking . . . the lower part of my body. I do not say making love, because this is not what he's doing. Copulating too would be inaccurate, because it would imply two people and only one is involved. Nor does rape cover it: nothing is going on here that I haven't signed up for. (94)

Offred's comment about forgiveness thus arises in the context of whether it is possible to forgive the Commander, who puts her life in peril by breaking the rules of their intercourse. On the one hand, he becomes an individual person rather than a thing to her, and she to him, which slightly eases her otherwise unbearable existence. On the other hand, she is completely in his power, and he can turn on her, or turn her in, at any moment, as happened to the previous handmaid. It may seem as if Offred is advocating forgiveness, but she goes on to record her childhood memory of a television documentary about the wife of a Nazi SS officer who was responsible for sending Jews to the ovens. Offred reflects that the wife "did not believe he was a monster. He was not a monster, to her. Probably he had some endearing trait: he whistled . . . he called his dog Liebchen. . . . How easy it is to invent a humanity, for anyone at all. What an available temptation" (145-46). The temptation of a woman to forgive a man is precisely what Offred abjures; forgiving would result in forgetting, and that is exactly what she records her narrative to prevent: her listeners must remember history and must not eradicate the memory of what has been done to the spirits and bodies of the regime's dissenters and its victims.

Docile Bodies: An Anatomy of Ideology

Offred neither forgives nor forgets; she rebels by keeping the past alive. What the regime would eradicate, she reinscribes. Her first words evoke the "afterimage" of a world long ago and far away: she remembers the basketball games and high school dances held through the decades in the gymnasium where she is imprisoned, which has been turned into a re-education center to indoctrinate handmaids in their new roles. "There was old sex in the room and loneliness, and expectation, of something without a shape or name. I remember that yearning, for something that was always about to happen . . . we yearned for the future" (3). The intensity with which teenagers yearned for the future is grimly ironic in retrospect, since that future has now arrived, emptied of hope, choice, possibility. The "something without shape or name" is desire, and Offred remembers her own "insatiability," a craving all the more poignant now, since desire is precisely what is banned in Gilead.

Her individual memories illuminate not just her intimate relations, but political and historical moments, ranging from her mother's feminist activism for abortion rights and against pornography, to her own combined roles as working woman, wife, lover, friend, mother, citizen. But

Gilead strips women of their individuality, categorizing them hier-
archically according to class status and reproductive capacity. They are in
fact, metonymically color-coded according to their function and their
labor: the Commanders' wives wear blue (a remnant perhaps of aristocracy's blue bloods); the handmaids wear red, the color of blood; and "econowives," distributed to lesser functionaries in the regime, wear multi-
colored dresses, to indicate that they have to perform multiple sexual
and housewifely functions. The very term "econowives" makes explicit
the hierarchical commodification of the female. Men without any status
are not "issued a woman, not even one" (18). The traffic in women
eliminates the individual female personality; she merely becomes an
interchangeable unit in the body politic.

The novel thus gives a new and ominous meaning to the phrase "the
body politic" by laying bare the devices by which subjects of the state are
ideologically constructed. Atwood implicitly inquires, "What is woman?"
The answer: a person of the female sex. Only in certain relations of
power and exchange does she become a servant, a womb, or a sexual
partner, as Simone de Beauvoir observes in *The Second Sex*, which may
have provided Atwood's donnée, for in trying to distinguish production
in the Marxist sense from biological reproduction, de Beauvoir observes:

> It is impossible simply to equate gestation with a service, such as
> military service . . . no state has ever ventured to establish obligatory
> copulation. . . . All that can be done is to put woman in a situation
> where maternity is for her the sole outcome—the law or the mores
> enjoin marriage, birth control and abortion are prohibited, divorce is
> forbidden.[14]

That is precisely the situation Atwood imagines: mass marriages are
arranged; divorce is prohibited; free will and individual choice cease to
exist. Like Héloïse, Mariane, and the many nuns in *The Three Marias*,
Offred takes the veil not from internal religious conviction but because
external pressures coerce her to harness her sexuality. The only difference between her existence and a nun's is that the latter is forced to be
chaste, whereas for Offred and all handmaids copulation is obligatory;
birth control and abortion are prohibited; woman is compelled to bring
forth or face death.

Apocalypse depicts what has been, what is, and what will be. Atwood
depicts what "woman" has been in the Judeo-Christian tradition, from
biblical times through the 1980s to the end of the next century. From
Medusa to the Virgin Mary, from the biblical handmaid Bilhah to Hester
Pyrnne, from Mary Webster[15] to Maryann Crescent Moon in 2195, the
novel assembles the constructions of "woman": monster, madonna,

witch, womb, whore, revolutionary, heretic, prostitute, servant, mother. Atwood's purpose is to show that revolutions come and go, but women's fates remain wholly unchanged. The three Marias share the same insight in *New Portuguese Letters,* as they similarly shift forward and backward through time, asking in a woman's diary entry from 1800:

> What woman is not a nun, sacrificed, self-sacrificing, without a life of her own, sequestered from the world? What change has there been in the life of women through the centuries? . . . We are living in an age of civilization and enlightenment, men write scientific treatises, and encyclopedias, nations continually change and transform their political structure, the oppressed raise their voices, a king of France has been sent to the guillotine and his courtiers along with him, the United States of America has gained its independence. . . . What has changed in the life of women?[16]

Rather than being progressive, history, for women, is both regressive and repressive. Atwood is unflinching in depicting the oppression of women before the coup as well as after: before the coup, women were not safe on the streets; portable "Pornomarts" were on every corner; "snuff" films celebrated the murder and dissection of female bodies. The new regime promises an end to rape, pornography, and violence. As Atwood observes, "A new regime would never say, 'we're socialist; we're fascist.' They would say that they were serving God. . . . You can develop any set of beliefs by using the Bible. . . . Repressive regimes always have to offer up something in return."[17] Women believed the regime's promises and participated in book-burnings, inadvertently colluding in their own enslavement; it is precisely the cooperation of feminists with right-wingers that helps bring about the fundamentalist coup: pornography is banned, but so are all civil liberties. Martial law is imposed and all undesirables—prostitutes, lesbians, and feminists like the narrator's mother—are forced to clean toxic wastes until they die from contamination. All are labeled "unwomen." Language thus defines reality, which is one reason that Offred spends so much time meditating about words, comparing their meanings before the coup and after, their arbitrariness and construction. Of the word *chair,* for example, she reflects "It can mean the leader of a meeting. It can also mean a mode of execution. It is the first syllable in charity. It is the French word for flesh. None of these facts has any connection with the others" (110). But in fact there is an associative connection, for the leaders of the revolution enforce their power by torturing the flesh of dissenters. Resisters receive no charity, no mercy; instead, they are executed.

The Handmaid's Tale functions as an anatomy of ideology, exposing the process by which one constructs, psychologically and politically, subjects of the state, and then enlists their cooperation in their own subjection. One begins at the level of the flesh. In the re-education centers, the handmaid is taught to have an entirely different relation to her own body, her "self." As Offred confesses:

> Each month I watch for blood, fearfully, for when it comes it means failure. I have failed once again to fulfill the expectations of others, which have become my own. I used to think of my body as an instrument of pleasure, or a means of transportation, or an implement for the accomplishment of my will. I could use it to run, push buttons of one sort or another, make things happen. There were limits, but my body was nevertheless lithe, single, solid, one with me.
>   Now the flesh arranges itself differently. I'm a cloud, congealed, around a central object, the shape of a pear, which is hard and more real than I am and glows red within its translucent wrapping. Inside it is a space . . . huge. . . . I see despair coming towards me like famine. To feel that empty, again, again. (73-74)

Atwood's purpose, like Ovid's in the *Metamorphoses,* "is to tell of bodies which have been transformed into shapes of a different kind"; here Offred's body is reduced to the womb, a reproductive factory.

The novel demonstrates the paradox that the ideology of the biological family really comes into its own when the complexity of a class society forces the kinship system to recede.[18] Since children are distributed like commodities, the biological kinship system has ceased to exist. But at the same time the patriarchs justify their reign of terror by trumpeting the ideology of the family to the heavens, basing it on an extremist's interpretation of the Bible. The closest corollary to the Gileadean system is slavery in the American South, when black women were similarly prized and priced as breeders. As in slavery, despite the woman's labor, the white slaveholders, like the men in Gilead, retain legal property rights over the product of the woman's body; religiously and legally, it is the man who "produces" the child, just as it has always been.

Bodies are turned into machines in the army, the school, and the hospital; in Atwood's novel, the Red Centers combine all three functions. They are run by the "Aunts," menopausal women whose job is to create a sisterhood and a women's culture, a grim parody of one of the quaint feminist impulses of the 1970s and 1980s. The Aunts are licensed to torture recruits who resist re-education. (This emphasis on the collusion of women with their oppressors is significant; one of the regime's strokes of genius is their discovery that the least expensive way to enforce its policies is by using women against each other.) The Red Centers are also hospitals, for here the handmaids practice Lamaze exercises and undergo drug and shock treatments. Their identities as women, wives, mothers, lovers are all erased through discipline, punishment, and torture. As Foucault asks, "Is it surprising that prisons resemble factories, schools, barracks, hospitals, which all resemble prisons?"[19] Offred is simultaneously a prisoner, a pupil to be re-educated, a patient who is forcibly subjected to monthly gynecological exams to optimize the chances of pregnancy. The novel thus condenses two of Foucault's major subjects: the birth of the prison and the birth of the clinic, the gaze of the panopticon and the gaze of the medical amphitheater.[20] In Gilead, all flesh is brought down to the level of the organism.

In revealing the inextricable connections between power and sexuality, Atwood demonstrates the validity of the observation that "Sexuality is not the most intractable element in power relations, but rather one of those endowed with the greatest instrumentality."[21] Offred's reckless trysts with Nick seem to refute Foucault's thesis, but when she is discovered, she says,

> I'll sacrifice. I'll repent. I'll abdicate. I'll renounce. . . . Everything they taught at the Red Center, everything I've resisted comes flooding in. I don't want pain. . . . I want to keep on living, in any form. I resign my body freely, to the uses of others. They can do what they like with me. I am abject. I feel, for the first time, their true power. (286)

Her predecessor's suicide under similar circumstances attests to the powerful mechanisms in force to control sexuality. In Gilead, all citizens are classified in binary categories that control and contain everyone: licit versus illicit sex; reproductive versus nonreproductive ovaries; white versus black; religious believer versus heretic. Homosexuals are executed as "gender traitors"; abortionists are hanged for crimes against the species; Jews must emigrate or convert; blacks are "resettled"; feminists and other deviants—Quakers, Baptists, Catholics, atheists, liberals, leftists—are "disappeared."

To make visible the invisible work of ideology and subjection, Atwood's archeological investigations uncovered two theocracies as models: Puritan Boston of *The Scarlet Letter* and modern Iran under the Ayatollah Khomeini. Like Hester Prynne, the handmaid is defined by her sexuality, literally marked as a scarlet woman. Like Hester, she lives in a utopia gone awry, where the prison and the cemetery are omnipresent. Hawthorne's "Custom House" seems to have inspired Atwood's preoccupation with the ways in which we subject ourselves to the prison houses of custom: repression is first horrific, but soon comes to seem necessary, then customary, and finally "natural." At one point, Offred offhandedly remarks that at present "only" two bodies hang on the wall in what used to be Harvard Yard. The present reality in all its horror is already coming to seem normal—even to her—and the next generation will have no memory, no means by which to measure the relative normality or abnormality of the regime. Indeed, time is carefully manipulated so that all remnants of the past, pre-Gilead reality are obliterated: there are no dates after the 1980s; all historical documents are destroyed, and the Gileadean regime periodically wipes out even its own computer records after various purges.

In a society under siege, when the brutal force of a coup prescribes the law of the land, subjects are defined solely by obedience: the subject who is constituted as subject is he who obeys. As Foucault observes:

> The historical moment of the disciplines was the moment when an art of the human body was born, which was directed not only at . . . the intensification of its subjection, but at the formation of a relation that in the mechanism itself makes it more obedient as it becomes more useful, and conversely. What was then being formed was a policy of coercions that act upon the body, a calculated manipulation of its elements, its gestures, its behaviour. The human body was entering a machinery of power that explores it, breaks it down and rearranges it. A "political anatomy," which was also a "mechanics of power," was being born.[22]

Disciplined like soldiers, the handmaids learn to control their bodies, to respond mechanically, to act as a collective unit. As with a soldier or a nun, each handmaid's body and gestures must reflect her status; she is commanded by signals, not by comprehension. Perhaps the closest model for the behavior desired of her is *dressage*—the leading of horses through their paces—which metaphorically signifies blind obedience.[23]

Obedience is also ensured through the careful regulation of time. As Offred notes, "the bell that measures time is ringing. Time here is measured by bells, as once in nunneries. As in a nunnery too, there are few mirrors" (8). Offred's bodily movements are minutely monitored: so many minutes in the bathroom; so many chances (three) to conceive. Her entire existence as handmaid consists of waiting: waiting for the monthly "ceremony" during which the Commander tries to impregnate her; waiting for the results; and, if they are positive, waiting to deliver the baby. Another way to ensure obedience is to enforce silence; since spies are everywhere, the entire society ceases to speak freely, and the handmaids are only allowed to speak in prescribed pious clichés.

Atwood portrays a regime in the process of establishing the mechanisms of repression that will eventually be invisible. At the moment, they can still be seen: executions still abound; checkpoints stop citizens from fleeing the city; police vans suddenly materialize on the streets and whisk unsuspecting citizens away. However, once Gilead works out the kinks in its repressive mechanisms, all citizens will, like the handmaids in their red habits, exist in a state of conscious and permanent "compulsory visibility" that will ensure the automatic functioning of power. The agents are called the Eyes, and eventually, as in Bentham's panopticon, surveillance will become permanent in its effects, even if discontinuous in its action, for the institutional gaze will be invisible but omniscient.[24]

Atwood's novel is thus an exemplary response to the challenge Michèle Barrett recently addressed to feminist literary critics:

> I can find no sustained argument as to why feminists should be so inter-
> ested in literature or what theoretical or political ends such analyses of
> literature serve. . . . Related to this is the inadequacy of feminist
> attempts to explore the ways in which material conditions have histori-
> cally structured the mental aspects of oppression.[25]

Atwood's aim, however, is precisely to demonstrate how material conditions structure mental oppression, for despite all Offred's efforts to remember her prior existence, she has begun to take on the perception the regime wants her to have of herself. When she sees a pregnant woman, for example, she feels the emptiness of her own womb and experiences a sense of failure, futility, and worthlessness. Her breasts become swollen and ache. This is exactly how the material and mental aspects of oppression work in concert, for the Red Center trains her to reflect in her material body the mental impression it strives never to let her forget: that she is nothing but a passive receptacle.

Although Offred internalizes the oppression to which she is subjected, she also resists it. She repossesses her body by making love with Nick, an act for which she could be executed; she is compelled toward him, "expecting at any moment to feel the bullets rip through me" (268). By telling him her real name, she unburies the body, the voice, the self that the regime sought to annihilate, and she demonstrates how uneradicable desire is. As de Beauvoir observes, "It is impossible to bring the sexual instinct under a code of regulations. . . . What is certain is that it does not permit of integration with the social, because there is in eroticism a revolt of the instant against time, of the individual against the universal."[26] In this way Offred defies the regime's definitions of her, for she and Nick "make love each time as if we know beyond the shadow of a doubt that there will never be any more, for either of us, with anyone, ever" (269).

Paradoxically, she also resists the regime by taking responsibility for her actions. Offred recognizes that she is guilty of numerous sins, albeit sins different from those defined by the regime. She castigates herself for not paying enough attention to the alarming signs of intolerance—religious, racial, and sexual—in her society before the takeover; and for colluding with the regime in order to survive. Her confession of these sins recalls one of the most remarkable characteristics of the female voice throughout epistolary literature, for from Héloïse to Mariane to Clarissa, heroines have used their letters to engage in merciless self-condemnation. Like Clarissa and the three Marias, Offred puts herself on trial.[27] She reveals her participation in the rite of "salvaging," for instance, which means that when a woman is hanged, Offred touches the rope in unison with the other handmaids, then places her hand on her heart "to show my unity with the Salvagers and my consent, and my complicity in the death of this woman" (276). She also confesses to sharing the sensations the regime wants her to have when a political prisoner is brought before the handmaids on trumped-up charges of raping and murdering a pregnant handmaid. In a ritual called particicution they rape and dismember him; only by an extraordinary effort of will does Offred restrain herself, but she nevertheless experiences the "bloodlust; I want to tear, gouge, rend" (279). And she memorializes both her complicity and that corpse in her text.

> I wish this story were different. I wish it were more civilized. I wish it showed me in a better light, if not happier, then at least more active, less hesitant, less distracted by trivia. I wish it had more shape. . . . I'm sorry there is so much pain in this story. I'm sorry it's in fragments, like a body caught in crossfire or pulled apart by force. (267)

While apologizing for the pain in her story, Offred emphasizes that the fact that she is unhappy is less relevant than the fact that she should have been more engaged in collective action to save her society from fanatics. She compares the present with the ominous signs of growing repression in the past before the coup.

> We lived as usual. Everyone does, most of the time. Whatever is going on is as usual. Even this is as usual, now. We lived, as usual, by ignoring. Ignoring isn't the same as ignorance, you have to work at it. Nothing changes instantaneously: in a gradually heating bathtub you'd be boiled to death before you knew it. (56)

She was an apathetic, self-absorbed member of the "post-feminist generation."[28] The passage is thus an example of the ways in which one can locate in the same situation the forces of oppression and the seeds of resistance, for while Offred in some respects internalizes the oppression the regime enforces, she simultaneously resists it by confessing her individual responsibility and by making the tape recordings. From *Clarissa* to

The Three Marias, the heroine's discourse simultaneously reveals her oppression and resistance, collusion and rebellion. That duality, indeed, is yet another hallmark of the female voice in epistolary literature.

Quakers and Catholics also resist the regime; even Southern Baptists start a civil war, which to Atwood proves that there is considerable resistance, even among groups one would have thought would support a fundamentalist takeover. Her view of the Southern Baptists, however, seems overly optimistic in reality, for the 14.6-million-member denomination in 1987 elected a leader who endorses a literal interpretation of the Bible, insisting that "the narratives of Scripture are historically and factually accurate." A moderate minister who dissented from the majority vote noted that the election "seems to reflect the agenda of the fundamentalist takeover."[29]

Thus another reason for feminist literary analysis is that novels like Atwood's are less about the "fearsome future," than about the "fearsome present," for she dismantles received ideas and unquestioned assumptions about religion, sex, politics, women's cultures—and feminism itself. Atwood audaciously creates a heroine who is in a very real sense responsible for the Gileadean coup: she is apathetic politically, complacent about women's struggle for equal rights, absorbed solely in her individual existence. All around her she sees racial hatred, religious intolerance, and sexual repression intensifying daily. If *The Handmaid's Tale* were solely a tragic tale of one woman's suffering, it would merely reinforce the emphasis bourgeois ideology places on the individual, but by focusing equally on the decimation of a culture and a race, Atwood expands the parameters of the epistolary mode. Perhaps the most chilling statement in the novel is that of Professor Pieixoto, who observes, "There was little that was truly original with or indigenous to Gilead: its genius was synthesis" (307). The repressions Gilead devises are a synthesis of all previous cultures: it borrows from the Spanish inquisitors, the Puritans, Khomeini's Iranian followers, the KGB, the CIA. Gilead borrows Hitler's tactics of encircling urban centers, persecuting the Jews, eliminating undesirables, and using female bodies as laboratories for genetic reproduction. Pieixoto comments, "The sociobiological theory of natural polygamy was used as a scientific justification for some of the odder practices of the regime, just as Darwinism was used by earlier ideologies" (306).

Since such ghastly practices come to seem normal while Offred is witnessing them, one inevitably wonders what hope there is of sustaining any sense of outrage nearly two centuries later. Because readers in the 1980s are closer to the period Offred describes, our horror at what may become our imminent destiny is proportionally greater; Pieixoto and his colleagues, however, look coolly back on a distant past. Whereas Offred sees nothing but pain in her narrative, two hundred years later, it is merely a source of quaint curiosity to the historians, archaeologists, and anthropologists who hear it. The immediacy of her danger and her descriptions of the evils she witnesses seem so remote in 2195 that her audience cannot even rouse itself to murmur against "the banality of evil"; nothing is condemned by Pieixoto, who warns: "We must be cautious about passing moral judgment upon the Gileadeans. Surely we have learned by now that such judgments are of necessity culture-specific. . . . Our job is not to censure but to understand" (302).

This statement is a direct contrast to Offred's own defiant outrage, for like survivors of other holocausts, she insists that we pay attention to the material conditions of the suffering of specific individuals in a particular historical moment:

> Maybe none of this is about control. Maybe it isn't really about who can own whom, who can do what to whom and get away with it, even as far as death. Maybe it isn't about who can sit and who has to kneel or stand or lie down, legs spread open. Maybe it's about who can do what to whom and be forgiven for it. Never tell me it amounts to the same thing. (134-35)

You can only forgive atrocities that you forget, and Offred reminds us never to forget, never to bury the horrors of history amid vague clichés in which there are no agents and no evils. Judgment is necessary, she insists, to prevent the past from repeating itself.

The archivist's myopia is ironically underscored by the last words of the text: "Are there any questions?" The novel leaves us haunted by myriad questions: What was Offred's eventual fate? What happened during the intervening century and a half to the United States and North America? The human race has survived, and the planet seems to have replenished itself—there are fish, oceans, forests—but what kind of society exists in 2195? Is it less sexist, racist, homophobic, fanatical? Is it more just? Or is it a telling comment that the archivist refuses to condemn Gilead as evil? Perhaps his society has merely perfected Gilead's "genius for synthesis," making the mechanisms of power and repression completely invisible—and thus all-pervasive. What, if anything, have we learned from history?

The novel resists closure, leaving us with disturbing questions rather than soothing answers. Atwood records the failure of humanism, liberalism, individualism, and feminism, but she offers no substitutes, no solutions, no comforting fictions of personal or political redemption—including feminist fictions. As Elaine Hansen observes, "This kind of fiction and feminism alike insists that we uncover and examine the contradictions, the disequilibrium and insufficiency masked by the sense of an ending."[30] Thus in form and content, Atwood purposely dismantles received ideas about the present, as well as about the past and future, a strategy that evokes Fredric Jameson's reflection on future fiction: "The reader will there find an empty chair reserved for some as yet unrealized, collective, and decentered cultural production of the future, beyond realism and modernism alike."[31] Atwood invents just such a decentered cultural production, for the narrative we read is a collective endeavor, made possible by the resistance movement that presumably rescues Offred, by her courage and defiance in taping her discourse, and by archaeologists and technicians who reassemble her speech. The concentric construction of Atwood's apocalyptic novel encompasses past, present, and future. She makes us into detectives, trying to reconstruct the political history from which Offred's daily chronicle emerges. We discover the struggles and tensions that resulted in the establishment of Gilead's theocracy, and with the appended historical notes, we see history portrayed in its vastest sense, projected into the next century.[32] Through this triple framework, Atwood decenters both history and narrative. By dialogically superimposing the archivist's writing over the heroine's speech, she decenters the representational status of writing while reaccentuating the epistolary postmark.[33]

Atwood's unique contribution to the long tradition of female voices in epistolary literature is to combine epistolary poetics with apocalyptic politics. Despite Gilead's attempts to ban desire, Offred's remains unvanquished. Despite the self-aggrandizement of masculine editors, the interventions of time, and the ideologues who sought to eradicate her, the distinctive female voice of Atwood's heroine remains. Her discourse is a defiant testimony of her innocence and culpability, her defiance and desire, her submission and rebellion to the history being rewritten before her eyes. Like Rennie, Atwood's heroine in *Bodily Harm,* her experiences of a brutal regime so radicalize her that she becomes "a subversive: She was not once but now she is. A reporter. She will pick her time; then she will report."[34] The novel is finally a testament to the urgency of the analytical project that lies at the interstices of feminism and literary theory, for the future Atwood describes is not distant. Instead, like 1984, it has already arrived. Atwood merely defamiliarizes the world around us in the 1980s: whether one thinks of the trials of surrogate motherhood, or the Vatican's recent doctrinal edict against anything but married "normal sexuality," or of the AIDS epidemic and its attendant repressions, or the resurgence of racial and religious intolerance—the seeds of hatred, violence, and repression are already prepared. Whatever "issue" is slouching toward Bethlehem may not yet be more than an embryo, but the seeds of disciplinary power and punishment of the body politic have already been sown. Like Foucault, Atwood is writing a history of the present.[35]

NOTES

1. Mary McCarthy, *New York Times Book Review,* 9 Feb. 1986, pp. 1, 35.

2. Margaret Atwood, *The Handmaid's Tale* (Boston: Houghton Mifflin, 1986), 227. Subsequent references to this text are cited parenthetically.

3. For an analysis of the *Heroides* as the locus classicus of epistolarity, see Linda Kauffman, *Discourses of Desire: Gender, Genre, and Epistolary Fictions* (Ithaca: Cornell University Press, 1986), ch. 1. See also Janet Altman, *Epistolarity: Approaches to a Form* (Columbus: Ohio State University Press, 1982), 118–20.

4. Altman, *Epistolarity,* 53. Chapter 2 examines the oppositions of confidence and dissimulation in epistolary fiction. The dissimulation and duplicity of epistolary heroines (Ovid's, Héloïse, Mariane, Clarissa, and the three Marias) are discussed in Kauffman, 17, 23–27, 31, 32, 40–44, 56, 61, 70, 74, 110, 138, 142, 145, 148, 154–56, 179, 187, 201, 207, 288, 301–2, 305.

5. Bernard Duyfhuizen, "Epistolary Narratives of Transmission and Transgression," *Comparative Literature* 37 (Winter 1985): 1–26.

6. See Frédéric Deloffre and J. Rougeot, "L'Enigme des *Lettres portugaises,*" in *Lettres portugaises, Valentins, et autres oeuvres de Guilleragues* (Paris: Garnier, 1962), v-xxiii. While in the editors' view the identification of Guilleragues as author is definitive, others argue that although no Portuguese original has ever been found, the work was at least inspired by authentic letters of a Portuguese woman. The controversy is far from being settled; Peter Dronke maintains in the *Times Literary Supplement* (5 Nov. 1976, p. 1397) that the entire issue "remains . . . wide open"; Yves Florenne, in "Introduction," *Lettres de la religieuse portugaise* (Paris: Librairie générale française, 1979), 77, argues for a female voice; Jean-Pierre and Thérèse LaSalle offer new evidence and additional letters by the same hand in *Un Manuscrit des lettres d'un religieuse portugaises: Leçons, interrogations, hypotheses,* Papers on French Seventeenth-Century Literature 6 (Paris: Biblio 17, 1982). See also Kauffman, ch. 3.

7. Frédéric Deloffre and J. Rougeot, eds., *Lettres portugaises, Valentins, et autres oeuvres de Guilleragues* (Paris: Garnier, 1962), 43, my translation.

8. Maria Isabel Barreño, Maria Teresa Horta, Maria Velho da Costa, *The Three Marias: New Portuguese Letters* (New York: Bantam, 1976), 158. The three Marias were prosecuted by the Caetano-Salazar dictatorship from 1972 to 1974. See Kauffman, ch. 8; on epistolary strategies of transgression, see Kauffman, 18, 27, 38–40, 49–50, 60, 64–68, 75, 78, 81–84, 89, 119, 132, 155, 229, 280–81, 289, 290–300, 310.

9. Margaret Atwood, "Circe/Mud Poems," in *You Are Happy* (Toronto: Oxford University Press, 1974; rpr. in *Norton Anthology of Literature by Women,* ed. Sandra Gilbert and Susan Gubar [New York: Norton, 1985], 2296–98).

10. Pierre Macherey, *A Theory of Literary Production,* trans. Geoffrey Wall (London: Routledge & Kegan Paul, 1978), 6.

11. See, for example, Peggy Kamuf, "Writing like a Woman," in *Women and Language in Literature and Society,* ed. Sally McConnell-Ginet, Ruth Borker, and Nelly Furman (New York: Praeger, 1980), 284–99; Nancy K. Miller, "The Text's Heroine: A Feminist Critic and Her Fictions," *Diacritics* 12 (Summer 1982): 48–53; and Kauffman, ch. 3.

12. In "Flaubert's Presuppositions," *Diacritics* 11 (Winter 1981): 2–11, Michael Riffaterre traces a causal connection leading from forbidden reading to adultery, and from adultery to prostitution or suicide:

> The first fatal step leads inevitably to the last fatal leap. These inseparable and complementary poles thus set the limits of the fictional space extending from an imaginary or metaphorical transgression (wicked thoughts nurtured by immoral and forbidden readings) to the most definitive of all actual or literal transgressions—the one that drags the heroine out of existence, and out of the text, simultaneously putting an end to what can be lived or to what can be told in words. The adulteress either commits suicide or sinks into prostitution.

13. *The Three Marias,* 219.

14. Simone de Beauvoir, *The Second Sex,* trans. and ed. H. M. Parshley (New York: Vintage, 1974), 65–66.

15. Atwood dedicates the book to Perry Miller, her professor of American literature at Harvard, and to Mary Webster, her Puritan forebear who was hanged as a witch but survived. "She had a tough neck," Atwood wryly observes.

16. *The Three Marias,* 154. Even after a junior officer's coup overthrew the Caetano-Salazar dictatorship in 1974, the women were still forced to stand trial, an injustice that further demonstrates the validity of their argument that revolutions do little to change women's oppression. See Kauffman, ch. 8.

17. Interview with Cathy N. Davidson, *Ms.* magazine, February 1986, pp. 24–26. Regarding the current feminist debate about pornography versus censorship, Atwood observes, "Women are in the position of being asked to choose between two things, neither of which is good for them. Why can't they have a third thing that is good for them . . . some kind of reasonable social milieu in which pornography would not be much of an issue because it would not be desired by men?"

18. Juliet Mitchell, *Psychoanalysis and Feminism: Freud, Reich, Laing, and Women* (Harmondsworth: Penguin, 1975), 378.

19. Michel Foucault, *Discipline and Punish: The Birth of the Prison,* trans. Alan Sheridan (New York: Vintage, 1979), 228.

20. See Foucault, *The Birth of the Clinic: An Archaeology of Medical Perception,* trans. A. M. Sheridan Smith (New York: Vintage, 1975).

21. Foucault, *Discipline and Punish,* 103.

22. Ibid., 138.

23. Ibid., 166.

24. Ibid., 195–228.

25. Michèle Barrett, "Ideology and the Cultural Production of Gender," in *Criticism and Social Change: Sex, Class and Race in Literature and Culture,* ed. Judith Newton and Deborah Rosenfelt (New York: Methuen, 1985), 65–85.

26. de Beauvoir, 65.

27. For an analysis of the trial motif in epistolary literature and the heroines' self-condemnation, see Kauffman, 44–45, 77–78, 133–36, 187–94.

28. See Susan Bolotin's "Voices from the Post-Feminist Generation," *New York Times Magazine,* 17 Oct. 1982, pp. 28–31, 103–7.

29. Atwood's comments appear in the *Ms.* interview; the Southern Baptists' Convention was reported by the *News and Observer,* Raleigh, N.C., 17 June 1987, pp. 1, 13A.

30. Elaine Tuttle Hansen, "Fiction and (Post)Feminism in Atwood's *Bodily Harm,*" *Novel* 19 (Fall 1985): 5–21.

31. Fredric Jameson, *The Political Unconscious: Narrative as a Socially Symbolic Act* (Ithaca: Cornell University Press, 1981), 11.

32. The novel embodies Jameson's concept of "symbolization," (75), for its structure consists of:

> three concentric frameworks [that] function to mark a widening out of the sense of the social ground of a text through . . . first, . . . political history, in the narrow sense of . . . a chroniclelike sequence of happenings in time; then of society, in the . . . sense of a constitutive tension and struggle between social classes; and ultimately, of history now conceived in its vastest sense of . . . various social formations, from prehistoric life to whatever far future history has in store for us.

33. Cf. Jameson, 285, 296. On Bakhtinian dialogism and epistolary reaccentuation, see Kauffman, 18, 23, 25, 33, 79, 82, 120, 282, 298.

34. Atwood, *Bodily Harm* (New York: Simon and Schuster, 1982), 265.

35. Foucault, *Discipline and Punish,* 31. Mary McCarthy disagrees. She sees nothing "in our present mores that I ought to watch out for unless I want the United States . . . to become a slave state something like the Republic of Gilead." *New York Times Book Review,* 9 Feb. 1986, pp. 1, 35. Has McCarthy perhaps lived in Paris too long?

13

No Body There:
on the Politics of Interlocution

ALICIA BORINSKY

 FEW LITERARY works will be perceived as being as far apart in their overall effect on the reader as Manuel Puig's *Heartbreak Tango* and Jacques Derrida's *La Carte Postale*. It is because of that very difference between them, so easily intuited at first reading, that their consideration together may shed light onto the ways in which the epistolary genre has changed in contemporary literature.

One of the works is by a "true" novelist, Manuel Puig; the other is by the writer most identified with an interest in the theoretical underpinnings of written language, Jacques Derrida. In spite of its stated intention of subverting the hierarchy separating what is commonly understood as literature from the discourse—called theory—that encompasses it, the work of Derrida is often cited as the ultimate instance of critical awareness, thereby exempting it from any questioning.[1] What if, instead of granting it that privilege vis-à-vis other texts, we refused it a special place and let it circulate, changed by meanings inflected by a very different sort of writing? This way of reading is, in itself, an understanding of literary criticism as a special kind of correspondence. Its locus is our contemporary library, where coexistent volumes are made to produce meaning for each other through our reading. In the forced familiarity imposed by the present, the reader becomes the ideal recipient of a correspondence trying to persuade and manipulate him or her. The two works considered are built, in each case, around an explicit epistolary conceit.[2]

How Good Is Woman's Love?

Throughout his numerous novels, Manuel Puig has paid increasing attention to popular culture as a tool for undoing the solemnity of "serious" literature. Among the startling effects of this borrowing from existent mainstream sources is his treatment of love, in which woman surfaces as a kind of countermuse in his frequently humorous, but also tragic, re-thinking of what is envisaged as essentially feminine. In his early novels, *Heartbreak Tango* and *Betrayed by Rita Hayworth,* he takes us to a Latin America where women—interested in the role models proposed by the radio and the movies—are seen as derivative characters for recurrent patterns of love. The clichés and joys of middle-class family life are presented through direct dialogue, letters, and school compositions in their capacities of seduction and entrapment.

Sentimentality, an interest in plot, gossip, and deceit permeate the almost suffocating intimacy of Puig's novels as he tries to situate their language close to the pleasures elicited by the sources of popular culture they evoke. In *Heartbreak Tango* several women are engaged in an exchange of letters. Their bond is simply stated: a newspaper from a provincial town announces the untimely death of a young man, Juan Carlos Etchepare. His mother and an old girl friend, Nené (now married and living in the "city" with her husband and children), write to each other, impelled by the nostalgia elicited by Juan Carlos's death. It is later revealed that Juan Carlos's sister, Celina, had been the actual author of the letters received by Nené, which she had signed with her mother's name. Thus, the subject of the novel shifts from an interest in the explicit retrospective materials presented by the letters, to the reasons for the hoax. A hatred between women suggested through the conceit is presented as more pressing than the love between Nené and Juan Carlos.

The dream of utmost happiness in *Heartbreak Tango* is serene domesticity but, when achieved by Nené through marriage to a dependable husband, it appears as flat and grey. In contrast, her infatuation with Juan Carlos is a measure of her capacity to have lived a higher form of love, almost an aesthetic denial of her present family. Tango lyrics, used as epigraphs in each chapter, tinge the women's conflict with irony and a sense of inevitability.[3]

The dead man, Juan Carlos, succumbed to the ravages of an illness that—in the best tradition of literary attractiveness[4]—causes him to get thinner and cough up blood. He is an enigmatic point of convergence for the sense of unease that Nené feels about her conventional married life and the driving resentment of the single Celina, who has become a schoolteacher. He stands for beauty and eroticism, while the women have been left with mere fragments, recollections of a past youth in a world cluttered by unfulfilled expectations (the schoolteacher Celina) and the flatness of being a housewife (Nené).

The hatred that Celina feels for Nené matches the unease that Nené feels for her. As the reader realizes the hoax on which the exchange of letters is based, the novel betrays its "real" subject: the suspicion that love will always be out of reach for women's discourse. Jean Carlos's death is a pretext for uncovering their own lack of daring. Even a provincial Casanova—Juan Carlos was a handsome heartbreaker of little intelligence—has enough power to show the inadequacy of women in relation to their object of desire.[5]

Is it all a joke? Are the letters, the sentimentality, the tangos there so that we may laugh? And, in that case, what would be the nature of our laughter? Puig's work as a whole is open to this sort of inquiry. *Heartbreak Tango* is persistent in its opacity regarding these issues; when summarized it yields humorous results, and when read it resists any distancing of its readership from its sentimentality. If there is a joke here, then, it would be on the reader caught in the same web as the characters.

The laughter is self-critical, an awareness of having been seduced. *Heartbreak Tango* takes us to its overall effect of women lying to each other (through the death of a man handsome but ridiculous) in a language articulated by a relentless common sense. Part of the sadness—as tangos often say—is that the love object, while not meriting the passion it elicits, is still infinitely more desirable than the person who pursues it. Here, of course, in a reversal of the tango tradition, the lost love object is a man, not a woman.

Signatures and Power

In *Heartbreak Tango* letters become what they perhaps always are: objects through which the characters attempt to create a presence for themselves with the hope of overwhelming the recipient, of according credence to something that might become true if the recipient accepted the invitation to continue the game and respond to the letters. This kind of game is a signing exercise, in which each letter is a dare to continue the exchange. The identities generated owe their solidarity to their faithfulness to the letter, to the coherence with which they cling to the univocity of their signatures. Letters—as we all know—are characters and they make up characters. It is the seduction of the characters represented and produced by the signatures that keeps the story running. The *fact* of letter exchange is an *effect* that grants presence to the signature.

The epigraph to the opening chapter of *Heartbreak Tango* in its English edition is a fragment from Homero Manzi's tango "Su Voz" (His Voice): "The shadows on the dance floor, / this tango brings sad memories to mind, / let us dance and think no more / while my satin dress / like a tear shines."[6] As is the tango, the novel is centered on the active forgetting of a supposedly unforgettable memory. In these lyrics by Manzi, one of the most nostalgic poets of tango, the dancers are shadows propelled by a memory they want to erase while, at the same time, they affirm it, since the very genre of their dance constitutes a rememoration of their loss. The shiny dress is like a tear—the novel unfolds that image in a retrospective and sentimental key.

The satin dress is like a tear: one *wears* one's sorrow. The attire makes emotion visible and embodies it; it makes up the right character for the dance. The correspondence among feeling, identity, and movement alluded to in these lines is an ideal searched for throughout Puig's novel. But such an easy, natural relationship to their medium of expression is to be denied to his female characters, who are trapped by the insufficiency of the commonplaces they are seemingly destined to use.

Once the novel has established a place for Juan Carlos's body ("The remains of Juan Carlos Etchepare were interred in the local burial ground, accompanied to their final home by a grief stricken funeral cortege"), the first letter is sent by Juan Carlos's old love, Nené. Its stated purpose is to send condolences to Mrs. Etchepare, Juan Carlos's mother. Through the letter we learn that Nené lives now in Buenos Aires, has a husband and two children, and had not seen Juan Carlos for nine years. We also learn about an unresolved problem between Nené and Celina and Mrs. Etchepare.

> I've been living in Buenos Aires for several years now, soon after I got married I came to live here with my husband, but this terrible news made me decide to drop you a few lines in spite of the fact that before my marriage yourself and your daughter Celina had stopped speaking to me. In spite of everything poor Juan Carlos always said hello to me, may he rest in peace. (10)

The letters that follow build an entanglement among the three characters. Celina, trying to get even with Nené after years of resentment, poses as her own mother by forging her signature. For Nené, what is explicitly at issue in the letters is the consecration of her past with Juan Carlos. She believes that the correspondence is the equivalent of erecting a monument to Juan Carlos: a loving girlfriend on one side and an aching mother on the other construct a friendship from the remains of their love and passion for a now dead man.

Much is said in the novel about Juan Carlos's body. He is so attractive that he is irresistible; he is a womanizer of such kindness that he leaves behind only love for him in the women he conquers.

Old letters written by Juan Carlos are presented as an archaeology of the female correspondence that frames them; they suggest the quality of Juan Carlos's presence in the past evoked by the letter writing after his death. They perform this function in a curious way, having to do with his identity as an author, with his signature. While Nené and Celina (the main letter exchangers) write well, with no spelling mistakes, with the correctness of good students,[7] Juan Carlos's writing abounds in spelling mistakes and capricious punctuation. He writes like an ignorant and unimaginative school dropout.

What is the effect of such "bad writing" on the perception of Juan Carlos as a character? The most immediate one is the production of a strong novelistic presence for him. He sounds more pure, less literary, than the characters that mention him. He does not need to write about anything in a "good" way; his task is fulfilled by merely *presenting* himself. The errors in writing, with the compassionate laughter that they elicit in the reader, the colloquial turns of phrase taken from the realm of the commonplace, are evidence of Juan Carlos's uncomfortable relationship to literature—the only medium through which we know him. The reader suspects that there is more to him, that the chunks of public language he is obliged to recycle in his letters are but a pale indication of his persona. Thus, by exaggerating his inadequacy with language, he emphasizes another level that remains all the more intense because of its invisibility: his body.

Juan Carlos does not need to write well. He is the first character in the novel to have achieved centrality in an event: his own death. Death constitutes the achievement of the illusion of presence and tangibility in the political interaction of *Heartbreak Tango*. The dead body is the decisive point of interlocution.[8] His letters stand as a confirmation of the fact that Juan Carlos will not write any more, but they are also, most importantly, confirmation of him as a *fact*.

Unlike Juan Carlos's, Celina's and Nené's identities are wavering. Celina forges her mother's signature and initiates the most explicit lie in the novel; she signs as another. In signing with her own name, Nené discovers that she would rather be another.

The novel closes with another body; Nené's signature is unfolded and delivered of the vagueness it carried throughout the novel when she dies. In this way she becomes, like Juan Carlos, central in an event. Juan Carlos's old letters are burnt in agreement with her will (old letters that she had wanted to take with her to her grave right until the day she died, when she seemingly attained a more singular self-definition). This change of mind means that her death is not the death of the Nené who signed the letters presented to us but of someone quite different. Juan Carlos's letters are again transcribed in fragments as they fly up into the air before turning into ashes, thereby creating a highly sentimental retrospective account of what we have read.

Only one among the characters of the epistolary exchange remains alive at the novel's end. It is Celina, the schoolteacher with enough mastery of the language to forge letters, incapable of becoming a character with the kind of weight that—we are told in *Heartbreak Tango*— only death can achieve. Hers is the power of plotting, of initiating a correspondence of which she will always be in control. Thus, the winner of the interlocutionary exercise of this novel is a participant whose victory is achieved by a most intense understanding of the nature of letter writing, so precise that she can manipulate the conventions of the genre by forgery.

Old Mail: Delivered and Returned

The original (Spanish) version of *Heartbreak Tango (Boquitas pintadas)*[9] contains an epigraph from a tango by Le Pera: *"Era . . . para mi la vida entera."* (she meant everything to me). The lyrics, transcribed as though they were part of an audible song, bemoan the kind of death suffered by one lover when his counterpart disappears. The loss is described as the taking away of life from the one who remains.[10]

A lover remains with a bundle of letters in Jacques Derrida's *The Post Card (La Carte Postale)*. This man signs with his own name but wonders why the person writing him back does not sign her letters. He reasons about his own signature and speculates about the kind of responsibility he is acknowledging in refusing to forge a name for himself.

As we read *Heartbreak Tango* we are aware of its being fiction. Its reconstruction of the past furthers the sense that it is an artifact, with music from the 1930s, letters from the 1940s, final death in the 1960s. The reader feels the safety of these literary conventions at work and enjoys the kind of repetitive, sentimental pleasures already suggested by the use of Le Pera's lines.

The Post Card, on the other hand, reads as though it could have taken place yesterday, around the corner.[11] The letters presented in the text produce the illusion of a breathless figure attempting to take shape. In other words, they *play against* the reader's awareness of fiction and search for an effect of naturalness.

The Post Card consists of a first part entitled "Envois," which presents letters from Derrida to someone whose responses are implied but not published; a second part, "Speculer sur Freud," a reflection dealing explicitly with the death instinct; third, "Le Facteur de la Vérité" (about Freud and Lacan); and, finally, an interview with René Major entitled "Du tout." Thus, the book is framed by two clearly interlocutionary instances: one side of a correspondence at the beginning and the transcription of an interview at the end. What are the consequences of this structure for the general understanding of what we read?

"Envois" is explicitly presented as a perhaps *unreadable* section of the book *(je ne sais pas si la lecture en est soutenable),* while "Du Tout" suggests the existence of a hypothetical, nonanalyzed aspect of Freud around which, nevertheless, the pyschoanalytic movement might have been built and mobilized. This tacitly acknowledged nonanalyzed view would be that which keeps psychoanalysis going by being inherited, transmitted intact, conveniently willed, consolidated, frozen, and encoded. According to Derrida, it would give structure and architecture to the movement. In the circuit of communication suggested here, this hypothesis performs the role of an ever replenished stock for the exchange.[12]

"Envois" presents another startlingly similar example of the "nonanalyzable," this time without explicitly discussing its function and consequences. It is represented by the hostile reaction to the rumor that the acknowledged signer of the letters (J.D) is "enanalyse" (written as single a word, *inanalysis*).

Why would it be so wrong to say that J.D is "enanalyse"? There are, of course, the obvious answers regarding discretion over intrusion in personal matters. But the role performed by this moment of "Envois" goes far beyond questions of propriety and undue curiosity; this is, after all, a confessional section of the book. Why should a rumor about J.D talking in a psychoanalytical session be condescendingly dismissed?

In the rereading of "Envois," as its meaning becomes inflected by the reflections about that dark, unspoken instance in the Freudian movement, a privileged blind spot emerges. It refers to J.D's signature, to his own status as author of both the letters in the fictional conceit and of the book of which they are only a part.

"Envois" sketches the meanderings of the construction of a secret, the careful emergence of something that, in order to remain truly hidden, needs to be ignored by someone who *recognizes* it in its unknowability. We read about J.D writing letters in public places, surreptitiously but at the same time aware that the possibility of being spied upon might sweep away the already fragile intimacy of the correspondence. He also makes calls to his lover from public telephones, hastily, while friends wait outside the telephone booth. They do not know whom he is calling, and yet they are essential to the illusion that J.D has an exclusive relationship, outside the public sphere, hidden from the surface like a purloined letter. Friends, strangers, family are special guests in "Envois"; they give tension to a correspondence that needs them the better to exclude them. The "Envois" may, indeed, be unreadable, as Derrida says in the prologue. What are the *practical* possibilities that make unreadability feasible? How could the correspondence be actually lost to scrutiny?[13]

J.D talks often about dying and suicide, about children and sterility, about ending the liaison that gives shape to the story by finally signing a last letter. J.D would like to shape an event, make a decision. In the letters he says that he would like to become a body (dead, consumed in his own anecdote, a character in his own correspondence, someone who might make us weep). Instead, he takes the writing and phoning in public places one step further and publishes the letters.

As one side of the correspondence appears in print, the secret is made public; that is, the public looks over the shoulder of the one writing the letters and keeps the exchange going in the incompleteness of its information. Thus, "Envois" attains its special unreadability: half of it will never be available in this book. In the same stroke, a new interlocutionary instance is opened; the spy has been promoted to recipient (*destinataire*) of the correspondence. Discretion is not the reason keeping half of the correspondence from appearing in the book; the publication of the volume has created its own "other side," represented by the reader and displacing the lover, now a mere pretext for this new exchange.[14]

At this different level, the questions about J.D's signature and the love mentioned in the letters circulate burnt, in a crypt, as a dark celebration of one of J.D's hopes. Thus, the crypt embodies both the beginning and the end of the book as it inflects the book with the fulfillment of its purpose.[15] The unknowability of Freud posited as the spine of psychoanalysis in "Du Tout" is matched by the unknowability of J.D in this book, somebody without the kind of univocal presence (as is whispered in the letters) needed to commit suicide.

The last letter of "Envois" closes this way: "Tomorrow I shall write to you again, in our foreign language. I shall not retain a single word and in September, without my even having seen it again, you will burn, you will burn it, it has to be you" (*Faut que ce soit toi*).[16] The title of the last section of the book provides the answer: "Du tout"—not at all. The correspondence has become secret for the lover; the "other side" is represented by an anonymous readership whose response will be fragmented, part of a silent current not quite able to shape narrative events. The epistolary conceit of *The Post Card* has dismantled its initial pretext in order to present a permanently elusive author (J.D: Derrida) who dares the reader to take part in the exchange. In this way, the love letters, returned to the wrong address, call for a critical reading eloquent about misdirection and partiality.

No Body

In *Heartbreak Tango* only Celina remains alive after the lovers' letters have been burnt. She is secretive about her own signature after having precipitated the plot through forgery. The letters turn to ashes, and the deaths of the authors of the correspondence close the novel for the reader, providing Celina's lie as a key for interpretation.

The Post Card offers a heterogeneous register for its halting faithfulness to the signing exercise; we have J.D—the fictional or real lover—and Jacques Derrida discussing Freud and being interviewed. The love affair that gives shape to "Envois" having been erased by time, its avatars come back in the sections devoted to the study of Freud (as well as in the interview), as a project to de-essentialize the notion of self by collapsing it into the interpretation of a signature.

The reader wishing *to see* Juan Carlos through Nené's nostalgic correspondence is disappointed; he or she will have to rely on imagination. The project of doing away with, erasing, the univocity of Jacques Derrida's signature in *The Post Card* has a startlingly opposite effect. The assimilation between that nonanalyzable aspect of psychoanalysis and Derrida *himself* as nonanalyzable presents us with the aporia of a dream of selflessness. In Derrida's book it is his own persona, his signature, that appears most prominently as the final point of interlocution. The woman who has generated the conflict and received the letters is obliterated.

Loved, silent, generating passion, and becoming the source for a writing that ultimately excludes her, she performs the role of the traditional feminine muse denied to the characters of *Heartbreak Tango*.[17]

J.D would have liked to die like Juan Carlos; he is, instead, condemned to an infinite correspondence with the reader. While Celina's clear-cut forgery produces a clear closure for interpretation, J.D's resistance to definition creates an illusion of authenticity that conspires against its own explanations. Celina's precise (and laughable) manipulation of the epistolary genre may be a manifold lesson to the J.D—or Derrida—who says that he would like to write as a woman.

NOTES

1. This is evident not only in the explicit role accorded to his writing, but also, at the most immediate level in the number of articles and books on literature in the United States that choose to open with epigraphs from Derrida. It is, of course, not Derrida's fault that his work has been accorded the place it has, and it is indeed paradoxical that this would happen to the very author who has sharpened the sense of written language as a permanently decentered polemical field that dismantles illusions of control and meaning.

2. Manuel Puig, *Heartbreak Tango,* trans. S. J. Levine (New York: Dutton, 1975). Unless otherwise indicated, all English quotations from the novel are from that edition; Jacques Derrida, *La Carte Postale* (Paris: Flammarion, 1980). I have provided my own translations into English.

3. Tango is a highly popular mode of expression in Latin America, especially in Argentina. The lyrics of tango have come to represent a mainstream philosophy. Confined in its beginnings to the marginal and the lumpen, tango evolved into an accepted middle-class art form. The use of poetry lines such as the ones presented in this novel fulfills the purpose of contextualizing and *predicting* the outcome of conflicts by framing them as part of a long-accepted and already commented tradition.

4. Juan Carlos's illness itself has been evoked many times in the tango tradition. The illness is usually attributed to women, often at the end of a life of prostitution. Susan Sontag in her *Illness as Metaphor* offers interesting insights into the attractiveness that this sick fragility creates in fiction.

5. Juan Carlos's untimely death represents a break in domesticity. He has been able to interrupt the normal course of events. Women, tied securely to the conventions of the middle class, are portrayed as lacking in imagination. In this novel, they are able to love the possibility of being different through Juan Carlos. The reader, though, is not presented with any reason for them to be loved in return.

6. The use of Homero Manzi's lyrics in the English version is an interesting change from the original.

7. Rhythmic contrasts separating writing styles constitute one of the main

sources of humor in this novel. School compositions, letters, and tangos in direct and indirect styles coexist with newspaper clippings. The uneasy transition from one kind of writing to another produces social commentary and laughter.

8. In doing this, Puig joins a long literary tradition. Death consecrates characters and renders them interesting as points of departure for narratives because their lives acquire the finality of a destiny.

9. Manuel Puig, *Boquitas pintadas* (Buenos Aires: Sudamericana, 1969).

10. The intimacy sensed by the listener (or reader) of tango is, to a great extent, generated by the sympathy for the grief of the writer of the lyrics. In this case, what is shared is a story of sentimental loss.

11. There are, of course, ways to date the occurrences by following Derrida's travels and recognizing his academic itineraries as well as the names of friends. The effect of immediacy has to do with the general reader's supposed ignorance of these references.

12. I have loosely paraphrased the following paragraph:

> Ce sera, cet inanalysé, cela aura été ce sur quoi et autour de quoi se sera construit et mobilisé le mouvement analytique: tout aurait été construit et calculé pour que cet inanalysé soit hérité, protégé, transmis intact, convenablement légué, consolidé, enkysté, encrypté. C'est ce qui donne sa structure au mouvement et à son architecture. (*La Carte Postale*, 547)

13. Can a book actually ever be lost? Can anything written be completely forgotten or obliterated? Borges has posed this question many times, with different responses, concerning the nature of repetition and rewriting. In his *Libro de arena*, he wonders how to lose a book, how to do away with it forever. After dismissing the possibility of burning it (this book was infinite and the character in the story fears that by setting it on fire he may burn the whole universe), he decides to put it in an arbitrary place in a library. Misdirection is also the road taken by Derrida with part of the correspondence of *La Carte Postale*.

14. Kierkegaard in his essay *On Repetition* gives a similar role to woman. She is necessary as a first stage, but romantic involvement has to give way to a higher relationship. For Kierkegaard, that higher relationship was first poetic, then religious, with male friendship as its ideal embodiment. In Derrida, the sex of the ideal reader (recipient) of the correspondence, once the woman has been left aside, remains unmarked.

15. In "Fors"—preface to *Le Verbier de l'homme aux loups* by N. Abraham and M. Torok (Paris: Flammarion, 1977)—Derrida reflects on the word *crypt*. Those ideas are closely related to the use he makes of it afterwards in *La Carte Postale*.

16. "Demain je t'écrirai encore, dans notre langue étrangère. Je n'en retiendrai pas un mot et en septembre, sans que je l'aie même revue, tu brûleras, toi, faut que ce soit toi" (273).

17. The praise for the woman in Derrida's book is, in the last analysis, a celebration of her silence, of her capacity to elicit passion through passivity. In a more recent volume, *feu la cendre* (Paris des femmes, 1987), Derrida returns to two aspects that we have discussed regarding his book: the gender of the recipient and the possibility of losing the correspondence. While the meditation on

gender makes explicit what the reader would otherwise need to extract as an interpretation of *La Carte Postale,* the comments on the trace left by writing simply restate the basic undecidability of textuality from Derrida's perspective. Although Derrida has become increasingly aware of the polemical field opened up by the attention to gender, his texts tend to mention it in a mode that is more self-critical than analytical.

14

Authorship and Authority: George Sand's Letters to Her Mother

KATHRYN J. CRECELIUS

GEORGE SAND'S correspondence can be considered among her finest works. The twenty-one volumes published so far by Georges Lubin in an impeccable edition, with more to follow, provide a mirror of Sand's times as well as her soul, depicting the major events of the nineteenth century, many from the vantage point of one who was personally involved in them. The list of Sand's correspondents reads like an international *Who's Who*. From England, Italy, Germany, and the United States, political and literary luminaries such as Elizabeth Barrett Browning, Giuseppe Mazzini, Heinrich Heine, and Karl Marx were all in touch with George Sand.

That George Sand's epistolary instincts were very strong is illustrated not only by her vast correspondence, but by the intrusion of the epistolary into her *oeuvre* as well. It is surely not coincidental that her first fictional work, the "Voyage au Mont d'Or" (1827–29), known today as the "Voyage en Auvergne," begins as a stillborn letter to her mother and turns out to be a journal, or a kind of letter to herself. Aurore Dudevant's next two works, "Histoire du rêveur" and *La Marraine*, begin as letters to another friend, Jane Bazouin, who desires to close the geographical distance between herself and her convent friend by possessing a text that she can read and reread.[1] In addition, letters play an important role in *Lélia* (1833), in which many dialogues read like written rather than spoken exchanges. *Jacques,* Sand's first epistolary novel, which appeared the next year, successfully revives an eighteenth-century genre. At the same time, she was writing to Alfred de Musset the real letters that would become part of the fictional *Lettres d'un voyageur* (1837), a work that stands at the confluence of five genres: fiction, nonfiction, correspondence, autobiography, and travel literature. Also in 1837, Sand began the *Lettres à Marcie,* fictional letters on a nonfictional topic— feminism—that were published in Lamennais's newspaper *Le Monde* until her introduction of the question of divorce caused him unceremoniously to halt publication. During the revolution of 1848, Sand's many publications included the "Lettres au peuple." Later epistolary novels are *Mademoiselle La Quintinie* (1863) and *La Confession d'une jeune fille* (1865). One of her posthumous publications was the *Nouvelles Lettres d'un voyageur* (1877). Clearly, Sand was at ease with the conventions of epistolarity, as Janet Altman has defined them.[2] Sand's ability to adopt the epistolary mode in her *oeuvre,* much as a ventriloquist throws his or her voice, indicates that a study of her correspondence as literature would be appropriate.

Like her contemporaries, Sand knew that "private" correspondence rarely remained so; even before she became famous, her friends shared and passed around her letters, as was often the case at the time. Letters were frequently written according to models that children learned in school or at home, and were thus not entirely spontaneous or personal, but already literary productions. A letter from Aurore Dupin's grandmother to the fourteen-year-old in her Parisian convent compliments the girl on a letter she wrote to her illegitimate half-brother, but instructs her on the proper format to use in addressing a social inferior.

> You wrote a charming letter to Hippolyte, but since you don't owe him any respect, you mustn't put his name on a line by itself. My dear, Sir, Madam go in the body of the letter and after you have written 3 or 4 words, but never later than the second line.[3]

Once she was a published author and known as such, Sand clearly recognized that her letters might become public property and might even be used against her. She frequently cautions her correspondents against allowing her letters to fall into the wrong hands. Such an incident did in fact occur in 1845, when a letter she sent to Bettina von Arnim was opened in transit and served as the basis of articles in the *Gazette de Leipzig* and the *Revue de Paris.*[4] Sand's awareness of the artificial and nonprivate nature of letters, in addition to her literary talents, makes a critical examination of her correspondence all the more necessary.

There are many ways of reading a correspondence. For those who prefer the synchronic approach, Sand's correspondence with certain individuals is available in several editions. Others enjoy reading a correspondence day by day, year by year, to see events in their proper order and refracted in their multiple versions. However one chooses to read a correspondence, one is always reading a text that was not conceived as a whole by its author, but rather written piecemeal. Unlike an epistolary novel, where the letters are intended to form a coherent *récit,* a correspondence is created as a fragmented work whose parts are separate in time and space. They are only reunited by an editor who seeks to gather all available documents, no matter how brief or seemingly uninteresting, which signify simply because they are part of a whole and provide useful clues regarding dates, times, places, and people, essential aspects of any correspondence.[5] A published correspondence, then, gives the reader an opportunity neither the author nor her individual correspondent had— that of reading a letter in context, as well as the chance to survey the correspondence with one person over a period of years. In both cases, a new text is born, assembled by the critic rather than the author, which can nonetheless be considered a valid exposition of the author's thought.

Previous studies of Sand's correspondence have focused on the letters written during a specific time frame.[6] I would like instead to take as my corpus Sand's letters to her mother, written over a period of twenty-five years. There are several compelling reasons for choosing this particular group of letters. First, the relationship between women authors and their mothers has received a great deal of recent critical attention and remains an important theme in feminist criticism. Furthermore, George Sand's relationship with her mother has been a dominant note in Sand criticism since Germaine Brée's 1976 article, "George Sand: The Fictions of Autobiography."[7] Yet despite the emphasis on her mother's importance, much remains to be said about the nature of maternal influence on Sand's development. Finally, since the seventeenth century, Madame de Sévigné's correspondence with her daughter has served as a model both of epistolarity and of motherly devotion, linking the two inextricably. It seems fitting to examine the question from its converse side, namely the nexus of epistolarity and filial sentiments, to see if a similar connection exists.[8]

Of all her correspondents, Sophie Dupin, George Sand's mother, was perhaps the one with whom she had the most complicated and uneasy relationship. In addition, it was for the most part a long-distance relationship, for after Maurice Dupin's accidental death in 1808, when his

daughter was four, Mme Maurice, as she was often called to distinguish
her from her mother-in-law, Mme Dupin, soon relinquished custody of
her daughter and returned to Paris. Therefore, there was reason for
daughter to write to mother. This move was motivated not only by the
Parisian's dislike for the country and the plebeian's conflict with her
aristocratic in-laws, but also by Mme Dupin's desire to be with her other
daughter, an illegitimate child borne before her meeting with Maurice
Dupin and who was not welcome in Mme Dupin Sr.'s home. Thus,
Aurore Dupin, the future George Sand, had cause to feel doubly abandoned by her mother and to believe that her mother preferred another
child to her. Sand's feelings about her mother at this time were in conflict, as fierce love and protectiveness mixed with jealousy of her sister
and anger at being deserted. The question of Mme Dupin's perceived
split loyalties to her two daughters resurfaces later in the correspondence
as Sand denies envying her half sister, with whom Mme Dupin lived for a
while.[9]

For a time, Aurore saw a great deal of her mother and spent a large
part of the year with her and her grandmother, either in Paris or at
Nohant. The first letter we have from Aurore to her mother is dated
1812 by Georges Lubin and expresses sadness at her mother's departure:
"How I regret that I can't say good-bye! You see how much this departure hurts me. Farewell, think of me and be sure that I will not forget
you" (*Correspondance* 13).[10] A second letter, no longer in existence but
the subject of a major scene in Sand's autobiography, *Histoire de ma vie*, is
the occasion for a description of the turbulent and ambivalent emotions
on both sides of this relationship. As Sand, the mature autobiographer,
notes about her mother's feelings at the time:

> I told myself that my mother didn't love me as much as she was loved
> by me. I was unjust this time, but, basically, it was the revelation of a
> truth that each day confirmed.[11]

Sand remembers a great deal about this letter, written in 1814, at least
about its physical nature, but she has forgotten the contents. "My impression is that never was a deeper and purer passion more naïvely
expressed" (*Oeuvres* 1:759).

The concrete aspect of the letter and its delivery take on a peculiar
importance in this scene. Aurore takes pains to place the letter behind a
portrait of her grandfather that hung in her mother's room, and asks that
a response be left in the same place. The next morning, there is no
answer, so that the portrait of the dead man serves as dead-letter office,
short circuit of communication. The response, which Aurore had envisioned as a permanent reminder of her mother and the plans she had

adumbrated to remove Aurore from Nohant and open a millinery shop with her two daughters, is lacking, just as the shop had only been a fantasy, albeit perhaps sincerely meant. Nothing remains of Mme Dupin this time, not even a token letter of affection. At this early date, a pattern of one-way, monologic correspondence has already begun in Aurore's writing to her mother.

Aurore turned for emotional support to her grandmother, Bonne Maman, whose traditional designation is here especially significant, given the shifting good mother/bad mother roles she and Mme Dupin played for Aurore. Her affection for her grandmother grew as the old woman became more feeble and dependent on her. This relationship was also fraught with ambivalence, however, for Aurore rightly understood that her separation from her mother was deliberately caused by her grandmother. "It seemed to me that I was physically and morally attached to my mother by a diamond chain that my grandmother vainly tried to break" (*Oeuvres* 1:743). Her adult view of this period and its complex relationships is the result of years of reflection and distance from the original events.

> [I] even believe that I would have needed a large dose of coldness or pride to judge calmly which one was more right or wrong in their quarrels, and I admit that it took thirty years to understand the situation and to cherish almost equally the memory of both women. (*Oeuvres* 1:744)

It is in light of this background of shifting emotions and custody arrangements that Aurore's letters and sentiments must be read.

There are no letters to her mother from Aurore's adolescence, unfortunately; the next extant letter dates from 1821, after Aurore had left the convent where she had spent two years completing her education and while she was nursing her grandmother through her final illness. It is by far the longest letter Aurore had written to anyone until then, and its tone is quite different from that of the bantering, friendly letters she was exchanging at the same time with her convent friends. Several years before Aurore Dupin even thought of earning her living by her pen, the writer's authority and control are clearly visible in this missive.

Mme Dupin had apparently heard that Aurore was leading too free a life, taking advantage of her grandmother's illness and consequent lack of supervision to run about in the country with inappropriate friends. Many of these allegations were likely true, although perhaps more innocent than Mme Dupin was inclined to believe. Aurore did experience much freedom from the kinds of constraints visited upon girls who were to become ladies; she rode horseback in pants, helped her tutor practice country medicine, and had male as well as female friends. Our incomplete knowledge of Sand's relationship with Stéphane Ajasson de Grandsagne, who may have fathered her daughter, Solange, six years later in 1827, allows room for speculation on the extent of their relationship in 1821. This letter could, among other things, be read as a denial of a liaison that went further than just friendship.

The letter begins "My dear Mother," and not "My dear (little) mama" (*Correspondance* 1:74), as do subsequent letters, and ends with the declaration that if her tone is more respectful than usual, it is not out of anger, but from the sense that she has passed the age of using the familiar *tu*. Henceforth, she will use *vous* in her letters, as she does in this one. This small linguistic detail, to which she herself calls attention, indicates an enormous psychological distance that she is deliberately establishing between herself and her mother. Indeed, this letter reads more like a lawyer's brief than a daughter's letter. She responds point by point to her mother's assertions, and utilizes various forms of the conditional to pose hypothetical situations, a prime use of rhetoric. Already, at seventeen, Aurore Dupin possesses the "persuasive style" Nancy Rogers has detected in Sand's work.[12]

There are no letters from the period following the grandmother's death two months later, when Aurore was again under her mother's legal control. This unpleasant time, when her mother threatened to lock her in a convent until her majority, and then left her for several months with friends whom Aurore did not know, is detailed in *Histoire de ma vie* and in a letter to Aurélien de Sèze (*Correspondance* 1:196–201). Her mother in some sense drove her to marry Casimir Dudevant, the first suitable candidate who presented himself, in order to obtain independence from her unstable guardian. Aurore soon learned that she had entered an even worse situation, from which it would take her fifteen years to escape.

The fourth letter to her mother, written in 1824 after Aurore's marriage and the birth of her son, Maurice, is concerned and witty, containing private jokes about Pierret, a friend (and perhaps more) of her mother's. The next letters are filled with news about Maurice and her trip to the Pyrénées. In the following letters, up to 1831, she is always concerned with her mother's health, and mentions her own small but nagging complaints. In the period just preceding the break with her husband and her move to Paris to begin a career, while she was beginning to write for herself and her friends, her health seems to become worse and her complaints more serious. "My dear mama, I have been unable to write for a long time because of an ophthalmia that has made me suffer for more than a month and of which I am not yet completely free" (*Correspondance* 1:630). Georges Lubin's note reminds us that although her eye condition was real, it did not prevent Aurore from writing to others during this same period. Four months later, Aurore recounts a serious episode to her mother.

> I would have responded earlier to your letter, my dear little mother, if I hadn't been very ill. They feared I had a cerebral fever, and for 48 hours I was I don't know where. My body was indeed in bed and seemed to sleep, but my soul was galloping on I don't know what planet. To speak simply, I was no longer there and I was no longer in touch with myself. (*Correspondance* 1:697)

Indeed, this illness resembles a death or an out-of-body experience recounted by those who have been near death. It is not difficult to see these illnesses as symptomatic manifestations of her domestic unhappiness, which only increased with the years. Yet, significantly, Aurore does not write of her marital dissatisfaction at all to her mother; she does not share her distress, but rather uses the illnesses as an excuse for not writing to Mme Dupin.

In these letters, she occasionally asks her mother to send her items that are more easily obtained in Paris, especially clothes, patterns, and cloth. Aurore orders an outfit for Maurice in 1826, and states: "I would like it to be in the *latest style*" (*Correspondance* 1:356). She also orders "a guimpe and a pair of long sleeves in a flesh-colored silk knit" (1:398). Later on, she asks about the newest fashion in dress sleeves: "I think that now they are cut with the grain and as wide on bottom as on top. But advise me, for I am very backwards" (1:512). Once Solange is born in 1828, she sends details about both children, noting humorously: "This is a mother's prattle, but you won't reproach me because you know what it means to me" (1:599).

Essentially, Aurore's letters during this domestic lull in her life fulfill the phatic function of language, as described by Roman Jakobson: they maintain contact between the two, without conveying much of a message.[13] Many letters refer explicitly to this function when they state that it has been a long time between letters—from the sender, from the recipient, or from both. On 23 December 1826 Aurore writes:

> You have left me a long time without news of you, my dear mama, and I have also waited a long time to thank you for your letter. But I have been so sick, and I am still, that it takes a lot of effort for me to write. (*Correspondance* 1:367)

On 2 August 1828 Aurore admits, likely in answer to a reproach from her mother:

> It is true that it has been a long time since I wrote you, my dear mama, but I haven't ceased asking Hippolyte for news of you. He could also

tell you that I asked him 3 times in a row for your address without receiving it. I looked in your last letters, but didn't find the address you said you mentioned. (1:453)

It seems odd that Aurore should not have her own mother's address. In a note to Sand's last letter to her mother, 9 July 1837, Georges Lubin remarks:

> One might ask if she [Sand] wrote to her very often. The preceding [letter] is from February 8. Of course, some letters could be lost, but it should be noted that George forgot the house number, a fact that doesn't indicate a very regular correspondence. (4:146)

Indeed, we have only seventy-three extant letters from Sand to her mother, out of the 1,557 she wrote between 1812 and the date of her final letter to Mme Dupin. In terms of number as well as content, Sand's letters to her mother play a minor role in her correspondence.

Aurore seems to write to her mother in spurts; often, two or three letters follow one after the other, then there is nothing for months. (It is true that we do not have their entire correspondence, but we certainly possess a good part of it.) Aurore habitually sends a New Year's greeting, often after 1 January. Therefore, it is surprising to read in 1836, during her separation trial:

> My dear Mama, I ask pardon for having forgotten that you like the formality of the New Year's greeting. I admit that I have never observed this formality without finding it *stupid,* because I find it *cold.* (3:278)

Thus, she subtly blames her mother for requiring a banal greeting, rather than excusing her own omission, part of her usual pattern of self-justification in these letters, in which an apology is only grudgingly given.

In 1831, the year Aurore moved to Paris, there is a clear change in tone in her letters to her mother. There are only four from this year, but they are noteworthy. Aurore's letters are cool, more calculated. She establishes an imaginary dialogue with her mother within the letters, addressing her directly, but there is no exchange. Rather, she tells her mother what she wants her to know and brooks no contradiction. Thus, she explains in a cavalier manner why she has moved to Paris, without entering into the details of, or reasons for, her new arrangement. "You ask what I am going to do in Paris; what everyone does, I think, enjoy myself, amuse myself, view the arts that one only sees there in all their splendor" (1:785).

A few months later, she does describe in a rather offhand and amusing fashion—that is, in a literarily conceived way—her own and her husband's separate life-styles. In neither letter does she mention her determination to earn her living by writing. She denies wearing pants, but in a passive manner. "They told you I was *wearing pants,* they deceived you; if you spent 24 hours here, you would see for yourself" (1:888). She blames others for calumniating her and deliberately misinforming her mother, and does not use *je* so much as *on,* them. Further on, she states, "Those who don't like it [her life-style] and would criticize me to you must be judged with your mind and with your motherly heart; both must be for me" (1:889). This unequivocal declaration leaves Mme Dupin little room for response, even should she have wanted to make one.

This strange letter is longer than usual and filled with allusions to what "others" think and say about Sand. She indirectly reproaches her mother for listening to them and not having confidence in her daughter's judgment. She obliquely shows how much she would have liked her mother's support by referring to her mother's own difficult social position many years previously. "How much good an indulgent and tender mother, who opened her arms to you at each new sorrow, would have done you!" (1:888). Sand justifies herself and her conduct in this letter, which is reminiscent of that of 1821, when she had also denied gossip about herself. As in the earlier instance, her self-defensiveness translates itself into verbal aggressivity and accusation, rather than apology.

This renewed assertive stance at a crucial time in her life can be linked to Sand's attitude toward writing and its disjunctive relationship to her mother. From her earliest compositions, which her grandmother sent to Sophie in Paris and which Sophie ridiculed, to the letter in the "Voyage" that could not be mailed, even by the fact that she talks about writing with her friends, and writes for them while mentioning nothing to her mother, we can deduce a negative connection between literature and the maternal. Even after becoming a published author, she mentions only in passing her works in progress. These 1831 letters show that as Sand began her career, Mme Dupin was now permanently excluded from Sand's inner emotions, although the author outwardly remained the dutiful daughter until Mme Dupin's death in 1837.

As Sand wrote full-time and became more famous, and also as the circle of her correspondents increased, she wrote less and less frequently to her mother. There is a flurry of letters in 1835–36, when Sand pressed her case for legal separation from Casimir. Like that of 1821 and those of 1831, these eight letters read more like a legal report than a daughter's correspondence. The letters have two purposes: first, to inform Mme Dupin directly of the steps Sand was taking and of the progress of the case; second, and perhaps more important, to tell her mother what to think about the affair and how to act, especially around Casimir.

Besides, you don't want me to lose this lawsuit, in which case I would
be under his control. I have a thousand chances to win, but just one can
go against me and it's enough to sink me. Be prudent, therefore, for he
probably will come to you in order to justify himself or to see what you
are thinking. Pretend, dear mama, to know nothing. (3:101)

"My dear Mama, I beg you, be careful and don't say to my husband out
of good intentions things that could be used against me without your
realizing it" (3:171). She chooses the imperative as her dominant mode
in these letters. There is even a self-righteous tone as Sand depicts
herself as a crusader for justice. Interestingly, she reminds her mother
that she is following her father's example as far as combatting social
opinion is concerned, linking herself with the paternal rather than the
maternal heritage. "I am my father's daughter, and I scorn prejudices
when my heart orders justice and courage. If my father had listened to
the idiots and fools of this world, I would not bear his name" (3:280).
Georges Lubin's note is revealing: "Sharp reminder of a time when
Sophie Delaborde was less conformist"; that is, when she lived with
Maurice Dupin without benefit of marriage. Aurore was born less than a
month after her parents' wedding, hence the reference to her bearing her
father's name. The implication that Sophie was less than supportive of
her daughter's separation and had to be rallied to her side contrasts with
the account of this episode in *Histoire de ma vie,* in which she is said to
have immediately espoused Aurore's cause.[14] This gap between correspondence and autobiography is not the only one, and will be discussed
below in more detail.

After the spate of letters about her separation, there are only three
more letters to her mother between 20 August 1836 and 9 July 1837.
Most of these eleven months were spent at Nohant far from her mother,
so that the lack of frequency in corresponding with her is readily apparent. The last letter was written a month before Mme Dupin's death and
expresses wishes for her recovery. This letter never reached her, as a
note from the mail carrier attests, either because Sand did not indicate
the house number or else because Mme Dupin had already moved to a
convalescent home (4:146). According to the autobiography, a letter
informing Sand of the new address had never arrived at Nohant (*Oeuvres*
2:398). For the second time in nine years, Sand did not know where her
mother was living. She soon left for Paris and saw her mother on her
deathbed, although she was at Fontainebleau the day Mme Dupin died.
This conjunction of private epistolary forgetfulness and public personal
attention sums up Sand's ultimate feelings about her mother. It is clear
that the conflicting childhood emotions have largely given way to indif-
ference and conventional behavior.

Perhaps her best and most honest assessment of her mother's complex character and their difficult relationship comes in a letter to her close friend Gustave Papet written five days after her mother's death.

> Poor little woman: shrewd, intelligent, artistic, angry, generous, a bit crazy, spiteful in little things and becoming good again in big ones. She made me suffer a lot and my greatest pains came from her. But she had truly made reparation recently, and I had the satisfaction of seeing that she finally understood my character and that she fully did me justice. I am aware of having done all I should have for her. (*Correspondance* 4:175)

This passage reveals the same attitude toward her mother as do the letters to Mme Dupin. Sand's "I" disappears, as the accent falls on her mother's faults (which were many, as we have seen): "She made me suffer, but she made up for it and finally understood me." With her mother's death, Sand feels vindicated at long last. Her final sentence is one of formal filial devotion, and the choice of verb is significant: she did all she *should* have for her mother. Under the circumstances, one might expect her to mention her love for her mother, but she does not. She speaks only of duty and self-justification, the two poles of her attitude toward her mother in these letters.

Sand's letters to her mother are, indeed, those of a writer. They are works of epistolary craft, written by one who was in command of her medium. She who could write openly and unabashedly to her friends reveals to her mother almost nothing of herself, her thoughts and feelings; there are no confidences of any sort in these letters. Except for those from the early years of her marriage, where there is little or no "message," Sand's letters to her mother are written at times of crisis— the illness of her grandmother, the beginning of a career, legal separation—and are prescriptive. Their habitual message seeks to persuade Mme Dupin to view her daughter as Sand sees herself, in ideal terms. It is evident that Sand is convinced that her mother really does not know her. "You know me very little I dare say, my dear mama," she writes in 1831 as she is about to go to Paris (*Correspondance* 1:887). There is no dialogue, and there is no evolution of the character Sand presents.

In some sense, there is no epistolary pact, that is, in Janet Altman's terms, "the call for response from a specific reader within the correspondent's world."[15] No answer to these letters is necessary or even possible, except perhaps acquiescence. In a bit of role reversal, this monologic attitude toward her mother is similar to that of a parent scolding a child. When a child is told to do something by an angry parent, there is no response to be made but yes; indeed, if there is any other answer, it is seen as "talking back" and is punished. In France, the parent might even switch from *tu* to *vous* to signify displeasure with the child as well as a withdrawal of intimacy; that is the same shift Sand makes—and maintains permanently—in her 1821 letter. Since this chilly daughter–mother relationship is in every way the opposite of Mme de Sévigné's passion for her daughter, it is not surprising that Sand voices a dislike for her seventeenth-century predecessor, "whom I don't really like, whatever they say about her" (*Correspondance* 1:736), although this curt dismissal might mask envy of a closeness she never experienced.

Examination of the corpus of Sand's letters to her mother reveals a side of their relationship very different from that presented in Sand's autobiography, as the two versions of Mme Dupin's attitude toward her daughter's separation have already attested. In *Histoire de ma vie*, Sophie Dupin is shown in a positive light as the victim of circumstances, poverty, and society's prejudices against the lower classes. Her relationship with Maurice Dupin is described in romantic terms as the union of a commoner with a past and an aristocratic officer. The happy end of the "novel" is marred only by the husband's untimely death. Both of Sand's parents come off well in her account as noble, loving, and defiant of social convention. Maurice demonstrates an egalitarian streak as he generously raises the daughter of a bird seller to his level, while Sophie is the redeemed "fallen woman" who expiates her past through her love and fidelity to her husband. The relationship with her daughter is also depicted for the most part in nostalgic terms; although Sand describes her mother's shortcomings, she excuses them and insists on her own love for Sophie, a sentiment missing from the letters. How can we explain the contradiction between the way Sand talks *about* Sophie in *Histoire de ma vie* and the way she talks *to* Sophie in the correspondence?

Sand's apologia for her mother's background can be linked in part to her strong sympathy for the poor and downtrodden, and stems from her very real understanding of the mechanism of social oppression, which she did so much to unveil and counteract. This knowledge itself derives both from what Sand knew of Sophie's own experience and from what she herself as a member of a privileged class had observed. The depiction of Sophie Dupin fits into a larger context that includes Sand's idealized portrait of her father, which occupies a large part of the autobiography, as well as the description of her social and political ideas, and must be evaluated in that light.[16] In order for Maurice to appear exemplary in his conduct toward Sophie, she too must be shown to be above reproach and thus worthy of his extraordinary behavior. Furthermore, with Mme Dupin's death, Sand no longer had to justify herself, but could feel she had achieved the maternal recognition she craved. Finally, *Histoire de ma vie* was begun ten years after Mme Dupin's death, during a period of personal and professional stability when the decades-old negative memories of Mme Dupin's capricious treatment of her daughter had perhaps started to fade.

Indeed, in a significant early text, the "Voyage au Mont d'Or," Aurore Dudevant limns the outline of an autobiography whose contours are astonishingly close to those of *Histoire de ma vie,* with an important difference. As has already been mentioned, Aurore casts about for literary forms before settling on the autobiography, and first chooses to write a letter to her mother, a heart-rending cry of despair that she immediately decides cannot be sent. " 'Oh my mother, what have I done to you? why don't you love me? . . . But you betrayed me, you lied to me. . . . You broke my heart' " (*Oeuvres* 2:504). Written during the period when Aurore was writing about her children and domestic matters to her mother, this letter, totally unlike those anodyne missives, is further proof of the control, even censorship, Aurore exercised over her letters to Sophie. Here Aurore unveils her real thoughts, and they are terrible, too terrible in fact, to be shared with the woman who inspired them and of whom Aurore is suddenly protective. Interestingly, the letter did go to the manuscript's recipient, who was thus privy to Aurore's feelings and before whom Aurore did not hesitate to bare her soul. In some sense, this is an indirect but still effective way of criticizing her mother, for Aurore could just as easily have not sent this letter to her friend at all. She manages to combine at the same time her two roles of dutiful daughter and wronged daughter.

After acknowledging how hurt her mother would be to receive this message, she goes on: "Ah I won't ever reproach you. I will cry in silence. You can grow old calmly" (*Oeuvres* 2:505). This is an indication of her force of character and refusal to own up to weakness, and is exactly the attitude of *Histoire de ma vie,* in which there is no reproach. The desire to weep silently to herself and not to speak against her mother is evidenced further on in the mini-autobiography she composes. Chapter 10 contains only two words, "My mother . . ." (*Oeuvres* 2:510). She cannot write anything about her mother, and sets this chapter up as a blank. This unfinished mention of her mother is a far cry from the ultimate role Sophie Dupin would play in *Histoire de ma vie* and is a better indication of Aurore's attitude toward her mother during the period in which she was corresponding with her. To the discrepancy between *Histoire de ma vie* and the correspondence, we can add one more distinction, that between the letters written for Mme Dupin and those Aurore kept to herself.

This unsent letter contains one particularity that links it with the letters of the correspondence. In seeking to understand why her mother does not love her, Aurore asserts: "I am good, though. I am good, you know so. I have a hundred faults, but I am basically gentle" (*Oeuvres* 2:504). This is essentially what she tries to prove to her mother in her letters, not in this pleading manner, but in a more insistent, commanding way. She is constantly combating the accusation (real as well as imagined) that she has not been good, that she has misbehaved, and tries to demonstrate her worth. The letter to Papet after her mother's death, cited earlier, stating that she finally had the satisfaction of convincing her mother, manifests the strength of this need and suggests that it was fulfilled only when her mother was no longer present to lodge criticisms. The child's desire for approval and understanding expressed to and for herself by the twenty-three-year old in the "Voyage" is transmuted in the correspondence into the adult's control and authority, another aspect of the role reversal described previously. Not only does she write to her mother as an adult to a child, but she must master the child within herself in order to do so. Between 1812 and 1821, she steels herself and buries her feelings of dependency in order to present an image of strength to her mother, determined never to admit the extent of her hurt. Not once does she allow the mask to slip in her mother's epistolary presence. Aurore Dupin essentially becomes her own mother in response to Mme Dupin's absence and lack of communication.

This role reversal is accomplished through language. Although she is the child, she speaks as an adult as early as her seventeenth year; she commands and ordains, and has power over rhetoric. She not only reverses roles with her mother, but she inverts grammatical structures as well. Sand constitutes herself not as a speaking subject in her letters, but as a grammatical object. "You don't have confidence in me, you misunderstand me." This subordinate linguistic position mirrors her psychological attitude of victim vis-à-vis her mother. Yet, paradoxically, this transposition also manifests her inner strength, rather than showing weakness, as does the letter in the "Voyage," in which the "I" dominates. Another, unavowed, reason for suppressing the letter in the "Voyage" is that it admits Aurore's need for her mother, something she is unable, or unwilling, to do openly, as the letter of 31 May 1831 shows.

By accenting "you" and not "I," Sand demonstrates how much she blames her mother for not treating her as she should have and reveals the depth of her rancor. She accuses her mother of not loving her, of abandonment, and of not responding to her, both literally and figuratively, as effectively as if she had done so directly. In blaming and accusing rather than complaining, though, she becomes powerful, active rather than passive. Her self-defensiveness turns into assertiveness, her vulnerability gives way to verbal force. She demonstrates the authority and sense of self that are the essential prerequisites of authorship, well before she begins to write for a living. In a negative way, through her daughter's perception of her as withholding support and nurturing, Mme Dupin contributed to the formation of George Sand the writer.

NOTES

1. I make the distinction in this article among Aurore Dupin, the child, Aurore Dudevant, the young married woman, and George Sand, the author.

2. Janet Gurkin Altman, *Epistolarity: Approaches to a Form* (Columbus: Ohio State University Press, 1982).

3. George Sand, *Correspondance*, ed. Georges Lubin, 2d ed. (Paris: Garnier, 1964), 1:24. (vol. 3, 1967, vol. 4, 1968). All translations are my own.

4. See *Correspondance*, 6:824–27; 7:305–6.

5. See Georges Lubin's remark about this aspect of editing a correspondence in Jean-Louis Bonnat and Mireille Bossis, eds., *Ecrire, publier, lire les correspondances: Problématique et économie d'un genre littéraire, actes du colloque international "Les Correspondances"* (Nantes: Publication de l'Université de Nantes, 1983), 180.

6. For example, Kristina Wingard, "Correspondance et littérature épistolaire: George Sand en 1834," in Bonnat and Bossis, *Ecrire, publier, lire*, 146–64; and Françoise van Rossum-Guyon, "Le Statut textuel de la correspondance de George Sand—l'époque d'*Indiana*, 1831–1832," paper delivered at the Seventh International George Sand Conference, Hofstra University, 1986.

7. Germaine Brée, "George Sand: The Fictions of Autobiography," *Nineteenth-Century French Studies* 4:4 (Summer 1976): 438–49.

8. It would be interesting to examine those letters of Mme Dupin that have come down to us, just as Mme de Grignan's responses to her mother have been scrutinized. Unfortunately, such a study is beyond the scope of this article.

9. See especially *Correspondance*, 1:886, 889.

10. Renate Karst-Matausch interprets this sentence as containing a veiled warning: " 'Think of me or else I will forget you.' " See "De la lettre aux lettres: Réflexions sur la genèse de l'écriture épistolaire chez George Sand," in Bonnat and Bossis, *Ecrire, publier, lire*, 155. Her discussions of this and the following letter complete mine, but our conclusions differ.

11. George Sand, *Oeuvres autobiographiques*, ed. Georges Lubin, 2 vols. (Paris: Pléiade, 1970, 1971), 1:762. All translations are my own.

12. See in particular Nancy Rogers's excellent article, "Style, voix et destinataire dans les lettres de George Sand avant 1837," in Bonnat and Bossis, *Ecrire, publier, lire*, 182–93. She describes the conditional mode as being especially persuasive (191).

13. Roman Jakobson, "Linguistique et poétique," in *Essais de linguistique générale* (Paris: Minuit, 1963), 217.

14. See *Oeuvres*, 2:397, and Georges Lubin's note, 2:1390.

15. Altman, *Epistolarity*, 89.

16. For a detailed discussion of the role of her father in Sand's work, see my *Family Romances: George Sand's Early Novels* (Bloomington: Indiana University Press, 1987).

15

"Trying To Do Without God": The Revision of Epistolary Address in The Color Purple

CAROLYN WILLIAMS

 IN HER FIRST letter to God, Celie recounts her rape at the hands of her Pa. Celie is fourteen at the time, and she prays to God for "a sign letting [her] know what is happening to [her]."[1] But the sign for which she prays is not forthcoming. That first letter initiates the story of Celie's unrelenting victimization, until little by little she manages—through identification with other women—to find her strength and identity. The epistolary form of Alice Walker's *The Color Purple* highlights this aspect of its content, since the letters themselves figure crucially in the plot. Toward the middle of the novel, Celie discovers that her husband, Mr. ——, has been hiding the letters from her sister, Nettie, and allowing Celie to believe that her sister is dead. Through Nettie's restored letters, Celie eventually learns that the man who raped her—thus motivating her correspondence with God—was not her Pa after all, but her stepfather. Her last letter to God at this point reveals the amazed disgust she feels upon realizing that her chosen correspondent could hardly have been paying attention to her letters at all:

Dear God,
    That's it, say Shug. Pack your stuff. You coming back to Tennessee
with me.
    But I feels daze.
    My daddy lynch. My mama crazy. All my little half-brothers and
sisters no kin to me. My children not my sister and brother. Pa not pa.
    You must be sleep. (163)

Surely the most striking feature of the novel's particular epistolary form
involves the shift in address that occurs at this point, as Celie turns away
from her first correspondent and begins instead to address her sister. In
her second letter to Nettie, Celie offers an explanation of her turn away
from God as addressee. True to the womanist philosophy of the novel,[2]
Celie's explanation involves the race and class as well as the gender
associated with a God who does not listen to "poor colored women."

Dear Nettie,
    I don't write to God no more, I write to you.
    What happen to God? ast Shug.
    Who that? I say. . . .
    Anyhow, I say, the God I been praying and writing to is a man. And
act just like all the other mens I know. Trifling, forgitful and lowdown.
    She say, Miss Celie, You better hush. God might hear you.
    Let 'im hear me, I say. If he ever listened to poor colored women
the world would be a different place, I can tell you.
    She talk and she talk, trying to budge me way from blasphemy. But
I blaspheme much as I want to.
    All my life I never care what people thought bout nothing I did, I
say. But deep in my heart I care about God. What he going to think.
And come to find out, he don't think. Just sit up there glorying in being
deef, I reckon. But it ain't easy, trying to do without God. Even if you
know he ain't there, trying to do without him is a strain. (175–76)

In the remainder of this crucial letter, Shug offers Celie a revised understanding of what "God" might be; and by the end of the novel, Celie has
managed to put Shug's revised notion of God into practice. On the level
of form as well as explicit content, this epistolary text performs the work
of "trying to do without God," and by the end, that work is no longer
such a "strain." The shift in Celie's address from God to Nettie, divinity
to humanity, figurative to real family, "father" to sister, male to female,
white to black, turns the novel in a new direction, toward the affirmative
"Amen" of its closure.

    Though Celie does not understand this until much later, the God
whom she initially addresses is identified with men from the start. The
choice of God as addressee, for example, is not made by Celie herself but

is urged by the man she calls Pa. His suggestion that God is the only "safe" confidant involves an explicit prohibition of the mother, as well as an implicit bond between the abusive human father and his God. This is clear in the italicized epigraph to the first letter, which suggests that Celie's text opens under the auspices of a voice other than her own: *"You better not never tell nobody but God. It'd kill your mammy"* (11). Celie follows this advice when she "protects" her mother from knowing the identity of her first child's father, and thereby, of course, she also protects the abusive father. "She ast me bout the first one Whose is it? I say God's. I don't know no other man or what else to say" (12). This refusal to identify the real father has the ironic effect of identifying that father with God; and this ironic association further serves Celie to explain to her mother when the child disappears. "Finally she ast Where is it? I say God took it" (12). Here "God" serves Celie as a mask for that other "he," who gives her children and then takes them away.

Recognizing the bitter irony of Pa's recommendation of God as correspondent depends on seeing Celie's simultaneous exclusion from and implication within the male network of power relations. She attempts to protect her mother from death by collaborating with the father's lies, but her mother dies anyway, and Celie then realizes that her death came as a result of the very lies she herself had helped to tell. "Trying to believe his story kilt her" (15). Celie's mother, weakened through repeated pregnancy, had never provided her daughter with a strong support against her Pa. But with her mother gone, Celie herself is left in the position of surrogate mother to her sister, Nettie, and Nettie becomes her primary female relation. She hopes to protect Nettie from her own fate. "I see him looking at my little sister. She scared. But I say I'll take care of you. With God help" (13). Her desire to protect her sister motivates Celie's marriage to Mr. ——, insofar as her motives figure at all in what is basically an arrangement of convenience between father and husband. Mr. —— turns out to be a fit successor to Pa, and Celie's plan to protect Nettie from Pa only puts her in danger from Mr. ——, who, like Pa, has his eye on Nettie. When she refuses his sexual advances, he sends her away and revenges himself on the sisters by plotting to keep Celie from receiving Nettie's letters (26, 119). In other words, he takes Celie's sister away from her, completing the process that Pa began of isolating Celie from the other women in her family.

Her isolation is the precondition of Celie's continued correspondence with God. The novel's epistolary form, in other words, is the most fundamental representation of a concern with women isolated from one another within the patriarchal network, a concern that is also elaborately thematized within the novel. Because of Pa and Mr. ——, there is no one safe to talk to, and the emblem of Celie's solitude becomes her choice of God as epistolary addressee. When parted from her sister by Mr. ——, she covers her sense of isolation by turning to God and to writing. "But I just say, Never mine, never mine, long as I can spell G-o-d I got somebody along" (26). Thus very early in the novel the functional analogy is established between God and the sister in the role of possible confidant. Here, "spelling G-o-d" is clearly meant to fill the gap left by the absence of the sister, as the first letter to God clearly substitutes for telling the mother. This formal substitution will be reversed later in the novel in the pivotal shift in address from God to Nettie. But until that moment signals Celie's decisive rejection of God as addressee, the ironic result is her correspondence with a confidant who only reinforces her passivity toward the male power structure.

The inadequacy of God as a confidant is underscored later in the novel when Squeak recounts the story of her rape by her uncle, the prison warden. Shug encourages her to unburden herself to her family by making fun of the only other alternative: "If you can't tell us, who you gon tell, God?" (95). Early in the story, however, Celie is caught up in just this mystification. Even then, the voices of other women—Nettie, Kate, Sofia—try to break through the mystified submission to her husband which Celie rationalizes with reference to God. "Well, sometime Mr. —— git on me pretty hard. I have to talk to Old Maker. But he my husband. I shrug my shoulders. This life soon be over, I say. Heaven last all ways." Sofia replies: "You ought to bash Mr. —— head open, she say. Think bout heaven later" (47). But since her sister is absent and presumed dead, Celie can think of rebellion only as futile, speech as impossibly dangerous. Her passivity and silence depend upon the absence of her sister and the lesson she reads in that absence. "I don't say nothing. I think bout Nettie, dead. She fight, she run away. What good it do? I don't fight. I stay where I'm told. But I'm alive" (29). Writing—as opposed to speech—seems safe, seems even the sign of ongoing life. Within this context, epistolarity itself must be seen to represent both the resignation of Celie's silence and its implicit strength: her silent refusal to lose her identity, despite her isolation.

According to the logic of epistolarity, all the while Celie addresses God in letters, God too is absent—not necessarily and definitively "deef," as Celie later complains, but distant and uncertain of response. Janet Altman has theorized the play of absence and presence that characterizes "epistolary mediation" in general.[3] Within this context, the wit of *The Color Purple* implicitly draws attention to a similarity between epistolary desire and prayer; both represent attempts, through language, to conjure presence from absence. In addressing God, Celie prays to read a sign of his presence in order to feel her own more clearly; if he were to answer her prayers, she would know herself, would know "what is happening to [her]" (11). Of course, God never answers, and the epistolary relation remains incomplete. For Celie, the practice of addressing God simply reaffirms her solitude; she is essentially writing to herself. *The Color Purple* is thus an example of an epistolary novel with close affinities to the journal, diary, or autobiographical confession.[4] As in those genres, here the practice of introspective letter writing records the disciplined process of increasing self-knowledge. In this case, however, self-revelation is at first referred to a principle of absolute exteriority—God— which is always paradoxically close to sheer interiority, and prayer always an exercise in attempted self-possession. The effect of this epistolary address is also similar to that of the poetic strategy of apostrophe or prosopopoeia, however, in which the lyric address of something absent, inanimate, or dead conjures the illusion of presence and voice but at the same time has the uncanny effect of reflecting absence back upon the lyric "I."[5] This feature of epistolary address, in other words, cuts across and complicates the fiction of increasing self-knowledge and self-presence, which is the generic mark of autobiography.

When she receives no letters, Celie must conclude that Nettie is not merely absent but dead, especially since the sisters have made a pact explicitly establishing letters as the sign of their ongoing life. Parting from her sister, Celie demands correspondence. "I say Write. She say, nothing but death can keep me from it. She never write" (26). Absence, the necessary precondition of any epistolary exchange, is here given its most ominous significance. Nettie's presumed death rationalizes Celie's continued address to God, and at the same time it provides the narrative opportunity for resurrection. When her letters do finally appear in the text, they appear suddenly, in a group that presents a more or less complete record of Nettie's life since the two sisters parted. The last letter in the group explains that "Pa is not our Pa," allowing Celie to revise her own personal history and forcing her to realize that God has never been adequate to her correspondence (162–63). Thus Nettie's figurative (and epistolary) reappearance from the dead gives Celie a new life as well. The first letter Celie writes to Nettie rather than to God (164–67) tells of a day "like it be round Easter," when she revisits their childhood home, now transformed, with flowering trees all around.

The figurative resurrection that takes place in Celie's life is of course made possible through her love for Shug. This is most obvious on the level of plot and theme, but it is true on the level of narrative form as well, for Shug is the route through which Nettie's letters are restored. They begin appearing two pages after Celie and Shug make love for the first time (109, 112). In terms of the plot, this is fully rationalized—after Celie tells her about Nettie, Shug figures out where the letters are—but in textual terms it seems like magic, as if the act of love has conjured Nettie's voice. The plot structure demonstrates the axiom that sexuality conjures the sister, for when each one falls in love—Celie with Shug and Nettie with Samuel—she tells her beloved all about her sister (112–13, 174). It is this chiasmic confidence—Celie's talking about Nettie with Shug while Nettie talks about Celie with Samuel—that causes the parallel but divided plots of the two sisters to come together again. Shug produces Nettie's letters, the last of which reveals to Celie that "Pa not pa." Through Shug, Nettie is restored; and through Nettie, Celie's children return, purged of an incestuous origin (though never of rape).

Celie's turn toward women overturns her earlier implication in the patriarchal network, and the revision in her epistolary address is the most graphic reminder of this shift. However, the sudden, pivotal shift in address is but the decisive register of an internal process of transformation, which begins before it and continues long beyond it. The awakening of Celie's sexuality begins the process of replacing God with the sister as addressee. Long before they become lovers, she feels for Shug's body a reverence that reminds her of prayer. "I wash her body, it feel like I'm praying. My hands tremble and my breath short" (53). But her sexual correspondence with Shug accomplishes what prayer could never do; it derives from and leads back to her increasing self-possession. Just before making love with Shug for the first time, Celie tells of her rape by Pa. For the first time, she experiences the comforting and responsive love of an attentive listener. This enables her to mourn her past life, to achieve the catharsis of tears, and to gain the intensified comprehension of her story afforded by the retrospective reenactment with another of her past losses (108).

Finally, the sexual correspondence with Shug metaphorically restores the familial—and definitively female—relations whose removal constituted the crisis of the novel's opening. While she combs out Shug's hair, for example, Celie is reminded of her mother and her daughter through the intimacy of this bodily attention (57). In one of the last letters to God she muses on what making love with Shug is like—"little like sleeping with mama . . . little like sleeping with Nettie," but different from both (110). This maternal network is drawn very close during Celie and Shug's first sexual encounter. "Then I feels something real soft and wet on my breast, feel like one of my little lost babies mouth. Way after while, I act like a little lost baby too" (109). In the moment of ecstasy, Celie finds within herself the capacity to enact her greatest loss and its restoration. Sexuality in this novel represents the principle of transference, substitution, and internalization. As Celie learns to love Shug, she finds her mother, sister, and lost babies within. No longer isolated, and full of her remembered relations, Celie begins to experience a sense of wholeness. "Dear God, Now I know Nettie alive I begin to strut a little bit" (138). At the end of the first letter addressed not to God but to Nettie, Celie reports Shug's summary of this compensatory vision. "Shug say, Us each other's peoples now, and kiss me" (167).

Celie's sense of wholeness is not complete until she manages to recognize both "God" and the absent sister within herself. "Trying to do without God," in other words, paradoxically involves an act of self-possession, of internalization, which cannot take place as long as she addresses God and thereby reinscribes an absence. Only after turning to address her sister as correspondent, and then almost immediately, Celie begins the work of radically redefining and internalizing God. Her "blasphemy" in rejecting God as addressee inspires Shug to put her through a catechism. She forces Celie to recognize that her God has been a white man, imprinted in her imagination by the pictures in "the white folks' white bible. . . . You mad cause he don't seem to listen to your prayers. Humph! Do the mayor listen to anything colored say?" After making the point that "God" is a culturally conditioned concept, Shug pursues a strategy of negativity, first rejecting race, then gender, as defining attributes of her God. "God ain't a he or a she, but a It" (177). Finally her iconoclasm goes far beyond Celie's "blasphemy" as she insists that God cannot be envisioned at all. God is absolutely interior, a matter of responsiveness, affirmation, love. Since It is inside, It includes Everything.

> Here's the thing, say Shug. The thing I believe. God is inside you and inside everybody else. You come into the world with God. But only them that search for it inside find it. . . . Don't look like nothing, she say. It ain't a picture show. It ain't something you can look at apart from anything else, including yourself. I believe God is everything, say Shug. Everything that is or ever was or ever will be. And when you can feel that, and be happy to feel that, you've found It. (177–78)

The impersonal pronoun "It," which names Shug's "God," as well as the internal sensation of being a part of everything else, is close to the euphemistic usage of "It" to refer to the sexual act; this association is explicit in Shug's remark that "when it happen you can't miss it. It sort of like you know what, she say, grinning and rubbing high up on my thigh" (178). In Shug's theology, sexual pleasure is the best metaphor for the state of ecstatic affirmation that characterizes God-as-Everything, for "Everything want to be loved" (178). In fact, the title of the novel comes from this second letter to Nettie, suggesting the crucial importance of

Shug's theology of love, admiration, and appreciation. "I think it pisses God off if you walk by the color purple in a field somewhere and don't notice it" (178).[6]

Unfortunately, the state of total responsiveness and affirmation is not easy to achieve, for the work of negation must constantly go on, in order to purge the world of the associations "man" has made.

> Man corrupt everything, say Shug. He on your box of grits, in your head, and all over the radio. He try to make you think he everywhere. Soon as you think he everywhere, you think he God. But he ain't. Whenever you trying to pray, and man plop himself on the other end of it, tell him to git lost, say Shug. (179)

"But this hard work, let me tell you," Celie comments. "He been there so long, he don't want to budge." In fact, this "hard work" is the work of this text. The narrative work of internalizing divinity is a familiar feature of a certain Protestant tradition in the English novel, a tradition in which *The Color Purple* still participates.[7] But the way that work gets done is of course particular to each narrative form. In *The Color Purple* the epistolary form enacts the effort to negate the corruption man has wrought upon "everything" and to address a female principle of totality and familiarity instead. The "Amen" that ends this crucial letter suggests again that Celie is finally really praying only when she begins writing to Nettie. The functional analogy established earlier between God and the sister is now fulfilled at the moment of its reversal, as the sister replaces God in the role of confidant. Addressing the sister instead is the route of detaching the concept of "God" from patriarchal oppression and allowing "It" to embrace "Everything." Paradoxically, the internalization of God accomplishes this massive externalization as "Everything." This revised divinity is no longer absent or distant, but close and familiar. "To do without God," then, is paradoxically to have "It" always readily available.

Meanwhile, through her experiences in Africa, Nettie too recognizes that "God" is a relative, culturally bound concept, for the Olinka have projected "roofleaf" as their divinity. Through the painful process of witnessing the colonization of the Olinka, she is forced to realize how powerless her own God really is (203). She too must come to the conclusion that divinity is internal, and therefore unrepresentable.

> God is different to us now, after all these years in Africa. More spirit than ever before, and more internal. Most people think he has to look like something or someone—a roofleaf or Christ—but we don't. And not being tied to what God looks like, frees us. (227)

Since Celie's letters to Nettie are never received, only the reader can see how thoroughly the two correspondents "answer" each other. The parallel plots of the two sisters' radically different lives work out elaborately parallel experiences of racism and sexism.[8] Through their work in the world, both Nettie and Celie accomplish the transformation, internalization, possession, and negation of God. But at the same time, each sister must achieve a similar sort of faith in relation to the other; the sister, too, must be internalized. Here again, the process of internalization depends upon absence. In the case of Celie's communications to Nettie as well as to God, the epistolary relation must remain unfulfilled in order for this crucial fiction of internalization to be enacted. In a sense, then, the epistolary form of *The Color Purple* is ironic throughout. A full epistolary exchange is never established, either with God or with Nettie, and the most profound motives of the narrative depend upon this fact. Meanwhile, the hope and faith that epistolary desire *might* be internally fulfilled sustain the epistolarity of the second half of the novel.

As correspondent, Nettie's position in relation to Celie is like Celie's position in relation to God: radical solitude prompts the address, and neither letter writer gets an answer. Nettie knows that Mr. —— is diverting the letters and that Celie has probably never heard from her. "I know you think I am dead," she explains, in the first letter from her produced in the text (112). Despite the lack of response, however, Nettie continues to write to her sister.

> I remember one time you said your life made you feel so ashamed you couldn't even talk about it to God, you had to write it, bad as you thought your writing was. Well, now I know what you meant. And whether God will read letters or no, I know you will go on writing them; which is guidance enough for me. Anyway, when I don't write to you I feel as bad as I do when I don't pray, locked up in myself and choking on my own heart. I am so *lonely*, Celie. (122)

Nettie takes up the practice of writing from Celie and reflects back to Celie a theoretical understanding of what that practice means. She has already learned what Celie, too, will learn: the figurative equivalence of prayer and epistolary address to the sister. Finally, she expresses through this equivalence the sense that re-externalizing the internal is the dynamic of conjuring presence, companionship, and correspondence.

> But always, no matter what I'm doing, I am writing to you. Dear Celie, I say in my head in the middle of Vespers, the middle of the night, while cooking, Dear, dear Celie. And I imagine that you really do get my letters and that you are writing me back: Dear Nettie, this is what life is like for me. (144)

In this figurative sense, the faithful continuity of Nettie's invocation keeps Celie alive to her, though after thirty years of this unfulfilled correspondence, she begins to imagine that Celie might be dead. But Samuel counsels her at this point to trust in God and to have faith of another, analogous sort as well, "to have faith in the sturdiness of [her] sister's soul" (227).

In the second half of the novel, after receiving Nettie's letters, Celie too learns to keep this faith "in the sturdiness of [her] sister's soul." A second time she is threatened with Nettie's death, when Mr. —— gives her the telegram from the Department of Defense saying that Nettie's returning ship has been sunk by German mines off the coast of Gilbraltar. "They think you all drowned. Plus, the same day, all the letters I wrote to you over the years come back unopen" (225). The return of Celie's unopened letters is an apt emblem of her sister's possible death, as the sudden appearance of Nettie's letters testified to her resurrection. At this point it seems that Celie's second correspondence will be as fruitless as her first. But her refusal this time to believe in Nettie's death is a mark of exactly how far she has come into her own. She, like Nettie, has learned to internalize her sister's presence.

> And I don't believe you dead. How can you be dead if I still feel you? Maybe, like God, you changed into something different that I'll have to speak to in a different way, but you not dead to me Nettie. And never will be. Sometime when I git tired of talking to myself I talk to you. (229–30)

Celie's explicit association of faith in her sister with the transformation of God emphasizes the parallel dynamic at work. And again, the thematic point is reinforced by the narrative form, which wittily exploits the temporal disjunction, or lag time, involved in any epistolary relation. Celie's faith in the sturdiness of her sister's soul is supported by a figure of her abiding presence, the evidence of her letters. "And no matter how much the telegram said you must be drown, I still git letters from you" (241).

Once more Celie must practice internalization as a compensatory technique, when Shug leaves with Germaine; and this final movement recapitulates and concludes this line of development in the novel. "Feel like I felt when Nettie left," writes Celie when Shug leaves earlier in the novel, emphasizing the association of Shug with her sister (76). After a time, Celie establishes an epistolary relation with Shug, and through this relation Celie learns both to do without Shug and at the same time to have her always within (236). No sooner has Celie accomplished the internal restoration of their relation than it is re-externalized—that is to say, rewarded in the plot—by Shug's appearance.

> And then, just when I know I can live content without Shug, . . . Shug write me she coming home.

Now. Is this life or not?
I be so calm.
If she come, I be happy. If she don't, I be content.
And then I figure this the lesson I was suppose to learn. (247–48)

The extravagant magic of the plot's resolution may seem more fundamentally grounded if we have appreciated "this lesson" of epistolarity, its fictive trick of conjuring presence. Celie's internalized recreations of "Everything" and everyone eventually issue in their external appearances in the plot. The work of internalization done, Celie is complete; her solitude has become a company, and the narrative represents this achievement in the dramatized reunion of the family.[9] After Shug returns, Nettie again turns out to be alive. The male characters, who were expunged from the narrative's good graces during its period of separatism,[10] are redeemed and given reformed characters. Celie's children are no longer lost but grown up and joined by their African counterpart. The parallel and divided plots of the two sisters are reunited. Time is figuratively reversed, and everyone feels young again. And epistolary address ceases altogether, for Celie's correspondent has returned.[11]

The closure of the epistolary form turns again on Celie's pivotal revision of address. Since she can no longer address Nettie, Celie returns to her earlier addressee, now thoroughly transformed, both internalized (as Spirit) and externalized (as Everything). "Dear God. Dear stars, dear trees, dear sky, dear peoples. Dear Everything. Dear God" (249). This last letter closes with "Amen," Celie's characteristic signature ever since the second letter to Nettie, the one in which she describes her transformation of God. Nettie has begged Celie to "Pray for us" (169), and the novel's last word is the close of that prayer. It is also the "Amen" of enthusiastic response to "Everything"—as in a church service or revival meeting one answers the arrival of the Spirit with the tribute of a loud "Amen."

This epistolary novel is framed at its outer edges by epigraphs that break the fiction of presence and refer us to its author. We find, on the last page of the text: "I thank everybody in this book for coming. / A.W., author and medium" (253). Alice Walker closes the book as if it had been one long letter to the reader and this were her signature. The usual effects of epistolarity are set in motion again at the edges of the text in order to assert authorial presence and at the same time to deny it. As "author" she claims the novel as artifice, an aesthetic form created by her own letter-writing hand; but as "medium" she refers authority to a power external to herself, who speaks through her. The conception of the artist as mediating the voice of a higher power is but one step removed from the conception of the artist as analogous to or a surrogate for God; both conceptions are traditional in romantic literature where, as feminist critics have pointed out, they operate to reserve authorial power in the male line.[12]

Here Walker's womanist revision of God has consequences for her vision of narrative authority as well. Through correspondence with the sister, the notion of God has been detached from the patriarchal chain of authorization, with the result that, when the female artist refers to her power as a "medium," she makes a claim at once more humble and at the same time more vast than the traditional male claim. She defers to Everything, and as a consequence her voice is multitudinous, democratic, and responsive; she speaks for Everything, and as a result everyone speaks through her.[13] The authority of her voice is grounded in its paradoxical assertion of deferral. She claims to have transcribed Celie's voice, to have listened carefully, to have responded. Walker's closing signature returns us to the opening epigraph of the novel, in which she introduces this epistolary fiction of presence with a gesture of deferring her own. Her dedication strikingly conflates life outside and inside the text; and it invites the reader to consider epistolarity as a paradigm for all creation. "To the Spirit: / Without whose assistance / Neither this book / Nor I / Would have been / Written."

NOTES

1. Alice Walker, *The Color Purple* (New York: Harcourt Brace Jovanovich, 1982), 11. Further references are given parenthetically in the text.

2. Alice Walker defines "womanism" in *In Search of Our Mothers' Gardens: Womanist Prose* (New York: Harcourt Brace Jovanovich, 1983), xi–xii. See also Chikwenye Okonjo Ogunyemi, "Womanism: The Dynamics of the Contemporary Black Female Novel in English," *Signs* 11:1 (1983): 63–80.

3. Janet Gurkin Altman, *Epistolarity: Approaches to a Form* (Columbus: Ohio State University Press, 1982), esp. 13–46.

4. Altman notes the similarities and differences among "pure autobiography," journal and diary novels, and certain epistolary forms. Ibid., 88–89, 112n.2.

5. Paul de Man, "Autobiography as De-facement," *MLN* 94 (1979): 919–30.

6. The choice of color is also coded to Walker's exposition of womanism. The axiomatic ratio "Womanist is to feminist as purple to lavender" emphasizes Walker's wish to intensify feminism by "universalizing" it. She restricts her definition of "universalist" to racial terms, but this color coding can only remind us of her strictly qualified emphasis on lesbian sexuality, her insistence that it must not translate as "separatist." *In Search of Our Mothers' Gardens*, xi–xii.

7. See Michael McKeon, *The Origins of the English Novel, 1600–1740* (Baltimore: Johns Hopkins University Press, 1987), esp. 95–96 and 315–37.

8. On the most general level, Nettie's voice seems to relate to Celie's voice as theory relates to practice (Nettie theorizes the practice of epistolary introspection which Celie begins) or as the explicit commitment to "uplift" (127) relates to the pure experience of racism. Most reviewers did not find Nettie's voice compelling. See for example Mel Watkins, "Some Letters Went To God," *New York Times Book Review,* 25 July 1982, p. 7. But in relation to Celie's voice, the lack of "color" in Nettie's voice may be seen as its point, spelling the losses as well as the gains of education, uplift, universalism.

9. On this dynamic in romance see Harold Bloom, "The Internalization of Quest Romance," in *Romanticism and Consciousness,* ed. Harold Bloom (New York: Norton, 1970), 3–24.

10. On this problematic feature of Alice Walker's womanist program, see note 6, above. A womanist is "not a separatist, except periodically, for health." *In Search of Our Mothers' Gardens,* xi.

11. Altman points to this situation as the codified comic closure of the epistolary novel. (The codified tragic closure turns on the death of the epistolary correspondent.) Altman, *Epistolarity,* 150, 165n.8.

12. See Sandra Gilbert and Susan Gubar, *The Madwoman in the Attic: The Woman Writer and the Nineteenth-Century Literary Imagination* (New Haven: Yale University Press, 1979) and Margaret Homans, *Women Writers and Poetic Identity: Dorothy Wordsworth, Emily Bronte, and Emily Dickinson* (Princeton: Princeton University Press, 1980).

13. Alice Walker describes this experience of narrative power in "Writing *The Color Purple*," in *In Search of Our Mothers' Gardens,* 355–60.

The Contributors

JANET GURKIN ALTMAN is professor of French at the University of Iowa. She has written on epistolary fictions in her book *Epistolarity: Approaches to a Form* (1982). Her other writings include articles on Laclos, Balzac, Proust, the pre-Revolutionary novel, diary fiction, and letter manuals, as well as a forthcoming book on Cocteau's filmmaking.

ALICIA BORINSKY teaches Latin American and comparative literature at Boston University, where she is associate professor of Spanish. Her most recent books are *Intersticios* (1986), *Macedonio Fernández y la teoría crítica* (1987), and *Mujeres Tímidas,* poems (1987). She is currently working on a book entitled *Theoretical Fables.*

JAMES CARSON, assistant professor of English at Kenyon College, recently completed his doctoral studies at the University of California at Berkeley. He is currently completing a book entitled *Surveillance and Sympathy in the Gothic Novel,* and has published articles on Mary Shelley's letters and epistolary fiction.

KATHRYN CRECELIUS specializes in nineteenth-century French literature and French women writers. She is the author of *Family Romances: George Sand's Early Novels* (1988), the first critical study of the novelist. She has also written on Mérimée, Antonine Maillet, and Hélène Cixous.

JULIA EPSTEIN is associate professor of English at Haverford College, where she teaches as well in the Comparative Literature and Gender Studies programs. She has published articles on epistolary literature, the picaresque novel, and relations between literature and science and medicine. Her book *The Iron Pen: Frances Burney and the Politics of Women's Writing* will be published in 1989.

ELIZABETH C. GOLDSMITH is associate professor of French at Boston University. She has written on the seventeenth-century writers Madame de Sévigné, Bussy-Rabutin, Madeleine de Scudéry, and

Madame de Villedieu. Her book *Exclusive Conversations: The Art of Interaction in Seventeenth-Century France* was published in 1988.

JULIE C. HAYES is associate professor of French at the University of Richmond. She has published several articles on Diderot and Sade and has just completed a book on sentimental theater in eighteenth-century France.

SUSAN K. JACKSON is assistant professor of French at Boston University. She has published on Beauvoir, Diderot, Rousseau, and on the novels and correspondence of Isabelle de Charrière. Her work in progress is a reading of the problematics of autobiography in Rousseau's occasional texts.

KATHARINE A. JENSEN recently received her Ph.D. from Columbia University and is now assistant professor of French at Louisiana State University. She has published translations of contemporary French feminist texts and articles on the writings of Madame de Villedieu and Madame de Sévigné. Her research interests include seventeenth-century French literature, women writers, and feminist theory.

LINDA KAUFFMAN is associate professor of English at the University of Maryland, College Park. She is the author of *Discourses of Desire: Gender, Genre, and Epistolary Fictions* (1986), and she has published numerous articles and reviews on modern literature and feminist theory. She edited *Gender and Theory: Dialogic Encounters* and is now working on *Special Delivery: Epistolary Modes in Modern and Postmodern Fiction*.

SUZANNE RODIN PUCCI is associate professor of French at the State University of New York at Buffalo. Her publications include *Diderot and a Poetics of Science* (1986) and several articles concerning representation in eighteenth-century literature and philosophy.

MARGARET F. ROSENTHAL is assistant professor of Italian at the University of Southern California, where she specializes in Renaissance comparative literature, women poets, and Venetian social history of the Renaissance. She is currently completing a book on the Venetian courtesan poet Veronica Franco.

PATRICIA MEYER SPACKS is professor of English at Yale University. She has published numerous articles on eighteenth-century English writers and on a wide range of other subjects including modern drama, satire, and autobiography. Her most recent books are *The Female Imagination* (1975), *Imagining a Self* (1976), *The Adolescent Idea* (1981), and *Gossip* (1985).

CAROLYN WILLIAMS is associate professor of English at Boston University. She has written feminist essays on Charlotte Brontë, George Meredith, and Virginia Woolf. Her book on Walter Pater's aesthetic historicism, *Transfigured World,* will be published in 1989.

SALLY WINKLE is assistant professor of German at Eastern Washington University. Her book *Woman as Bourgeois Ideal: A Study of Sophie von La Roche's 'Geschichte des Fräuleins von Sternheim' and Goethe's 'Werther'* will be published in 1989.

Index